CHILDREN'S BIBLE STORIES

Share the greatest stories ever told

Senior Art Editor Sheila Collins
Project Editor Steven Carton
Managing Art Editor Diane Peyton Jones
Managing Editor Linda Esposito
Category Publisher Laura Buller
US Senior Editor Rebecca Warren

Publishing Director Jonathan Metcalf
Associate Publishing Director Liz Wheeler
Art Director Phil Ormerod

Pre-Production Producer Lucy Sims
Senior Producer Gemma Sharpe
Jacket Designer Ira Sharma
Jacket Editor Manisha Majithia
Picture Researcher Nic Dean

Old Testament Consultant Dr. Jean-Marc Herimerdinger
New Testament Consultant Dr. Steve Motyer
Historical Consultant Dr. Philip Parker

DK India
Senior Art Editor Anjana Nair
Art Editor Nidhi Mehra, Priyanka Singh, Swati Katyal, Devan Das
Assistant Art Editor Gazal Roongta, Ankita Mukherjee, Aanchal Singhal, Payal Rosalind Malik, Namita
Managing Art Editor Arunesh Talapatra
Production Manager Pankaj Sharma
DTP Manager/CTS Balwant Singh
DTP Designer Rakesh Kumar
Jackets Editorial Coordinator Priyanka Sharma
Managing Jackets Editor Saloni Singh
Picture Researcher Surya Sankash Sarangi

This American edition, 2021
First American edition, 2013
Published in the United States by DK Publishing
1450 Broadway, Suite 801, New York, NY 10018

20 21 22 23 24 10 9 8 7 6 5 4 3 2 1
001–322072–Mar/2021

Published in Great Britain by Dorling Kindersley Limited.

A catalog record for this book is available from the Library of Congress.

ISBN: 978-0-7440-2877-5

Printed in the UAE

For the curious
www.dk.com

This book was made with Forest Stewardship Council™ certified paper—one small step in DK's commitment to a sustainable future. For more information go to www.dk.com/our-green-pledge

CHILDREN'S BIBLE STORIES

Share the greatest stories ever told

Stories retold by
Sally Tagholm

All other text by
Andrea Mills

Illustrations by
Julian De Narvaez

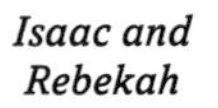

Isaac and Rebekah

Contents

Ancient jar used to store oil

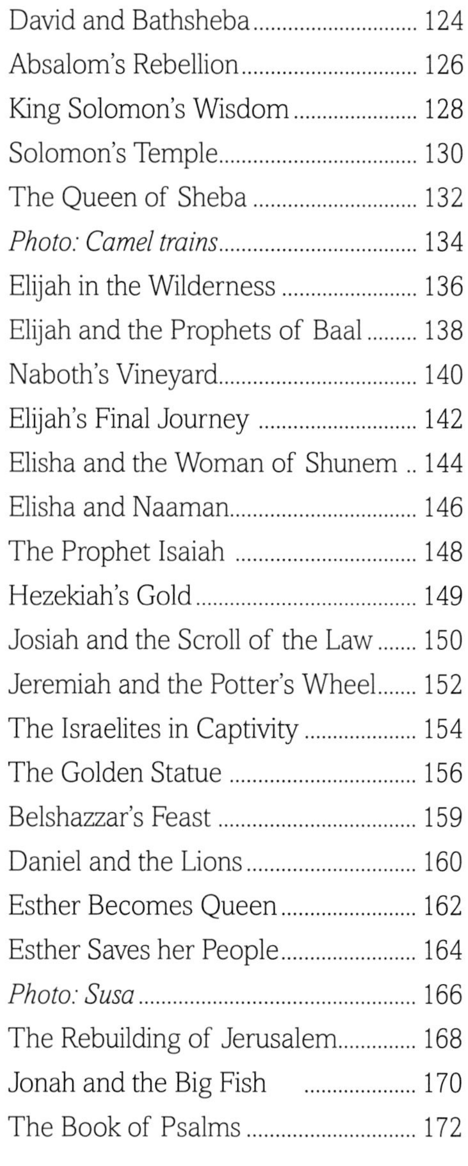

Decorative box used for keeping special Shabbat spices

Absalom's long hair gets caught in a tree

The three Wise Men

Judas betrays Jesus

Terracotta amphora, used to store wine

Roman gladius (short sword)

The Books of the Bible

Translated into more than 2,000 languages, the Bible is the most read book in the history of the western world. Its name comes from "biblia," the Greek for "books," because the Bible consists of 66 books. These are the sacred texts of Judaism and Christianity, telling the story of God and His people.

Two Testaments
The Bible is divided into two "testaments," a translation of the Hebrew word for "covenant" (an agreement between God and His people). The Old Testament (above) is the story of the Israelites and their relationship with God. The New Testament details the life of Jesus and the early spread of Christianity.

Unearthing scriptures
Artifacts of great religious importance have been discovered by archaeologists. Among them are the Dead Sea Scrolls, which contain parts of the Old Testament and other religious texts from as early as the 3rd century BCE. Almost 1,000 scriptures were found in caves at Qumran, on the West Bank (left).

Authors of the Bible
Not all of the authors are known. The books were written over 16 centuries and many do not mention an author's name. The Book of Isaiah may have been written by the prophet himself (left), but some think it was written and edited by more than one person.

Link between the Testaments
Many Christians believe that the Old Testament predicts the coming of Jesus. One example is Jesus entering Jerusalem on a donkey, which fulfills a prophecy that foretells the coming of the Messiah.

St. Jerome and the hidden books
In the 4th century CE, St Jerome (right) translated the Bible into Latin. He decided that some Jewish books written between the Old and New Testaments, called Apocrypha ("hidden books"), did not carry enough authority, so he did not include them.

Lindisfarne Gospels
During the Middle Ages, Bibles were copied carefully by hand and decorated with ornate illustrations. The Lindisfarne Gospels (below), created by an English monk named Eadfrith in the 8th century CE, are a beautiful example of this style.

King James Bible
An English translation of the Christian Bible was made by 47 scholars from the Church of England between 1604 and 1611. Translated from Greek, Hebrew, and Latin, the epic work became known as the "authorized" or "King James Bible." This rare fourth edition (below) was printed by Robert Barker of London in 1634.

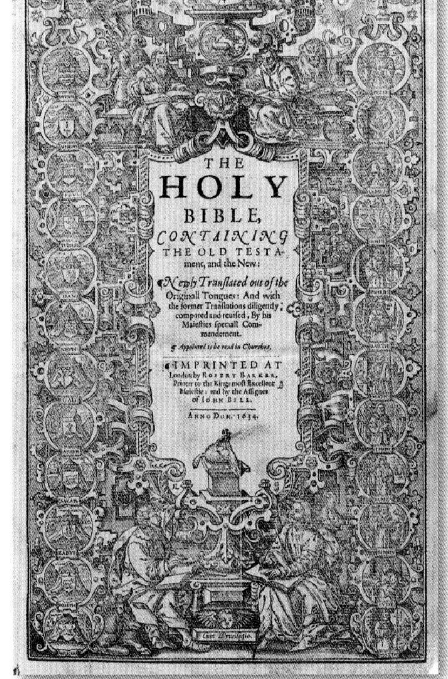

THE
HOLY
BIBLE,
CONTAINING
THE OLD TESTAment, and the New:
Newly Translated out of the Originall Tongues: And with the former Translations diligently compared and reuised, By his Maiesties speciall Commandement.
Appointed to be read in Churches.
IMPRINTED AT London by ROBERT BARKER, Printer to the Kings most Excellent Maiestie: and by the Assignes of IOHN BILL.
ANNO DOM. 1634.

Bibles in print
The print industry was transformed in the 1440s by German publisher Johannes Gutenburg. His new invention of print with moveable type (left) was meant to look as if it had been handwritten. Thanks to Gutenberg, the Bible became available to a mass audience. Since then, billions of copies have been printed, making the Bible the biggest-selling book of all time.

Adam and Eve
The Bible's first agreement is between God and the first people, Adam and Eve (above).The Tree of Life represents their covenant. Adam and Eve will receive immortality—symbolized by the Tree of Life—if they protect the Lord's creation. However, Eve is tempted by the forbidden fruit of the Tree of Knowledge of Good and Evil, and they become cut off from God.

The Covenants

The main theme of the Bible is a book of covenants (formal agreements) established between the Lord and His people. While the Old Testament describes God's covenants with individuals and the Israelites, the New Testament focuses on His son, Jesus Christ, who offers a new covenant to the world. Sacred occasions and special signs from God mark each covenant.

Noah and the flood
God becomes angry at the corruption and wickedness taking over the world, so He sends a devastating flood to wipe out humanity. Sheltered on the ark, righteous Noah and his family (right) are the only ones spared. The Lord agrees to send no more floods and sets a rainbow in the sky as a sign of this covenant between Him and humankind.

Abraham
God makes a covenant with childless Abraham (left). He promises him the leadership of a great nation and says his descendants will inherit the Promised Land. All God wants in return is the faith of Abraham and his people. This covenant's sign was male circumcision, an operation still performed on Jewish boys today.

Moses and the Ten Commandments
Treated as slaves by the Egyptians, the Israelites lose faith in the Lord. God responds by taking them out of Egypt, led by His servant Moses (shown left talking to God, who is inside a burning bush). God gives the Israelites a strict code of moral laws, called The Ten Commandment They must keep these laws, and in return,God promises to protect them

Joshua and the Stone of Shechem
With the Promised Land conquered, the Israelite leader Joshua renews the covenant with God. He promises Israel will keep to the law of Moses and ignore false gods. Joshua erects a stone at Shechem (left), saying it "will be a witness against you if you are untrue to your God."

David and the Kingdom of Israel
God's covenant with David guarantees David's throne "will be established forever," turning the Israelite tribes into a kingdom, with David at the head of an everlasting dynasty. David responds by making Jerusalem (below) the City of God, an earthly companion to God's Kingdom in Heaven. David's son Solomon builds a temple there as a sign of this covenant.

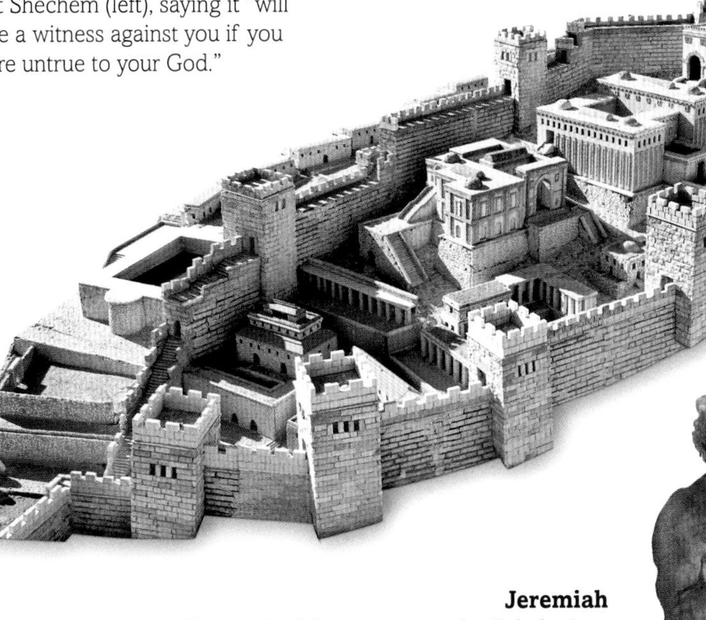

Jeremiah
During the 6th century BCE, the Babylonians destroy the holy city of Jerusalem. The prophet Jeremiah (right) understands that this is God punishing people for disobeying His sacred covenants. But Jeremiah says in future God will create a new covenant with Israel in which He will offer them forgiveness for their sins.

Jesus and the New Covenant
The promise given to Jeremiah comes true. When Jesus dies, humanity is offered a new covenant. All who believe in him will receive complete forgiveness for past sins and the gift of eternal life on the condition that they remain faithful and good. This covenant is celebrated at the Last Supper (left), when Jesus shares the wine (symbolizing his blood) with the disciples.

Lands of the Bible

All of the events of the Bible take place within these maps. Most of the stories are based in the Holy Land: called the Promised Land in the Old Testament, and where Jesus lived and preached in the New Testament.

Index of Places

The places on the large map are indicated through grid references with uppercase letters and Arabic numbers (eg, C6). The places on the Holy Land map are indicated by lowercase letters and Roman numbers (eg, dii).

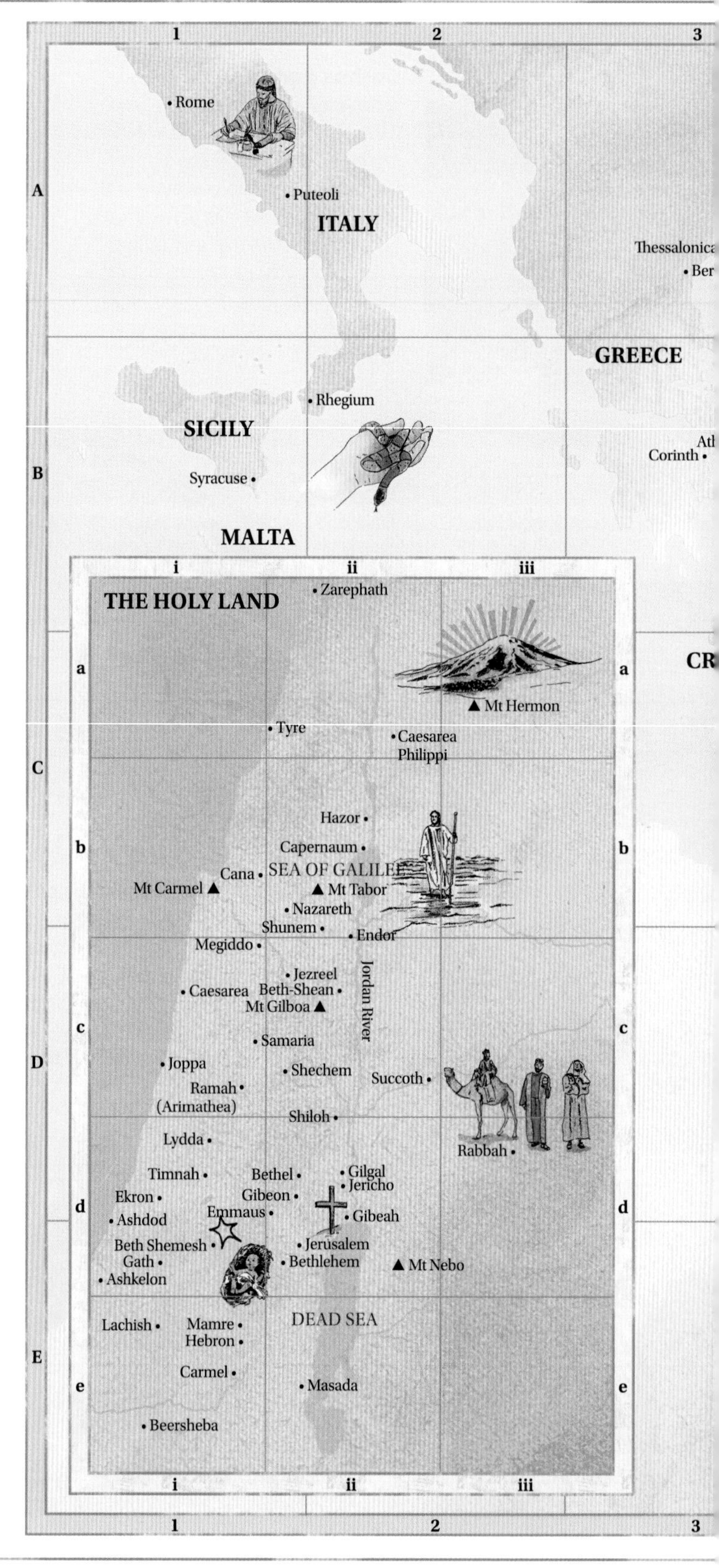

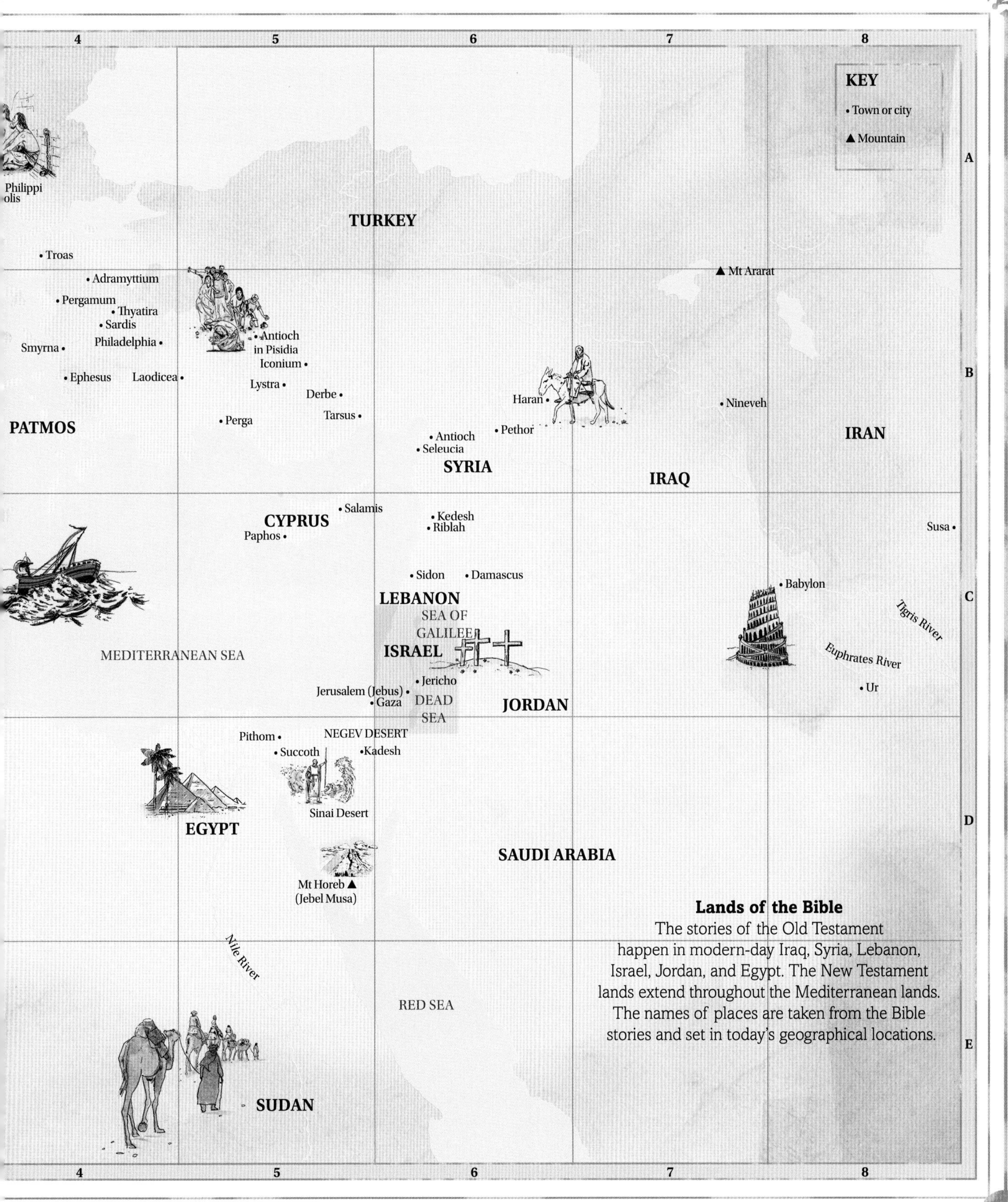

Lands of the Bible

The stories of the Old Testament happen in modern-day Iraq, Syria, Lebanon, Israel, Jordan, and Egypt. The New Testament lands extend throughout the Mediterranean lands. The names of places are taken from the Bible stories and set in today's geographical locations.

The Old Testament

And God said, "This is the sign of the covenant I am making between me and you and every living creature with you, a covenant for all generations to come: I have set my rainbow in the clouds, and it will be a sign of the covenant between me and the earth."

Genesis 9:12–13

Old Testament

A collection of books about God's relationship with the Israelites make up the Old Testament. This is the holy book, called the Tanakh, of the Jewish people, and the first half of the Christian Bible. Divided into three parts, it was mostly written between the 8th and 3rd centuries BCE.

The Torah
The first five books of the Old Testament are called the Torah, meaning "instruction," or the Five Books of Moses (after Israel's first great leader). The text details the laws that the Israelites had to keep, as well as their history up until they entered the Promised Land. The Torah Scroll (left) is the most important object in a synagogue. This scroll is from the Heichal Shlomo, the main synagogue of Jerusalem.

The Prophets
Both historical narratives and prophetic messages are contained in the Nevi'im ("prophets") section. Prophets were people of devout faith who voiced God's will, such as Daniel and Elijah (left). They warned of the dangers of ignoring God and also correctly predicted many events, such as the coming of the Messiah.

The Writings
The last part of the Old Testament is called Ketuvim ("writings"). It consists of 11 books written in a range of styles, such as songs, poems, wise words, and short stories that reflect on human existence. Three of the books (Proverbs, Ecclesiastes, and Song of Songs) were said to have been written by King Solomon. This illustration (right) shows the idea, taken from Ecclesiastes, that "for everything there is a season."

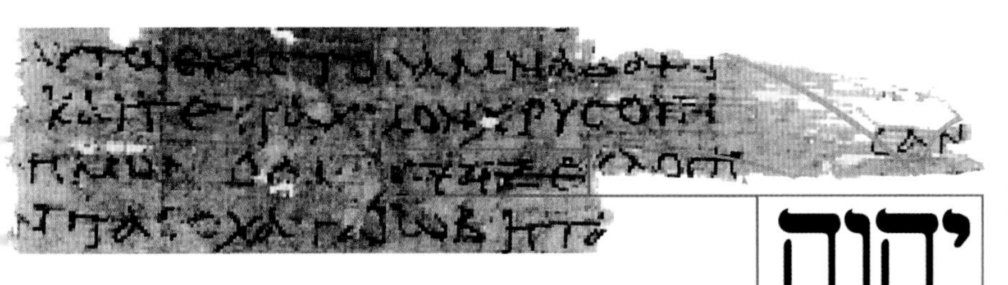

The name of God
The most sacred word in the Old Testament is the name of God. It was spelled YHWH (left inset), as written Hebrew did not have vowels. The pronunciation is unknown because the word was regarded as too sacred to speak aloud. Over time, Jews forgot how to say it, but names such as Jehovah, the Lord, or God are common today.

Solomon's Temple
Some of the Old Testament books describe worship in the Temple of Jerusalem, where animal sacrifices were offered to God. King Solomon (above) is shown here bringing the Ark of the Covenant, which contains the Ten Commandments, into the Temple.

Synagogue
After Solomon's Temple was destroyed by the Romans in 70 CE, the Jewish religion came under review. There were no more priests or sacrifices. Instead, the synagogues, such as this one in Hungary (right), became the focus for prayer and religious study, under teachers called rabbis.

The Creation

In the beginning, God created the heavens and the earth. It was a dark and watery place at first, with no form, no shape, no beginning, no end. The entire surface of the earth was covered with deep black water.

There was no life, but the Spirit of God hovered over the dark face of the waters and He said, "Let there be light." And there was light. He separated the light from the darkness and called the light day and the darkness night. And that was the first day.

On the second day, God said, "Let there be a space above the earth to separate the waters below from the waters above." And He called it sky.

On the third day, God said, "Let the water under the sky be gathered to one place and let dry ground appear." He called the dry ground land and the waters seas. At once, trees, plants, and shoots burst through the ground. And God saw that it was good.

On the fourth day, God said, "Let there be lights in the sky to separate day from night and to mark the seasons and days and years." He made a great shining orb, which He called sun, to light the day. And He made a paler companion, which He called moon, to shine at night. Around the moon He placed the stars like jewels.

On the fifth day, God said, "Let the water teem with living creatures and let birds fly across the sky." And He created all the creatures of the sea and all the feathered birds of the air. And God saw that it was good.

On the sixth day, God said, "Let there be living creatures on the land." And He covered the earth with creatures of all shapes and sizes, from the tiniest flea to the mightiest lion. Then God said, "Let us make man in our image, in our likeness, and let them rule over the fish of the sea and the birds of the air, and over all the creatures that move along the ground." And He made the first man and blessed him, saying, "Be fruitful and increase in number." God looked at everything that He had made in heaven and earth and He was pleased.

On the seventh day, His work was complete, so He rested and He blessed the day and made it holy.

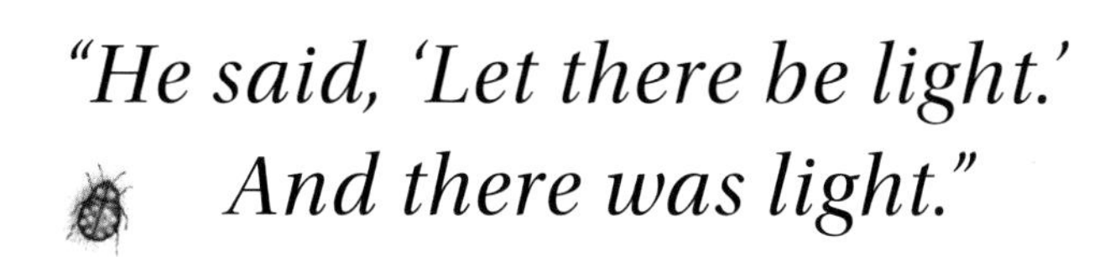

"He said, 'Let there be light.' And there was light."

Shabbat
The seventh day is the Jewish day of rest, called *Shabbat* in Hebrew. It begins every Friday at sunset and ends on the following Saturday night. A special ceremony called *havdalah* ("separation") marks the end of the day, when the sweet-smelling spices used during the day are stored in spice boxes like this one (above) until the next *Shabbat*.

Understanding the story

In the first books of Genesis, God creates the Universe in seven days, and each day is dedicated to a different feature of the Universe. The story serves as evidence of God's supremacy and of the harmony and wholeness of the Universe. The number seven has since come to represent perfection.

The Garden of Eden

The Lord God made a beautiful garden in Eden for the man He had created. It was watered by a sparkling river and was green and shady—an earthly paradise.

Forbidden fruit
The forbidden fruit symbolizes temptation, and Eve believes eating it will grant her knowledge. The Bible does not say what the fruit is, but it is often depicted as an apple since, in Latin, the words for apple ("*malus*") and evil ("*malum*") are very similar.

Cherubim
The cherubim are usually depicted as sphinxes with wings or lions with human heads. They act as God's protectors, singing His praises and assisting His work on Earth. In Eden, they prevent humans from returning to eternal life.

There were trees heavy with fruit so that the man would never go hungry, and in the middle of the garden stood the Tree of Life and the Tree of Knowledge of Good and Evil. And the Lord God named the man Adam and took him to his new home. He told him that he must take care of it. "You are free to eat from any tree in the garden, but you must not eat from the Tree of Knowledge of Good and Evil, for when you eat of it you will surely die." He brought the beasts of the field and the birds of the air to Adam and asked him to give them names. But, although God was very pleased with His work so far, there was one thing that still worried Him. Adam was on his own in the world.

One day, God made Adam fall into a deep sleep and, while he was dreaming, cut open his side and took out one of his ribs. Then, He closed him up again and made a woman out of the bone. The man and the woman stood there happily together in the Garden of Eden.

Now, of all the animals that God had created, the craftiest was the snake. As soon as he spotted the woman in the Garden of Eden, he slithered down the tree and hissed at her, "Did God really say that you must not eat from any tree in the garden?"

The woman told him what God had said to Adam about the Tree of Knowledge. "How ridiculous!" spat the snake. "You won't die! When you eat from the Tree of Knowledge, you will become wise and you will be like God! You will know good and evil."

Tempted by the fruit that would make her wise, the woman picked one and sank her teeth into its juicy flesh. Then she gave it to Adam and he ate it all. At once, their eyes were opened and they realized that they were naked. Full of shame, they found some fig leaves that they sewed together to hide their nakedness. They were so ashamed that they ran and hid in the trees when they heard the Lord God walking in the garden in the cool of the day. "Where are you?" called God.

"I heard you and I hid," admitted Adam. "I was afraid because I was naked." And when God asked him who had told him he was naked, Adam replied, "The woman you put here with me—she gave me some fruit from the Tree of Knowledge and I ate it."

"The snake tricked me and I ate from the Tree!" cried the woman. Then, the Lord God cursed the snake and banished him from the Garden of Eden.

To the woman He said, "With pain you will give birth to children." And, turning to Adam, He said, "Through painful toil you will eat of the ground all the days

Eve gives Adam the forbidden fruit in German painter Lucas Cranach the Elder's oil painting "Adam and Eve" (1526).

of your life. Dust you are and to dust you will return."

The Lord God made clothes for Adam and his wife, whom He named Eve because she would become the mother of all the men and women.

And He said to them, "You now know good and evil. Whatever happens you must not eat from the Tree of Life or you will live forever."

And He banished the pair from the paradise garden. At the gates of the Garden of Eden, God put winged cherubim and a fiery, ever-turning sword to guard the way to the Tree of Life. Adam and Eve could never return.

"You must not eat from the Tree of Knowledge of Good and Evil."

Understanding the story

The first humans, Adam and Eve, ruin the tranquility and harmony (peace and innocence) of Eden by disobeying God's will. They exert free will in eating the forbidden fruit, but, in doing so, they have also chosen independence from God. God confirms this separation by expelling them from His earthly paradise.

Cain and Abel

After Adam and Eve had been banished from the Garden of Eden, their first son, Cain, was born. Time went by and Eve gave birth to another boy. They named him Abel.

As the two brothers grew toward manhood, Cain worked in the fields, taking care of the crops, while Abel roamed the hills looking after the sheep and lambs. They both made offerings to the Lord, Cain bringing the fruits of his crops and Abel bringing the finest meat from his lambs. The Lord was greatly pleased with Abel's offerings, but not with his brother's. Cain could not believe it! He was filled with anger—against God, against his brother, and against the unfairness of life.

"Why are you so angry?" God asked. "Do what is right and all will be well. But if not, sin is lurking at your door, ready to devour you. Watch out!"

But Cain was possessed with murderous thoughts and lured his brother to a field far from home. There he attacked and killed him. The Lord asked where his brother was and Cain replied, "I don't know. Am I my brother's keeper?"

God, who sees everything, said, "Cain, what have you done? Your brother's blood cries out to me from the ground where it was spilled. You are cursed—as long as you live. You are an outcast from man and from God, condemned to wander the world for the rest of your days."

"My punishment is more than I can bear," wailed Cain. "I have lost everything, driven from the land and from God. I am homeless and will spend my life on the road, at the mercy of murderers."

But the Lord reassured him that anyone who killed him would suffer the most terrible vengeance—seven times greater even than his own punishment. He put a special mark on Cain to keep him safe. Cain went on his way to the land of Nod, east of Eden.

Understanding the story

Jealous of God's preference for his brother Abel, Cain commits a terrible sin by killing his brother. God banishes him from Eden. He also gives him a mark that protects him from being killed and serves as a constant reminder of his crime.

Offerings
The Bible states that firstborn animals and the first crops of the harvest are fitting offerings to God. It is unclear exactly why God rejects Cain's offering, but it is likely that they were not the first crops, which were deemed the best.

Noah and the Flood

Adam's descendants increased and multiplied, and so did their wickedness and corruption.

The Lord saw it all and said, "I will wipe humankind, whom I have created, from the face of the earth for I am grieved that I have made them."

But Noah was different. He alone was righteous. The Lord spoke to him telling him that there would be a great flood. He instructed him to make a huge ark out of cypress wood and to cover it with tar, inside and out, to make it seaworthy. Noah and his wife, and their three sons and their wives, must go into the ark and they would be saved. With them, they must take two of every kind of bird or creature—one male and one female—that walked or creeped or slithered across the earth and plenty of food to go around.

Noah listened and did exactly what the Lord God had commanded him. With the help of his three sons, Shem, Ham, and Japheth, he worked patiently, day and night. Bit by bit the great ship took shape

Cypress wood
God requests that the ark be built with the wood of cypress trees. This wood was recognized for its durability, and it was a symbol of immortality in ancient times. The wooden ark represents God's protection and is Noah's salvation.

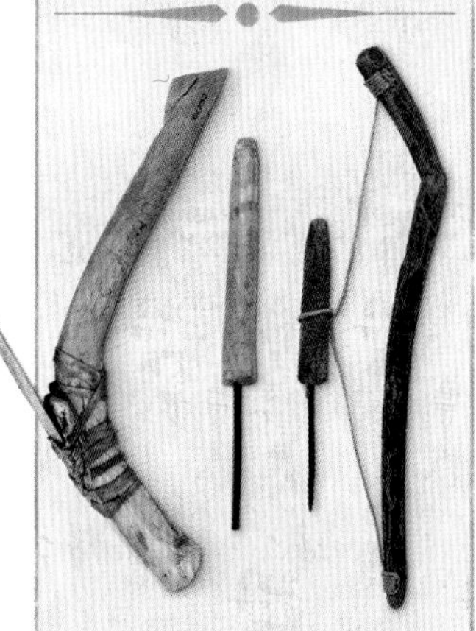

Boat-building tools
These 3,000-year-old tools were typical of the ones used by Middle-Eastern workmen to construct boats. The adze (left) was used to hack and plane wood, while the bow drill (right) made holes for pegging wood. The chisel (center) is an early version of the tool still used today.

Mount Ararat
There is no agreement as to where the ark ran aground. Perhaps the most popular suggestion is Mount Ararat (above), which lies in the Ararat mountain range in modern-day Turkey. Archaeological expeditions have sought to unearth the ark there, but it has never been found.

Olive branch
When the dove returned with the olive branch, it showed Noah that life had begun to thrive on Earth once more, and, as such, the olive leaf symbolizes a peaceful new beginning. The image of a dove with an olive branch in its beak is still a common symbol for peace.

as they skilfully sawed and smoothed and planed the cypress timber, then hammered and coated the ark with pitch. At last it was finished.

And God said to Noah, "Seven days from now I will send rain on the earth for forty days and forty nights, and I will wipe from the face of the earth every living creature that I have made." Noah quickly set to work to find the creatures that God had told him he must save and lead them into the safety of the ark. And when the very last pair had scurried in, Noah and his wife followed them. And, just at that moment, the clouds gathered and the heavens opened.

It rained and it rained and it rained, and steadily the waters crept over the face of the earth. Almost every living thing perished apart from Noah and the animals on the wooden ark. Then, after many days, God sent a strong wind that raced and whistled around the world, drying up the water. Slowly but surely, the levels began to drop.

One day, the ark shuddered to a halt. It had run aground on the top of Mount Ararat, surrounded by a vast expanse of sea. Noah wondered whether there might be any dry land over the horizon. So he chose a raven and launched the bird into the air to search for land. But it flew back. Noah tried again, this time choosing a dove. But she returned to the ark, too. Seven days later, he sent her out again and she flew back, triumphant, with an olive leaf.

When the earth had emerged once more, God spoke to Noah. "Come out of the ark, you and your wife and your sons and their wives. Bring out every kind of living creature that is with you so they can multiply on the earth."

So they all came out of the ark for the first time in many months. Noah built an altar to the Lord and made sacrifices on it. The Lord was pleased and said, "Never again will I curse the ground because of humankind, even though their heart is inclined toward evil from childhood. And never again will I destroy all living creatures, as I have done."

A beautiful rainbow appeared as he made a covenant with them that life on earth would never again be destroyed by flood. And he said, "I have set my rainbow in the clouds, and it will be the sign of the covenant between me and the earth. Whenever the rainbow appears in the clouds, I will see it and remember the everlasting covenant."

Understanding the story

Unhappy with the sinfulness and immorality of man, God decides to cleanse the Earth by sending a flood to destroy mankind. He only spares the righteous Noah (whose name means "comfort" in Hebrew) and his family. The flood brings chaos to the Earth, but from this discord springs order and a new beginning.

"Noah listened and did exactly what the Lord God had commanded him."

Map of Mesopotamia
The world's very first cities, dating back to 4000 BCE, are marked on this map, including Babel, which is thought to be Babylon. They were all built in Mesopotamia (shaded orange)—which is now mostly modern-day Iraq.

Mud bricks
Since stone and mortar were scarce in Mesopotamia, the bricks were made by mixing mud and straw together, before placing the mixture in wooden molds. Left to dry out in the sunshine, the mixture formed its distinctive brick shape. This method is still in use today.

The Tower of Babel

After the great flood, centuries passed and Noah's descendants gradually peopled the earth. Generation followed generation, and the clans of his sons, Shem, Ham, and Japheth, flourished and prospered.

They spread in every direction, all speaking one common language so that, wherever they went, they could understand each other. And in the east they found a wide and fertile plain in Shinar, which became known as Babylonia. They settled there, and life was pleasant. "Come, let us build a city, with a tower that reaches to the heavens, so that we may make a name for ourselves and not be scattered over the face of the earth," the people said to one another. After all their wanderings, this seemed a good idea. It would be the first city to be built since the flood, and the tower would be its crowning glory, admired by the whole world. It would be made of bricks instead of stone, and it would climb up to the stars.

They mixed mud and straw to make the bricks, baking them in the sun, and stirred vats of bitumen, like molasses, to use as mortar. Teams of builders set to work and, slowly, the city began to take shape.

And the tower rose steadily from the ground, climbing higher and higher into the sky, as if it wanted to reach heaven itself. The finest craftsmen decorated the tower with precious stones. Steep flights of steps zigzagged breathtakingly up and up, through the clouds to the very top. The people marveled at their great achievement and congratulated each other. Even the eagles, flying above, looked down in astonishment.

But the Lord was not pleased with the vanity and pride that He saw. "After this, nothing will be impossible for these people. They are reaching too high! I will bring them down to earth and confuse them so that they no longer speak the same language," He said. And suddenly, the air was filled with a terrifying noise. It was the deafening babble of thousands of voices, each speaking a different language. Nobody could understand what anyone else was saying. Panic-stricken, people shouted and screamed, trying to make themselves understood, but the words that came out made no sense. It was a hideous chorus that shook the city to its foundations and gave it the name of Babel.

Confused and unable to communicate with each other, the people were not able to go on building their city. Instead, they were scattered over the face of the earth, speaking their different languages.

"The Tower of Babel" (1563), oil on canvas, by Flemish painter Peter Bruegel the Elder (1525–1569)

Understanding the story

In the ancient world, the people of Babylonia claimed to be the center of the world, and in this story, they build a great tower to show God their genius and power. God punishes them for their arrogance and vanity by making it impossible for them to communicate, so preventing them from building their city and forcing them to scatter.

Abram's Journey

Abram was seventy-five years old and he lived in Haran, not too far from the Euphrates River in Mesopotamia. He was married to Sarai but, to their great sadness, they had no children.

Euphrates River
The longest river in western Asia is the Euphrates, covering about 1,700 miles (2,700 km). It begins in the mountains of eastern Turkey, crosses Syria, and flows southeastward through Iraq. In ancient times, the Euphrates River flooded the flat plains of Mesopotamia every year. Settlements developed as people began digging canals and reservoirs to channel and store the river's water.

One day, the Lord came to Abram and told him to leave his country and move to the land of Canaan. "I will make you into a great nation and I will bless you," He promised. "I will make your name great and I will bless those who bless you, and whoever curses you, I will curse. And all the peoples on the earth will be blessed through you." So Abram set off, taking with him Sarai, his nephew Lot, and their servants. The camels were laden with all their possessions and their flocks straggled behind. When they arrived in Canaan, they traveled as far as the great tree of Moreh at Shechem.

There, the Lord appeared to Abram. He promised, "To your offspring I will give this land." And Abram built an altar there and gave thanks. Then he went on toward the hills east of Bethel and built another altar to the Lord. After this, he continued his wandering toward the Negev and beyond.

Finally, Abram came back to the place near Bethel, where he had built the altar. But, by now, after so long traveling, Abram and his nephew, Lot, were not seeing eye to eye. They both had large flocks of sheep and goats and there was never enough good grazing to go around. Their herdsmen were constantly at each others' throats. At last, Abram said to Lot, "Let's not quarrel. There is plenty of land. Let's part company. You

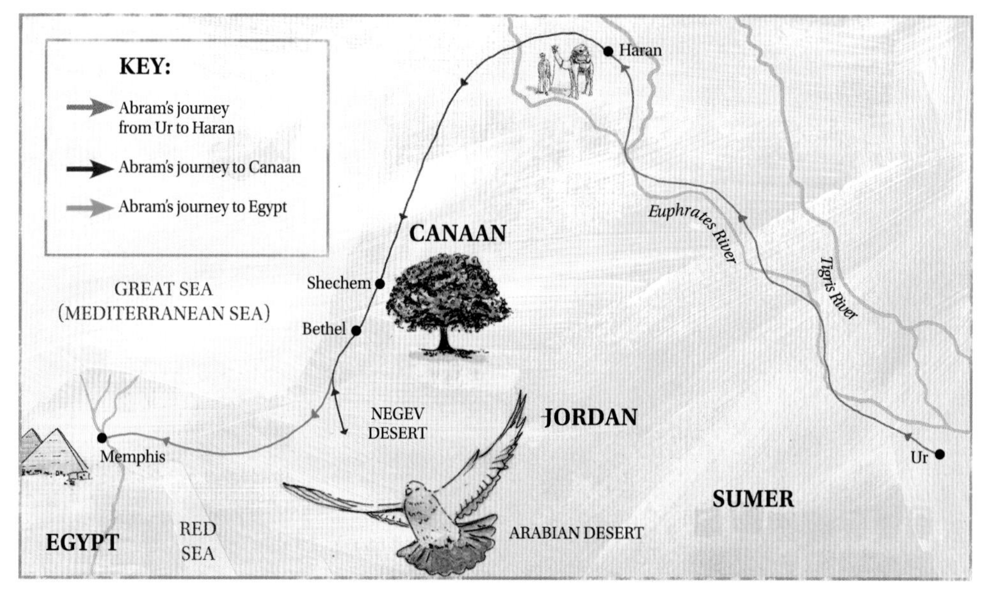

Abram's travels
Abram's birthplace was Ur, one of the main cities of Sumer in southern Mesopotamia. Greek for "the land between the two rivers," Mesopotamia was located between the Tigris and Euphrates rivers. Abram's family later traveled to Haran where they settled. Following God's covenant with Abram, in which he is promised a new country, he leaves Haran and sets off for Canaan. Abram later went to Egypt to escape a famine in Canaan.

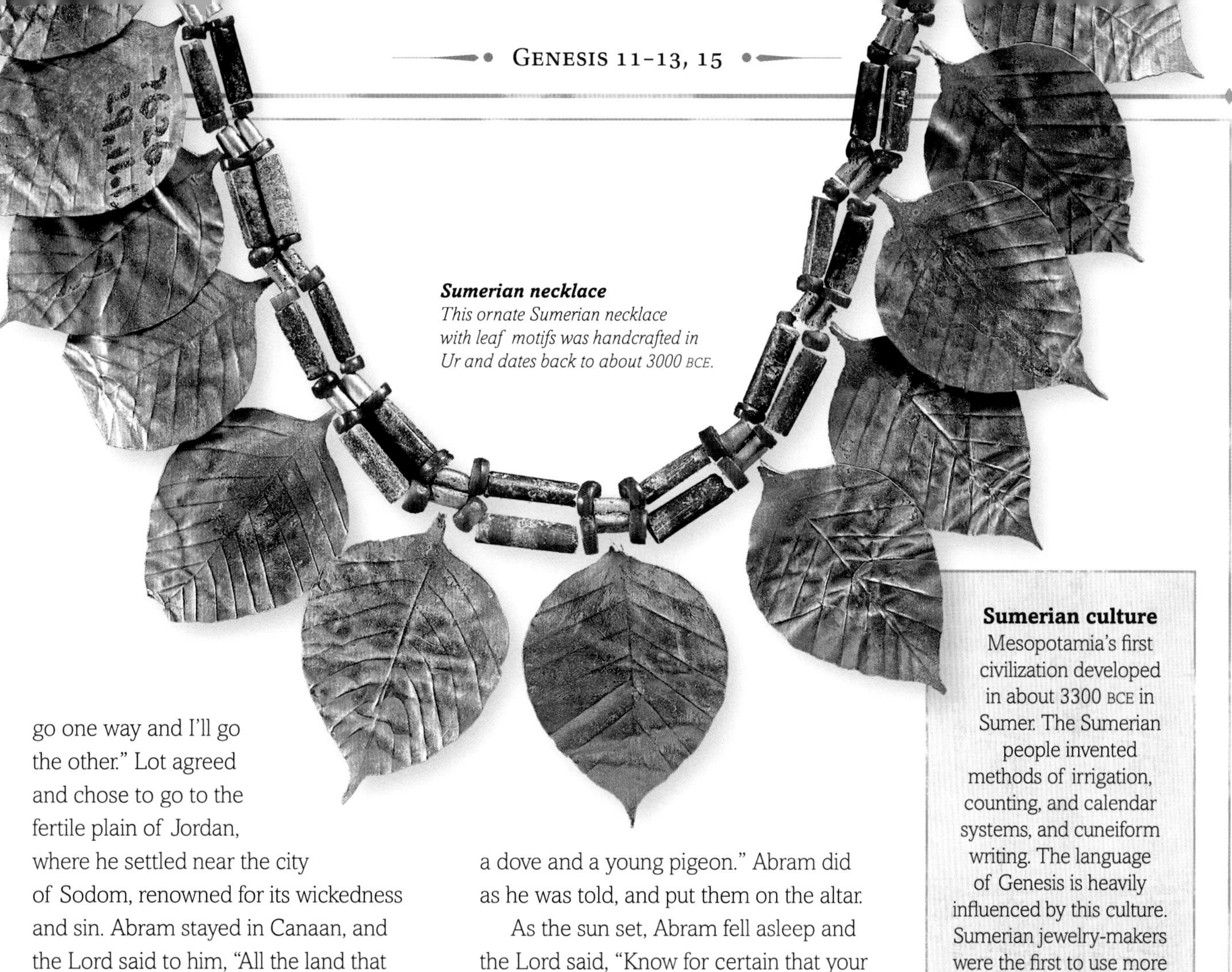

Sumerian necklace
This ornate Sumerian necklace with leaf motifs was handcrafted in Ur and dates back to about 3000 BCE.

go one way and I'll go the other." Lot agreed and chose to go to the fertile plain of Jordan, where he settled near the city of Sodom, renowned for its wickedness and sin. Abram stayed in Canaan, and the Lord said to him, "All the land that you see—north, south, east, and west—I will give you and your offspring forever." But Abram replied, "What can you give me since I remain childless?"

The Lord promised him that, one day, he would have a son and heir, and that he would have as many descendants as stars in the sky. Then the Lord sealed His promise to Abram, "Bring a heifer, a goat, and a ram—each three years old—and a dove and a young pigeon." Abram did as he was told, and put them on the altar.

As the sun set, Abram fell asleep and the Lord said, "Know for certain that your descendants will be strangers in a country not their own and they will be enslaved and ill-treated for four hundred years." "When darkness had fallen, a smoking brazier with a blazing torch appeared in front of Abram. And in this way the Lord made a covenant with him and promised, "To your descendants I give this land from the river of Egypt to the great river, the Euphrates."

Sumerian culture
Mesopotamia's first civilization developed in about 3300 BCE in Sumer. The Sumerian people invented methods of irrigation, counting, and calendar systems, and cuneiform writing. The language of Genesis is heavily influenced by this culture. Sumerian jewelry-makers were the first to use more complex techniques, working with precious metals and beading.

"All the land that you see... I will give you and your offspring forever."

Understanding the story

God promises to bless Abram's people and make them into a great nation. Abram endures many hardships, but he follows God's instructions because he has complete faith in His promise. Unlike the people of Babel, his trust will be rewarded, and his descendants will become the nation of Israel.

Abram's Two Sons

Ten years had passed since Abram arrived in the land of Canaan with his wife, Sarai, and still they had no children. They were old now, and perhaps it was impossible.

They had, however, a young Egyptian maidservant named Hagar, and one day Sarai went to her husband with a plan. Abram should take Hagar as his wife and have a child with her. At least they might be able to start a family like that. Abram agreed and, before long, Hagar was pregnant. But as soon as she knew she was going to have a baby, Hagar got ideas above her station and began to be rude toward her mistress.

Sarai complained to Abram, "I put my servant in your arms and now that she knows she is pregnant, she despises me!"

"Do what you think best," replied Abram. So Sarai began to treat her maidservant with such cruelty that Hagar ran away to hide in the desert. An angel found her weeping by the side of a spring, and Hagar told him the whole story. He said that she must go back and that she would have a son named Ishmael. So Hagar returned and gave birth to Abram's son, who was named Ishmael. Abram was eighty-six years old at the time.

Thirteen years later, the Lord appeared to Abram again and made a covenant with him. "You will be the father of many nations. No longer will you be called Abram; your name will be Abraham. I will establish my covenant as an everlasting covenant between me and you and your descendants after you for the generations to come, to be your God and the God of your descendants after you. I will give you the whole of Canaan as an everlasting possession." And He went on to say that, as a sign of the covenant, every male must be circumcised and that, from now on, Sarai must be known as Sarah. "I will bless her and will surely give you a son by her," He added.

"But I am nearly one hundred years old! And Sarah is ninety!" said Abraham.

The Lord replied, "Sarah will indeed give you a son and you will call him Isaac. I will establish my covenant with him as an everlasting covenant for his descendants after him." And He said that He would also bless Ishmael. "He will be the father of a great nation. But my covenant I will establish with Isaac, who will be born next year." And that very day, Abraham and Ishmael—and every male in the household—were circumcised as the Lord had ordered.

Some time later, Abraham was sitting at the entrance to his tent, near the great trees of Mamre, when the Lord paid him a visit. It was the middle of the day and the heat was intense. Abraham noticed three men standing nearby in the full glare of the sun. He went and greeted them, bowing low on the ground, and invited them to rest in the shade of the trees. "I will get water so that you can wash your feet and please let me

Desert life
Abram and his people led a simple life. A supply of water and pasture for the animals were all they needed. Their existence was nomadic, moving from one place to another. They slept in tents and sometimes used camels to help carry their loads.

Animal skins
Animal skins similar to those used by Hagar and Ishmael are still in use today. This Egyptian woman is making buttermilk by shaking a goatskin backward and forward, churning the milk inside.

give you something to eat," he said. He hurried back into the tent and asked Sarah to bake some bread with the finest flour. Then he ordered the servants to kill a tender young calf and prepare it for the strangers, and to bring some curd and milk. They enjoyed their meal in the shade of the trees and asked Abraham, "Where is your wife, Sarah?"

"There, in the tent," he replied.

The Lord said, "I will surely return to you about this time next year and Sarah, your wife, will have a son." From the tent, Sarah heard these words and laughed to herself at the thought.

And the Lord was not pleased and said to Abraham, "Why did Sarah laugh? Nothing is impossible for God." And, sure enough, when it was time, Sarah gave birth to a boy. They named him Isaac and, when he was eight days old, Abraham circumcised him. "God has brought me laughter and everyone who hears about this will laugh with me," rejoiced Sarah.

But one thing spoiled her joy—and that was Ishmael. She did not like the way he taunted Isaac. She asked her husband to get rid of him and his mother, too. Abraham was saddened by this, but the Lord told him not to worry. "Listen to what Sarah says, because it is through Isaac that your line will be continued. I will take care of Ishmael."

So, early next morning, Abraham gave Hagar some food and water and sent her on her way with Ishmael. It was not long before their food ran out and their water skin ran dry, and Hagar knew that they could not last long in the desert of Beersheba. She put her son under a bush and walked away. She could not bear to watch him die. Then she collapsed on the ground, shut her eyes, and wept.

An angel spoke to her from heaven, saying, "Don't be afraid. Go back to the boy and lift him up and take him by the hand. God will not let him die. He will become the leader of a great nation!" At that, Hagar opened her eyes and saw a well full of sparkling water in front of her. She filled her water skin to the brim and took it back to Ishmael. And God looked after him as he grew up in the desert. He was strong and fearless. In time, his mother found a wife for him from Egypt, the land of her birth.

Three strangers paid Abraham a visit

Understanding the story

While Abram's devout faith means he will wait for God to keep His original promise, Sarai's impatience and lack of trust in God leads to hasty action. The following conflicts and divisions suggest this is not the Lord's wish, and the resulting baby is not the prophesized son. God carries out His promise, by giving Abram (meaning "exalted father") the name Abraham (meaning "father of a multitude of nations"), and granting him and Sarah a son, Isaac.

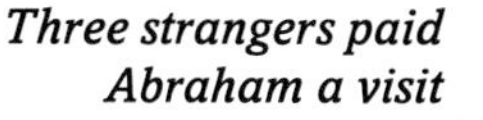

Sodom and Gomorrah

The twin cities of Sodom and Gomorrah, on the fertile plains of the Jordan River, were awful places. Awash with sin, the people led wicked lives, satisfying every desire.

The Lord saw it all and made up His mind to destroy the cities and wipe them from the face of the earth. But Abraham asked Him, "Will you sweep away the righteous with the wicked? Just suppose that there are fifty God-fearing people who live there?" The Lord agreed and said He would spare the cities. Apologizing for his boldness, Abraham pressed Him further. Exactly how many—or how few—righteous people would it take for God to show mercy and to spare the cities? In the end, the Lord replied, "For the sake of ten, I will not destroy Sodom and Gomorrah."

That evening, two angels disguised as men arrived in Sodom, and Abraham's nephew, Lot, was sitting by the city gates. He greeted the visitors, bowing low on the ground. "My lords, please do me the honor of coming to my house. You can wash your feet there and spend the night, then go on your way in the morning." At first, they refused, wanting to stay in the square, but Lot insisted and, in the end, they agreed. The angels went home with him, and Lot prepared a splendid meal for them and baked loaves of special bread without any yeast.

But as darkness fell, a great crowd of thugs surrounded the house, looking for trouble. "Where are those nice young men who have just arrived?" they jeered. "We'll show them a good time!"

Lot bravely went out to confront them. "No, my friends," he said. "I have two beloved daughters. I would rather give them to you than let anything happen to the guests who are staying under my roof."

"You don't belong here, anyway," they shouted. "Just you wait! We'll give you a good seeing to, as well!" They surged forward to grab him, but the angels managed to reach out from the doorway and pull him inside to safety just in time. And then the angels blinded the mob so that suddenly none of them could see. Sightless, they stumbled over each other in the dark, arms outstretched like sleep walkers, trying to find their way home.

The angels said to Lot, "Do you have any other family here? Sons or daughters or sons-in-law? Get them out because we're going to destroy the place!" Immediately, Lot hurried to talk to his sons-in-law and told them that the Lord was going to raze the city to the ground. But they thought he was joking and took no notice.

Dead Sea
The area where Sodom and Gomorrah are likely to have been is now a dry, sulfurous land by the Dead Sea. Yet, in the past, the region was fertile and thriving. It was also home to many people, as the discovery of five ancient ruined cities has shown.

As dawn broke, the angels begged Lot to save himself. "Hurry! Take your wife and your two daughters and leave! Otherwise you will all perish!" But Lot hesitated. Then the two angels took him and his wife and their two daughters, and led them to safety outside the city walls. There they told them that they must run for it. "Don't look back, whatever you do, and don't stop on the plain! Flee to the mountains or there's no hope!"

"No!" said Lot. "You have shown great kindness to me in sparing my life. But I can't flee to the mountains. It is too far. Let me take refuge in that little town over there on the edge of the plain. It's called Zoar." The angels agreed and told him he would be safe there.

By the time that Lot reached Zoar, the Lord had put His plan into action. He began the destruction of Sodom and Gomorrah. It was a terrifying sight as burning sulfur rained down from the heavens on the two cities, turning them into one gigantic inferno. Flames licked high in the air, devouring everything in their path. There was no escape. Everything that lived or breathed there died an agonizing death that day and the surrounding plains were reduced to charred and blackened cinders.

Hospitality
Hospitality was a matter of life and death in ancient times, as travelers relied on strangers offering them food and drink to survive. Even today, Bedouin people (above) welcome visitors with the words, "You are among your family."

Lot's wife
Lot's wife is punished for looking back at the city of Sodom when she is turned into a pillar of salt. This distinctive salt rock column (above) is called "Lot's wife," and it can be seen on Mount Sodom, standing over the salty waters of the Dead Sea.

Salt
The Dead Sea has no outlet, so the minerals, such as salt, that flow into it stay there forever. These minerals remain after the water has evaporated, producing crystal formations visible both in the water and on the shore.

And Lot's wife forgot what the angels had told them and, as she fled from the flames, she turned around for one last look. Immediately, she was rooted to the ground and turned into a pillar of salt, never to move again. The next morning, Abraham got up and looked down. There was no sign of the two cities. It was as if they had never existed.

Understanding the story

The destruction of Sodom and Gomorrah demonstrates the power of God's justice. Lot's kindness and hospitality are his salvation. He didn't know that the men who came to Sodom were angels, but he risked his life to protect them. However, Lot's wife becomes a pillar of salt as a permanent reminder of what happens when God's word is disobeyed.

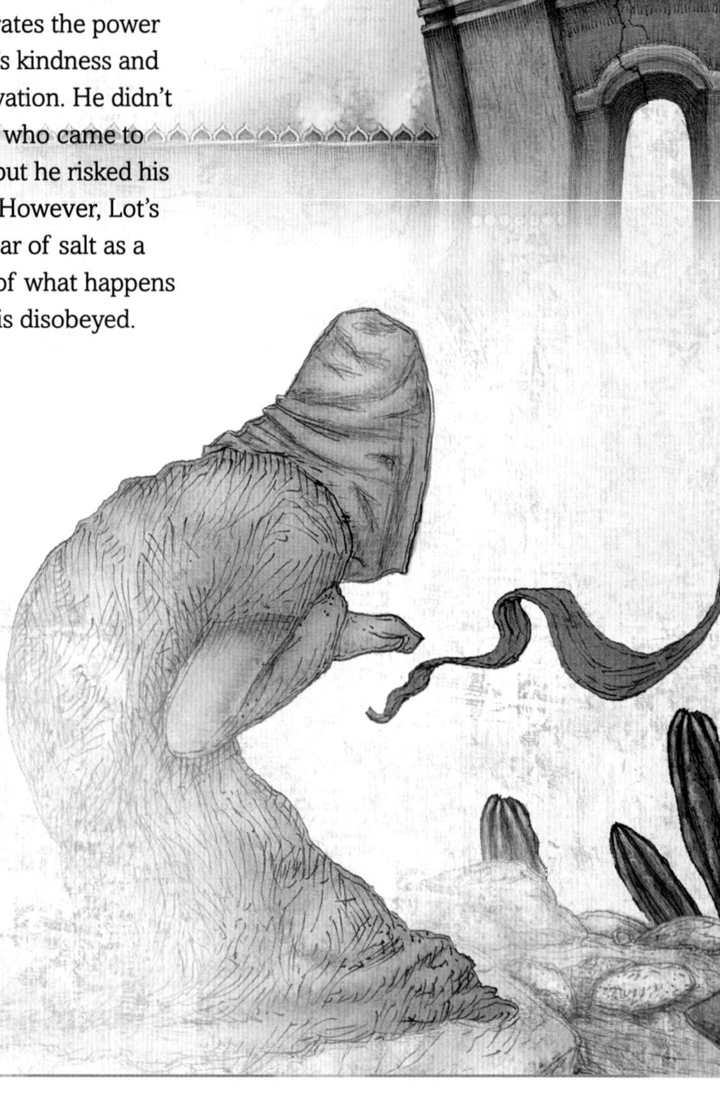

The Sacrifice of Isaac

The Lord came to Abraham again and gave him the ultimate test of his faith. "Take your beloved son, Isaac, and go to the mountains of Moriah. Sacrifice him there as a burnt offering. I will show you where."

Early the next morning, Abraham got up, with a heavy heart, and prepared to make the long journey through the desert. He packed food and water, then saddled his donkey and set off from Beersheba with Isaac and two servants. Slowly they traveled through southern Canaan until the mountains loomed before them. It took them three days, but to Abraham it seemed a lifetime.

They stopped in the foothills to cut some firewood from the trees, choosing young branches of chestnut and poplar, which would burn well on the altar. Abraham told the servants to wait. "Stay here with the donkey while the boy and I go up there. We will worship and then we will come back to you."

He gave the bundles of wood to Isaac to carry on his back. It was a heavy load for the young boy, but he did not complain. Abraham took a sharp knife and a blazing torch to light the fire on the altar. Father and son trudged up the steep path, side by side, but Isaac was puzzled. He said to Abraham, "The fire and the wood are here, but where is the lamb that we are going to sacrifice?"

"God himself will provide the lamb for the burnt offering, my son," replied Abraham quietly, avoiding his eyes. They continued up the mountain and when they got to the highest peak, Abraham finally stopped and built an altar out of stone. He took the wood from his son and arranged it on top. Isaac watched him curiously and looked around. There was no sign of a lamb or any other creature that could be offered to God as a sacrifice. Abraham went over to his son and gripped him tightly. He took a length of rope and tied him up so that he could not move. Then he laid the boy on the altar.

With a breaking heart, Abraham reached for his knife and held it high in the air, ready to plunge it into his son. But just at that moment, the angel of the Lord called out from above, "Abraham! Abraham! Do not lay a hand on the boy. Do not do anything to him. You have proved your love of God. You were willing to sacrifice your son for Him."

Abraham dropped the knife and released his son, embracing him tenderly. Then he looked around and saw a mountain ram that had got its horns caught in a bush. Abraham went over and untangled the animal, then slit its throat and offered it

Negev Desert
The Negev Desert is a rocky desert that covers more than half of modern-day Israel. As with Moses and Jesus after him, Abraham's time in the desert is a symbol of intense suffering and being tested by God.

Burnt offering
Complete commitment to God could be demonstrated by making a burnt offering—the sacrifice and burning of an animal until only ashes remained. This Israelite altar was a typical site for such burnt offerings to the Lord.

Golden statue
This golden statue is one of a pair excavated from a royal tomb in Ur, and dates from about 2500 BCE.

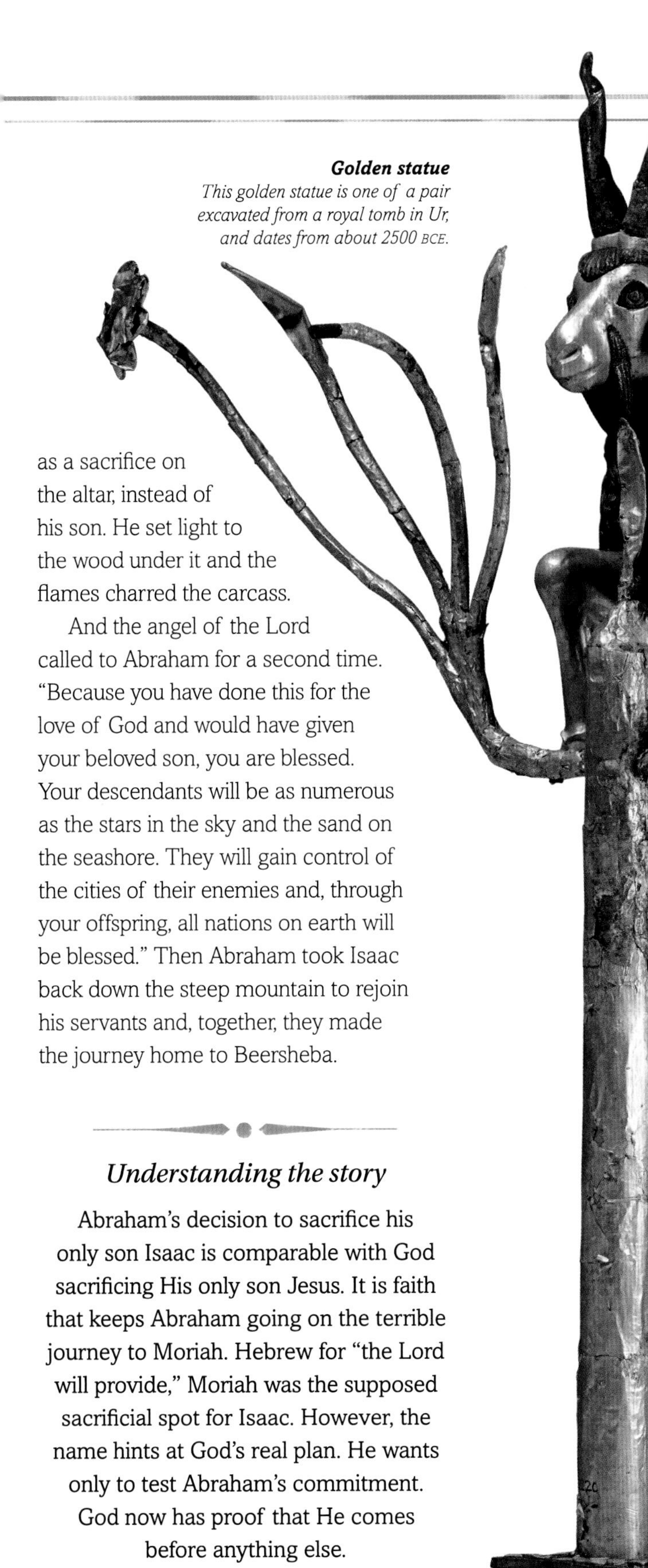

as a sacrifice on the altar, instead of his son. He set light to the wood under it and the flames charred the carcass.

And the angel of the Lord called to Abraham for a second time. "Because you have done this for the love of God and would have given your beloved son, you are blessed. Your descendants will be as numerous as the stars in the sky and the sand on the seashore. They will gain control of the cities of their enemies and, through your offspring, all nations on earth will be blessed." Then Abraham took Isaac back down the steep mountain to rejoin his servants and, together, they made the journey home to Beersheba.

Understanding the story

Abraham's decision to sacrifice his only son Isaac is comparable with God sacrificing His only son Jesus. It is faith that keeps Abraham going on the terrible journey to Moriah. Hebrew for "the Lord will provide," Moriah was the supposed sacrificial spot for Isaac. However, the name hints at God's real plan. He wants only to test Abraham's commitment. God now has proof that He comes before anything else.

Ram
Though God has spared Isaac, Abraham must still make a burnt offering. With limited options on the mountain, he finds a ram caught in a bush. The killing and burning of the ram until nothing remains show the Lord that Abraham is keeping nothing for himself. All his love and belief are with God.

Dome of the Rock
This foundation stone is where it is believed Abraham was intending to sacrifice Isaac. Today, a Muslim shrine called the Dome of the Rock stands on top of it, in Jerusalem. The location is steeped in Biblical history, with both Solomon's Temple and Herod's Temple later built nearby.

Carrying jars
Rebekah carries her jar on her shoulder when she goes to fetch water. Many women living in remote parts of the world still carry jars or other containers on their heads or shoulders. This makes it easier to manage a heavy load.

Camels
The harsh conditions of desert life pose no problem for a camel. This hardy animal has adapted well, with three stomachs able to hold up to 15 gallons (70 liters) of water. If food is limited, fat is stored in the humps. Long, strong legs help them carry loads.

Isaac and Rebekah

Abraham was a very old man by now and he was blessed in every way. But he knew that he would not live forever and that there was still one thing that he must sort out before he died.

He called his most trusted servant and asked for his help. "Please put your hand on your heart and swear that you will go back to the country where I was born and find a wife for my son Isaac. I do not want him to marry anyone from around here in Canaan."

The servant pointed out that it might not be easy to persuade a young woman to leave her home and family so far behind. "Why don't I take your son with me back to the country you came from?" he asked.

"No," answered Abraham. "Whatever you do, don't take Isaac with you. The Lord, the God of heaven, will send His angel with you to help find a wife for my son."

So Abraham's loyal servant set out on his mission, taking ten of his master's camels, laden with gifts. He headed for the town in northwest Mesopotamia, where Abraham's brother, Nahor, lived.

He arrived just as the young women were coming down to the well with their jars to fetch water. He stopped, and his camels kneeled down on the ground after their long journey.

And Abraham's servant looked at the young women gathering around the well and he prayed, "O Lord, help me! How will I know who is the one? Please give me a sign. Could it be the one who offers me a drink from her jar and offers to water my camels?"

As he was praying, a beautiful girl arrived, carrying her jar gracefully on her shoulder. She knelt down and drew some water from the well, and Abraham's servant hurried up to her and asked for a drink. "Of course. You are welcome, my lord!" she said. "And what about your camels? They must be thirsty, too." After he had drunk, she emptied all her water into the trough and ran back to the well for more so that the camels could have a good drink.

Abraham's servant was so pleased that he reached into his bag of gifts and gave her a solid gold nose ring and two heavy gold bracelets. "Whose daughter are you?" he asked. "Please tell me, would there be a room in your father's house where I could spend the night?"

She replied that she was called Rebekah and that she was the daughter of Bethuel and the granddaughter of Nahor. She said that he was welcome to stay the night in her father's house and ran back to tell her family. Her brother, Laban, went straight out to meet the stranger. He knew immediately that the stranger was blessed by the Lord and welcomed him into the house, offering him food.

But Abraham's servant would not eat before he explained why he had come. "I am the servant of Abraham. He has one son, Isaac, and I have been sent to find him a wife here, in the country of Abraham's birth. And the Lord has led me to Rebekah, the granddaughter of my master's brother. She has been chosen."

Laban and Bethuel listened, knowing that it was the will of God, and they answered, "Here is Rebekah. Take her and let her become the wife of your master's son, as the Lord has directed."

And the servant gave more jewelry to Rebekah—both gold and silver—and beautiful embroidered clothes. He also gave special gifts to her brother and mother. They would have liked Rebekah to stay with them for a few more days to say goodbye, but Abraham's servant was in a hurry to get home.

Rebekah took her maidservants and her old nurse, and together they set off, with Abraham's servant, to start a new life in Canaan. When they eventually arrived it was dusk, and Isaac was praying by himself out in the fields. He opened his eyes as the camel train approached and saw Rebekah for the first time. Soon afterward, Isaac and Rebekah were married, and Isaac loved his wife dearly. And she comforted him greatly after the death of his mother, Sarah.

Dowry bag
A dowry was a gift for the bride's father to show the groom's appreciation for taking his daughter. It was usually money or precious goods. A bride was also given a dowry (in a bag similar to this Afghan example) from her father to help with married life.

Understanding the story

Abraham sends his trusted servant to find a wife for his son Isaac, but he is really putting his faith in God to determine the outcome. The servant asks God to help him find a bride, and his prayers are answered in the form of Rebekah's extraordinary kindness and generosity toward the servant, which show that she is the perfect choice. Abraham, his servant, and Rebekah all demonstrate their commitment to God.

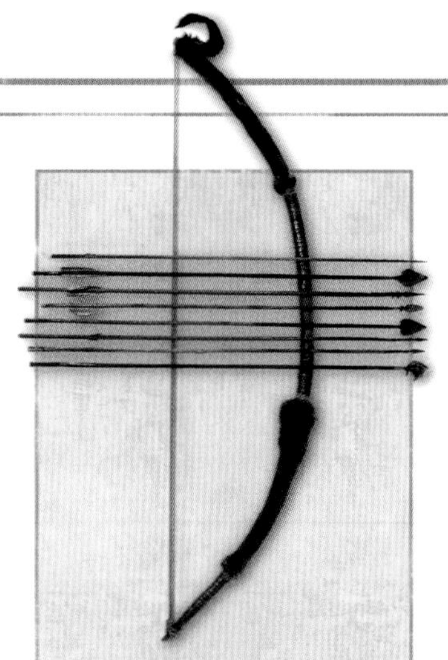

Hunting weapons
Esau used bows and arrows to hunt animals. The bows were crafted from wood and bone, while the arrows were made of reeds or wood with a tip of flint, bone, or metal. Arrowheads were sometimes dipped in poison. Game included wild goat and deer. Ancient hunters also used nets and traps.

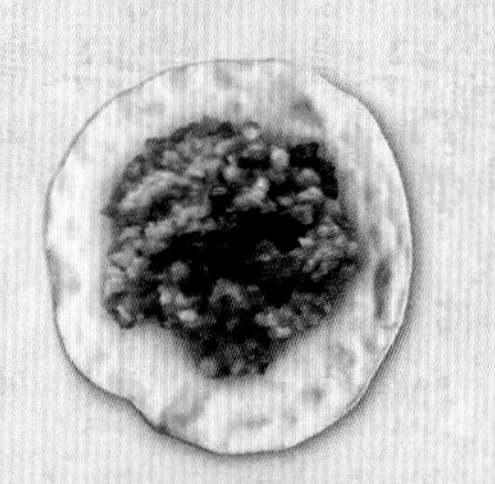

Lentil stew
A standard meal in ancient times, lentil stew was usually eaten with unleavened bread. Esau trades his right to the family's estate for a bowl of stew, but, more importantly, he gives up his right to inherit God's covenant with his grandfather Abraham.

Esau and Jacob

Isaac was forty years old when he married Rebekah, but for many years they remained childless.

They prayed to the Lord and, at last, after nearly twenty years, she became pregnant with twins. As they grew inside her, they kicked and jostled, and she asked the Lord why this was happening? He replied, "Two nations are in your womb, and two peoples from within you will be separated. One people will be stronger than the other, and the older will serve the younger."

When the time came, Rebekah did indeed give birth to twin boys. The first was bright red and covered in hair from his head to his toes and they named him Esau. The second was smooth and slippery as an eel and they named him Jacob.

The twins grew up side by side, but Esau became a hunter, skilful with his bow and arrow, while Jacob preferred to stay at home and help his mother. He was her favorite, while Esau was dearer to his father's heart.

One day, Jacob was stirring a lentil stew when Esau rushed in, famished. "Quick! Give me some stew!"

"I will," replied Jacob. "But only if you give up your rights as the firstborn son and give them to me."

"I can't see what good my rights are anyway," retorted Esau. "You can have them, with pleasure." Then Esau tucked into a bowl of stew.

The years passed and Isaac lost his sight. He called to his son, Esau, and said, "My son, I am an old man and death is approaching. Go and catch some wild game for me. Prepare my favorite dish. Then I will give you my blessing before I die."

Rebekah overheard his words, but she wanted Jacob to receive the blessing instead of Esau and she thought of a plan. She told Jacob to find two young goats and bring them to her. She would prepare a delicious meal. Then Jacob could take it to his father and receive his blessing. But Jacob protested, "Esau is hairy and I am smooth-skinned. What if my father touches me? He would know I was tricking him and would curse me." His mother told him not to worry, saying any curse would fall on her.

So Jacob fetched the goats and Rebekah prepared the meal. She dressed Jacob in Esau's clothes and disguised his hands and the skin of his neck with hairy goatskins. Then Jacob took the dish to Isaac. But Isaac hesitated, confused. "Come near so I can touch you, my son," he said. "The voice is Jacob's, but the hands are Esau's. Are you really my son Esau?"

"I am," lied Jacob.

So Isaac sat up and ate the food. When he had finished, he put his hand on Jacob's head and gave him his blessing. "May nations serve you and peoples bow down to you. Be lord over your brothers and may the sons of your mother bow down to you."

Jacob received the blessing and ran out of the tent, glad to get away. Soon after,

Esau arrived with a plate of food. "Here I am, father. Esau, your firstborn. I've got the food you asked for." Isaac gasped in horror, knowing that he had been tricked by Jacob.

"Your brother came and took your blessing," he cried. "I cannot take it back."

"He has deceived me twice," replied Esau bitterly. "He took my birthright and now he's taken my blessing."

Isaac nodded. "I have made him lord over you and have made all his relatives his servants," he said sadly.

And Esau wept. "Do you only have one blessing, my father? Bless me, too."

But Isaac knew that the Lord's word was in the blessing he had given to Jacob and it could not be altered.

From that day on, Esau hated his brother. He planned to kill him as soon as their father was dead and the days of mourning were over. When Rebekah heard about Esau's plot, she went straight to Jacob and warned him. She told him to hide in her brother's house far away in Haran. "Stay there until Esau's fury subsides. I'll send word when it's safe for you to come back." Jacob fled immediately.

"Your brother came and took your blessing."

Understanding the story

Tensions between the brothers start in the womb. Esau demonstrates that he is not fit to lead by swapping his inheritance, which includes God's covenant, for some food. God's promise that Rebekah's younger son would rule the older one is kept when Jacob receives Isaac's blessing. Although the blessing is achieved by deceit, it is still valid.

Jacob's Ladder

Jacob continued on his journey from Beersheba to Haran and, when the sun dropped low in the sky, he stopped to rest for the night.

He found a smooth stone and put it under his head, like a pillow, and lay down under the starry sky. He was tired from traveling and fell into a deep sleep. He dreamed that he saw a magnificent stairway reaching steeply through the clouds to heaven. A procession of angels glided up and down the steps. And at the very top of the stairway stood the Lord, looking down at Jacob.

"I am the Lord, the God of your father Abraham and the God of Isaac," He said. "I will give you and your descendants the land on which you are lying. Your descendants will spread out to the west and to the east, to the north and to the south. All peoples on earth will be blessed through you and your offspring."

Jacob woke up early the next morning, refreshed after his sleep, and he remembered his dream. "The Lord is in this place and I didn't know," he said to himself, shivering with fear. "This is the House of God and that is the gate to heaven." To mark the site of his sacred vision, Jacob took the stone that he had used as a pillow and made a memorial stone. Then he poured some oil over it and named the place "Bethel," which means "House of God."

And he made a vow, saying, "If God watches over me on this journey so that I return safely to my father's house, then the Lord will be my God and this stone that I have set up will be God's house."

"He dreamed that he saw a magnificent stairway reaching steeply through the clouds to heaven."

Understanding the story

In Jacob's dream, God is standing at the top of a stairway to heaven. God repeats the promise He first made to Jacob's forefathers Abraham and Isaac, and affirms that Jacob will receive the covenant, too. Jacob also realizes the link between the God of his ancestors and the people on Earth, and that God can be encountered anywhere.

Haran
A center for trade and commerce, Haran was also one of the main cities of the moon-god Sin. The site of Haran today is in southeast Turkey, where the ruins of the Temple of Sin, including this striking tower and arch, can be found.

Ziggurat steps
Jacob's dream of a stairway to heaven closely resembles the steep outdoor staircases found on many ancient Mesopotamian pyramid-shaped temples, known as ziggurats. Religious altars or shrines were probably built on the top.

Jacob dreams of a procession of angels in "The Dream of Jacob" by Italian painter Alessandro Allori (1535–1607).

Jacob and Rachel

Jacob left Bethel, where God had appeared to him in a dream, and continued on his way. It was a long journey across the Jordan River to Haran in northwest Mesopotamia, where his mother's brother, Laban, lived.

When at last he arrived, he saw a well in the middle of a field, covered by a large stone. Around it, a few flocks of sheep lay sleeping in the sun. The shepherds watched over them, chatting to each other. Each day, toward sunset, when all the flocks had gathered, the shepherds rolled the stone away from the mouth of the well to reveal the cool water deep below. Then they would draw the water up and fill the troughs so there was plenty for all the thirsty sheep.

Jacob greeted the shepherds and asked them if they knew Laban. "We do indeed," they replied. "And here comes his daughter Rachel with the sheep."

But Jacob could not understand why the shepherds were hanging around, doing nothing. "Look," he said, "the sun is still high in the sky and the rest of the flocks won't be gathered for hours. Why don't you water your sheep now and then you'll be able to take them back to pasture?"

"No, we can't water them until all the flocks are gathered," they replied. "Only then will we roll the stone away."

Jacob turned and saw Rachel, the beautiful young shepherdess, walking toward the well, guiding her flock before her. His heart leapt at the sight of his lovely cousin. He went over to her, bowing low, and introduced himself, saying he was the son of Rebekah and the nephew of her father, Laban. He embraced her and kissed her. And, despite what the shepherds had told him, he rolled the stone from the mouth of the well and drew water for her sheep.

Rachel ran home to tell her father and her older sister, Leah, about the visitor, who had arrived so unexpectedly. They were curious to see him, and Laban rushed out of the house to find him. He threw his arms around his nephew and welcomed him, overjoyed to meet him. Together, they went back to the house and Jacob explained why he had come from Beersheba and told him the whole story about his twin brother, Esau.

"You are my own flesh and blood," said Laban. "You must stay with us here." Jacob agreed, happy to remain in his uncle's house and to help him. He would also be near Rachel with whom he had fallen in love. He worked hard from morning until night, helping with the livestock and tending the crops in the fields.

"He would also be near Rachel with whom he had fallen in love."

Understanding the story

Jacob continues his journey and goes to live with his uncle Laban. He is honest in telling his family the whole story about his brother, Esau. Laban welcomes him as his own flesh and blood. Jacob finds happiness in his uncle's affection and his love for his cousin Rachel. He toils away to keep his place in their home.

Jacob's Wedding

After a month, Laban came to Jacob, his nephew, and said, "You have been working hard for several weeks now. But, just because you are my own flesh and blood, you should not work for nothing. How can I pay you?"

Jacob replied, "I'll work for you for seven years in return for your youngest daughter, Rachel."

Laban looked at him and thought for a moment. Then he said, "It is better that I give her to you than to a stranger. Stay here with me."

Jacob worked hard for the next seven years but, because of his deep love for Rachel, the time slipped by so quickly that it seemed more like seven days. At the end of this time, Jacob went to Laban and said, "Uncle, give me my wife. I have worked for you for seven years, as promised, and I want to marry her now."

Laban agreed and started to plan a splendid wedding feast, with the best dishes and the finest wines. The celebrations

"I'll work for you for seven years in return for your youngest daughter, Rachel."

"Jacob with the Daughters of Laban" (1787) by French painter Louis Gauffier (1762–1801)

Veil

It was customary for brides to wear veils over their faces on wedding days. This was how Jacob mistook Leah for Rachel. The veil represents purity and modesty, as well as respect for God. Laban's deception echoes Jacob taking advantage of his blind father, Isaac.

"Finally, to her great joy, she found she was pregnant and she gave birth to a son who was named Joseph."

would go on for a week, with music and singing and dancing. Everybody would be invited.

When the great day came, Jacob watched proudly as his bride took her place by his side. She was dressed in the most beautiful embroidered robes and wore a heavy jeweled veil, which concealed her face completely. He took her hand.

That night, as darkness fell, they retired early to bed, leaving Laban and their guests to carry on feasting and drinking. But the next morning, when Jacob opened his eyes and turned over to kiss his new wife, he could not believe his eyes. He saw with horror that it was not Rachel, but her older sister Leah, lying by his side.

He rushed to find Laban, shouting, "What have you done? You tricked me! You deceived me! I worked for seven whole years for Rachel and you have given me ugly old Leah."

Laban replied, "It is not our custom here to give the younger daughter in marriage before the older one. We will finish celebrating your marriage to Leah and then, at the end of the week, you can also have Rachel as your wife. But only if you promise to work for another seven years."

And so, a week later, Rachel became Jacob's wife. He loved her from the bottom of his heart and he worked happily for another seven years.

Although Jacob was not in love with his first wife, Leah, she quickly became pregnant and gave birth to their first son, who was named Reuben. And, before long, she went on to have three more sons—Simeon, Levi, and Judah. It was hard for Rachel, who was still not pregnant, and she watched her sister with increasing jealousy. "Give me children or I will die!" she implored Jacob.

"Do you think I am God?" he replied angrily. In desperation, Rachel took her maidservant, Bilhah, and gave her to Jacob as a wife. "Marry her so that she can bear children for me so that, through her, I too can build a family."

Bilhah had no difficulty in conceiving and, nine months later, gave birth to a son named Dan. And the next year she had another son named Naphtali. Jacob also fathered two more sons with Leah's servant, Zilpah, and they were named Gad and Asher. And Leah herself bore him two more sons, Issachar and Zebulon, and finally a daughter named Dinah.

All these years Rachel had waited, grieving that she had not been able to give her husband a son. Finally, to her great joy, she found she was pregnant and she gave birth to a son who was named Joseph.

Understanding the story

Jacob discovers that he is not always the master of deception. As he tricked his brother in order to get the blessing, his uncle now tricks him into marrying the wrong daughter, as well as working for another seven years without pay. Despite these setbacks, Jacob fathers 12 sons, who will become the leaders of the 12 tribes of Israel.

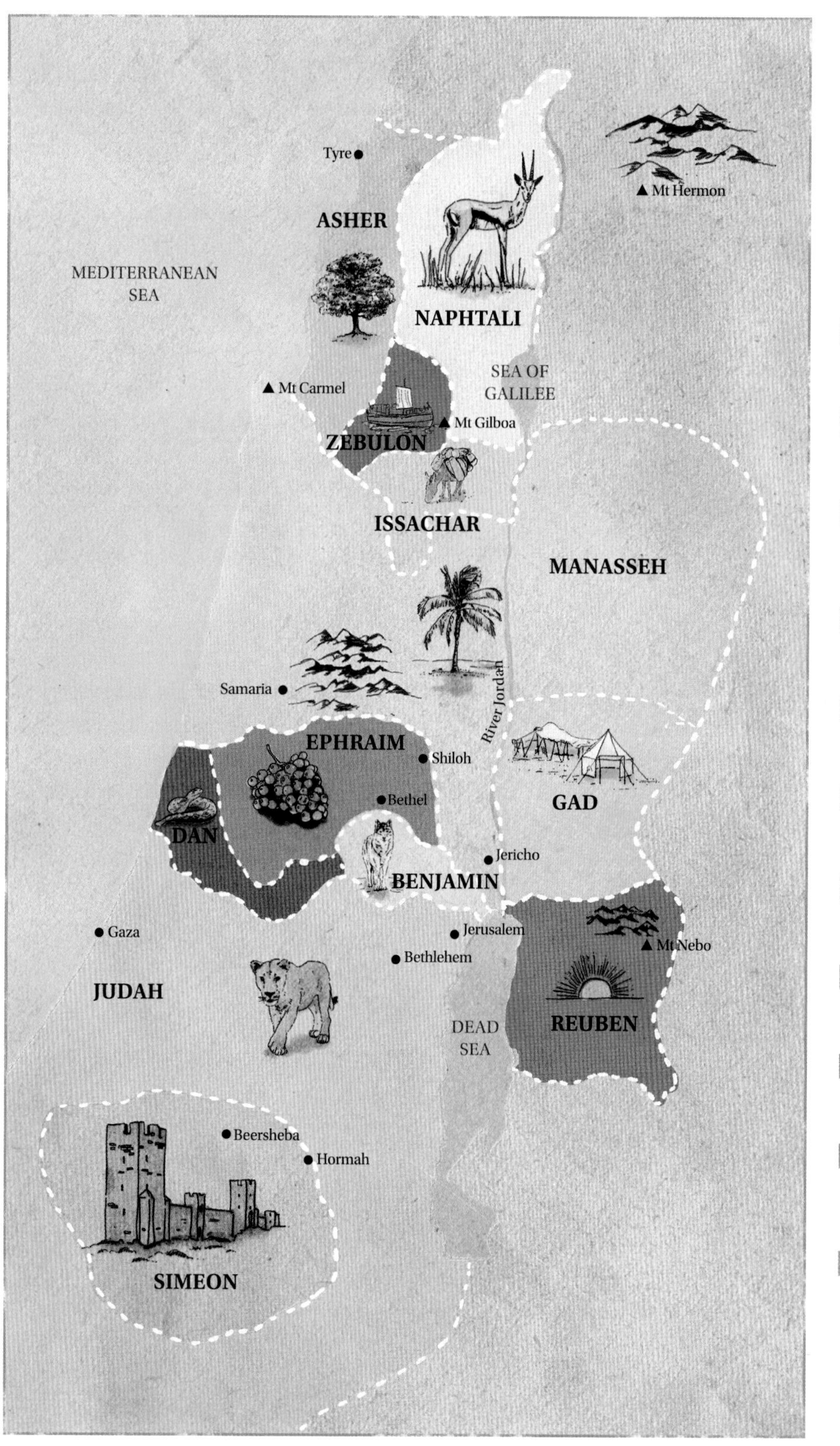

Tribes of Israel

This map shows the kingdoms of the 12 tribes of Israel. These tribes were descended from the 12 sons of Jacob. Each tribe had its own identity and territory after Canaan was conquered. The Levite tribe was the exception without a territory.

12 TRIBES OF ISRAEL

REUBEN
Jacob's eldest son was known for his kind heart. He was given the territory east of the Dead Sea.

SIMEON
The second son of Jacob, Simeon had prophetic powers. He inherited the southern part of Canaan.

JUDAH
The fourth son of Jacob, Judah became the greatest tribe, with the largest area of the Promised Land.

DAN
Dan's territory on the Mediterranean coast meant that his tribe became known for seafaring.

NAPHTALI
Joseph's sixth son inherited land on the eastern side of Galilee. His tribe were brave warriors.

GAD
Jacob's seventh son, Gad and his tribe settled in the central region of Transjordan.

ASHER
Asher was given western Galilee, which contained some of Canaan's most fertile and prosperous land.

ISSACHAR
The ninth-born son, Issachar, and his tribe came to be known for study of the Torah.

ZEBULON
Zebulon's tribe became merchants, and had a close relationship with their neighbor, Issachar.

JOSEPH
Joseph was the eleventh son and his father's favorite. Joseph received two areas, one for each of his sons—Ephraim and Manasseh.

BENJAMIN
The twelfth and youngest son, Benjamin was given land east of the Judean hills.

LEVI
Instead of receiving land, Levi's tribe were committed to serving God as priests.

Jacob's Return

"A man suddenly appeared out of the night and lunged at him, gripping him by the throat."

In time, Jacob wanted to go home to Canaan, but his uncle, Laban, persuaded him to stay in Haran. Over the years, he had come to rely on his nephew.

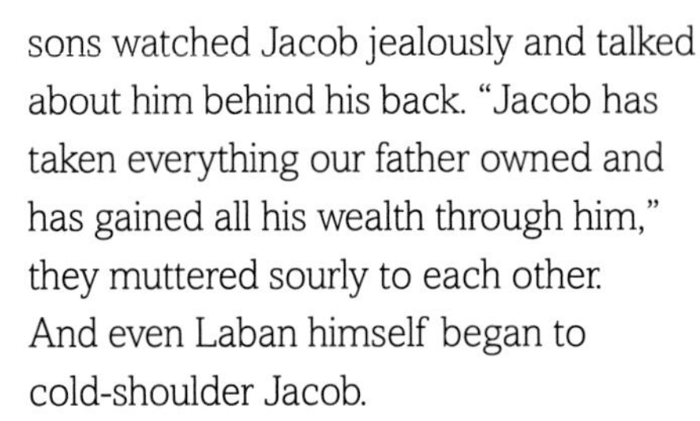

But Laban was not always honest with Jacob and sometimes tried to cheat him. Despite this, Jacob had built up large flocks and herds of his own and was now wealthy in his own right. Laban's sons watched Jacob jealously and talked about him behind his back. "Jacob has taken everything our father owned and has gained all his wealth through him," they muttered sourly to each other. And even Laban himself began to cold-shoulder Jacob.

Then the Lord came to Jacob and said, "Go back to the land of your fathers and to your relatives. I will be with you."

Jacob immediately sent for his wives, Rachel and Leah. "You know that I have worked for your father with all my strength, yet he has cheated me out of my wages. However, God has not allowed him to harm me. And God has told me to leave and go back to my native land."

Rachel and Leah listened and prepared to leave with their children and all their worldly possessions. Then, without a word, they left, driving their flocks and herds ahead of them across the Euphrates to the mountains of Gilead.

When Laban discovered that they had gone, he chased after them and finally caught up with them seven days later. "Why did you deceive me and run off like that?" he asked Jacob. "You didn't even let me kiss my grandchildren and daughters goodbye!"

The two men talked and argued long into the night, but eventually they settled their differences, calling God to bear witness. Early the next morning Laban kissed his grandchildren and daughters goodbye and blessed them. Then he set off and returned home.

Jacob took his family and continued the long journey to Canaan. When they drew near he sent a message to his brother Esau, whom he had fled from so many years before. Soon, news came back that Esau was coming to meet him with a force of four hundred men.

"O God of my father Abraham, God of my father Isaac," Jacob prayed, "I am unworthy of all the kindness and faithfulness you have shown me. Save me, I pray, from the hand of my brother Esau!"

Jacob chose his finest animals and sent them ahead with his servants, as a gift to Esau. Then he took his wives and children and all their possessions across the Jabbok River and told them to wait for him there. He spent the night alone, and as he sat, deep in thought, a man suddenly appeared out of the night and lunged at him, gripping him by the throat. Jacob gasped and fought back, pinning him to the ground.

They wrestled, on and on, grappling with each other like silent shadows, evenly matched. At last, the sun's rays started to creep over the horizon and the man said, "Let me go, for it is daybreak. What is your name?"

Jacob told him his name and the man replied, "Your name will no longer be Jacob, but Israel, because you have struggled with God and with man and have overcome." With these words He blessed Jacob and disappeared into thin air.

Israel means "he struggles with God" and Jacob realized that he had seen God face to face and that his life had been spared. He went straight to rejoin his family—just in time to see Esau approaching with all his men. Telling his wives and children to stay behind, Jacob went to meet his brother, bowing low before him seven times. Without hesitation, Esau threw his arms around his neck and kissed him warmly, saying that he did not need the animals that Jacob had sent him.

"No, please, if I have found favor in your eyes, accept this gift from me," Jacob replied. "For to see your face is like seeing the face of God, now that you have received me favorably. Please accept the present that was brought to you, for God has been gracious to me and I have all I need."

Understanding the story

Abraham and Isaac accepted God as their Lord immediately, but Jacob often experienced conflict over his faith. This is why he is named Israel, meaning "he struggles with God." The mysterious stranger he wrestles with is really a representation of God. God promised to look after Jacob, and He does not let him down. With his new name, he is a changed man who now accepts God completely.

Wrestling
Wrestling is the only sport mentioned in the Bible. Men often settled their scores and showed their strength in wrestling matches. This sport featured at the ancient Olympic Games of Greece, as depicted in this relief (above). Jacob does not know he is wrestling with God, and therefore, wrestling his own faith.

Jabbok River
Jacob sends his family ahead across the Jabbok River to give himself time for quiet contemplation. Today it is called the Zerqa River. The fast-flowing waters of the river flow into the Jordan River 15 miles (25 km) north of the Dead Sea.

Joseph's Dreams

Joseph lived with his father, Jacob, and his brothers in the land of Canaan. Jacob loved all his sons, but Joseph was his favorite.

His father had given Joseph a beautiful coat, intricately woven with the colors of the rainbow. Joseph wore it all the time. Everybody knew that he was the apple of his father's eye and Joseph's brothers hated him for it.

One night, Joseph had a dream and he told his brothers about it. "We were binding sheaves of corn out in the field when suddenly my sheaf rose and stood upright. Your sheaves gathered round mine and bowed down to it." His brothers were incensed. "So you want to rule us, do you?" they jeered. A few nights later, Joseph had another dream and he

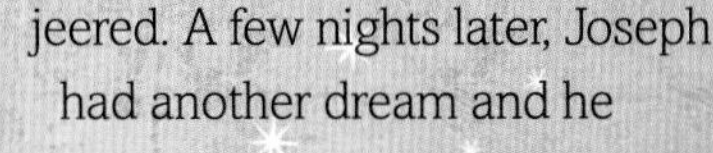

Joseph's coat
Joseph's ornate coat was probably made of a rich, quality cloth woven with colored threads, as seen in this Egyptian tomb painting of Asians. Their clothes differed from those of the Egyptians, who wore more simple clothes and designs.

Dyes
The description of Joseph's coat suggests it was dyed in a range of vibrant shades. These colorful dyes came from natural sources. Red was from the kermes insect, orange from the saffron flower, purple from mollusk shells, and blue from pomegranate rinds.

foolishly told his brothers about it. “This time the sun and the moon and eleven stars were bowing down to me.”

He also told his father, who was not pleased. “What is this dream? Do you think the whole family will actually come and bow down to you?”

Joseph’s brothers went to look after their father’s sheep and goats in the north of the country. After some days, Jacob asked Joseph to go and see that all was well. When the brothers saw Joseph approaching, they saw their chance. “Here comes that little dreamer,” they said. “Let’s kill him and hide him in one of these pits. We’ll say a wild animal attacked him.”

But Reuben, who was a kind man and liked his brother, pleaded with the others, “By all means, throw him into the pit, but don’t kill him.” When Joseph finally reached his brothers, they pounced on him and ripped off his coat. They put him in the pit without any food or water.

The brothers sat down to eat their meal that evening, unsure of what to do. And then they saw a caravan of Ishmaelite merchants on the horizon. One of the brothers, who was named Judah, said, “Do we really want to kill Joseph? He is our own flesh and blood. Why don’t we sell him? Then we’ll be rid of him, without laying a hand on him.” His brothers agreed.

So, they pulled Joseph out of the pit and offered him to the merchants. A price was agreed, and he was sold and hoisted on to a camel, bound for Egypt.

The brothers slaughtered one of the goats and smeared the blood on Joseph’s tattered coat before going home. They showed the coat to their father saying, “We found this. Do you think it could belong to Joseph?”

Jacob recognized the blood-stained bundle and cried, “It is my son’s coat! An animal has devoured him.” And he mourned for his beloved son. Meanwhile, Joseph had reached Egypt. He was sold to Potiphar, one of Pharaoh’s most important officials.

Traded goods
Ishmaelites were Arabian merchants descended from Abraham’s son Ishmael. Slave trading was far less common than the trade of spices and aromatic resins between Arabia and Egypt. Fennel seeds (top) were sold as a medicinal ingredient, while myrrh resin (bottom) was part of the anointing and embalming process for dead bodies.

Jacob is grief-stricken when he sees Joseph’s bloody coat

Understanding the story

Sibling rivalry leads to Joseph’s downfall. His jealous brothers don’t like the preferential treatment he receives or the implications of his dreams. When Jacob sees the blood-stained coat, he fears the worst for his favorite son. But the brothers’ plan to kill Joseph is in contrast with God’s plan for him. Joseph’s destiny lies in Egypt, and God is with him.

Joseph the Slave

Joseph, who had been taken to Egypt from Canaan and sold as a slave, worked hard for his new master, Potiphar.

The Lord was always by Joseph's side, and Joseph was good at whatever he did. His master, who was captain of Pharaoh's guard and a man of great standing, was impressed. Before long, he made Joseph his own personal attendant and put him in charge of the whole household.

Now, Joseph was a very handsome man, and Potiphar's wife took a shine to him. Eventually, her passion running high, she tried to seduce him. Joseph spurned her advances. "My master trusts me. How could I betray him? How could I sin against God?"

But Potiphar's wife would not take no for an answer, believing herself to be irresistible. Day after day she pursued him, and day after day he refused her. At last, in desperation, she cornered him and tore at his cloak. Terrified, Joseph turned and fled, leaving his cloak in her hands. Scorned and rejected, Potiphar's wife called the servants and told them that Joseph had tried to ravish her. "Look! When I screamed, he left his cloak behind and ran!" Then she rushed to tell her husband the story. Potiphar was horrified and ordered Joseph to be thrown into prison.

But the Lord watched over Joseph. The prison warder liked the new inmate. Soon, Joseph was put in charge of all the other prisoners and, before long, he was running the place.

There were two very special prisoners, the royal baker and Pharaoh's chief cupbearer. Before they were criminals, they had specific duties. The cupbearer had to taste Pharaoh's food and drink in case it was poisoned, and the baker made the household's finest sweetmeats.

One morning, while doing his rounds,

Women in Egypt
The most powerful Egyptian women enjoyed a very high status, reflected in this mural from the tomb of Sennedjem, where Sennedjem's wife, Iyneferty, is shown as of almost equal stature to him. Women were able to own and manage property, and make important decisions.

Cupbearer
The pharaoh's cupbearer held a high-ranking and trusted position. His job was to taste the pharaoh's food and drink to ensure they were not poisoned. The pharaoh would have drunk from cups like this typical Egyptian glazed earthenware vessel.

"How could I sin against God?"

Joseph saw the two of them sitting in their cells with long faces. He asked what was the matter. "We both had really odd dreams last night," they answered, "but there is nobody who can interpret them."

"Tell me your dreams," said Joseph.

The chief cupbearer began with his. "I saw a vine with three branches. As it budded, it blossomed and its clusters ripened into grapes. Pharaoh's cup was in my hand, and I took the grapes and squeezed them into the cup for him."

Joseph explained the dream. "The three branches are three days. Within three days, Pharaoh will restore you to your position and you will put his cup in his hand, just as you used to do." And he added, "Please, when you are back in favor, remember me and mention me to Pharaoh. Try to get me out of prison. I have done nothing to deserve it." The cupbearer agreed.

Then the baker described his dream. "On my head were three baskets of bread. In the top basket were baked goods for Pharaoh, but the birds kept flying down to eat them."

Joseph interpreted the dream. "The three baskets are three days. Within three days, Pharaoh will hang you on a tree, and the birds will eat away your flesh." The baker looked at him, doubtfully.

Now, Pharaoh's birthday was in three days time and he gave a feast for all his officials. He ordered the release of the chief cupbearer and the royal baker from prison. Then he summoned them to court and gave the cupbearer back his old job, but told the baker that he would be hanged, just as Joseph had said. Sadly, the cupbearer was so happy to be restored to his position that he forgot to tell Pharaoh about Joseph's plight.

Understanding the story

Joseph proves his good character by repelling the advances of his master's wife. Though Joseph is thrown in prison, God remains with him. Though the meanings of Joseph's own dreams have yet to be revealed, his interpretations of the cupbearer and baker's dreams come true. This suggests that in the future, Joseph's dreams will also come to pass.

Pharaoh's Dreams

Two long years had passed and Joseph was still in prison. The chief cupbearer had forgotten about him completely and, far from home, there was no-one else to spare Joseph a thought.

One night, in the royal palace, Pharaoh had a strange dream. He was on the banks of the Nile and seven sleek, well-fed cows waded out of the water and began to graze among the bulrushes. Then seven more cows followed them out of the water—but these poor creatures were gaunt and their ribs stuck out pitifully from their hides. They opened their starving mouths and ate all seven of the sleek, fat cows.

That same night, Pharaoh had another dream. Seven ears of plump, healthy corn were growing on a single stalk. Then another seven ears of corn sprouted, but these were scorched and shriveled and they devoured the seven healthy ears of corn.

Pharaoh was troubled. He could not understand what his dreams meant, but knew that they were important. He sent for the royal dream interpreter, who was much revered and practiced in such matters, but even he was baffled. Then Pharaoh issued a decree, summoning all the wise men in Egypt. They came from far and wide and listened to Pharaoh's dreams, but they too were perplexed.

Then, the chief cupbearer suddenly remembered the young Joseph, who had interpreted his dream so perfectly a long time ago in prison. And he felt bad that he had forgotten Joseph for so long. He told Pharaoh, and Joseph was released from prison and summoned to court.

Joseph bowed down before Pharaoh, who said, "I had a dream and no one can explain it. But I have heard it said that when

Pharaoh's throne
Pharaoh had a lavish throne for religious ceremonies and other special occasions. The throne represented his power and authority, and it was often placed on a higher step or level to show the lofty position of the ruler. This ornate gold-plated example was discovered in the treasures of the boy-king Tutankhamun's tomb.

you hear a dream, you can interpret it."

"I cannot do it," replied Joseph, "but God will give Pharaoh the answer he desires."

So Pharaoh told Joseph about his dreams, and Joseph explained that they were the same dream. They had been sent by God in two different forms because the message they contained was so important. "The seven good cows are seven years and the seven good ears of corn are the same seven years. The seven thin cows that came up afterward and the seven worthless ears of corn are the next seven years."

Joseph said that seven years of great plenty would come to Egypt, but then seven years of famine would follow. And he warned Pharaoh, "The abundance in the land will not be remembered, because the famine that follows will be so severe." And he went on to advise Pharaoh that he should find a wise man and put him in charge to make sure that, during the good years, one fifth of the harvest was saved and stored so that there would be enough food when the famine came.

Pharaoh was impressed by Joseph's words. "Can we find anyone like this man?" he asked. "Someone with the Spirit of God? Since God has made all this known to you, there is no one more discerning or wise than you. You shall be in charge of my palace, and all my people are to submit to your orders. You will be my second-in-command. I hereby put you in charge of the whole of Egypt."

With that, Pharaoh took off his signet ring and put it on Joseph's finger. He dressed him in fine robes and placed a gold chain around his neck. And together, they rode in a magnificent chariot, Joseph by Pharaoh's side, for all to see.

Just as Joseph had predicted, seven years of plenty followed, and the fertile land, watered by the Nile, produced food in abundance. The fields were full of wheat and barley, the fruit trees groaned with figs and pomegranates, and the vines were heavy with the sweetest grapes. Joseph traveled all over the country, making sure that a good proportion was stockpiled and saved for the bad years that he knew lay ahead. Huge quantities of grain were stored in granaries in every town and city.

Then, after seven years, the Nile dried up, the land shriveled and shrank back into itself, and the relentless famine began. But, although the crops failed year after year, there was food for everybody in Egypt and, thanks to Joseph, no one went hungry.

Pharaoh's chariot
Joseph had the honor of riding with Pharaoh in his chariot, a remarkable change in his fortunes. Royalty and high-ranking officials traveled in style in ceremonial chariots, such as the one above, which belonged to Tutankhamun.

Drought record
The Famine Stela, discovered on Sehel Island in the Nile River, recorded information about a seven-year drought and famine that affected ancient Egypt while Pharaoh Djoser was on the throne (c. 2686–2667 BCE). This seven-year famine ties in with Pharaoh's dreams.

Understanding the story

Pharaoh's disturbing dreams are of particular significance because the Egyptians believed that their nation's fate depended on the pharaoh's fate. When Pharaoh's own dream interpreter cannot tell him the meaning of his dreams, Joseph can. Joseph makes it clear that it is God who is providing the answer.

The pharaoh
The Bible gives no clues to the identity of the pharaoh in the story of Joseph. The most famous pharaoh was Rameses II (ruled 1279–1213 BCE), who erected more statues of himself than any other king.

So Pharaoh said to Joseph, "I hereby put you in charge of the whole land of Egypt." Then Pharaoh took his signet ring from his finger and put it on Joseph's finger. He dressed him in robes of fine linen and put a gold chain around his neck. He made him ride in a chariot as his second-in-command, and people shouted before him, "Make way!"

Genesis 41:41–43

Joseph the Governor

Famine gripped the land, spreading from country to country. Soon, it arrived in Canaan, which Joseph had left so many years before.

Famine
This sad statue of a desperate man begging was discovered in Egypt and dates from the Middle Kingdom (2040–1640 BCE). When the water levels of the Nile River dropped, the crops could not flourish and many people starved to death.

His aged father, Jacob, had heard the rumor that there were great mountains of grain far away in Egypt. So ten of Joseph's brothers made the long journey to Egypt, but the youngest, who was named Benjamin, stayed at home with his father.

Now, although they did not know it, their brother Joseph was the most important governor in all Egypt and was in charge of selling grain. When the brothers arrived, Joseph recognized them. He did not let on, however, and asked them where they came from.

"From the land of Canaan," they replied nervously, not recognizing him.

"You are spies!" Joseph accused them. "You have come to snoop and pry!"

"No, my lord," they protested. "We were twelve brothers, all the sons of one father who lives in Canaan. The youngest is now with our father and one brother is no more."

"I don't believe you! I think you're spies!" retorted Joseph. "But I will test whether you are lying or not. You will not leave unless your youngest brother comes here. One of you must go and get him. The rest of you will stay here in prison. Then we will see if you're telling the truth!" But, for the time being, he put them all in prison.

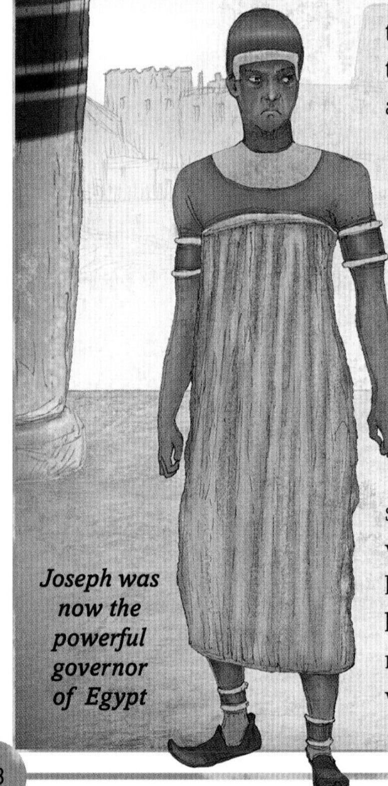

Joseph was now the powerful governor of Egypt

After three days, Joseph went to them, relenting slightly. "If you really are honest, as you say, one of you can stay here and the rest can go back home and take grain to your starving household. But then you must bring back your youngest brother to prove that you are telling the truth."

The brothers looked at each other, bewildered. "This must be some kind of punishment for what we did to our brother so long ago," they said. Reuben, the kindest of the brothers, who had pleaded with the others to spare Joseph's life, said, "Didn't I tell you not to sin against that boy?"

Deeply moved, Joseph turned away from them to hide his tears. When he had composed himself, he turned back and chose Simeon to be held in prison. Then he gave orders for their bags to be filled with grain and for the silver they had brought with them to be hidden amongst it. He also arranged for food to be given to them for their journey. The brothers loaded up their donkeys and set off for Canaan.

When they stopped to rest that night, one brother opened his sack to give his donkey a few handfuls of grain and he found the piece of silver buried there. He showed it to the others in amazement and they looked at each other uncertainly, and said, "What does this mean?"

They continued their journey and at last arrived in Canaan. As they were emptying their bags, they found the silver hidden in each one and they shivered with fear, not knowing what was going on. They told their father, Jacob, the whole story and begged him to let them take their youngest brother, Benjamin, back to Egypt. But Jacob, distraught at the thought of losing him, refused.

Recording harvest
Grain gathered at harvest time was stored in large granaries, with clerks given the job of noting and documenting the stock. This clerk, part of a larger frieze, is writing down the annual harvest tally so all records are kept up to date.

Understanding the story

The power balance has shifted and Joseph, governor of Egypt, is now in charge. Joseph forces his brothers to confront their past and each other, so they can all be reconciled. Simeon's detention in Egypt reminds the brothers of how they treated Joseph. The story proves that it is never too late to change direction. Though the brothers were jealous and aggressive, they see the error of their ways.

"Didn't I tell you not to sin against that boy?"

Joseph orders Simeon to be taken to prison

Benjamin
Jacob had 12 sons, but his favorite was the youngest. Benjamin (meaning "son of my right hand") was the only one born in Israel. His father predicted great things for Benjamin's descendants, who went on to form a tribe, called the Benjamites. King Saul of the Old Testament and Paul of the New Testament were the best-known Benjamites.

Silver cup
To steal a silver cup was a major crime in ancient Egypt. Silver was a highly prized and relatively rare metal compared to gold, which was more readily available. Silver supplies were limited because the metal was imported into Egypt from Syria. This theft was particularly serious because the cup was the property of Joseph. As the Pharaoh's deputy, he was the second most important person in Egypt.

The Silver Cup

The famine continued and, in time, the grain that Jacob's sons had brought from Egypt had run out.

Jacob wanted his sons to go back again to buy more, but Judah reminded him that, this time, they would have to take their youngest brother, Benjamin. They had made a promise to Joseph, the governor of Egypt. "Why did you tell him that you had a young brother in the first place?" grumbled Jacob, who was very fond of his young son.

"He asked all about us and our family," his sons protested. "He wanted to know if our father was still alive and if we had another brother. How were we to know he would insist we brought our brother to him?"

Then Judah spoke to his father, "I myself will guarantee Benjamin's safety. If I don't bring him back, I will bear the blame all my life."

Reluctantly, his father agreed. "So be it. But you must keep on the right side of this governor. Take gifts with you and take twice as much silver this time, for you must return the silver you found in your sacks. And take your brother. May God Almighty grant you mercy."

When the brothers arrived in Egypt, they presented themselves to Joseph. As soon as Joseph saw Benjamin, he said to his chief steward, "Take these men to my house, slaughter an animal and prepare a feast. They will eat with me at noon."

The brothers could not understand why they were being treated with such favor. Perhaps it was a trick and they were going to end up as slaves? And then, the steward brought in Simeon, who had been left behind in

Silver bowl
This Ancient Egyptian bowl dates from 3rd to 1st century BCE. It shows a daisy in its center surrounded by petals or leaves, which was a typical decoration style for containers in this period.

prison, and the brothers threw their arms around him, relieved that he was safe.

Joseph arrived and, bowing low, the brothers gave him the gifts from Canaan. He received them graciously, but could not take his eyes off Benjamin. Unlike the others, Benjamin and he shared the same mother and they were real brothers. Tears welled in Joseph's eyes at the sight of him, but he pulled himself together and ordered the food to be served. It was a feast, but the brothers were astonished as Benjamin was given five times as much as anybody else.

Afterward, Joseph gave instructions for their sacks to be filled with food and grain and for their pieces of silver to be hidden amongst it. And then he ordered that his own special silver cup should be put in Benjamin's sack.

The brothers headed home, but had not gone far before Joseph's chief steward caught up with them, accusing them of stealing his master's silver cup. The brothers protested their innocence. "Why would we steal silver or gold from your master's house? If any one of us is found to have it, he will die. And the rest of us will become your lord's slaves." Gladly, they opened their sacks and the steward peered inside them. When he saw the silver cup in Benjamin's sack, he pulled it out and brandished it high in the air. The brothers looked at Benjamin in disbelief. They returned to Joseph's house. "How can we prove our innocence?" asked Judah, sadly. "We are all your slaves."

"No!" answered Joseph. "Only the man who had the cup will be my slave. The rest of you must return to your father."

Judah pleaded with him, explaining how precious Benjamin was to their father. "Please let me stay here as your slave in place of Benjamin. How can I go back to my father if he is not with me?"

At this, Joseph broke down. He sobbed, "I am Joseph! Your brother Joseph! The one you sold into Egypt. But don't be angry with yourselves. It was to save lives that God sent me ahead of you. It was not you who sent me here but God." And he gave them a message for their father, "God has made me lord of all Egypt. Come here to me. You shall live in the region of Goshen—you, your children, and grandchildren, your flocks and herds, and all you have. I will provide for you because five years of famine are still to come."

When Jacob heard the news he could not believe that his beloved son, Joseph, was still alive. And he was now the governor of Egypt and was offering the family refuge. He exclaimed, "My son Joseph is alive! I will go and see him before I die!"

"It was to save lives that God sent me ahead of you. It was not you who sent me here but God."

Understanding the story

Joseph recognizes that his rise to power in Egypt was God's will all along. As his family gather together and his brothers prove themselves to be changed men, Joseph remembers his past dream. It all becomes clear. The stars and sheaves of corn represented the 11 brothers now working for him. Again, his dream comes to pass.

Moses in the Bulrushes

Since the time of Joseph, the children of Israel had thrived and prospered in the land of Egypt. Generations came and went and they multiplied, spreading far and wide throughout the fertile country.

But one day, a new Pharaoh, who had never heard of the Israelites' famous ancestor, Joseph, came to the throne and was consumed with fear. "Look," he said to his counselors, "the Israelites are everywhere. There are far too many of them. If war breaks out, they will side with our enemies."

He ordered that the Israelites be forced to labor, building stone cities with their bare hands. But the more cruelly the Israelites were treated, the quicker they multiplied. Then Pharaoh had a better idea. He ordered that all male children born to Israelite women should be put to death at birth. But the midwives took no notice. "Why have you let the boys live?" thundered Pharaoh.

"Israelite women aren't like Egyptian women," the midwives said. "They are healthy and give birth before the midwives arrive."

At his wits' end, Pharaoh declared, "Every boy that is born must be thrown into the Nile, but let every girl live!"

Now, there was a couple who belonged to the tribe of Levi and the wife had just given birth to a son. She could not bring herself to comply with Pharaoh's cold-blooded order and, for three months, she hid her baby son at home. But as the infant grew bigger and noisier it became impossible. So she fetched a basket and made it watertight. Then she laid her baby in it and took it to the banks of the Nile, hiding it in the bulrushes. Her young daughter went with her to keep watch.

Soon, Pharaoh's daughter came to bathe in the river and caught sight of the basket. She sent a maid to fetch it and, as she lifted the cover, the baby whimpered sweetly and her heart melted. "It must be one of those poor Israelite babies," she said.

At that moment, the baby's sister asked innocently, "Shall I get one of the Israelite women to nurse the baby for you?" Pharaoh's daughter agreed. So the baby

Victory steles

Steles were upright slabs crafted to commemorate special events. The Merneptah Stele (above) includes pictures and text for King Merneptah (c. 1213–1203 BCE), and is the only Egyptian source to mention the Israelites as a settled people.

Papyrus boats

The Hebrew for "basket" is used in the Bible to describe both Noah's ark and the container in which baby Moses was found. It actually means a papyrus boat. Small boats made of strong reeds were used to transport people and goods on the Nile River.

was brought up by his real mother, and when he grew older Pharaoh's daughter adopted him as her own. She named him Moses, which means "to draw out," because she had drawn him out of the water.

Understanding the story

The birth of Moses came almost 300 years after Joseph's death, during a period in which the Israelite population expanded greatly. The pharaoh feels under threat from the Israelites and is determined to destroy them. It is the pharaoh's daughter who rescues and raises the baby boy. Moses will go on to lead the Israelites and save them from slavery.

Sinai Desert
With fine sand, bare rocks, and high plateaus, the Sinai Desert is a spectacular place. Desert conditions are harsh, however, with high daytime temperatures dropping to below freezing at night. Despite this, it has been home to Bedouin tribes for thousands of years.

YHWH
God's name "I AM" is spelled with the four Hebrew letters YHWH and is known as the "Tetragrammaton." YHWH is usually written out as "Yahweh" and is taken from the Hebrew verb "to be." It translates as "the one who is always there," which reflects the Lord's eternal presence.

Moses is Called by God

Moses grew up in Pharaoh's palace and was treated as if he was the son of the princess. But he was a thoughtful young man, who never forgot that his birth parents belonged to the Levite tribe of Israel.

One day, he went out and saw the Israelite slave gangs dragging huge slabs of stone out of the quarry. From morning until night they worked in the scorching sun. Suddenly, one of the slaves collapsed on the ground. The Egyptian slave driver went over and kicked him. When the poor man still did not get up, the slave driver gave him a savage beating. Moses, unable to bear it, rushed over and, glancing around to make sure that no one saw, killed the cruel slave driver. Then, filled with horror at what he had done, he dug a large hole in the sand and buried the body.

The next morning, Moses went back and saw two Israelites arguing. One of them grabbed the other by the throat. Moses went up and separated them, asking them why they were fighting.

"Who are you to judge us?" one replied. "Are you going to kill me, just as you murdered that Egyptian yesterday?"

Moses was filled with terror. Word would soon spread and everybody would know about his crime. And when the news reached Pharaoh, Moses knew that his own life would be in danger. He gathered a few belongings and left Egypt, fleeing across the Sinai Desert until he reached the land of Midian. He settled there, far from danger.

One day, Moses was sitting by a well when seven young women came to draw water for their flocks. The local shepherds tried to stop them, but Moses came to their rescue and helped them get water. They were grateful and took him to meet their father, who was a priest named Jethro. He welcomed Moses and asked him to stay. In time, Jethro gave his daughter, Zipporah, to Moses in marriage.

Moses helped his father-in-law to look after the sheep. One day, he took the flocks across the desert to graze by the sacred mountain of Sinai. He sat down to rest and started to sleep. Suddenly, he sat bolt upright and saw a blazing bush in front of him. Although the flames crackled through the branches, they did not even singe them.

Moses crept nearer and then he heard the Lord's voice coming from the middle of the burning bush. "I am the God of your father, the God of Abraham, the God of Isaac, and the God of Jacob. I have seen the misery of my people in Egypt and am concerned about their suffering. So I have come down to rescue them from the hands of the Egyptians and bring them to a land of their own, flowing with milk and honey. I am sending you to Pharaoh to bring my people, the Israelites, out of Egypt."

Moses was amazed and filled with terror. "But how can I do that?" he asked. "Who am I that I should go to Pharaoh and bring the Israelites out of Egypt?"

"I will be with you," God reassured him. "Say that the God of their fathers has sent you and that His name is 'I AM'. "

And God said Moses must tell Pharaoh that Egypt would be cursed, and plagues would sweep the land, if he did not let the Israelites go.

"But what if he doesn't believe me?" protested Moses.

God told Moses to throw his staff on the ground, which he did at once. Immediately, it turned into a snake, writhing and hissing in the dust. "Pick it up by the tail now," said God. Moses lifted it up at arm's length, and the serpent turned back into a wooden staff.

"Now go," God told him. "Take your brother, Aaron, with you. He is coming to meet you. I will tell you both what to say. And take your wooden staff— it will help you to perform miraculous feats."

"I am sending you to Pharaoh to bring my people, the Israelites, out of Egypt."

Understanding the story

Though Moses lives the life of Egyptian royalty, he never forgets his own people, demonstrated by him killing the Egyptian slave driver for mistreating the Israelites. God's presence is sometimes symbolized by fire to show His power, and here He appears to Moses inside a burning bush. By telling Moses to lead the Israelites to the Promised Land, God shows that He has not forgotten His chosen people either.

Moses Warns Pharaoh

Beating a slave
At first, the Egyptians looked after their Israelite slaves. But as the number of Israelites increased, the Egyptians felt threatened. They began to mistreat their slaves, by making them work harder and punishing them regularly.

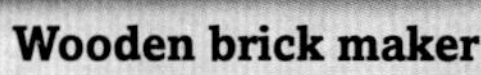

Wooden brick maker
This wooden brick mold was used to make many Egyptian buildings. Equipped with a handle, the mold has the distinctive brick shape still used in construction today. Workmen molded the bricks from mud, sand, and straw, before drying them in the sun.

After so long in the land of Midian, Moses said goodbye to his father-in-law, Jethro, and set off for Egypt, just as God had told him. He took his wife and sons.

The landscape was bleak and barren and the sun beat down relentlessly. Moses carried the wooden staff that God had given him. As they approached the great holy mountain of Sinai, they could see Moses's brother, Aaron, coming to meet them. They greeted each other warmly and Moses told his brother that God had spoken to him, and had sent him back to Egypt to lead the Israelites out of slavery.

As soon as they got back to Egypt, Moses and Aaron called the elders of the Israelites together and said that the Lord had sent them to rescue their people. When they heard this, and that the Lord was concerned about their misery, the elders bowed down to worship. Then Moses and Aaron went to Pharaoh in his splendid court. "The Lord, the God of the Israelites, has spoken to us," they said. "He told us to take His people into the desert to offer sacrifices to Him. If we do not do this, He may strike you all with plagues or with the sword."

Pharaoh was angry. "Who is this Lord that I should obey and let the Israelites go?" he shouted. "Why are you keeping them from their work?" Incensed, he summoned his chief slave drivers and ordered them to make the Israelites work even harder. From now on they were not to be given straw to make the bricks. And so the slaves were forced to scavenge in the fields for any stubble they could find.

Moses and Aaron were worried. But God reassured Moses and gave him a message for the Israelites. "I am the Lord and I will bring you out from under the yoke of the Egyptians. I will free you from slavery.

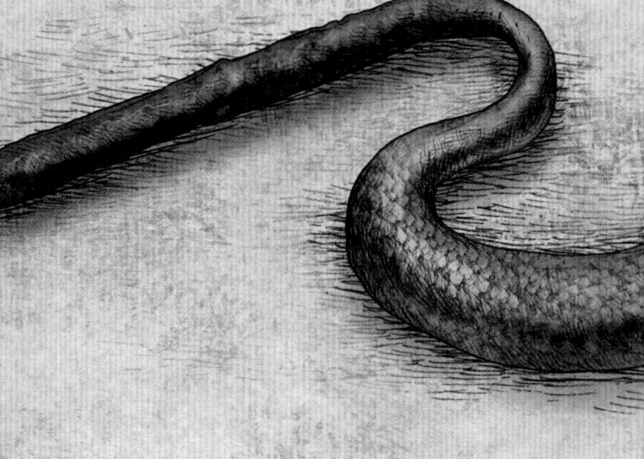

And I will bring you to the land I swore with uplifted hand to give to Abraham, to Isaac, and to Jacob." The Israelites listened in disbelief.

God told Moses to go back to Pharaoh. "Say everything I command you, and your brother Aaron is to tell Pharaoh to let the Israelites go out of his country."

And Moses and Aaron did as the Lord had told them. But, still, Pharaoh would not listen. So then Moses told Aaron to throw down his wooden staff. As it touched the ground, it became a serpent. Not to be outdone, Pharaoh called his wise men and told them to throw down their staffs, too. At once, they turned into a mass of serpents. But Aaron's snake opened his mouth and swallowed the other snakes with relish. Pharaoh watched but was not impressed.

Then God said to Moses, "Go to the Nile tomorrow and wait for Pharaoh. Strike the water with the staff and the water will turn to blood." Moses and Aaron did as the Lord had said and the Nile became a river of blood. It was a terrible sight. But it was not just the Nile that turned red. Blood filled the streams, the ponds, and the reservoirs. Pharaoh watched, unmoved. He returned to his palace without a backward glance.

Serpent god
The Egyptians worshipped a variety of gods, including the serpent god Sito. It is a symbolic moment when Aaron's serpent eats up the Egyptian serpents. This is a sign that God has control over the Egyptian gods. They are far less powerful than the Lord.

Understanding the story

The Lord's miracles and Aaron's appointment as spokesman combine to make Moses accept the role God offers him. But the Israelites' treatment under the Egyptians gets even worse when Moses asks the Pharaoh to let them go. Moses's staff (shepherd's crook) is called the "staff of God" in the Bible. For Moses, it symbolizes God's power, demonstrated when it becomes a serpent and turns the Nile's waters to blood.

"He may strike you all with plagues or with the sword."

Nile
The Nile River was the lifeblood of ancient Egypt. The annual flooding of the river made the soil on its banks very fertile, meaning that fruit and vegetables could grow there. Boats carried people and goods along the river.

The Plagues of Egypt

Seven days passed and still Pharaoh would not release the Israelites. Moses and Aaron, after speaking with the Lord again, pleaded with Pharaoh, telling him that the Lord would send a plague of frogs if he did not let the slaves go.

But Pharaoh did not listen. So, the next day, Aaron held his wooden staff over the Nile, as God had commanded, and suddenly a great croaking sound came from the river. An army of frogs emerged from the waters, hopping out in their thousands, up the banks and over the land, covering it like a shiny green carpet. They swarmed everywhere—even into Pharaoh's palace, as the guards watched in horror. They jumped by Pharaoh's feet and on his throne.

This was too much, and Pharaoh called Moses and Aaron, saying, "Pray to the Lord to take the frogs away from me and my people. I will let your people go to offer sacrifices to the Lord." The Lord heard and the frogs died instantly. They were swept up and piled into heaps that rotted in the sun. But Pharaoh broke his word and did not release the Israelites.

So Aaron struck his staff on the ground once more, as God had told him. The dust turned into millions of gnats, which took off in a cloud, biting any Egyptian man, woman, or child they could find. Pharaoh's magicians went to him, swiping the dreadful insects away, and said, "This is the finger of God." But, although he had been bitten badly himself, Pharaoh would not release the Israelites.

Then Moses went to Pharaoh again, telling him that the Lord would send a swarm of flies next. They would plague the Egyptians and their animals, but would not bother the Israelites. And the next day a dense black cloud of flies appeared, blotting out the light. At this, Pharaoh relented and said to Moses and Aaron, "Go, sacrifice to your God here in this land."

But Moses replied, "No, the sacrifices we offer to the Lord, our God, would be detestable to the Egyptians. We must make a three-day journey into the desert to offer our sacrifices there." Pharaoh agreed, and the flies died immediately.

Again Pharaoh went back on his word, and so the Lord sent a terrible disease that killed all the Egyptians' livestock. But Pharaoh would not let the Israelites go.

Then the Lord said to Moses and Aaron, "Take handfuls of soot and toss them high in the air, in front of Pharaoh. It will drop as fine dust all over Egypt and give everyone terrible boils." The brothers did as He said and everyone, except for the Israelites, broke out in boils. Pharaoh himself was covered in boils, but still he would not relent.

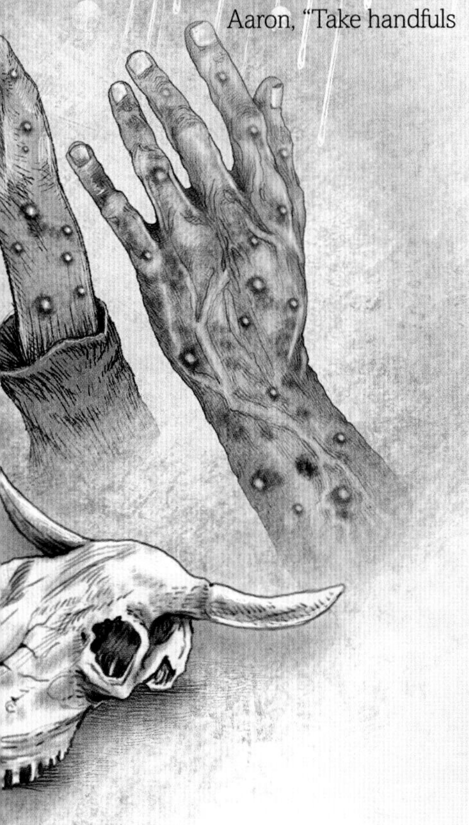

Next, the Lord sent a violent storm, with hailstones as big as rocks, and after that a plague of locusts that devastated the country, gobbling up the crops and stripping the leaves from the trees. Again Pharaoh said he would let the Israelites go, but again he broke his promise.

And then the Lord said to Moses, "Stretch out your hand toward the sky so that darkness will be spread all over Egypt." Moses did as he was told and the sun went out, blanketing the whole country, except for the area where the Israelites lived.

Pharaoh summoned Moses and Aaron again. When they finally found him in the pitch black, Pharaoh said, "Go, worship the Lord. Even your women and children may go with you. But leave your flocks and your herds behind." Moses protested at this, saying they needed to take their animals with them to be used as sacrifices. Infuriated, Pharaoh changed his mind, shouting, "Get out of my sight! If I ever see you again, I will kill you."

Understanding the story

In Hebrew, "plague" means "lash" or "blow," so God's plagues are clearly punishments. As plague after plague is unleashed, the Egyptians are left in turmoil. They worshipped the sun in a variety of forms, which is why the plague of darkness is terrifying to them. Still, the pharaoh refuses to release the Israelites.

The Tenth Plague

The Lord told Moses that He would bring one last plague to Egypt. It would be so terrible that Pharaoh would go down on his knees and beg the Israelites to leave.

At midnight, each firstborn son in Egypt would die. Even the livestock would not be spared—the firstborn cattle and sheep would also die. But the Israelites would not suffer and not one of their children would be harmed. Moses approached Pharaoh yet again, as he had done so many times before, to plead for the Israelites' freedom and to give him God's chilling message. But Pharaoh did not believe him, and Moses came away seething with rage.

Then the Lord told Moses and his brother, Aaron, that from now on this would be the beginning of the Israelites' year, instead of the first month of harvest. It was early spring and that night there was a new moon. On the tenth day of the first month each Israelite household must choose the best firstborn lamb and prepare it for slaughter. It should be a one-year-old. Four days later, at dusk, the lamb must have its throat slit and its blood was to be used to mark the door of the house. That night there should be a feast, with the meat

Bitter herbs
Israelites ate bitter herbs deliberately to remind themselves of how bitter and terrible their slavery had been. The bitter herbs that they ate were probably sour salad vegetables. In ancient Egypt, these included dandelions, chicory, and lettuce. Today, horseradish is the most popular choice to represent the bitter taste.

Passover feast
Jewish people celebrate Passover every year. Families gather together to feast on symbolic foods and remember the Israelites' last night in Egypt. On the menu is roasted lamb, unleavened bread, charoseth (nut and apple paste), horseradish and lettuce, eggs, and salt water.

"The Tenth Plague", oil on canvas, by German painter Johann Heiss (1640–1704)

roasted over the fire and eaten with bitter herbs and special bread, made without yeast.

God said that this would be the very night when He would pass through Egypt and all the firstborn sons, cattle, and sheep would die. But He would see the bloody marks on the Israelites' doors and they would be safe.

Moses listened and then summoned all the elders of the Israelites to him. He told them what was going to happen in two weeks' time and told them what they must do. "It will be known as the Passover sacrifice to the Lord, because He will pass over the houses of the Israelites in Egypt and spare our homes when He strikes down the Egyptians," he said. "And from that time on the Passover feast must be celebrated for all times."

So, two weeks later, the Israelites slaughtered their lambs and roasted them over the fire. They smeared their doors with blood, then tightly closed them against the night, uncertain of what was to come. They feasted on the roasted meat with bitter herbs—wild lettuce, endive, and nettle—and unleavened bread.

At midnight, when the moon hung heavy in the sky, the Lord passed silently over Egypt, just as He had promised, and killed all the firstborn sons as they lay sleeping. And He wiped out all the firstborn cattle and sheep, too. After He came and went, the dead lay in their beds and in their cots and in their fields.

Howls of grief were heard as the people discovered their lifeless sons. Soon, a wailing filled the air as the scale of the horror was revealed. Sorrow and terror swept the country. Not one Egyptian household had escaped the massacre—not even Pharaoh's. Beating his breast, he summoned Moses and Aaron and sobbed, "Leave my people, you and the Israelites! Go, worship the Lord as you have requested. Take your flocks and your herds and go! Have pity on me!"

The Israelites left immediately, asking the Egyptians for silver and gold and clothing, as Moses told them to do. They had lived in Egypt for four hundred and thirty years and, at last, they had been released from their slavery. Six hundred thousand men, women, and children set off on foot, with their flocks and herds, at the start of their long journey.

Understanding the story

God's last plague shows the Egyptians His supreme power. The pharaoh finally sets the Israelites free and begs for God's mercy. The event becomes known as Passover because the Lord "passed over" the Israelite homes and they escaped the Egyptians' punishment. Bitter herbs are to remind the Israelites of the bitterness of their slavery. Unleavened bread is symbolic of the speed with which the people left Egypt—with no time for their bread to rise.

"It will be known as the Passover sacrifice to the Lord."

Egyptian mummy
Before Joseph died, he made his brothers swear an oath to take his remains back to Canaan with them. Moses kept the promise. After Joseph's body was embalmed, he was taken to Canaan in an Egyptian mummy case like this.

Red Sea
Though the Red Sea usually looks blue, dying algae in its waters turn it reddish-brown from time to time. God allows Moses to command its waters, demonstrating God's power over the seas, which He created on the third day.

The Crossing of the Red Sea

So the Lord led His people out of Egypt and through the desert, on their way to the land of Canaan. It was a huge group, with all the different tribes and clans of Israel.

The Israelites took what few cattle and sheep they had with them, and their donkeys were piled high. They were careful to avoid the land of their enemy, the Philistines, and went the long way around, toward the land that God had promised their forefathers. They took with them, too, the bones of Joseph, which had been carefully preserved. An oath had been sworn, long ago, that the bones would be taken back to Canaan to be buried by the side of his father, Jacob.

The Israelites traveled eastward, a vast human river creeping through the harsh desert landscape. Then they turned southward toward the Red Sea. And the Lord was with them and He guided them during the day with a pillar of cloud. By night, He led them with a pillar of fire, like a beacon, so they could see the path.

In Egypt, Pharaoh had a sudden change of heart. "What have we done?" he asked. "We have let the Israelites go and lost our slaves. Prepare the chariots!" At once, the army was assembled and Pharaoh set off in pursuit of the Israelites, with six hundred of his finest chariots and the fastest horses. They pounded through the desert in a cloud of dust, with thundering hooves.

The Israelites, camping on the shores of the Red Sea, felt the earth tremble and looked at each other in fear. Then they saw the Egyptians charging toward them, their armor glinting in the sun.

The Lord said to Moses, "Tell the Israelites to move on. Raise your staff and stretch out your hand over the sea to divide the water. The Israelites will be able to go through the sea on dry ground." And the great pillar of cloud and fire, which had guided the Israelites on their journey, moved behind them, protecting them from their pursuers.

As Moses stretched out his hand over the Red Sea, a strong east wind whipped up out of nowhere and the waters parted to reveal a path that stretched all the way across to the other side. The Israelites hurried along the muddy track as fast as they could. Huge walls of water towered above them, to their right and to their left. They crossed in their thousands and arrived on the other shore.

The Egyptians followed, driving their chariots toward the sea. But the wheels got stuck in the mud of the seabed. They could not move.

Then the Lord said to Moses, "Stretch

"The Deliverance of Israel" by Irish painter Francis Danby (1793–1861) shows the Egyptian army engulfed by the sea.

out your hand over the sea so that the waters may flow back over the Egyptians and their chariots." Moses obeyed, and the walls of water crashed together, meeting in a sea of boiling foam. The path across the Red Sea vanished, as the waters swallowed the entire Egyptian army.

The Israelites, watching from the other side, embraced and gave thanks. And Moses's sister, Miriam, took her tambourine and led the women in singing and dancing. "Sing to the Lord for He is highly exalted. The horse and its rider He has hurled in the sea!"

"Raise your staff and stretch out your hand over the sea to divide the water."

Understanding the story

The Exodus of the Israelites from Egypt is the start of God's plan for His people. The dramatic parting of the waters, the safe crossing of the Israelites, and the subsequent destruction of the pursuing Egyptian army are proof of God's power. The pillars of cloud and fire are symbols of His presence and protection throughout the journey to the Promised Land.

God Provides

After the Israelites had crossed the Red Sea, Moses and Aaron led them up into the Desert of Shur.

For three days they walked under the scorching sun, and, by the time they reached the spring at Marah, their throats were parched and dry. They rushed to the water, but it was foul and undrinkable and they looked at Moses. "What are we meant to drink?" they asked him.

The Lord showed Moses a special tree. He snapped off a piece of wood and threw it into the spring. Immediately, the water became sweet and pure. The Israelites tried it again and this time drank gladly and quenched their thirst. Refreshed, they continued on their way to Elim, where there were twelve springs and seventy shady palm trees. They slept well that night under a clear, starry sky.

Then Moses and Aaron led them on their way through the dry and stony wilderness. The landscape was so different from the green valley of the Nile River, which they had fled. There, although their lives as slaves were hard, at least the food was plentiful. Here, there was nothing, and their supplies had run out. "If only we had died by the Lord's hand in Egypt," they grumbled at Moses. "There we ate all the food we wanted.

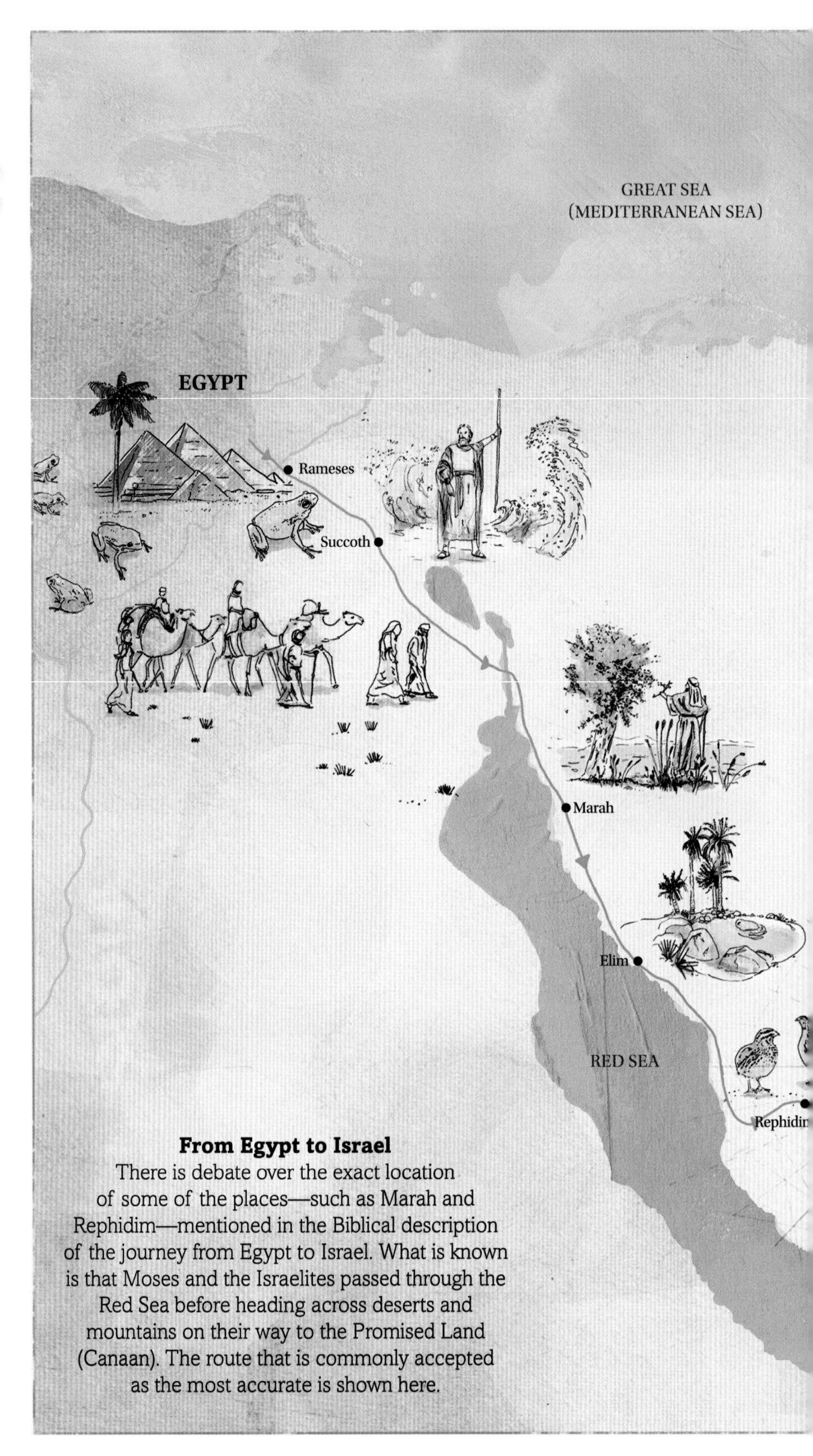

From Egypt to Israel
There is debate over the exact location of some of the places—such as Marah and Rephidim—mentioned in the Biblical description of the journey from Egypt to Israel. What is known is that Moses and the Israelites passed through the Red Sea before heading across deserts and mountains on their way to the Promised Land (Canaan). The route that is commonly accepted as the most accurate is shown here.

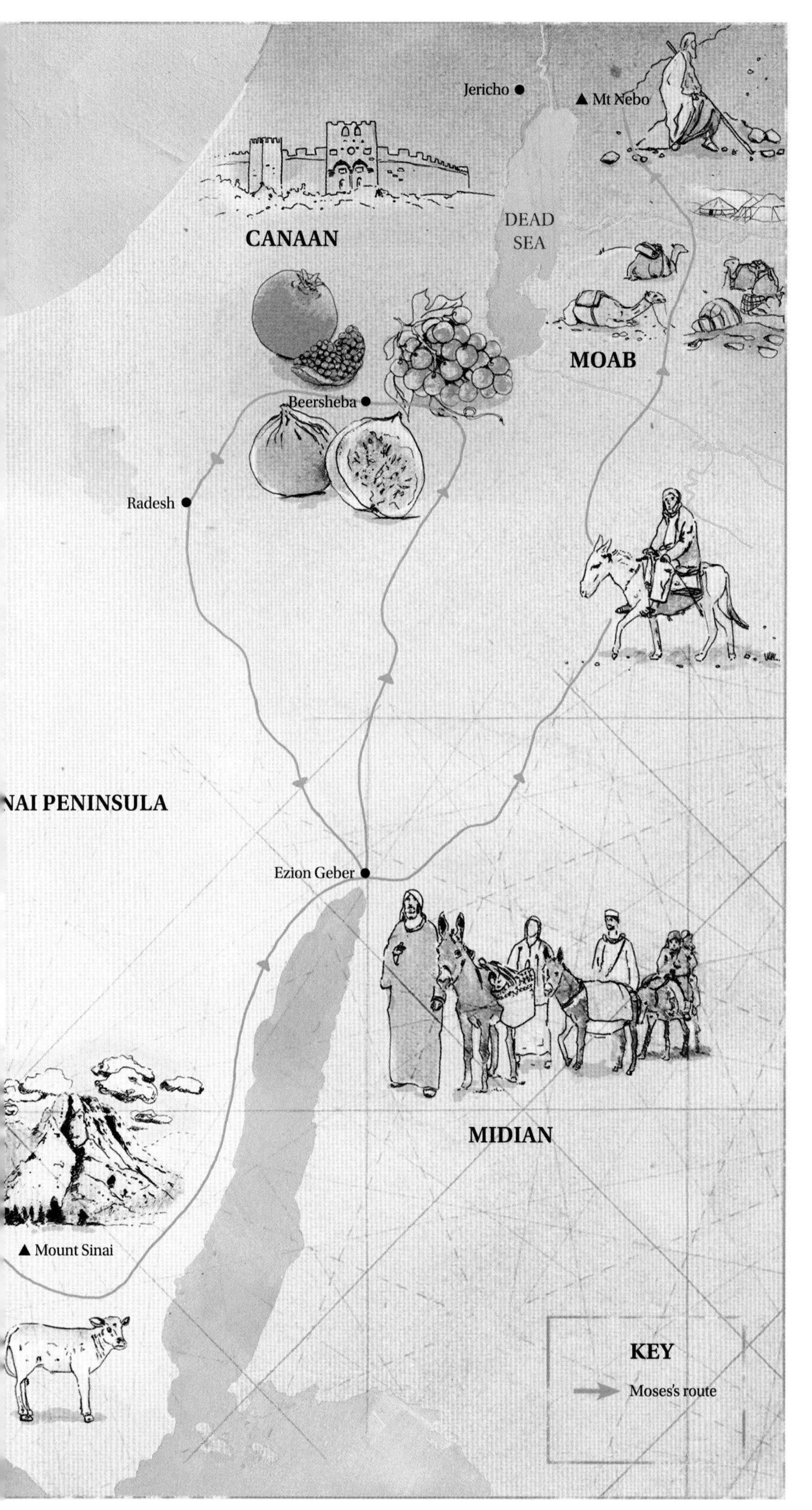

You have taken us to a desert to starve."

Then the Lord spoke to Moses and Aaron again and said, "I will rain down food from heaven for you. The people are to go out and gather it each day. At twilight they will eat meat and in the morning they will have as much bread as they want." Moses and Aaron repeated God's words, saying, "In the evening you will know that it was the Lord who brought you out of Egypt and in the morning you will see the glory of the Lord, because He has heard you grumbling against Him. Who are we? You are not grumbling against us, but against the Lord."

That same evening, as the sun began to set, a huge flock of quails appeared in the distance on their long migration across the desert. They flew toward the Israelites' camp, swooping lower and lower on tired wings, and finally dropped to the ground, exhausted by their journey. The plump little bodies rained down in their thousands, the soft brown feathers matching the sand where they fell. They lay there motionless, waiting to be caught. The Israelites lit their fires and prepared the birds, roasting them over the flames. The flesh was succulent and, after so long without food, the Israelites feasted to their hearts' content.

The next day, the Israelites woke up to find that the ground was covered with strange white flakes that looked like thick frost. They were puzzled, and Moses told them, "It is the bread the Lord has given you to eat, and you are to gather it each morning. Take just as much as you need for that day—no more." It was the color of coriander seed and tasted delicious, like the sweetest honey. The Israelites had never seen anything like it and they called it manna. But some people were greedy and ignored the instructions. They grabbed

Quail
These small, speckled birds fly over the Sinai Peninsula on their migrations between Europe and Africa. The distance is so great that they often get tired and must rely on the wind to carry them.

Manna
It is not clear from the Bible text what manna (Hebrew for "What is it?") actually is. While some people believe it is the sweet substance released from insects living off the Tamarisk Bush in the Sinai Peninsula, others believe it is the sticky resin produced by several desert plants, including this hammada shrub (below).

"How long will you refuse to keep my commands and instructions?"

as much as they could and stuffed it in their bags. After a few hours the smell was terrible and the manna was alive with white maggots.

On the sixth day, Moses told them they could take enough manna to last them two days. "Tomorrow is to be a day of rest, a holy Sabbath to the Lord. Six days you are to gather but not on the seventh."

Nevertheless, a few people disobeyed and went out at dawn the next day to look for manna. But the manna had vanished into thin air. And the Lord said to Moses, "How long will you refuse to keep my commands and instructions?"

Then the Israelites traveled on further through the desert under a burning sun, and they camped at Rephidim that night. They were tired and thirsty and went to Moses to complain again. "Why did you bring us out of Egypt to make us die of thirst?" they moaned.

Moses did not know what to do. He appealed to the Lord again. "What am I to do with these people?" he asked. "They are almost ready to stone me."

The Lord told him to walk ahead, taking with him his wooden staff. "I will stand there before you by the rock at Horeb," the Lord said. "Strike the rock and water will come out of it for the people to drink." Moses went on and found the spot. He hit the sheer rock face and immediately a stream of crystal-clear water gushed out, sparkling in the sun.

Understanding the story

Hunger and thirst cause the Israelites to question their faith in God, but He shows His presence by miraculously providing food and water. In spite of God's actions, the people still doubt Him. God did not give food for the seventh day because it was set aside for worship and rest, just as He commanded during the Creation.

Moses Receives God's Laws

"You will be my treasured possession."

Three months after the Israelites had left Egypt, they came to the sacred mountain of Sinai, where the Lord had appeared to Moses in a burning bush many years before.

And the Lord called to him now, from the top of the mountain, and Moses went up to meet Him. The Lord gave Moses a message saying, "You have seen what I did in Egypt and how I carried you here on eagles' wings. If you obey me fully and keep my covenant, then, out of all the nations, you will be my treasured possession. Although the whole earth is mine, you will be for me a kingdom of priests and a holy nation."

Moses went down and summoned the elders, telling them what God had said.

Mount Sinai
The holy mountain of Sinai is where God gives Moses the Ten Commandments. It is thought to be the mountain Jebel Musa or "Mountain of Moses" in the south Sinai Peninsula, in modern-day Egypt. The red granite mountain stands 7,500 ft (2,300 m) in height.

Aaron
In this illumination from an 18th-century Hebrew Bible, Aaron is depicted as the first High Priest. God selects Aaron and his sons to lead the rituals of worship and sacrifice on His behalf. Aaron was the forefather of the Israelite priesthood.

Then the Lord called Moses to Him again and said that, in three days time, He would come down from the heavens in a thick cloud and speak to him in front of all the Israelites.

Three days later, the sky suddenly darkened. Peals of thunder crashed high above and lightning flashed from the heavens. A deafening trumpet blast ripped through the air. The people huddled together in terror, but Moses went to them and led them to the bottom of the mountain. From the middle of the cloud of smoke the Lord spoke to Moses, and told him to come up with his brother, Aaron. Before he went, Moses said to the Israelites, "Do not be afraid. God has come to test you so that the fear of God will be with you to keep you from sinning." Then the two brothers climbed higher and higher into the thick cloud, where God was waiting. He said to them:

"I am the Lord your God and these are my commandments:
You shall have no other gods before me.
You shall not bow down to idols or worship them.
You shall not misuse the name of the Lord your God.
Remember the Sabbath day by keeping it holy.
Honor your father and your mother.
You shall not murder.
You shall not commit adultery.
You shall not steal.
You shall not give false testimony against your neighbor.
You shall not covet your neighbor's house or his wife or his belongings."

When he had finished, the Lord told them to go down and to make an altar at the bottom of the mountain. He went on to give them some more laws and said that an angel would go with the Israelites on their journey to the Promised Land. Moses and Aaron went back down to their people, who had been waiting and repeated the Lord's words. "Everything that the Lord has said, we will do," said the people. So Moses wrote all the Lord's words down in the Book of the Covenant.

They built an altar with twelve stone pillars, one for each of the twelve tribes of Israel, and they made burnt offerings to God. The best young bulls were sacrificed, and Moses sprinkled some of the blood on the altar and some over the people, saying, "This is the blood of the covenant that the Lord has made with you in accordance with all His words."

Then Moses and Aaron went up the mountain again. This time they took with them Aaron's two sons, Nadab and Abihu, and seventy of the Israelite elders. When they reached the top, God was waiting for them, standing on a beautiful sapphire floor. And God said to Moses, "Come here and I will give you tablets of stone with the laws and commands I have given you written on them." And Moses went into the cloud and stayed on the mountain for forty days and forty nights.

Sefer Torah
The distinctive crown shape symbolizes the ruling power of the law. The scroll is sewn on to two wooden rollers, making it easier to read.

Understanding the story

For the Creation, God creates order from chaos using ten commands, and here God gives order to Israel with the Ten Commandments. God's speech takes the same form as an ancient royal treaty: first there is an introduction identifying the king, then a historical section follows before the terms are set. The Book of the Covenant is the constitution of Israel, establishing how people should relate to God and each other.

"I am the Lord your God and these are my commandments"

Code of law
Handwritten scrolls that proclaim God's commands became codes of law for people to read and live by. This Sefer Torah scroll is used in the ritual of Torah-reading at Jerusalem's main synagogue, Heichal Shlomo.

The Golden Calf

With Moses staying on the mountain for such a long time, the Israelites thought he was never coming back.

Apis bull god
The golden calf is based on the Apis bull—the Egyptian god of fertility. Apis was worshipped in the form of a living bull. Pagan gods were often represented as bulls in ancient times because of their strength and power. This detail showing the Egyptian deity Horus and the Apis bull was found near Teti's Pyramid in Saqqara, Egypt.

They went to his brother, Aaron, and said, "Please make us a god. We need someone to worship! Moses brought us out of Egypt, but we don't know what has happened to him. He has deserted us!"

Aaron listened and thought for a little while. Then he told them to bring whatever gold jewelry they had to him. Obediently, they took off their necklaces, slipped off their bracelets and their rings, and unclipped their earrings. They even searched in their bags for any gold trinkets that they might have hidden at the beginning of their journey. They gave it all to Aaron.

The pile of gold grew, glittering in the sun, and Aaron took it and poured it into a great vat. It looked like an enormous treasure chest. He placed it over the fire, melting the gold into a thick paste. Then he let it cool slightly and molded it into the shape of a young calf. When he had finished, it bore a passing resemblance to the Egyptian bull god Apis. The Israelites watched, impressed by his skill.

Then, Aaron built an altar for the golden calf, and the next day the people worshipped their new idol. They made sacrifices to it and put burnt offerings on the altar. And they feasted and drank and danced through the night.

Moses had been on the mountain for forty days, and the Lord told him that he must go down to his people again. "They have been quick to turn away from what I commanded and have made themselves an idol cast in the shape of a calf. Now, leave me alone so that my anger may burn against them and destroy them," He said.

But Moses pleaded with the Lord to

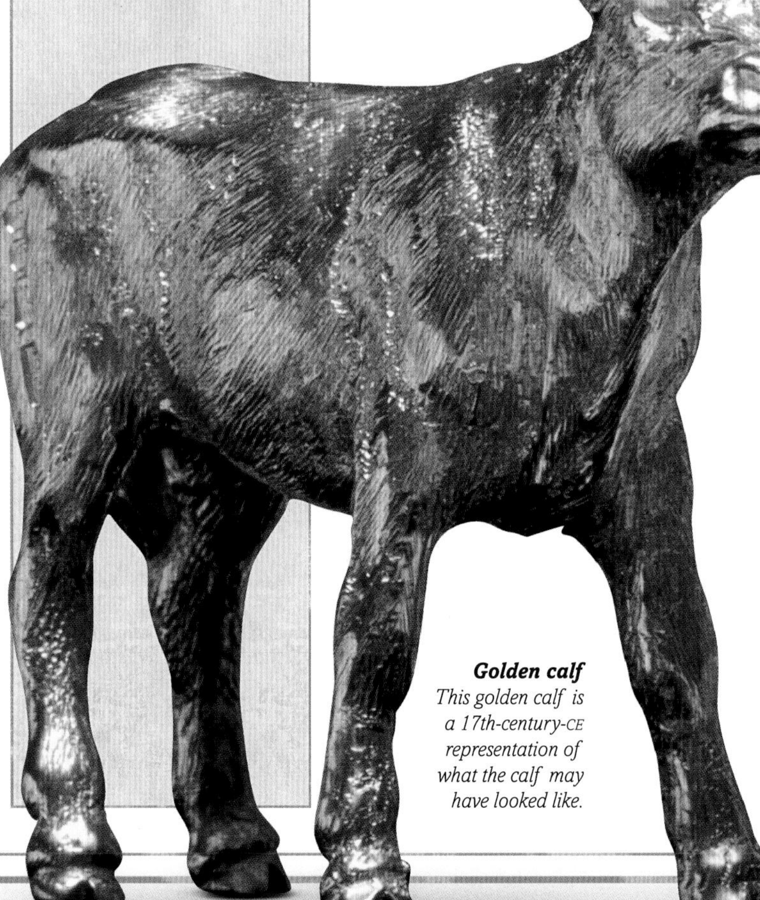

Golden calf
This golden calf is a 17th-century-CE representation of what the calf may have looked like.

spare the Israelites. He reminded Him of His promise to make their descendants as numerous as the stars in the sky in the land of Canaan. The Lord listened carefully and relented.

Moses left Him and went back down the mountain, taking with him the two stone tablets that the Lord had given him, inscribed with the Lord's own writing. He had engraved the Ten Commandments on both sides. As Moses got to the bottom of the mountain, he could hear music and singing. It got louder and louder and, when he neared the camp, he saw, with horror, the shiny golden calf standing by the altar and the Israelites drinking and reveling around it. In anger, Moses threw the stone tablets to the ground, smashing them into pieces.

The Israelites looked at him in stunned silence. Then, Moses went straight over to the golden calf and hurled it into the fire. It melted in the heat, the body writhing and bubbling in the flames. When it had cooled, he took the golden cinders and pounded them into a fine powder, which he mixed with water and made the Israelites drink.

Then, he confronted his brother, Aaron. "What were you thinking of?" he shouted furiously. "How could you allow them to do this?" Moses could see that the Israelites were out of control. They were a danger to themselves and had become a laughing stock to their enemies.

Moses went to the entrance of the camp and summoned the people to him. "Whoever is on the side of the Lord, come to me!" he shouted. And the people of the Levite tribe were the only ones who came to his side. Everyone else stood back and looked the other way. He told the Levites that they must take their swords and teach the rest of the Israelites a lesson. There was a terrible massacre that day as the Levites killed at least three thousand of their kinsmen.

Afterward, Moses congratulated the Levites and said to them, "You have been set apart today and the Lord has blessed you." Then he went back up the mountain to speak to the Lord and to ask for His forgiveness. "Oh what a great sin these people have committed," he said. "They had made themselves a god of gold. But, now, please forgive their sin!"

"Go, lead the people to the Promised Land and my angel will go with you," replied the Lord. "However, they have sinned and I will punish them when the time is right!" And He told Moses to write the Ten Commandments on two new tablets of stone to replace the ones that had been broken.

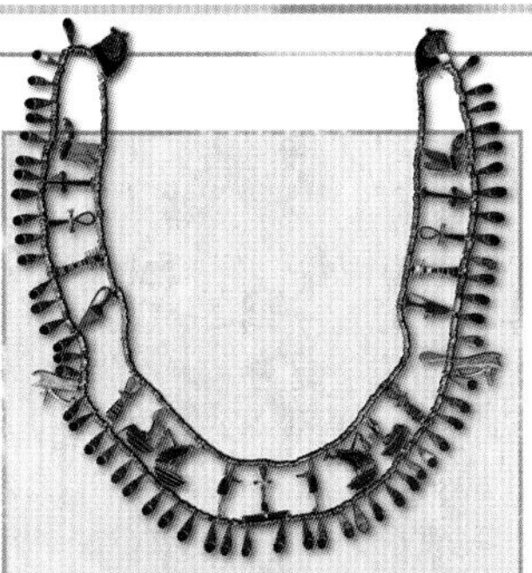

Egyptian jewelry

Ancient Egyptians were skilled at crafting jewelry. Extracted metals, such as gold and silver, were processed and inset with semiprecious stones. This gold necklace (from c. 1880 BCE) belonged to Egyptian Princess Khnumet and is decorated with carnelian, lapis lazuli, and turquoise.

Levites

Descended from Aaron, the tribe of Levi was one of the 12 tribes of Israel, and the only one not to worship the golden calf. The Lord rewarded this loyalty by making them priests and giving them 48 cities where they organized worship and took care of the temples. As a result, many tombstones of Levites are distinguished by hands symbolizing the blessing of the priests (above).

Understanding the story

Many pagan civilizations showed their gods as bulls because they symbolized power. By worshipping the golden calf, the Israelites are breaking the second commandment of the Covenant Law. God tells Moses to inscribe the commandments on two tablets in keeping with the Middle Eastern tradition of writing two copies of a treaty—one for the king and one for his subjects.

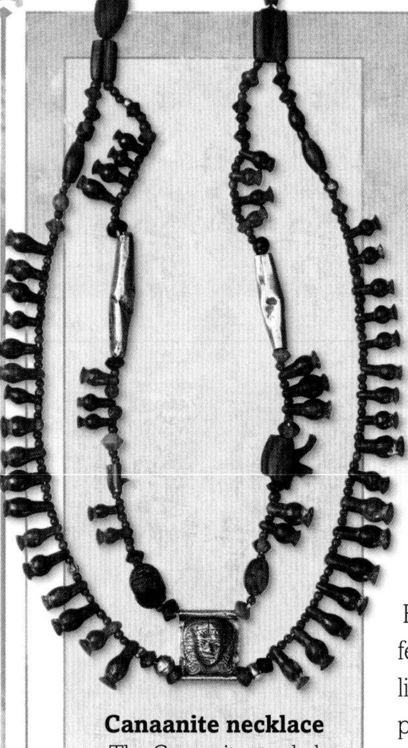

Canaanite necklace
The Canaanites traded with Egypt as early as 3300 BCE. Items of jewelry, such as the necklace (above), were commonly traded. The Canaanites used a lot of gold and jasper, a tough red stone, in their designs.

Balaam's Donkey

After many years, the tribes of Israel were finally allowed to go to the Promised Land of Canaan.

They arrived on the plains of Moab, fresh with victory over the neighboring Amorites, and camped in their thousands along the Jordan River, across from Jericho. Balak, who ruled Moab, was horrified at the sight of them. He sent his envoys with a message and a fee to the famous soothsayer Balaam, who lived on the banks of the Euphrates. "A people has come out of Egypt; they cover the face of the land and have settled next to me. Come and put a curse on them because they are too powerful. Then I can defeat them and drive them from my country."

Balaam received the message and slept on it. In the night, the Lord came to him and said, "Do not go with these men. You must not put a curse on the tribes of Israel because they are blessed and are the chosen people." So Balaam told the envoys that he could not help them and they returned, unsuccessful, to Balak.

But the king refused to give up and sent the most distinguished princes in the land to Balaam. They offered Balaam great riches, but he replied, "Even if Balak gave me his palace filled with silver and gold, still I could not go against the word of the Lord my God. Stay here tonight and I will find out what the Lord says."

That night, God spoke to

Balaam to see what was in his heart. "Go with these men, but you must obey me and do only as I say," He told him. So, the next morning, Balaam saddled his favorite donkey and set off with the princes back to the land of Moab. But God was not pleased that Balaam had gone.

Suddenly, as they plodded along the dusty road, the angel of the Lord appeared, sword in hand, to stop Balaam. The little donkey saw him and shied off the road. But, full of his own self-importance, Balaam was blind to the apparition. He cursed and beat the donkey to get her back onto the road.

Then the angel appeared again, blocking a narrow path that snaked between two vineyards, with walls on each side. Again, the donkey saw the angel and squeezed against the wall to avoid him, crushing Balaam's foot in the process. As before, Balaam did not even glimpse the angel and beat the donkey.

For the third time, the angel appeared, standing in the middle of the path. It was impossible to get past. The little donkey's legs folded under her and she collapsed to the ground. Once again, Balaam saw nothing and he beat the donkey to within an inch of her life. At this point, the donkey opened her mouth and asked, "What have I done to make you beat me?"

"You have made a fool of me!" he shouted. "If only I had a sword, I would kill you now."

Then suddenly, the Lord removed the veil from Balaam's eyes and he saw the angel, gleaming sword in hand. Terrified, Balaam fell to the ground.

"Why have you beaten your donkey?" asked the angel. "I would have killed you, if she had not saved you. But I would have spared her." Balaam begged forgiveness and the angel told him to continue with the princes to Balak in the land of Moab. "Go with these men but speak only what I tell you," he said.

When Balaam arrived, he was met by the king. "I have come here as asked," the soothsayer said, "but I can speak only the words that God puts in my mouth." Together, they went up to the mountains where they could see the tribes of Israel below. There, they built seven great altars and put a bull and a ram on each one as offerings. Then Balaam left Balak and his princes with the sacrifices and climbed higher to the most solitary peak to meet the Lord. When he came down again, the charred offerings were still smoldering and Balaam delivered God's message, blessing the people of Israel instead of cursing them.

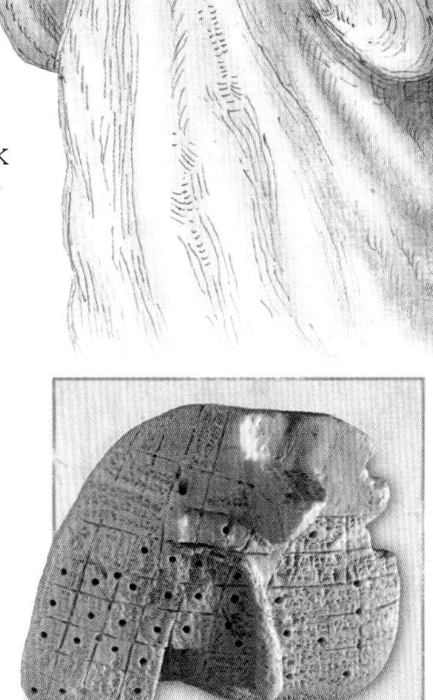

Fortune-telling tool
Though Balaam believed in God, he was known to use curses and make predictions. Unusual artifacts were used for these occult practices. This clay mold of a sheep's liver was a typical aid to foreseeing the future in ancient times.

Understanding the story

Balaam is known for his powerful curses, but these are forbidden under Moses's Law. The curses are unable to contradict God's will anyway. While the donkey is faithful, Balaam is initially blinded by greed. When the angel bears a sword, Balaam sees the light. He asks for forgiveness and ends up blessing the Israelites. God ensures Balaam and his donkey are part of His commitment to keeping the covenant promise.

The Promised Land

The Israelites were camped in the Paran Desert, near Canaan, and the Lord told Moses to send some scouts ahead. Moses picked twelve men, one from each of the tribes of Israel, and sent them on their way.

"Go through the Negev and into Canaan," Moses said to them. "Check out the lie of the land and see what the people are like."

The twelve men set off, traveling through the arid landscape until they got to Canaan. They reached Hebron and the Valley of Eschol, which was fertile and green. The trees were heavy with fruit. They cut a gigantic bunch of sweet grapes from the vines, so heavy that it took two men to carry it. They also took juicy pomegranates and luscious figs. Altogether, they spent forty days exploring Canaan, before returning to Moses and the Israelites.

When they got back, the scouts reported that Canaan was a beautiful country that did, indeed, flow with milk and honey. But ten of them, who liked to stir up trouble, made up a story that Canaan was full of giants who lived in walled cities.

"We can't attack them—we wouldn't stand a chance!" they said. "They are much stronger than us. Beside them, we look like grasshoppers!"

Two of the scouts, named Caleb and Joshua, remained silent. The rest of the Israelites looked at each other grimly. "If only we had died in Egypt," they sighed, looking at Moses and Aaron. "Or in this desert. Why did the Lord bring us to the Promised Land if we are going to be killed? Why don't we go back to Egypt?"

Caleb and Joshua then told their story. They said that the inhabitants of Canaan were not giants and that it would be an excellent place to live. "Do not rebel against the Lord," they pleaded. "And don't be afraid of the people who live in Canaan. We will easily get the better of them. The Lord is with us." But no one believed them and some talked about stoning them to death.

The Lord heard the tribes of Israel complaining yet again and was saddened and angry. "How long will these people treat me with contempt?" He asked Moses.

"How long will they refuse to believe in me, in spite of the miraculous signs I have shown them?" He said that, as a result of their sins, they would be condemned to wander in the desert for forty years before being allowed to enter the Promised Land of Canaan. "In this desert you will die, every one of you who has complained so much. Not one of you will enter the land I swore to make your home—except Caleb, son of Jephunneh, and Joshua, son of Nun. But your children will reach Canaan and will enjoy the land that their parents will never reach."

The years went by and the tribes of Israel wandered in the bleak and inhospitable wilderness. Moses grew old and he realized that, after all this time, he would not live to cross the Jordan River and get to Canaan. He summoned Joshua and, in front of everyone, said to him, "Be strong and courageous, for you are the one who must lead the people into the Promised Land. And you must divide it between them. Do not be afraid, the Lord will be with you."

Moses told the Israelite people to follow God's Law, the Ten Commandments, which were written down on two tablets of stone and kept in the Ark of the Covenant—a magnificent golden chest, guarded by two cherubim with outstretched wings. The Israelites carried the Ark with them wherever they went on their wanderings. When they stopped to set up camp, the Ark was put in the most sacred place, deep within the holy tabernacle—the brightly colored tent that was set up for worship.

The same day, Moses went to Mount Nebo in Moab, just across from the city of Jericho. Although he was very old, his body was still strong and his eyes were keen. He climbed slowly up the high mountain and the Lord showed him the land of Canaan, which had taken so many years and such hardships to reach. He stood at the top and saw the Promised Land, at last. It stretched across the Jordan River and the Salt Sea all the way to the waters of the Great Sea in the west. And the Lord said to him, "This is the land I promised on oath to Abraham, Isaac, and Jacob. You have now seen it with your own eyes, but you will never reach it."

And Moses died that day in Moab, one hundred and twenty years after he had been found as a tiny baby, hidden in the thick bulrushes of the Nile River in Egypt. The Israelite people grieved for thirty days, weeping and mourning. They knew that there would never be another prophet like him in the history of Israel.

Grapes
The Israelites loved the juicy grapes from Canaan. They dried them as raisins, boiled them into syrup, and pressed them to make wine. As explained at the Last Supper, wine was a symbol of Christ's blood.

Pomegranates
The pomegranate became a symbol for the delights of the Promised Land. It is used as a motif on the walls of Solomon's Temple and the robes of the High Priest.

"How long will they refuse to believe in me, in spite of the miraculous signs I have shown them?"

Understanding the story

The Israelites who reject God's Promised Land are condemned to wander the desert for 40 years. These 40-year periods are significant because the number 40 represents a period of testing. Only Joshua and Caleb give accurate reports of Canaan, and God rewards their faith by granting access. Joshua (meaning "The Lord is Savior") will become Moses's successor, leading Israel to salvation.

Then Moses climbed Mount Nebo from the plains of Moab to the top of Pisgah, opposite Jericho. There the Lord showed him the whole land... Then the Lord said to him, "This is the land I promised on oath to Abraham."

Deuteronomy 34:1–2, 4

Jericho
Known as the "City of Palms,"
Old Testament Jericho stood in a lush oasis.
Excavations reveal ancient cities built and
destroyed, one above another.

Rahab and the Spies

After the death of Moses, the Lord told Joshua that the Israelites should get ready to cross the River Jordan and enter the land of Canaan.

“It will all be yours—from the desert to the Lebanon and from the Euphrates River to the Great Sea in the west,” He said. “No one will be able to stand up to you. As I was with Moses, so I will be with you. I will never leave you or forsake you. But always be careful to obey the laws that my servant Moses gave you!”

Joshua told his people the Lord’s message but, first, he sent two spies ahead to Jericho on the west bank of the Jordan. Jericho was the most important city in the whole of Canaan. The two men set off through the desert, at dead of night. Guided by the moon and the stars, they crossed the river and drew near to the city. The two spies hid among the palm trees until the sun began to rise. Then they slipped quietly through the city gates, just as they opened, mingling with the noisy traders and merchants. Like shadows, they flitted through the narrow streets and past the temple, hearing fearful talk about the Israelites on every corner.

Rahab ties a scarlet ribbon to her window

But the spies needed somewhere to lie low. They found a little house in the city walls that was perfect. It belonged to a woman named Rahab. She invited them in and told them to make themselves comfortable, offering them food and water. And soon, she agreed to help them.

By now, the ruler of Jericho had heard a rumor that some spies might have gotten into the city and he was worried. He knew what a danger the Israelites were. They had wreaked death and destruction on the neighboring Amorites, and everybody had heard how the Lord had parted the waters of the Red Sea for them. He sent his henchmen to search every house in Jericho from top to bottom.

Rahab had taken the two spies up to the roof of her house and had hidden them under some flax that she was drying in the sun. The henchmen arrived and asked her if she had seen the men. “They did come here,” replied Rahab, smiling sweetly at them, “but I didn’t know who they were. If only I’d known!” They searched her house anyway and climbed the steep steps up to the roof. All they saw were large

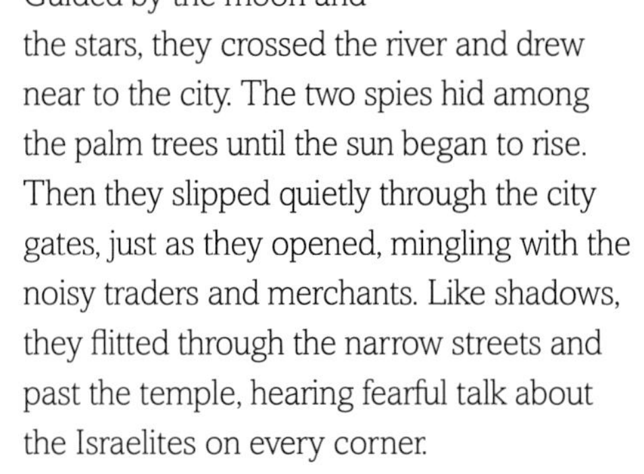

Flax

Linen was made from flax plants. The stems were placed in water, then left to dry out in the sun. Once the fibres were dry and separated, the threads were woven together to create linen. The spies hid under the drying flax at Rahab’s house.

Steep walls

Canaan lies between the Mediterranean Sea and the Jordan River. The Bible featured all six of Canaan’s geographical lands – the coastal plain, fertile foothills, central highlands, the Plain of Megiddo, Galilee, and the Jordan Valley. Fortified towns with steep, protective walls dominated these lands.

bundles of plants laid out to dry. The men left to search the house next door.

When they had gone, Rahab climbed up to the roof and gave the two spies the all clear. They emerged cautiously from the piles of flax and dusted themselves off. Rahab looked at them and said, "I know that the Lord has given this land to the Israelites. We have all heard about you. We are frightened! Please be kind to me and my family. Haven't I been kind to you? I beg you to spare my father and mother, my brothers and sisters."

The men smiled at each other and nodded. "A life for a life!" they replied. "Help us to escape and we will help to save you when we attack Jericho." They told her to tie a scarlet ribbon in her window when she heard that the Israelites were advancing. It would be a sign, and she and her family would be spared. But she must swear that she would not betray them. She agreed, thankfully, and went to find a thick rope.

They waited till the middle of the night when all was quiet and still in the city. Then they tiptoed to the window. Rahab took the rope and dropped it silently out of the window, tying it firmly to a thick beam inside. Then, one after the other, the men climbed down and landed outside the city walls. "Go to the hills and hide!" Rahab whispered. "They'll never find you there!" The spies stayed hidden for three days in the hills. Then they returned to Joshua and told him what had happened.

Understanding the story

God reassures Joshua of His eternal presence on the journey to Canaan with the Israelites. The two spies sent to Jericho agree a bargain with Rahab—she will help the spies, and they in turn will spare her when the Israelites attack. The scarlet ribbon on the window will protect Rahab just as the lambs' blood daubed on the Israelites' doors did on the night of the tenth plague in Egypt.

"Go to the hills and hide!"

Ancient Jericho
In Joshua's time (c. 1400 BCE) Canaan was divided into walled city-states, each with its own king. Lying close to the Jordan River, Jericho is the location of the world's oldest walled city first built in c. 8000 BCE. These ruins at Tell es-Sultan are evidence of settlements between c. 9600 BCE and 1400 BCE.

Shophar
In this story, the priests blow on their shophars when storming Jericho. Today, the instrument is traditionally blown at the start of Rosh Hashanah, the Jewish New Year. The blasting sounds of the shophar can still be heard in synagogues on holy days. Crafted from a ram's horn, it was steamed to make it more malleable, before the wide end was bent into the typical shape of a trumpet.

The Battle of Jericho

The two spies got back from Canaan, and they told Joshua that the country was gripped by fear.

So the Israelites moved forward and made their camp by the side of the Jordan River. Joshua spoke to the assembled group. "The Ark of the Covenant will go first, carried by the Levite priests. You must follow it—but at a distance. As soon as the priests set foot in the river, the waters will stop flowing. There will be a path of dry land to the other side and you will all be able to cross safely."

Three days later, the priests led the way, carrying the Ark, which contained the two stone tablets with the Ten Commandments written on them. Sure enough, as soon as they stepped in the water, the river stopped flowing and they walked to the middle. They waited there with the golden Ark glinting in the sun, and the Israelites started to walk across.

Joshua chose twelve men, one from each tribe. He told them to stop in the middle of the dry path, where the priests stood, and to pick up a stone. They did this, and carried the stones to the other side. When all the Israelites had crossed, the priests came with the Ark. As they stepped onto the bank, the river began flowing again.

They set up camp at Gilgal on the plains of Jericho. Joshua took the twelve stones and set them in the earth as a memorial to the people of Israel. Now the forty thousand Israelite soldiers were gathering. It was a fearsome sight. The king of Jericho ordered the city gates to be shut tight and bolted.

Then the Lord said to Joshua, "Go to Jericho with your soldiers and march around the city once. Take the Ark with you. Seven priests must walk in front of it, sounding their trumpets. Do the same for six days. Then, on the seventh day, march around the city like this seven times. At the end, the priests must sound a long trumpet blast and everyone must shout together, as loud as they can."

And so, the soldiers advanced on Jericho and marched around the city walls. The priests sounded their trumpets in front of the Ark. The walls shook, and inside the people watched in terror. For six days,

This 5th-century-CE mosaic from the Basilica Santa Maria Maggiore, Rome, Italy, shows the fall of Jericho.

the Israelites marched. On the seventh day, they marched around the city seven times and the priests raised their trumpets. A long, mournful blast filled the air. At this, Joshua gave the signal and the Israelites shouted at the tops of their voices.

But as the chorus faded away, another sound could be heard. A rumble came from the city walls and it grew louder. Suddenly, cracks appeared in the stone and bricks. The Israelites watched as the walls collapsed, crashing to the ground.

Without its great wall, Jericho was at the mercy of the Israelite soldiers. They rushed in and killed every living thing. The soldiers knew where Rahab lived, because of the scarlet ribbon in her window, so she and her family were spared.

"Go to Jericho with your soldiers and march around the city once. Take the Ark with you."

Understanding the story

As the Red Sea parted during the Exodus, the Jordan River stops flowing so the Israelites can cross to Jericho. The 12 stones stand for the 12 tribes of Israel. The seven-day siege represents completion, reflecting God's people finally inheriting the Promised Land.

The Call of Gideon

Baal
The worship of pagan gods and goddesses grew popular among the Canaanite people. Their chief deity was Baal (meaning "lord"), who controlled the weather. He was associated with rain and storms, and is often depicted holding a lightning bolt. As Baal had the power to bring heavy rain or drought, the Canaanites believed their fertile lands could only flourish under his influence.

For seven years, the tribes of Israel suffered at the hands of their neighbors, the Midianites. The Lord told the Israelites that they were being punished because they had been worshipping false gods.

One day, a young Israelite named Gideon was busy at work, threshing wheat. From the shade of a great oak tree a tall figure approached him. He greeted Gideon courteously and said, "The Lord is with you, mighty warrior!"

"But, sir, if the Lord is with us why does He allow our enemies, the Midianites, to overrun our country?" Gideon asked. "The Lord has abandoned us!"

The stranger smiled and said, "The Lord has chosen you. You are to save Israel from the Midianites. The Lord will be with you!" Gideon shook his head in disbelief.

He went to get some food for the stranger. The man had sat down to rest under the oak tree and, when Gideon approached, he asked him to put the dishes on a rock just by him. He then tapped the food with the tip of his wooden staff and a bright flame shot out of the rock and the food disappeared. And then the stranger vanished into thin air himself. As Gideon stood staring in wonder, it slowly dawned on him that he had seen an angel.

That night, Gideon smashed the altar that his father had made to the god Baal. He also cut down the wooden Asherah pole, which was sacred to the goddess Asherah. Then, with the help of his servants, he made a new altar to the Lord and sacrificed a fully grown bull on it.

In the morning, when the people saw that Baal's altar had been destroyed and that the Asherah pole had vanished, they were angry. They discovered that Gideon was the culprit and called for his blood. But his father, Joash, replied, "If Baal really is a god, he can defend himself when someone destroys his altar!" The people listened and agreed.

The Midianites and their allies from the east had now joined forces. They were camping in the Valley of Jezreel. Gideon knew the moment had come, and he took his trumpet and blew it loud and clear, calling the Israelites to arms.

Thousands of men came to join him. Next morning, he led them all to the Spring

Bronze Baal
This statue shows the Canaanite god Baal striking a warrior pose. It was probably crafted in the 14th century BCE in Ugarit, Syria, when the worship of the pagan god was at its height.

of Harod at the foot of Mount Gilboa, and they made their camp. To the north, the Midianites were gathered in the valley near the hill of Moreh.

But now the Lord said to Gideon, "You have too many men. I do not want my people to forget me and to think that it is their strength alone that will bring victory over the enemy. If some of your men are having second thoughts, let them go." And twenty-two thousand of Gideon's men turned around and left. There were still ten thousand soldiers, but the Lord said again, "There are too many! Take them down to the water and see who drinks using their cupped hands. They shall stay with you. But those who drink kneeling down shall be sent away." After this, Gideon was left with only three hundred men.

Gideon blows his trumpet to call the Israelites to arms

Later, at dead of night, he crept toward the Midian camp. From inside a tent Gideon could hear a man talking. "I had a dream last night," he said. "A round loaf of barley bread came tumbling into our camp. It hit the tent with such force that it collapsed."

And another voice replied, "That must be Gideon, the son of Joash, the Israelite. We've heard about him! God has promised him victory!"

Gideon rushed back to his men. "Get up!" he shouted. "I know the Lord is with us! He will destroy the Midianites for us!" He gave them all trumpets, jars, and torches, and silently they approached the enemy camp. On Gideon's order, they blew their trumpets and smashed their jars. Then they held their torches high in the air, lighting the darkness, and shouted loudly into the night. The Midianites woke up, confused and terrified. They did not know what the noise was or what the strange lights were. In panic, they drew their swords and turned on each other, and then led into the night.

"The Lord has chosen you. You are to save Israel from the Midianites."

Understanding the story

Gideon is a poor farmer's son, and his father has given up on God. He seems an unlikely champion to save the Israelites from their powerful enemy. Gideon follows God's guidance without hesitation, even when he is asked to send away all but three hundred men. By putting his trust in God, Gideon brings his people to victory.

Camels

The story of Gideon includes the first mention of camels being used in warfare (Judges 6:5). These animals were better suited to the hardships involved in desert battles. For long-range attacks, Midianite soldiers rode camels while firing arrows and thowing spears. This relief from Nineveh shows warriors fighting on camels.

Spring of Harod

This spring at the foot of Mount Gilboa is where Gideon observed his soldiers' drinking styles. Those who cupped the water in their hands rather than dipping their faces into it were chosen to do battle. God may have considered them more alert and ready for war.

Samson and the Lion

The Philistines swept through the south of Canaan, where the tribes of Dan and Judah lived. They brought their gods and they set up altars to them.

Honey
Mainly eaten as a sweet treat, honey and honeycomb were also highly valued in medicine. In the Bible, honey is often given as a present because it was a symbol of abundance and prosperity.

Philistines
The most dangerous enemy of the Israelites were the Philistines, who lived in southwest Canaan from 1200–600 BCE. They had a mighty army, but were also known for crafting beautiful pottery, such as this striking beer jug.

Although the Israelites feared the invaders, they began to worship their gods. So the Lord decided to punish them by allowing the Philistines to stay for forty years.

Manoah belonged to the tribe of Dan and he lived in the village of Zorah. He was faithful to the Lord but, to his great sadness, he had no children. One day, his wife was working in the fields when a stranger suddenly appeared. He told her that he had come from God and announced that she was going to have a son. "The boy is to be a Nazarite and his hair must never be cut," he said. "He will be set apart from other children and will dedicate his life to God. He will be the one who will start to save Israel from the Philistines."

Manoah's wife listened in amazement and rushed to find her husband. She told him the joyful news, and Manoah wanted to hear it for himself. He prayed to the Lord, and the messenger came back and repeated his words. Then Manoah invited him to stay for something to eat. He also asked him his name.

"Why do you ask my name?" the man asked. "It is beyond understanding. I am happy to stay, but do not give me food. Make an offering to the Lord, instead."

So Manoah took a young goat and sacrificed it on the altar, with an offering of grain. The divine messenger rose to the heavens in the smoke and disappeared. Manoah realized that their visitor had been the angel of the Lord.

In time, their baby boy was born and they named him Samson. He was blessed and, from the very first moment, his life was dedicated to God. As the years went by, Samson grew tall and strong and his hair grew longer and longer. But he fell in love with a beautiful young Philistine woman who lived in the fortress town of Timnah in the Sorek Valley. His parents were not pleased.

One day, Samson was on his way to Timnah when a young lion jumped out from the undergrowth in front of him. Samson felt an incredible strength surge through him. He knew it came from God. He grabbed the animal's throat and killed it with his bare hands. He left it lying there and carried on his way.

Days later, when he was coming back along the path, he saw the lion's carcass still lying there. He could hear a loud buzzing. He bent down and saw that, inside the rib cage, there was a bees' nest oozing with honey. He broke off a chunk of the

honeycomb and ate most of it on his way home. There was just a small corner left to give to his parents, although he did not tell them where it came from. Still his parents would not agree to their son marrying a Philistine, and Samson knew he would have to go ahead without them. He arranged the wedding feast, which would be held at his bride's house in Timnah. Her kinsmen and friends were invited, and thirty young Philistine men. The feast lasted seven days, with singing, dancing, and games from morning until night.

But, although Samson loved his bride, he felt alone among the Philistines. He knew that some of the men mocked him. He wanted to outwit them and made up a riddle. "If you give me the answer by the end of the celebrations, I will give you each a set of the finest clothes," he told them. "If you fail, you have to give me thirty sets of the finest clothes—one from each of you." And then he gave them the riddle: "Out of the eater comes forth meat; out of the strong comes something sweet."

For three days, his guests scratched their heads. Defeated, they asked the new bride to coax the answer from her husband. They even threatened to burn her house down. She went to her husband and sobbed, "You don't really love me at all, do you? If you did, you'd tell me the answer to that stupid riddle."

Samson finally relented. She told her friends and, that evening, when Samson put the riddle to them again, one of them stood up with the answer, "What is sweeter than honey? What is stronger than a lion?"

When Samson heard this, he knew he had been cheated by the Philistines and tricked by his wife. In a rage, he headed for the walled city of Ashkelon. Mad with fury, he ambushed thirty Philistines and slit their throats. He stripped off their clothes and took them as payment for the wager he had been cheated out of by his wife and her friends. He returned to his father's house, and his wife was given to one of his friends.

"The boy is to be a Nazarite and his hair must never be cut."

Understanding the story

A Nazarite was someone dedicated to God for a special purpose. They never cut their hair because it was considered the source of life. Samson's survival against the lion reflects the strength of God in him. Miraculous feats can be achieved with God. However, Nazarites were forbidden to touch dead bodies so they could remain pure to do God's work. When Samson eats honey from the lion's carcass, he breaks the first of many rules.

During the wedding feast, Samson poses a riddle to the Philistines

Samson and Delilah

Mighty Samson was feared and hated by the Philistines. He had harassed them for years, killing thousands.

When he fell in love again with another Philistine beauty, Delilah, his enemies saw their chance. The five most powerful lords sidled up to her with words of temptation. "We will each give you eleven hundred pieces of silver if you can find the secret of Samson's strength."

Now, Delilah's love for Samson was great, but her greed and her fear of the scheming lords were even greater. When Samson came to see her, she flattered him, "You are afraid of nothing, my love, and your strength is legendary. What is your secret, my sweet?"

Samson smiled gently to himself. "If I was tied up with seven new bowstrings, all my strength would disappear and vanish into thin air."

Delilah persuaded him to try it out for fun. What Samson didn't know was that the Philistines were waiting next door. He went along with the game pretending to lose his strength and turn to jelly. Then, to test him, Delilah warned, "The Philistines are coming!"

Samson leapt up, snapping the knotted bowstrings as if they were the flimsiest of fairy cobwebs. "Why did you lie to me?" shouted Delilah. Samson laughed. The truth was, he said, that he had to be tied up with thick ropes that had never been used before. Again, Delilah persuaded him to play the game with brand new ropes. But as she was tying the last knot, she screamed, "The Philistines are coming!" Samson broke free immediately.

Desperate with rage, Delilah asked him again. Samson told her that if she wove his long hair into her loom he would lose his strength. The next evening, when he had fallen asleep near her loom, she set to work, weaving his hair. Then she cried, "The Philistines are coming!"

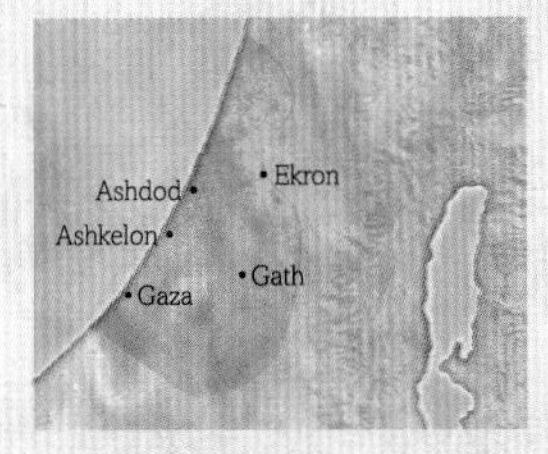

Philistine empire
By about 1050 BCE, the Philistine empire reached the peak of its power. Seizing land from the Israelites, the Philistines settled on Canaan's southern coast. This map shows their territory (shaded orange) and their five major cities.

Weaving
The process of weaving is the entwining of threads to produce cloth. Delilah would have used a horizonal loom similar to this one to weave Samson's hair into her fabric.

Delilah weaves Samson's long hair

Samson woke and tore free of the loom.

Delilah still would not give up. "How can you say you love me when you tell me nothing but lies?" she sobbed.

At last, Samson relented and told her his deepest secret. "I am a Nazarite and my life is devoted to the service of the God of Israel. As a token of obedience, I took a vow that my hair must never be cut. If I were robbed of my hair, I would lose all my strength."

The next evening, after dinner, Samson fell asleep contentedly on Delilah's lap. Suddenly, one of the Philistines crept in and cut off all his long hair. Staring in horror at his shaven head, Delilah screamed again, "The Philistines are coming!"

And this time they did come, and Samson woke up, helpless and weak as a kitten, unable to defend himself. The Philistines dragged him away and blinded him with burning spikes and threw him into prison in shackles. Day in and day out, he was put to work grinding corn, but day in and day out his hair began to grow back.

Understanding the story

Samson's bad behavior is comparable with the Israelites, who have turned away from God and worshipped idols. Samson allows a woman rob him of the sign of God's calling, but he will discover that his true strength lies not in bowstrings or his uncut hair, but in God.

Samson in the Temple

The Philistine lords assembled in the great temple to give thanks to Dagon, the fish god, for delivering Samson into their hands.

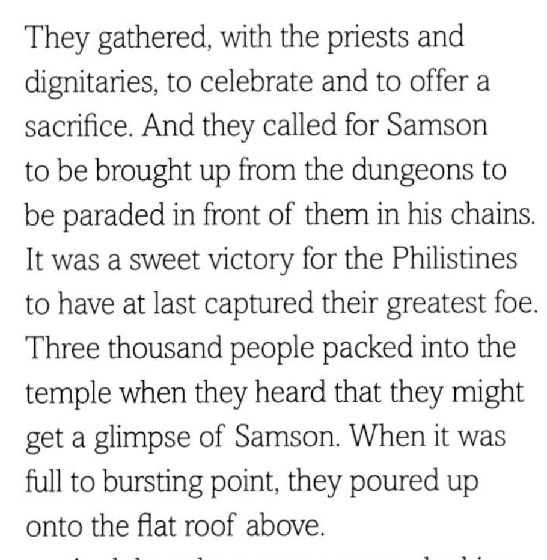

They gathered, with the priests and dignitaries, to celebrate and to offer a sacrifice. And they called for Samson to be brought up from the dungeons to be paraded in front of them in his chains. It was a sweet victory for the Philistines to have at last captured their greatest foe. Three thousand people packed into the temple when they heard that they might get a glimpse of Samson. When it was full to bursting point, they poured up onto the flat roof above.

And then there was a great clanking sound, and Samson was led out of prison by his jailer. He shuffled into the temple, with blinded eyes and manacled hands and feet. Everybody craned their necks to see him. They jeered, then started to prod and beat him. And the great warrior was forced to dance on his toes to the sound of his own chains. It was a pitiful spectacle. Gasping, Samson asked his jailer to take him to rest against the temple pillars.

Then he prayed to the Lord, "O Sovereign Lord, remember me. O God, please strengthen me just once more. Let me get revenge on the Philistines for my two eyes."

Samson was standing between the two great central columns, which supported the whole of the temple. Then he braced himself, arms outstretched between the columns, and cried, "Let me die with the Philistines!"

Samson pushed with all his might and the two pillars trembled, bringing the roof down with a crash. Soon, the other pillars gave way like a pack of cards. Everyone in the temple and on the roof—who had taunted Samson just a few moments before—was crushed to death.

When Samson's kinsmen heard the news they searched for his broken body amongst the ruins, then took him home. They buried him in a tomb next to his father, Manoah. With his death, Samson had killed more Philistines than he had during the whole of his lifetime.

Understanding the story

Although Samson has not always heeded God's word, he still turns to Him in times of trouble. Samson's last request is to take revenge for his blindness. The Lord responds, showing His mercy, but also using Samson's perceived weakness to the benefit of the Israelites. As the Philistines taunt and jeer Samson, God gives him the strength he needs to tear down their temple.

"Let me die with the Philistines!"

Ruth and Naomi

There was a famine in Judah, and Elimelech took his family from their home in Bethlehem to live in the land of Moab, beyond the Salt Sea.

He grew old and died there, leaving his wife Naomi with two sons. Both sons married Moabite women—one was named Orpah and the other was named Ruth. Then, sadly, both her sons died and Naomi lived with her daughters-in-law.

In time, Naomi heard that the famine had passed in Judah and she decided to go back, with both of her daughters-in-law. All three of them set off, but Naomi suddenly had second thoughts. How could she take the young women away from their own people? "Go back, both of you! May the Lord show kindness to you, as you have shown kindness to your dead and to me," she said.

They both protested and wept, but Naomi would have none of it. She had made up her mind. Orpah turned around, kissing her mother-in-law goodbye, but Ruth still clung to Naomi and insisted on going with her. "Where you go, I will go and where you stay, I will stay. Your people will be my people and your God, my God," she said. So the two women traveled on together and they arrived in Bethlehem just as the harvest was beginning. Naomi's relatives welcomed her home with open arms.

Ruth joined the workers in the fields and picked up any grain that was scattered behind the harvesters. She gathered as much of the leftover grain as she could, working hard from morning till night. And Boaz, who was a relative of Elimelech, came back from town and saw the young girl working in his field. He asked his foreman who she was, then went over to talk to her. "You are welcome to collect any grain you can find," he said. "I will tell my men to look after you. Help yourself to water from the jars whenever you feel like it. It's hot work!"

Ruth bowed down low on the ground. "How kind you are. Why have I found such favor in your eyes?" she asked. "I am a foreigner." Boaz replied that he had heard about her kindness to her mother-in-law, Naomi. He invited her to sit down and eat with the harvesters.

That evening, Ruth took the grain she had gathered back to Naomi, together with some food that had been left over from the meal. She told her mother-in-law how kind Boaz had been to her. "The Lord bless him!" said Naomi. "He is one of the very best!" And each day, Ruth went back to the same fields and worked there until the harvest was finished.

Naomi knew that Boaz admired Ruth and she decided that he would make a good husband for her. "Wash and perfume yourself and put on your best clothes," Naomi told Ruth. "Go and lie at his feet tonight after he has finished

Harvest law
When gathering the harvest, farmers in Israel were not meant to reap the outer edges of their fields, nor take the harvest "gleanings" (leftover grain). Instead, they were expected to leave both for the poor to collect.

An ancestor of David
Ruth has an important place in the Bible. Her righteousness led to her marriage to Boaz, and, as a result, she became the great-grandmother to Israel's King David, from whom Joseph, Mary's husband, is descended.

Émile Lévy's "Ruth and Naomi" (1859) shows Obed being welcomed warmly by Naomi.

threshing and wait until he is asleep."

Ruth did as she had been told and lay down beside Boaz. In the middle of the night, Boaz woke up and was startled to find a woman lying at his feet. "Who are you?" he asked.

"I am Ruth. I have come to ask for your protection."

Boaz was delighted, and said, "The Lord bless you! Everyone knows you are a woman of noble character. You have not run after younger men, whether rich or poor. And now, don't be afraid. I will take care of you." Before long they were married and Ruth gave birth to a son, who was named Obed.

Everybody was pleased for Naomi, who had no grandchildren of her own. "Praise be to the Lord!" they said. "May this baby become famous throughout Israel. He will sustain you in old age. Your daughter-in-law loves you and is better to you than seven sons!"

"Go back, both of you! May the Lord show kindness to you, as you have shown kindness to your dead and to me."

Understanding the story

Ruth is a foreigner in Bethlehem, but her faith in the God of Israel, together with her kind heart and hard work, are rewarded. Her marriage and the birth of a son bring hope and happiness. As Naomi and Ruth go from despair to fulfillment, the village goes from famine to feast. The bountiful harvest sees Bethlehem living up to its name, "House of Bread."

Shiloh
Before Jerusalem became the religious capital of Israel, Shiloh was the main center for worship. The tabernacle was the scene of religious festivals and sacrifices. It was also where Eli trained Samuel. Archaeological ruins are all that remain there today.

Priest's breastplate
As High Priest of Shiloh, Eli wore a bejeweled breastplate. This woven square was encrusted with 12 gemstones—ruby, topaz, beryl, turquoise, sapphire, emerald, jacinth, agate, amethyst, chrysolite, onyx, and jasper. Each was inscribed with the name of a tribe of Israel.

Samuel is Called to Serve God

Elkanah had two wives, Peninnah and Hannah. Each year they all went to Shiloh to make a sacrifice and to worship in the tabernacle, with its great pillars.

Hannah was beautiful, the apple of her husband's eye, although she had not given him any children. She sat by his side at the feast and he gave her all the choicest meat. Peninnah watched, green with envy. She had given her husband children, so why was she not his favorite? She went to Hannah, taunting her cruelly, "You'll never have a baby, will you? What kind of wife are you?"

Hannah was reduced to tears. She fled to the tabernacle where Eli, the high priest, was sitting on a chair. He watched her. "O Lord! Remember me!" she prayed. "Please give me a son! I will give him to the Lord for all the days of his life, and his life will be dedicated to you." She was in such a state that Eli got up from his chair and went to her. He asked her if she was drunk? "Not so, my lord," Hannah replied. "I am a woman who is deeply troubled. I was pouring out my soul to the Lord."

Hannah prays to the Lord for a son

Eli smiled at her and said, "Go in peace. May the God of Israel grant you what you have asked Him." Before long, Hannah discovered that her prayer had been answered and she was going to have a baby. In time, she gave birth to a son and she named him Samuel, which means "Asked of the Lord."

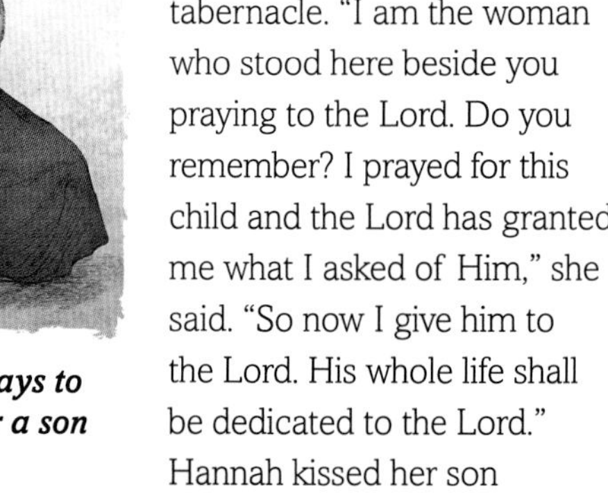

The time came for Hannah to take Samuel to Shiloh. When they got there, she approached Eli in the tabernacle. "I am the woman who stood here beside you praying to the Lord. Do you remember? I prayed for this child and the Lord has granted me what I asked of Him," she said. "So now I give him to the Lord. His whole life shall be dedicated to the Lord."

Hannah kissed her son goodbye and handed him to Eli. From that day on, Samuel helped the high priest with his duties. Samuel wore a special linen tunic, with an embroidered belt, just like the other priests.

Each year, when Hannah came back with her husband to Shiloh, she brought a coat she had made for Samuel to wear. And Eli blessed her, saying, "May the Lord give you children to take the place of the one you prayed for and gave to the Lord." And the Lord blessed Hannah with more children.

Samuel respected the Lord and worked hard, helping Eli as he grew older. But Eli's own sons, who were priests, were dishonest and stole offerings that were meant for the altar. Their father begged them to mend their ways, but they took no notice.

One day, Eli had a visitor with a message from God, "I chose your ancestors out of all the tribes of Israel to be my priests. Why do you honor your sons more than me? Why do you allow them to grow fat on offerings that belong to me? They have brought shame and disgrace on the name of the Lord." Eli listened, but did nothing.

In the middle of the night, Samuel heard his name being called. He ran to Eli who said, "I didn't call you! Go back to sleep!"

Samuel jumped back into bed and was just drifting off to sleep when he heard the voice again. "Samuel! Samuel!" it called.

He ran back to Eli, who said, "You must be dreaming. Go back to bed, my child!" Obediently, Samuel did as he was told and had just fallen into a deep sleep when he heard the mysterious voice again, calling "Samuel! Samuel!" Frightened, he ran to Eli again. The old man sat up and knew that it must be the Lord. He told Samuel to listen to the voice if he heard it again.

Samuel obeyed and, when he heard his name being called again, he said, "Speak, Lord, for your servant is listening."

"You must tell Eli that he and his bloodline are doomed! His sons are sinful, and he failed to stop them."

The next morning, Samuel told Eli what God had said. Eli replied sadly, "He is the Lord. He knows best!" And, as Samuel grew to manhood, the Lord was with him, and all the tribes of Israel knew that he was the prophet of the Lord.

"His whole life shall be dedicated to the Lord."

Understanding the story

Like Sarah, Rebecca, and Samson's mother, Hannah's infertility is resolved by God. All four women hope for a child and eventually their wishes come true. Each of their children has been chosen by God for a special purpose on Earth. Hannah's son Samuel is the first great prophet after Moses. Like all prophets, Samuel's role is to proclaim God's word and guide people towards righteousness.

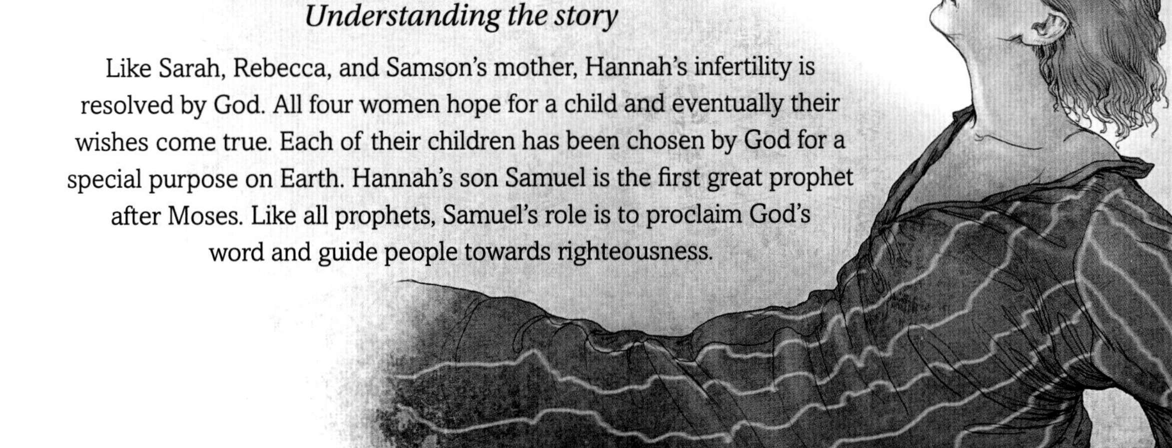

"They have sent us the Ark of the God of Israel to kill us!"

The Ark is Captured

The Philistines and the Israelites fought a battle on the Plain of Sharon. At least four thousand Israelites died, and the survivors asked, "Why did the Lord bring defeat upon us today at the hands of the Philistines?"

Iron weaponry
The Philistine armies were very organized and fierce. Their ironworking skills also gave them a great advantage in war. Harder than bronze and easy to find, iron was suited to weaponry. The use of iron daggers (above) and swords dealt a tough blow to the Israelites on the battlefield. Over time, the Israelites also worked out how to use iron.

That night, the elders talked together, knowing that the Lord had deserted them. They decided, as a last resort, to bring the Ark of the Covenant from the tabernacle in Shiloh. They believed it would save them from their enemies.

They sent a messenger to Shiloh and, before long, the golden Ark arrived in their camp. It was brought by the high priest's two sons, Hophni and Phinehas, and was a magnificent sight. The soldiers stared in amazement and a great cheer filled the air. The ground shook. The Philistines heard the cheer from the other side of the plain and they wondered what was going on. When they found out that the Israelites had the famous Ark of the Covenant by their side, they were filled with terror. "A god has come into their camp!" they said. "We must attack!"

They advanced on the Israelites again and a battle was fought at Ebenezer. The slaughter was terrible and the Ark did not help the Israelites. Thirty thousand of them died on the battlefield, including Hophni and Phinehas. The Ark was captured by the Philistines.

Eli, the high priest, who was ninety-eight years old, was saddened by the news of his sons. But when he was told that the Ark had been captured, he fell off his chair and broke his neck. And so, the Israelites lost the high priest, as well as the Ark.

The Philistines took the Ark to the town of Ashdod and put it in the temple beside their great god, Dagon. In the morning, when they went there to pray, they saw with horror that the statue of Dagon had fallen to the ground in front of the Ark. Dagon's head and hands lay smashed on the threshold of the temple. The Lord then sent a plague of boils and a plague of rats to torment the people of Ashdod. These brought terrible disease and death.

The Philistines knew that it was all the fault of the Ark. "What shall we do with it?" they asked each other. They persuaded the neighboring town of Gath to give the Ark a home. As soon as it arrived there, plague and pestilence hit the town, and the people could not wait to get rid of the Ark. They sent it on to Ekron but, as it was carried through the town, the people shouted, "They have sent us the Ark of the God of Israel to kill us!"

The Philistine lords called an emergency meeting. The Ark had been with them for seven months now and had brought nothing but death and destruction. "How can we send the terrible thing back?" they asked each other.

The lords conferred, then told the people, "Do not send it back empty. Send a guilt offering to the God of Israel. That will do the trick." They told the people to make five gold boils and five gold rats, and put them in a chest beside the Ark, on a cart pulled by two cows. If the cart went, of its own accord, toward Beth Shemesh, where the tribe of Dan lived, then the Lord of Israel had brought the plagues. If it went the other way, the plagues had happened by chance.

Before long, a cart carrying the Ark and a chest of gold boils and gold rats set off. The cows headed straight for Beth Shemesh. The Israelites could not believe their eyes when they saw the cart. It stopped right by them and they placed the Ark on a rock, with the chest containing the gold boils and gold rats by its side. They sacrificed the two cows as offerings to the Lord.

From there, the Ark of the Covenant was taken to Kiriath Jearim in Judah, which was to become its home for the next twenty years. A shrine was made for it and a man called Eleazar, from the tribe of Levi, was consecrated to guard it.

Understanding the story

The Ark of the Covenant symbolizes God's eternal presence and power. The Israelites assume the Ark will deliver victory against the Philistines, but instead they suffer bloody defeat. The Philistines treat the Ark as a captured idol, but the belief that their gods are more powerful than the God of Israel is short-lived. God shows both nations that He cannot be manipulated and the fate of their countries is in His hands.

Model of the Ark
Featuring a pair of cherubim extending their wings in protection, this model's design is based on the description of Israel's holiest object in the Bible. The Ark contained God's Ten Commandments.

Ephraim countryside
Ephraim (meaning "fruitful") was a mountainous but fertile area. Saul was looking for the lost donkeys in the nearby hills. This region was familiar to Saul because it was where he was born and raised. Ephraim was also the name of Joseph's second son, whose descendants became one of Israel's largest tribes.

Pharaoh Psusennes
When the Israelites were demanding their own king, Pharaoh Psunennes I (c 1039–993 BCE) was on the Egyptian throne. He brought stability to Egypt, restoring peace after a civil war and carrying out temple reconstruction. His power was absolute.

Saul, King of the Israelites

Times were hard for the tribes of Israel and they quarreled with each other all the time. There was discontent—and powerful enemies on every side.

The elders gathered and came to their prophet Samuel at his home in Ramah. "You are getting old and we do not think that your sons can carry on in your footsteps," they said. "We need a king, not a prophet, to lead us."

Samuel did not like the idea of a king at all and he prayed to the Lord. "Listen to them," replied the Lord. "It is not you they have rejected but me. Just as they have rejected me from the moment that I brought them out of Egypt. They have forsaken me and worshipped other gods. But warn them what kings are like."

Samuel repeated God's words to the elders, but they took no notice. "We want to be like other nations, with a king to lead us and fight our battles."

The Lord told Samuel to do as the people asked. He said that He had chosen a young man named Saul, from the tribe of Benjamin, to be the first king of Israel. "I have decided to give my people a king. Anoint Saul as leader of all my people. He will deliver them from the hands of the Philistines."

The next day was much like any other for Saul. He had no idea what was in store. Some of his father's donkeys had gone missing and he was searching for them in the hills. When he came to the town of Zuph and heard that a seer had just arrived to bless the sacrifice, his ears pricked up. He thought that the seer might be able to use his special powers to help him find the donkeys. As Saul went into the town, he saw an old man walking slowly up the hill. He asked him where he could find the seer. The man replied, "I am the seer." And, as if he could read Saul's mind, he went on, "Do not worry about your donkeys—they have been found. Come with me to the holy place where I am going to bless the sacrifice. You have been chosen to be the first king of Israel."

Saul listened in amazement. "But I am a Benjamite from the smallest tribe of Israel. And my clan is the smallest clan of the tribe of Benjamin. Why me?" Samuel smiled but did not answer the question. He just led him up to the holy place at the top of the hill.

After the sacrifice had been made, there was a splendid feast. Saul sat in the place of honor at the head of the table and was given a special piece of meat by Samuel that had been set aside for the prophet himself.

The next day, Samuel took a large

horn that was filled with oil, perfumed with spices and myrrh. He poured it slowly over Saul's head, saying, "The Lord has anointed you king of Israel, leader of all His people." And then he went on, "Now you must go home. You will meet two men who will tell you that your donkeys are found, but that your father is worrying about you. Then, by the great tree at Tabor, you will see three men with three goats, three loaves of bread, and a skin of wine. They will give you two of the loaves. Then you will go on and meet some prophets, chanting to the sound of lyres, tambourines, flutes, and harps. Join them and you too will prophesy. The Spirit of God will come upon you."

Samuel said goodbye to Saul and blessed him, telling him that he would meet him in seven days' time. Saul went on his way and, sure enough, all the things that Samuel had predicted came true.

Samuel summoned all the people to Mizpah to make the great announcement that a king had been chosen. But as they assembled in their thousands, Saul was nowhere to be seen. Eventually, he was found hiding behind some bags, pale with fear and apprehension. Reluctantly, he came out and stood by Samuel, head and shoulders above the rest of the crowd. "This is your king!" the prophet declared. "He has been chosen by the Lord."

Everybody cheered and shouted, "Long live the King!" But some people looked doubtful and shook their heads. Then Samuel explained the rules of kingship and wrote them down on a scroll that he dedicated to the Lord.

People had come from all over the country to see their new king, to swear allegiance, and to bring him gifts. But some of the Israelites were not happy with their new king. "How can he save us? We've never even heard of him," they hissed. "And he's a Benjamite, of all things. He was so frightened he went and hid when he was proclaimed king!"

Samuel anoints Saul as leader of all God's people with special oil from a horn

Understanding the story

When Samuel anoints Saul with oil, the process represents his consecration to God. He is now blessed to be the king. The Israelites have a leader to unify their tribes and save them from their enemies. But the people and the land still ultimately belong to God. Israel's king differs from those of other countries because Saul is ruling only as God's representative on Earth.

Saul's Downfall

"The Lord has chosen someone else now and will make him leader of His people."

Soon after Saul had been proclaimed king, the Ammonites besieged the great walled town of Jabesh, a few miles east of the Jordan River in Gilead.

It was a rich and fertile part of the world, and Nahash, the Ammonite king, wanted to drive the Israelites from their stronghold. He surrounded the walls with his troops. For weeks, nothing could get in or out of the town, and the food began to run out. The people were starving and their thoughts turned to surrender. Eventually, they sent messengers down to Nahash saying that they would make a treaty. But Nahash replied, "I will only make a treaty with you on the condition that I gouge out the right eye of every single man in the town!"

When the elders of Jabesh received this ghastly message they asked for seven days grace. Then, at dead of night, they sent messengers out of the city to tell their kinsmen of their plight. When the news reached Gibeah, where Saul lived, he was just coming back from the fields with his oxen.

Saul listened in horror and, burning with rage, snatched the messenger's gleaming sword and plunged it deep into the oxen. He sent the scraps of meat, like bleeding messages, all over the country, calling the Israelites to arms. In response, the tribes of Israel flocked to Saul's side. But it took more than five days for them all to arrive and only one day was

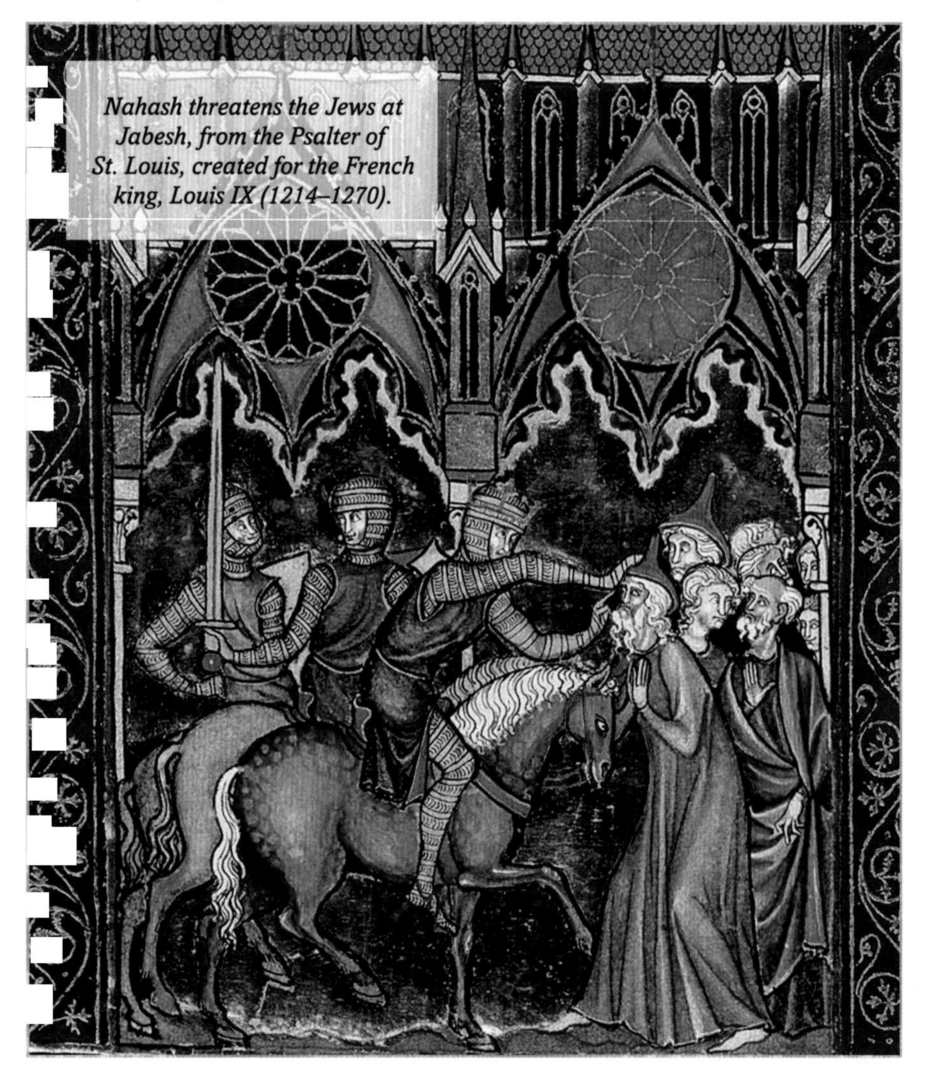

Nahash threatens the Jews at Jabesh, from the Psalter of St. Louis, created for the French king, Louis IX (1214–1270).

left before every man in Jabesh would lose an eye.

Saul sent word to the besieged city that help was on its way. When they received the message the people of Jabesh told the Ammonites that they would surrender the next day. Meanwhile, Saul divided his men into three companies and headed toward Jabesh. Then, at dead of night, they surrounded the Ammonite camp. At daybreak, the Israelites sounded their trumpets and swept in. The Ammonites, sleepy and unprepared, were swiftly defeated.

But, despite this triumph over the Ammonites, Saul was king of the Israelites in name only. For years the tribes of Israel had been under the thumb of the rich and powerful Philistines. Saul longed to free his people, but his army was small and his weapons were few compared to the might of the enemy. His son, Jonathan, was one of his most important lieutenants. He was stationed at Gibeah, near a small Philistine outpost that caused him nothing but trouble.

One day, infuriated by the insults of the officer in charge of the enemy outpost, Jonathan attacked it, killing all of the Philistine soldiers there. News of the bloodshed soon spread and, before long, the entire Philistine army was being mobilized against the Israelites.

Saul waited at Gilgal with his men quaking at his side. But he could not give the order to join battle before a sacred offering had been made to the Lord. The prophet Samuel had said that he would be there within a week to make the blessing. As the days went by and the tension rose, some of Saul's men fled in fear. Finally, on the seventh day, unable to wait any longer, Saul made the offering himself. And, just as he finished, Samuel arrived and said, "What have you done?"

"You had not arrived when you said you would, and my men are deserting me," Saul replied.

Samuel looked him straight in the eye and said, "You have not obeyed the Lord. If you had, your kingdom would have lasted forever. The Lord has chosen someone else now and will make him leader of His people." With that, the prophet turned around and left. Saul watched him go, aghast, as the full meaning of his words sank in.

Understanding the story

Saul acts in haste because his army is disappearing as the Philistines grow stronger. Though Saul was king, he was really working under Samuel's leadership because God spoke via His prophets. Impatience makes Saul ignore Samuel's command, which proves his lack of faith in God. In addition, the Law of Moses states that only a priest can make offerings, so again Saul's behavior is disobedient. As a result, God chooses a new leader.

Gibeah
During Saul's reign, Gibeah (the word is similar to the Hebrew word for "hill") was his hometown and the capital city of Israel. Gibeah is now identified as Tell el-Ful. This hill is located on the Central Benjamin Plateau, which lies 3 miles (4.8 km) north of Jerusalem.

Animal sacrifice altar
In ancient times, animal sacrifice was a common ritual throughout the Middle East. The Canaanites crafted rectangular or oval altars from uncut field stones. This is an example of an oval altar. Most altars were constructed on "high places," such as hilltops.

God Chooses David

Saul reigned over the Israelites for more than forty years, but, because he did not always obey God's commands, God decided to choose a new king for His people.

"I will tell you which one to anoint."

The prophet Samuel remembered the day, long ago, when he had anointed the young Saul as king. He had not seen him for many years now and was saddened. God said to him, "How long will you mourn for Saul? You know I have rejected him as king of Israel. Fill your horn with oil and be on your way. I am sending you to find a farmer named Jesse in Bethlehem. I have chosen one of his sons to be king." He told Samuel to take a heifer with him and to invite Jesse and his sons to the sacrifice. "I will show you what to do," He said. "I will tell you which one to anoint."

So Samuel traveled to Bethlehem in Judah. When he arrived, the elders greeted him in awe. They did not know why the great prophet had come to their village. "Do you come in peace?" they asked, bowing down before him.

"Yes, I have indeed come in peace," Samuel replied. "I have come to make a sacrifice to the Lord."

They took him to find Jesse, who was a descendant of Boaz and Ruth. Samuel asked Jesse to call his sons together. The humble farmer was amazed, not knowing why he and his sons had been singled out. Samuel invited them all to the sacrifice, but first he consecrated them to God. One by one, the young men stepped forward. The first, who was named Eliab, was tall and handsome and Samuel thought that he must be the one whom God had chosen. But God said, "Do not consider his appearance or his height. This is not the one. Man looks at the outward appearance, but the Lord looks at the heart."

Jesse called his next son, who was named Abinadab, to step forward. He was also a fine young man, but Samuel said, "The Lord has not chosen this one either." Then it was the turn of the third son, named Shammah. But he was not the one, and Samuel shook his head. All seven of Jesse's sons came to Samuel in turn, but none of them were chosen. The great prophet was puzzled and said to Jesse, "Are these really all the sons you have?"

"There is another one," replied Jesse. "He is the youngest—still a child really. He is named David and he is out in the fields looking after the sheep."

Samuel asked him to send for his last and youngest son immediately. He waited calmly, holding the horn of holy oil in his hand. In a little while the door burst open and a young boy ran in. He was a fine looking child with ruddy cheeks and blue eyes. Samuel looked at him and heard the voice within him saying, "This is the one I have chosen. Anoint him."

So Samuel poured the perfumed oil over David's young head and anointed him in

Star of David
The Star of David (or Shield of David) is the symbol of Israel. In 1948 it was officially adopted for the modern state flag. Though its origins do not relate directly to David, his historic importance resulted in the star being named after him. The star has been seen on tombs of the 3rd century CE, but its first mention was not until the 12th century in a Jewish text.

"Samuel Anoints David," 2nd-century-CE tempera on plaster from the National Museum of Damascus, Syria

front of his father and his seven brothers. They watched in silence, hardly able to believe their eyes. And from that day on, the Spirit of the Lord was with David wherever he went and whatever he did.

Understanding the story

God decides David will be Saul's replacement as King of Israel. Though a young shepherd may seem too inexperienced to be the country's ruler, God knows David has the necessary qualities. David cares for his sheep by feeding them, guiding them, and protecting them from danger. This is exactly what God wants for His people.

David and Goliath

The Philistines and the Israelites drew up their battle lines above the Valley of Elah in Judah and faced each other from the peaks of their separate hills.

Out of the Philistine camp emerged a terrifying figure. He was at least nine feet (three meters) tall, with legs like tree trunks and fists like hams. He was called Goliath and he came from Gath. He wore a massive bronze helmet and a heavy suit of armor. A huge javelin was slung on his back, while he clasped an iron-clad spear. He bellowed across the valley, "I defy the ranks of Israel this day! Choose one man to come and fight with me, King Saul. I dare you! If he is able to kill me, the Philistines will become your servants. But if I kill him, then you will become our slaves."King Saul and the Israelites listened in horror. Who could take on the Philistine giant? For forty days, Goliath appeared each morning and each evening and repeated his challenge.

One morning, David arrived in the Israelites' camp, bringing food for his brothers, who were soldiers with King Saul. He saw Goliath for the first time and heard his words. "Who is this monster who dares to threaten the army of the Lord?" he asked. The Israelite soldiers told him about Goliath. David went to the King and said that he would take up the giant's challenge.

"You can't fight this Philistine brute," smiled King Saul.

"But I am the keeper of my father's sheep and I am used to protecting them," David protested.

Saul reluctantly agreed. "Go and the Lord be with you," he said. He gave David his own tunic, a coat of armor, a bronze helmet, and a sword. David tried on his unfamiliar finery, but then shook his head and took it all off. He ran down to the valley and chose five smooth stones from the stream. He put them in his leather pouch and moved toward the giant. Goliath could not believe his eyes. "What's this? I ask for a man and they send a shrimp!"

David replied, "You come against me with sword, spear, and javelin, but I come against you in the name of the Lord Almighty, the God of the armies of Israel, whom you have defied. I am not scared of you." And with that he fished the largest stone out of his pouch and put it in his sling. He whirled it around and let the stone fly. It sped through the air and reached its target, sinking into Goliath's forehead. The giant screamed and crashed to the ground. David ran to him, took his sword, and cut off his head. Triumphantly, he lifted it high in the air. The Philistines fled in terror. The Israelites pursued them, hacking them down as they went. Then they returned to plunder the Philistines' camp.

Valley of Elah
This scenic spot in Judea was also a battlefield. The Philistines and Israelites assembled their armies on facing hills either side of the narrow Valley of Elah and prepared to do battle. The valley takes its name from the type of trees that grow in nearby woodland.

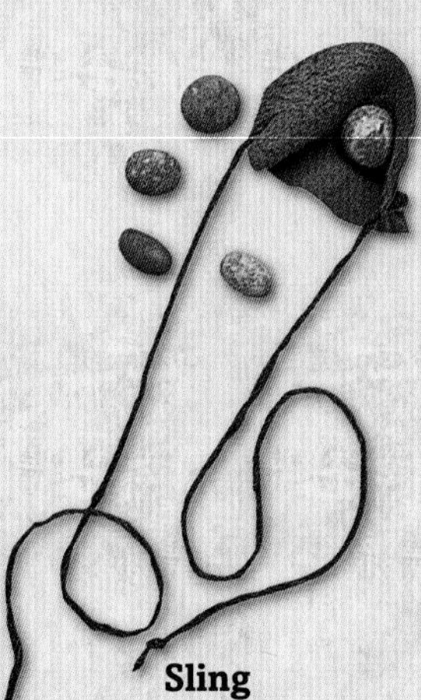

Sling
Though the sling was a deadly weapon of war, the shepherd David would have used it only to fire stones at wild animals endangering his flock. A stone was placed in the sling before the two ends were whirled above the head at great speed. When one end was released, the stone flew toward its target with devastating impact.

Understanding the story

Ancient battles were sometimes decided by one-on-one combat. Each side would choose a champion to represent them. The outcome was seen as being the will of the gods. Saul is scared of the champion Goliath, but the new leader David is fearless because he has complete trust in God. With only a sling for a weapon, David defeats the giant, proving that God protects those who keep faith in Him.

Saul Turns Against David

After David had killed the Philistine giant, Goliath, he was invited to live with King Saul in Gibeah. It was very different from the life he had been used to as a humble shepherd boy in the fields around Bethlehem.

From the very first day, he and Saul's son, Jonathan, were inseparable. Jonathan loved David and shared everything with him—giving him his finest clothes as well as his sword and bow. And Saul, seeing how close the two young men were, made David an officer in the army, just like Jonathan. He gave him command of more than one thousand men, and David led them on the battlefield with great success.

And, in time, Saul's daughter, Michal, fell in love with David and they were married.

David's fame spread throughout Israel and Judah. His triumph over Goliath was the stuff of legends and would never be forgotten. Women sang and danced to the music of their tambourines and lutes and cymbals. "Saul has slain his thousands!" they chanted. "And David has slain his tens of thousands!"

Although Saul had grown fond of David and knew how highly regarded he was, his heart sank and his stomach tied itself in knots when he heard these words. "They say that David has killed tens of thousands, but that I, their king, have only slain thousands!" he said to himself. "That young man will be after my kingdom next!"

And, in his heart, Saul despaired because he knew that the Lord, who had chosen him so long ago, had now deserted him. He did not understand why. All his years as king and all the battles he had fought seemed to stand for nothing. He was afraid of David and knew that the Lord was with him. He kept a jealous and wary eye on his young son-in-law.

One day, David was playing his harp, filling the air with sweet and soothing music. Saul listened, his eyes heavy, almost dropping off to sleep. But suddenly, as if possessed, he leapt to his feet. The hatred that had quietly gnawed away at him for so long erupted like a volcano. He seized a spear and hurled it at David's head. It missed by a hair's breadth and sank deep into the wall. David looked at Saul, stunned and unable to move. Incensed, Saul grabbed another spear and tried again, but this time David was prepared and dodged nimbly aside, then ran away as fast as he could.

He reached his house and told his wife, Michal, what had happened. She seized her husband tightly and cried, "You must escape while you can! You must not stay here another moment! They will find you here and you will not stand a chance!" And, when night had fallen, she lowered David out of the window on a rope, and he fled into the darkness. Then, she found a life-sized statue and put it in David's bed. She arranged goats' hair on its head and drew the covers up over it so that it looked just like a man fast asleep.

Saul's men arrived at the crack of dawn the next morning. They hammered on the door, asking for David. Michal let them in and whispered, "He is ill in bed. Please do not disturb him!" They pushed her aside and crept up the stairs, opened the bedroom door and tiptoed silently toward the bed. They pounced, swords at the ready, and pulled the covers off, only to discover that they had been tricked by a statue and a handful of goats' hair.

By then, David was far away from Gibeah. He had gone straight to the prophet Samuel at his home in Ramah and told him the whole story.

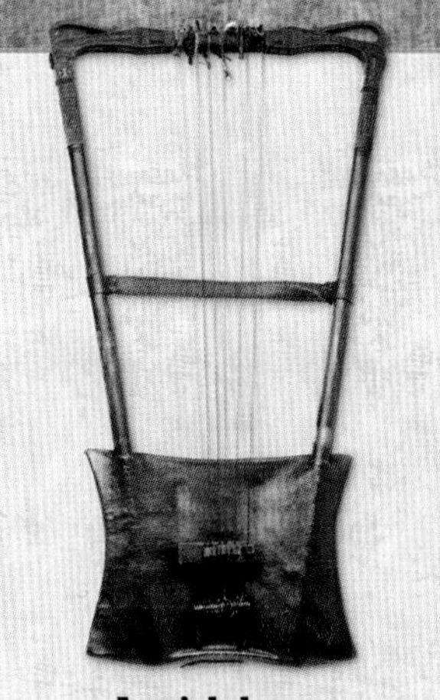

Jewish harp
David's harp playing helped to soothe the Saul. Ancient versions of the harp were made of animal skin stretched over a soundbox with strings attached to the frame.

"In his heart, Saul despaired because he knew that the Lord, who had chosen him so long ago, had now deserted him."

Understanding the story

Saul cannot cope with God's rejection. He becomes tormented by jealousy and believes David is going to take his throne. In a fit of rage, he attacks David, who escapes to safety because God is on his side. Saul tries repeatedly to kill David, but finds it is not possible to defy God's will.

David the Outlaw

Rosh Chodesh
The Jewish calendar was a lunar calendar, so the new moon festival, called Rosh Chodesh, was a time to celebrate the start of the month. Work came to a halt, offerings were made, and trumpets were blown during the festival.

David had fled from King Saul and taken refuge with the prophet Samuel at Ramah. He knew that Saul was determined to kill him and that his life hung by a thread.

One night, he left Samuel and went secretly back to Gibeah to talk to Jonathan, his great friend and the king's son. "What have I done?" he asked. "What is my crime? How have I wronged your father and why does he want to kill me?"

"You are not going to die!" said his friend. "I would know. My father tells me everything."

"Your father knows how close we are. Would he tell you if he was going to kill me?" retorted David.

Jonathan promised to do his best to find out what his father was thinking. He would find David and let him know, with a signal, whether King Saul still wanted to kill him. The two friends said goodbye, and David fled to the fields.

It was the new moon festival the next day and everybody came to the feast with King Saul. But, when they sat down to eat, there was one empty place at the table. Saul looked at Jonathan but said nothing. The following day, when David had still not appeared, Saul asked Jonathan, "Where is David? Why has he not come to eat with us either yesterday or today?"

Jonathan excused his friend, saying that David had gone home to Bethlehem to make a sacrifice with his family. Saul stood up and banged the table in fury. "You are on his side, aren't you? I am ashamed of you!" he shouted. "You must go and find him. Bring him to me! He must die!"

Jonathan felt his blood boil. "Why should he die?" he protested. "What

To warn David that his life is in danger, Jonathan fires an arrow into the air

has he done?" And he got up and stormed away from the table.

The next morning, as they had arranged, Jonathan went to the remote field where David was hiding. He fired an arrow high in the air. It landed far away in the distance—way beyond the place where David had concealed himself. This was the signal. It meant that David's life was still in danger and that he must flee far away.

David came out from his hiding place and, sadly, the two young men embraced and wept. "Go in peace, for we have a sworn friendship with each other in the name of the Lord," said Jonathan. They both knew that they would never see each other again.

Jonathan turned and went back to Gibeah. David set off in the other direction, heading for the hills far away by the Salt Sea. It was a long and difficult journey by foot through the desert. But, just after he passed the oasis of En Gedi, he saw the perfect place to hide—a cave, tucked neatly into the crags where the wild goats lived. Its entrance was concealed by big boulders and it stretched back into the darkness. As time went by, men came to join David and soon he had a band of four hundred followers.

When Saul heard that David was hiding in the desert of En Gedi with a band of loyal men, he set off to hunt him down. He took three thousand soldiers with him. He was determined not to let David get away again. As they neared the Salt Sea, Saul went inside a cave to shelter from the sun. It was the Cave of Adullam, where David and his men were hiding. They watched Saul from the depths of the cave, where the darkness concealed them completely. David knew that his enemy had been delivered into his hands. He could creep up and kill him just like that.

Instead, he tiptoed up to Saul and cut a corner of his robe. But he immediately felt stricken with guilt and said to his men, "The Lord forbade that I should do such a thing to my master, the Lord's anointed, or lift my hand against him."

When Saul left the cave, David followed him and called out, "My Lord the King!" Saul turned in astonishment and David went to him, bowing low. "See, my Lord," he said. "Look at this! It is a corner of your robe. I just cut it off. I could easily have killed you at the same time, but I could not harm someone who has been anointed by the Lord."

Saul looked at the scrap of material. He was overcome by shame. "You are more righteous than I am. I have treated you badly. May the Lord reward you well for the way you treated me today. I know that you will surely be king and that the kingdom of Israel will be yours."

Hideouts
Many natural caves like this one could be found in the En Gedi landscape. These were ideal hideouts for David and his followers. The darkness gave them protection, while the viewpoint made it easy to see an enemy advancing.

"I know that you will surely be king and that the kingdom of Israel will be yours."

Understanding the story

Jonathan accepts that David will be Saul's successor because this is God's will, but Saul has lost his faith and refuses to accept David. Though David has the opportunity to kill Saul, he cannot, because Saul is God's anointed king. When Saul realizes that David has spared his life, he is overcome with guilt at his own behavior. He finally accepts the Lord's wishes and recognizes that David deserves to be king.

Samuel
Samuel became a prophet after receiving messages from the Lord as a boy. Though he warned of the dangers of a ruling monarch, Samuel did as the Lord asked and anointed Saul and David the first two kings of Israel. He did not write the two books of Samuel, but they were named after him as recognition for his part in Israel's history.

Mount Gilboa
Situated in northern Israel overlooking the valley of Jezreel, Mount Gilboa is more like a ridge than a mountain. It was the scene for the bloody battle between the Israelites and the Philistines. The area is steeped in Biblical history but tarnished by tragedy, with Saul and his sons all dying here.

The Death of Saul

The great prophet Samuel died and was buried at home in Ramah. All of Israel mourned, including King Saul.

He had not seen Samuel for many years but, in the past, the prophet had guided him in everything he did. Now, the Philistines were gathering their forces yet again to take on Israel. When he saw the might of the enemy, Saul was overcome with terror. He could not eat and he prayed to the Lord for guidance. But there was no answer.

In desperation, Saul longed to contact Samuel. But he had banished the people who might have been able to help him. The sorcerers and magicians had been expelled. Saul asked his attendants if anyone had secret powers to summon up the spirit of Samuel. "I think there is still an old witch who lives in Endor—not too far away," one replied.

That night, when everyone was asleep, Saul disguised himself in a cloak of sackcloth. He took two of his men and they set off for Endor. When they found the witch's shack, Saul knocked on the door. There was no reply—except for a sudden scream from a screech owl. They knocked again and waited, chilled to the bone. At last, the door creaked open and an old woman beckoned them in. A fire crackled in the hearth and a black pot bubbled in the flames. Shivering with fear, Saul told her why he had come.

She refused to help. "Surely you know what King Saul has done? He tried to get rid of us. He is scared of our powers. This must be a trap. Do you want to get me killed?"

Saul reassured her, "As surely as the Lord lives, you will not be punished for this."

Reluctantly, the witch agreed to help and asked him who he was trying to get in touch with. Saul replied, "The great prophet Samuel, who died not long ago."

She peered at him in the gloom and let out a piercing scream. "You have tricked me!" she shrieked. "You are Saul, aren't you?"

"Do not be afraid," said Saul. "What do you see?"

She croaked, "I see a spirit coming up out of the ground. It is an old man with a white beard and he is wearing a robe." Immediately, Saul knew that it was Samuel.

"I am in such distress!" he cried. "The Philistines are gathering to fight again and God has deserted me. I beg you to tell me what to do."

Samuel answered, "Why do you consult me now that the Lord has turned away from you? He has given your kingdom to David because you were disobedient. He will hand over both Israel and you to the Philistines. Tomorrow you and your sons will die!"

Saul collapses in fear in "Saul and the Witch of Endor" by Anglo-American painter Benjamin West (1738–1820).

When he heard these words, Saul collapsed in a heap on the ground, weak with fear. He had not eaten anything all day and all night. The old witch saw what a terrible state he was in. "Let me give you something to eat so that you can get your strength back." When the meal was ready, Saul and his men tucked in gratefully. And that same night, before the first light of dawn filled the sky, they set off to rejoin their army in the camp.

The next day, the massed ranks of Philistines attacked the Israelites on Mount Gilboa, above the valley at Jezreel. It was a decisive victory for them and, before long, hundreds of Israelites lay dead. Hundreds more had fled for their lives. Saul's sons, Jonathan, Abinadab, and Malki-Shua, were killed, and Saul himself was mortally wounded. He turned to his armor bearer and asked him to finish him off. "Draw your sword and kill me!" he pleaded. "Do not leave it to those Philistine brutes!" But the armor bearer was terrified and would not do it. So Saul took his own sword and fell on it, dying just as Samuel had prophesied.

After the battle, the Philistines cut off Saul's head and stripped him of his armor. Then they took his body, together with the bodies of his sons, and put them on display on the walls of their great fortress at Beth Shan for all to see.

But, when the people of Jabesh in Gilead heard, they went straight there and took the bodies away. Saul had saved them many years before and this was the least they could do. Respectfully, they carried the bodies back home. They buried their bones under a tamarisk tree and fasted for seven days.

Understanding the story

Saul is completely hopeless and alone, and turns to a practice he had outlawed himself when he visits the witch of Endor. Samuel's ghost predicts Saul's tragic ending the next day. All of Saul's bad and selfish decisions have taken him to this point. God is no longer on his side, and Samuel is no longer alive for him to turn to. Wounded and defeated, Saul kills himself on the battlefield, surrounded by bloodshed.

David is King

When David heard that Saul and his son Jonathan had died, he was grief-stricken and composed a beautiful lament.

"Your glory, O Israel, lies slain on your heights.

How the mighty have fallen!
Saul and Jonathan—
In life they were loved and gracious
And in death they were not parted.
They were swifter than eagles,
They were stronger than lions."

After Saul's death, David was anointed king of Judah. Saul's surviving son, Ish-Bosheth, was made king of the tribes of Israel to the north. And so the country was divided—Judah in the south and Israel to the north. They warred constantly, but David and his people grew stronger and stronger. Eventually, Ish-Bosheth was killed and David was made king of all the tribes. He was thirty years old and he had already ruled Judah for more than seven years.

David wanted to establish a new capital, so he took his men and marched from Hebron in Judah to the great walled city of Jerusalem. It was a natural stronghold, sandwiched between Judah and Israel, and surrounded by three valleys. But the Jebusites, the Canaanite tribe who lived there, barred the gates firmly against the intruders.

The Israelites camped out while David devised a strategy. There was a long water shaft that went to the heart of the city—the perfect route. He sent a few of his men and, with the help of their scaling hooks, they climbed the shaft, emerging within the city walls.

The men unlocked the gates and the Israelites poured in and captured the city. David made it the capital of his kingdom and it became known as the City of David. He became more and more powerful because the Lord was always with him. He built a splendid new palace out of cedar wood and stone, with plenty of room for his wives and all their children.

With great rejoicing, the Ark of the Covenant was brought to Jerusalem. It was accompanied by a huge procession of people singing and dancing. Joyfully, they played their harps, lyres, tambourines, and cymbals as the Ark was carried through the great walls into the city. David took off his royal finery to join in the celebrations. But one of his wives, Michal, who was the daughter of Saul, watched from the window and did not like what she saw. "How the King has distinguished himself today!" she shouted at him sarcastically. "Taking off his royal robes in front of those slave girls. How vulgar. Whatever next?"

David looked up at her and said, "I am celebrating before the Lord, who chose me as king of Israel rather than your father or anyone from his house. I will be even more

Music in worship
Ancient worship included songs praising the Lord, accompanied by music. Temple musicians played a variety of instruments, such as cymbals, pipes, drums, and harps. This Assyrian carving shows two harpists playing.

Dancing
In Biblical times, the Israelites often danced to show their love of God. The Hebrew word used for dancing in the Old Testament invoked the idea of tuning and whirling. Dance is still a part of celebrations today. The Hora (above) is traditionally danced at Jewish weddings.

undignified if I want to." And with that he turned away and carried on dancing and praising the Lord.

The Ark was put into the innermost part of the tabernacle, its new home in the middle of the city. And David gave thanks, sacrificing a bull and a fattened calf. He made the offerings to the Lord in front of everyone. Then he blessed the people in the Lord's name and gave each of them a loaf of bread and a little cake made of raisins and dates.

"I am celebrating before the Lord, who chose me as king of Israel"

Understanding the story

Under David, the tribes of Israel are united, and a new kingdom is established. When David brings the Ark containing God's commandments into Jerusalem, he acknowledges that God is the true ruler of Israel. This act makes Jerusalem the religious capital of Israel. Unlike Saul, David obeys and worships God. He dances at the celebration, marking his commitment to God and the union of his people in the Promised Land.

This section from "Tapestry of David and Bathsheba" (c. 1510–1515) shows David dancing barefoot before the Ark.

The City of David

Today, the gold-topped Muslim shrine, the Dome of the Rock (far right), shines brightly next to the excavated City of David. King David captured Jerusalem from the Jebusites. It made a perfect royal capital, as it was protected by valleys on three sides and had a good water supply.

David then took up residence in the fortress and called it the City of David. He built up the area around it... And he became more and more powerful, because the Lord God Almighty was with him.

2 Samuel 5:9–10

Bathing
David watches Bathsheba as she bathes. In ancient times, bathing was considered good for body and mind. The Bible encourages bathing as a ritual of cleansing and purification. After washing and drying, it was customary for women to rub scented oil into their skin. This clay figure of a woman bathing dates back to about 1000 BCE.

David and Bathsheba

It was spring and the Israelite troops had won a decisive victory over the Ammonites. They were now besieging the walled town of Ramah under their commander-in-chief, Joab.

David had stayed behind in Jerusalem, not far away. One evening, he was walking on the roof of his palace, deep in thought. Suddenly, he noticed a beautiful woman not far away. She was washing herself and combing her long, dark hair. David gazed at her, entranced. He asked his attendant to find out who she was. "Isn't she Bathsheba, the daughter of Eliam and the wife of Uriah, the Hittite?" he replied.

Although she was the wife of one of his most loyal soldiers, David sent for her and courted her with sweet words. And soon, she told him that she was carrying his child. At once, David sent a messenger to summon Uriah back from the battlefield. He came to the palace and told David what was going on in Ramah. David listened, thanked him, and sent him home for the night. But, the next morning, when he got up, he discovered that Uriah had slept on the floor at the entrance to the palace with the servants.

When David asked him why, Uriah replied, "My master, Joab, and all his men are in their camp, ready to risk their lives for their country. How could I go home to eat and drink and lie with my wife? I would never do such a thing."

David persuaded Uriah to stay for another day. They drank wine together and talked late into the night. Once again, Uriah slept on the palace floor. But David could not sleep. He got up as soon as the first hint of daylight crept through his window and went up to the roof of the palace. It was his favorite place to think things out. Pacing up and down, he remembered the first time he had seen Bathsheba. And then, he made up his mind. He went down and wrote a letter to Joab, asking him to put Uriah in the front line of battle, where the fighting would be fiercest. David sealed the letter and put it into Uriah's hands, telling him to take it to Joab. Uriah was to deliver his own death warrant.

When Joab received the message, he carried out David's orders. And, when the Israelite troops attacked the city, Uriah died alone in the first moments of battle. Bathsheba heard that her husband had died and she grieved deeply for him. But, after the time of mourning was over, she agreed to marry David and, before long, gave him a baby son. But the Lord had seen all this and was not pleased. He sent the prophet Nathan to David to show him how badly he had behaved. Nathan told David a story:

Bathsheba washes herself and combs her long hair

"Once upon a time there was a rich man and a poor man. The rich man had large flocks of sheep, but the poor man had nothing at all—except for one tiny ewe lamb. He had brought her up from the moment she was born because her mother had died and she was weak and sickly. She shared the poor man's food, drank from his cup, and even slept in his arms. She was like a daughter to him.

"A traveler arrived at the rich man's house, tired and hungry after a long day on the road. But the rich man was so mean that he did not want to slaughter even one of his many, many sheep. Instead, he took the poor man's precious, solitary lamb and slit her throat. Then he prepared a good meal for the traveler."

David was shocked and appalled when he heard this story. "He should die!" he shouted. Nathan looked at him and replied, "You are that man, David. You were anointed king of Israel and given everything. You struck down Uriah the Hittite and took his wife to be your own. Why did you despise the word of the Lord by doing what is evil in His eyes?"

"I have sinned against the Lord," David replied.

"You are not going to die, but the Lord is going to bring calamity out of your own household," answered Nathan.

Soon after, David and Bathsheba's baby was gripped by a terrible fever. David pleaded with the Lord to spare his child. He fasted and prayed. But after a week, the baby died. David finally washed and changed his clothes, and asked for something to eat. And, in time, Bathsheba gave birth to another son. They named him Solomon and he was much loved by God.

Perfumed oil
After bathing, women often scented themselves. Perfume was made by dropping petals and seeds into hot olive oil. This was strained and left to cool, creating a sweet-smelling fragrance that was bottled to wear on special occasions.

Just as David had hoped, Uriah is killed in battle

Understanding the story

The Ten Commandments apply just as much to King David as anyone else. When he commits adultery with Bathsheba and arranges Uriah's death, God is angry at his immorality. God's punishment is the death of David and Bathsheba's baby. David has learned a very difficult lesson and he repents his sins. In time, God shows forgiveness and the couple go on to have another baby.

Absalom's Rebellion

King David had several different wives and fathered many children. The eldest son was named Amnon.

When he became a man, Amnon fell in love with his half sister, Tamar. She was young and beautiful and the daughter of Maccach, whom David had married when he was king of Judah. But he knew that his love was hopeless and that, according to the Law of Moses, he could never marry her.

One day, pretending to be ill, Amnon persuaded his father to send Tamar to him in his bedroom. When they were alone, he grabbed her. She struggled and tried to fend him off. Afterward, he sent her away in disgrace. She fled, broken and ashamed, and took refuge in the house of her true brother, Absalom. When David found out what had happened, he was furious, but did nothing to punish his son. But Absalom resolved to avenge his sister's honor. He ordered his men to kill Amnon when he was senseless with drink.

When David heard that his eldest son had been murdered and that another of his sons was responsible, he tore his clothes in grief and wept. He did not know what to do. Absalom fled immediately and went into hiding in the city of Geshur, where his mother came from. He stayed there for three years. David thought about him often and longed to see him, despite everything. Finally, Absalom was allowed to return to Jerusalem.

By now, Absalom was a very handsome young man, with long, dark hair that curled around his shoulders. He was admired wherever he went. But he was also ambitious and cold-hearted. He was determined to take the crown from his father.

Some people were not happy with the way David was running things and Absalom did his best to make things worse. "If only I were in charge," he would say when he heard someone complaining. "Then you could come to me and I would put things right." Gradually, the conspiracy gathered strength, and Absalom decided to go to Hebron, taking two hundred men with him. From there, he secretly sent messengers far and wide, calling the tribes of Israel to his side against David. And then he proclaimed himself king and challenged his father to battle.

David could not believe it. "We must leave the city immediately and prepare for battle," he told his officials. So David left Jerusalem with his entire household and all his men, making their way across the Kidron Valley toward the desert. They crossed the Jordan River and made their camp in Gilead. Absalom followed with his men.

That night, David talked to the three commanders in charge of his men and said, "Be gentle with Absalom, for my sake."

The next morning, the battle had begun. The fighting was long and bloody but, finally, Absalom and his army admitted defeat. More than twenty thousand soldiers died and the rebels who survived fled. Some of them were badly injured and did not manage to flee very far. Absalom himself was unhurt and managed to escape on a mule. But, terrified by the noise of the fighting, the mule bolted through the thick oak wood, and Absalom's hair got entangled in some low branches. He was left dangling in midair.

One of David's soldiers saw Absalom swinging helplessly from a tree and he went straight to Joab, the commander-in-chief, to tell him where he was. "What? You saw Absalom? Why didn't you kill him there and then? I would have given you ten shekels and a warrior's belt!"

But the soldier replied, "I would not have lifted a hand against the King's son—even if you gave me one thousand shekels. The King told us to be gentle with Absalom for his sake." So Joab stormed off, taking three javelins with him, and headed straight for the tree where Absalom was hanging. Without hesitating, he plunged all three of the javelins deep into Absalom's heart. Ten of his armor bearers finished him off. They took his body and buried it in a big pit in the middle of the forest and covered it with rocks.

When David heard the news of his son's death, he wept. "Oh my son Absalom!" he cried. "If only I had died instead of you!"

Hair
It was normal for the men and women of Canaan to keep their hair long. This carving shows an Assyrian man with a typically long hairstyle. Hair was often tightly curled into braids.

Hollow head
During the Bronze Age, javelins were made by fitting a spearhead into a metal cast with a hollow socket to take the shaft. By the time of David, metalworking had developed and stronger iron heads were used.

Understanding the story

God believes that everyone should be punished for their sins fairly and consistently, regardless of family ties and affections. David should have punished his sons' crimes but his love for them makes him weak. Though Absalom plots against his father and many Israelites switch their allegiance to him, David still wants him to be treated gently. When Absalom dies, David wishes it were he instead, so his son could be spared.

King Solomon's Wisdom

"Please help me to govern your people and to distinguish between right and wrong."

After forty years reigning over Israel, David lay dying. He gave his son Solomon some advice. "Be strong," he told him. "Show yourself to be a man and observe what the Lord requires. Walk in His ways and keep His decrees and commands, His laws and requirements, as written in the Law of Moses."

Crown
The ultimate symbol of authority and power, a crown is passed from one ruler to the next. As Solomon takes the crown, David advises him to be faithful to God, so their dynasty can continue. This ornate gold crown was buried with a princess in Afghanistan in the 1st century CE.

When the time came and David died, Solomon became king and married the daughter of Pharaoh, the king of Egypt. And the Lord appeared to Solomon one night in a dream and said, "Ask for anything you want. I will give it to you."

Solomon thought long and hard. "You have made me king of your great people, after my father David. Please help me to govern your people and to distinguish between right and wrong. Please, Lord, give me wisdom."

The Lord was pleased with Solomon's answer. He said, "If you walk in my ways and obey my commands as David your father did, then I will give you a wise and discerning heart so that there will never have been anyone like you, nor will there ever be."

Soon after, two women came before Solomon as he sat on his throne. They were in a terrible state as they clutched and fought over a bundle. Arguing and spitting at each other, they appealed to King Solomon for help in settling their dispute. At last they calmed down and managed to tell him their story, bit by bit. They lived together in the same house and had given birth to baby sons within three days of each other. But during the night one of the babies had died in his sleep. Each woman claimed that it was the other one's baby that had died. The two women pointed angrily at each other.

"Don't believe a word she says!" shouted

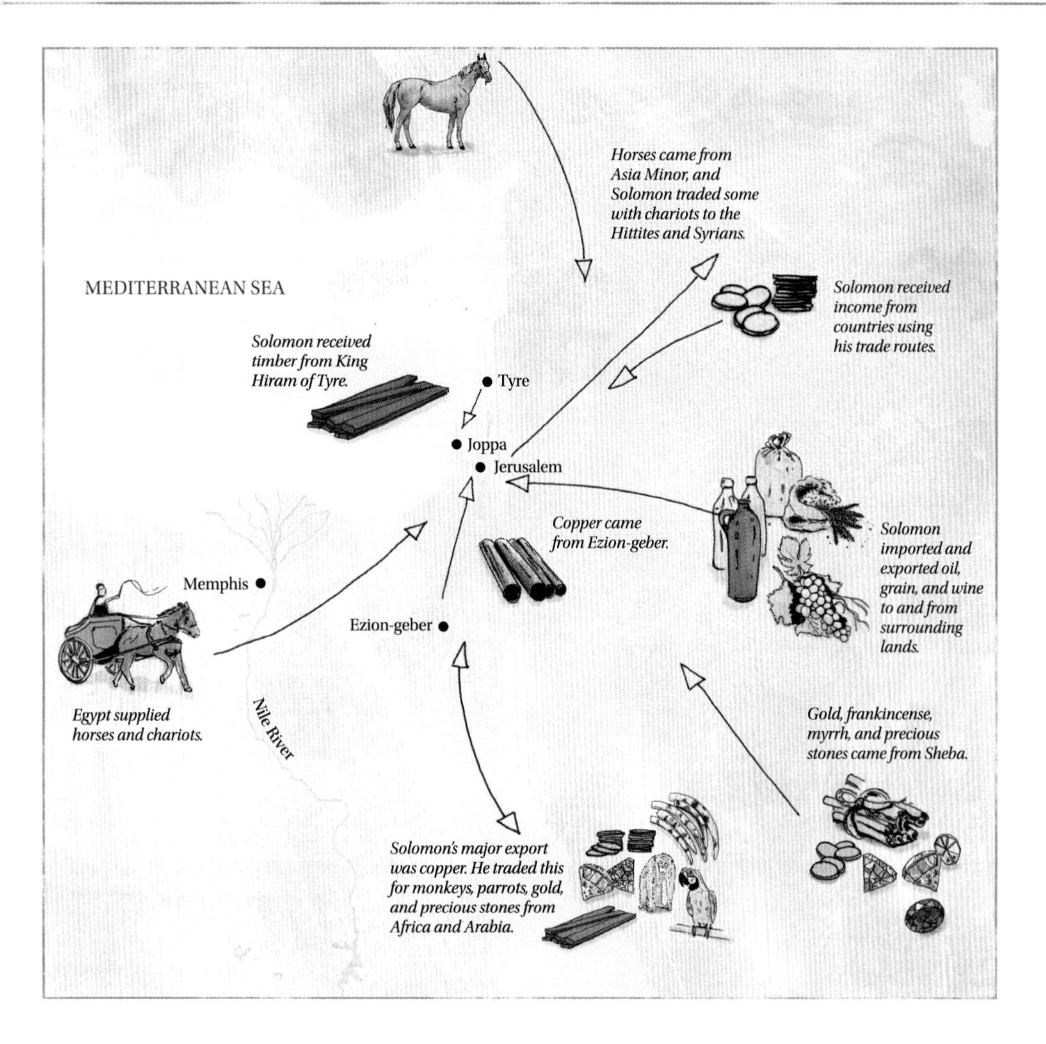

Royal trade routes
Aside from his great wisdom, King Solomon was known for his promotion of trade with neighboring kingdoms and countries. His kingdom became very wealthy as a result. His primary method of trading was by sea, and he established a great fleet of ships at Ezion-geber. He also used camel trains to cross over land.

the first woman. "It was her baby that died. Then she crept into my room, stole my baby, and put her dead son in his place."

"That's not true! What terrible lies! Your baby died and mine is alive. Here he is. You can see he's mine!" sobbed the second woman.

Solomon asked an attendant to get a sword and ordered, "Cut the infant in two and give one half to the first woman and the other half to the second woman. That should keep them happy."

The first woman shrieked in horror and fell to the floor sobbing. "Please, my Lord! Do not harm the baby. Give him to her. I don't mind. Whatever you do, don't kill him!"

But the second woman snarled, "Go ahead! Cut him in half! Neither one of us shall have him. See if I care."

Then Solomon in his wisdom spoke and gave his ruling. "Do not kill him. Give the baby to the first woman. She is his mother."

When the people of Israel heard of the judgement of Solomon, they were pleased and looked at him with great respect. They knew such wisdom could come only from God.

Understanding the story

Solomon accepts that he is lacking in the skills necessary to be king. God is pleased when he asks for the gift of wisdom. If the ownership of a property were in dispute, the judge would split it evenly between opposing sides. When Solomon proposes this solution with the baby, he cleverly reveals the true mother. His display of wisdom earns him the people's respect and admiration.

Transporting timber
Cedar was a highly valued timber in ancient times because it was strong and hardwearing. The inner walls of Solomon's Temple were built of cedar. This 8th-century-BCE relief from the palace of the Assyrian ruler Sargon II shows Phoenician oarsmen transporting exports of cedar on their rowing boats.

King Solomon
Although plans for the Temple were first started under his father David, Solomon was chosen by God to build it as, unlike his father, Solomon had not spilled blood in battle. Under his leadership, the Israelites enjoyed peace and success, and the Temple became a symbol of Solomon's reign.

Solomon's Temple

It was four years since Solomon had succeeded David and become King of Israel. His thoughts started turning toward the Temple that his father had longed to build.

The Temple would replace the tabernacle as a place of worship and provide a permanent home for the Ark of the Covenant. For years, David had worked on the idea, drawing up detailed plans for its construction in the heart of Jerusalem.

Solomon sent envoys with a message for King Hiram of Tyre. "You know that my father David was never able to build a temple because of the constant demands of war. Now there is peace, and I am going to build a temple in the name of the Lord my God. So please order cedars of Lebanon to be cut for me."

Hiram was pleased, saying, "Praise be to the Lord today for He has given David a wise son to rule over his nation." They made a treaty. Hiram would send cedar, pine, and craftsmen, and in return, Solomon would give him wheat and oil for his household.

Laborers were conscripted from all over Israel. Altogether, more than thirty thousand men were sent off in shifts to help cut down the great cedars of Lebanon and float them on huge rafts across the sea.

Meanwhile, eighty thousand stonecutters were sent to work in the quarries up in the hills, hewing vast blocks of stone for the foundations and the outer walls of the Temple. Another seventy thousand men transported the stone down to Jerusalem, overseen by their foremen. It was very hard work but, finally, in the month of Ziv (the second month of the year), Solomon laid the foundation stone. It took four long years before the foundations were completed and another three years to build the Temple.

Gradually, the magnificent building took shape with Solomon supervising everything. When it was finished it was twice as big as the old tabernacle. The walls inside were lined with fragrant cedar wood and overlaid with gold, while the floor was made of pine. Beautiful cherubim, palm trees, and garlands of flowers decorated the walls and the altar. All the furnishings of the Temple were made of gold.

An inner sanctuary, the Most Holy Place, was partitioned off at the rear of the Temple for the Ark of the Covenant. Two splendid golden cherubim, carved out of olive wood, spread out their huge wings. They would be the permanent guardians of the Ark. Two huge bronze pillars supported the roof at the entrance of the Temple, their capitals festooned with chains and hundreds of bronze pomegranates.

The Temple was finished in the eleventh year of Solomon's reign. When all the preparations had been made, the Ark of the Covenant, containing the Ten Commandments, was brought in by the priests, the elders of Israel, and the leaders

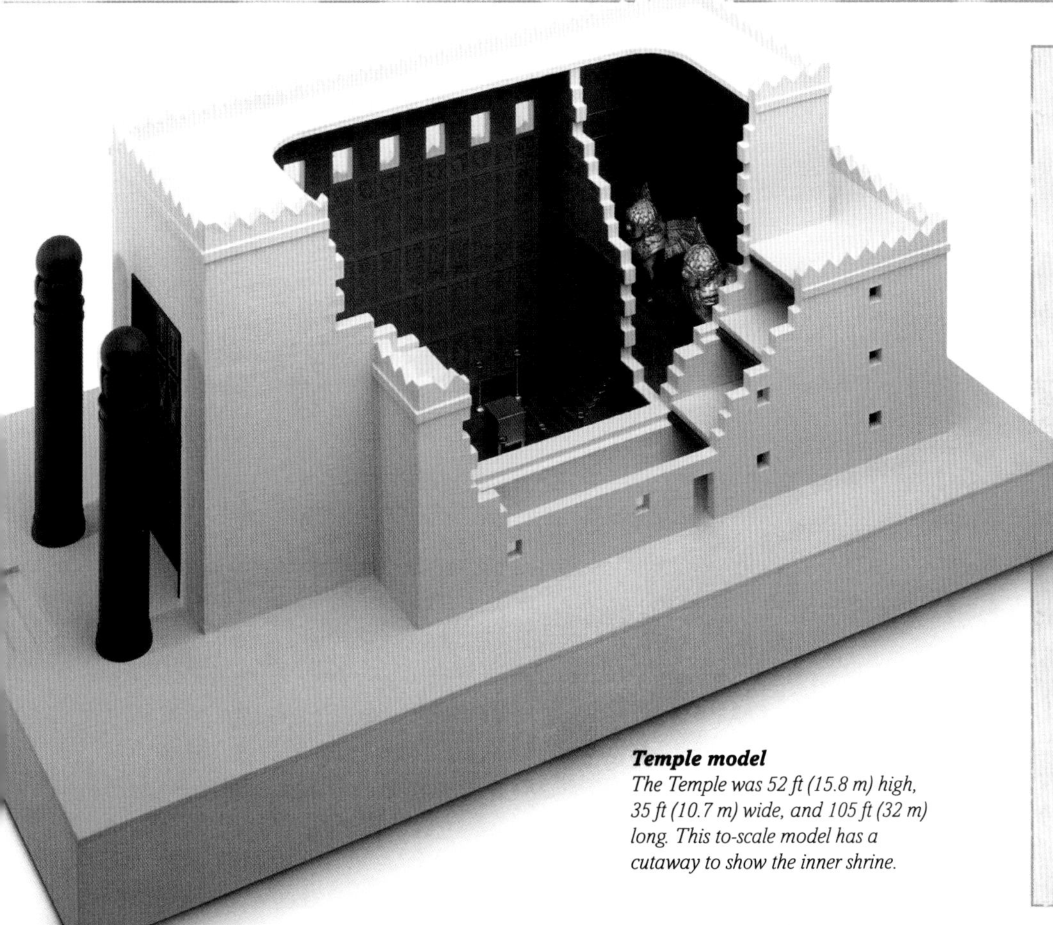

Temple model
The Temple was 52 ft (15.8 m) high, 35 ft (10.7 m) wide, and 105 ft (32 m) long. This to-scale model has a cutaway to show the inner shrine.

Temple plan
Solomon's Temple followed the basic design plan seen in earlier Canaanite temples. Walls were lined with cedar, while floors were laid with cypress. The walls and floors were overlaid with gold. The grand entrance was flanked by two bronze columns standing about 33 ft (10 m) in height. Doors were crafted from olive wood and decorated with carvings from nature. Gold overlay gave a sparkling finish. A porch led the way to a great hall called the Holy Place. Beyond it was a small inner shrine called the Holy of Holies.

of all the tribes. The priests entered the Most Holy Place and laid the Ark underneath the outstretched wings of the cherubim.

When they withdrew from the sanctuary, a great cloud suddenly appeared from nowhere, filling the Temple from the floor to the ceiling, and the priests could not carry on with the service. It was the Glory of God filling the House of God. Afterward, Solomon stood in front of the altar and said a prayer of dedication to God. He blessed all the people of Israel, and they offered sacrifices to the Lord.

"Now there is peace, and I am going to build a temple in the name of the Lord my God"

Understanding the story

Solomon's Temple takes seven years to build—the number that represents perfection and completeness. With the Ark safely inside the inner sanctuary, the presence of the Lord is confirmed when the great cloud fills the Temple. Solomon completes the building work that his father, David, had planned, making Jerusalem the focus of religious life. The Temple in Jerusalem becomes God's permanent home.

The Queen of Sheba

King Solomon ruled over the people of Israel for more than forty years. During his reign, people were prosperous and there was plenty to eat.

Israel was divided into twelve districts, and they each paid King Solomon a tribute. His own tribe, Judah, was exempt from tax. The kingdom stretched from the Euphrates River in the north to Egypt in the south. It was the land that God had promised Abraham many years before.

Solomon was richer and wiser than any other king on earth. People came from all over the world to seek an audience with him and to hear the wisdom that God had given him. Year after year they came, bringing with them gifts for the king. When the Queen of Sheba heard about the wisdom and the wealth of Solomon, she could not believe it. She decided she must see King Solomon for herself and she must test his wisdom. So she set off from Sheba, on the southwest tip of Arabia, and journeyed through the desert and north along the trade route known as the King's Highway to Jerusalem. She traveled with an enormous caravan of camels, laden with rich and exotic gifts for Solomon.

When the Queen of Sheba arrived in Jerusalem, Solomon greeted her from his magnificent throne. He showed her around his splendid palace and his stables with their thousands of horses and chariots. He took her to see his huge collections of shields, all hammered out of beaten gold. And then they returned to the throne room and he listened to all her questions. He answered them with great wisdom. Nothing was too difficult or too much trouble for him.

The Queen of Sheba was overwhelmed—by his wisdom and by the magnificence of the surroundings. "The report I heard in my own country about your achievements and your wisdom is true. But I did not believe these things until I came and saw with my own eyes. In wisdom and in wealth you have far exceeded the report I heard," she said. "O Praise be to the Lord your God, who has delighted in you and placed you on the throne of Israel!"

And she gave him the gifts she had brought with her—one hundred and twenty talents of pure gold and huge quantities of precious stones and spices. And, in turn, Solomon heaped lavish presents on his visitor, to take back with her to Sheba.

Spices

The Queen of Sheba's wealth was probably from trading goods. Spices and aromatics were very popular, particularly pepper (above), myrrh, frankincense, and cinnamon (left). They were used for a variety of things, from food preparation and perfumes, to ointments, and burial practices. A large amount of Sheba's tax revenue came from trading spices.

Precious stones

Precious metals and gemstones were also traded as luxury goods. As well as gold, carnelian (below left) and coral (below right) were particularly valuable for use in jewelry. The vast quantities of gemstones that the Queen of Sheba brought for King Solomon suggested they were part of a trade agreement with Israel's ruler.

"Solomon and the Queen of Sheba" by Frans Francken the Elder (1542–1616)

"In wisdom and in wealth you have far exceeded the report I heard."

Arabian origins
It had long been claimed that the Queen of Sheba ruled over Ethiopia and Egypt. However, experts now think that she was from southwest Arabia, in what is modern-day Yemen. She might have looked and dressed like this Yemeni woman (above) in traditional dress.

Understanding the story

Word of Solomon reaches far and wide. The Queen of Sheba decides to visit to witness his wealth and wisdom for herself. The wise words of Solomon and the grandeur of his palace do not disappoint. All the queen's questions are answered and her expectations are exceeded. The king and queen's meeting is a happy one, as she recognizes that Solomon has been truly blessed by the Lord.

When the queen of Sheba heard of Solomon's fame, she came to Jerusalem to test him with hard questions. Arriving with a very great caravan—with camels carrying spices, large quantities of gold, and precious stones—she came to Solomon and talked with him about all she had on her mind.

2 Chronicles 9:1

Camel trains
Known as the "ship of the desert," the camel is ideal for crossing oceans of desert sand thanks to its ability to endure the extremes of temperature and scarcity of water. This camel train is traveling across Erg Chebbi, in the Sahara Desert.

Elijah in the Wilderness

After the death of Solomon, his son Rehoboam became king of the Israelites. But the tribes of the north had not been happy for a long time.

"Now I know that you are a man of God!"

Under the rule of Solomon they had been subjected to high taxes. They thought that things might get better now, but their hopes were soon dashed. "My father laid on you a heavy yoke. I will make it even heavier," their new king told them with satisfaction. So the tribes rebelled against their new ruler. And soon, the kingdom was split in two once more, with Israel in the north and Judah in the south.

In time, Omri became the king of Israel and he made Samaria the capital. He made an alliance with Phoenicia through the marriage of his son Ahab to Jezebel. She was the daughter of the ruler of Sidon, and she encouraged her new husband to worship her god Baal. When he became king, Ahab built temples and altars to the pagan god.

The prophet Elijah foretold what was in store for the people of Israel, because they had turned away from the Lord. He said that there would be a drought lasting for many years, and, with it, famine. Elijah went to King Ahab in Samaria and warned him, "As the Lord the God of Israel lives, whom I serve, there will be neither dew nor rain in the next few years except at my word," he said.

And God spoke to Elijah. "Leave here, turn eastward, and hide in the Kerith Ravine, east of the Jordan River. You will drink from the brook, and I have ordered the ravens to feed you there." Elijah did just as God had told him and lived happily by the stream, being fed by the ravens and drinking the water. All around, the crops failed and the people began to starve. But then the stream dried up, and the Lord said to Elijah, "Go at once to Zarephath in Sidon and stay there. I have commanded a widow there to supply you with food."

So Elijah went to Zarephath in Sidon, the land where Queen Jezebel had come from. As he approached the gates of the town, he saw a woman stooping down and gathering sticks. Elijah went up to her and greeted her. "Would you bring me a little water in a jar so that I may have a drink?" he asked her. "And please, if you would be so kind, bring me a piece of bread."

She shook her head. "I don't have any bread," she said. "All I have is a handful of flour in a jar and a little oil in a jug. It is hardly enough for me and my son as it is!"

"Don't be afraid," replied Elijah. "Make a small cake of bread for me and then make something for you and your son. The Lord will make sure that the flour and the oil do not run out until the rain comes." The widow looked at him doubtfully, but did as he said. And, sure enough, her flour and oil did not run out, and there was plenty of food for her and her son and Elijah until the rain came.

But, some time later, her son fell ill and, no matter what the woman did, he got worse and worse. Finally, one night, he stopped breathing completely and she said to Elijah, "What do you have against me? You have let my son die! And you call yourself a man of God!"

Elijah looked at her calmly and told her to give him her son. Gently, he carried the boy upstairs and laid him out on the bed, cold and still. Then he stretched over the little body three times and cried, "O Lord my God, let this boy's life return to him!" And immediately the boy's chest started moving and the color returned to his cheeks. His eyelids fluttered, as if he was waking up from a dream. Finally, he stretched and opened his eyes.

Elijah carried him down and gave him to his mother. "Look, your son is alive!" he said.

The widow could not believe it and clutched the boy to her tightly. "Now I know that you are a man of God!" she cried to Elijah.

Understanding the story

God brings drought and famine to punish the Israelites, but also to demonstrate His power over Baal, the pagan god of rain. In the face of this disaster, the people suffer greatly. The prophet Elijah never loses his faith in God and, as a result, his supply of food and drink never run out. When the woman blames Elijah for her son's death, he brings the boy back to life in the name of the Lord, and she then shares his belief in God.

Ravens
In the Old Testament, ravens were considered dirty. But God gives these creatures a purpose by sending them to feed Elijah. They ensure that he does not go hungry, proving that even the most humble creature has a part in God's plan.

Oven
Clay ovens speeded up the breadmaking process. Before that, people spread the bread on clay molds over the embers of a fire, and used metal lids to cover it. Animal dung or grasses were probably used as fuel.

Elijah and the Prophets of Baal

The drought in Israel had lasted for three years. It was a punishment from the Lord because the Israelites had been worshipping the pagan god Baal.

The prophet Elijah went to see King Ahab in Samaria again. Ahab greeted him rudely, saying, "Is that you, the troublemaker, the thorn in Israel's side?"

"I have not made trouble for Israel," replied Elijah. "But you and your father's family have. You have abandoned the Lord's commands and have followed Baal. Now summon the people from all over Israel to meet me on Mount Carmel. And bring the four hundred and fifty prophets of Baal, who eat at Queen Jezebel's table."

Ahab sent word and summoned the people and the prophets to Mount Carmel. Elijah stood before them all and said, "You cannot worship both God and Baal! How long will you waver between them? If the Lord is God, follow Him. But if Baal is God, follow him." But nobody said anything.

Elijah continued, "I am the only one of the Lord's prophets left, but Baal has four hundred and fifty of them." And, although there were so many of them and only one of him, he challenged them to a contest to see who the true God was. The prophets were to make an altar to Baal. Then they were to place a sacrificial bull on top—but they must not set fire to it. He would do exactly the same, but his altar would be to the Lord. "Then you call on the name of your god and I will call on the name of the Lord, and we will see who wins," he said. "The true God will set the fire on His altar alight."

He let the prophets of Baal go first. They called their God's name from early morning till the middle of the day. And they danced around and around the altar they had made. But there was no response. The wood on the altar remained unkindled, and the calf lay on top of it uncooked.

Elijah could not resist taunting them. "Shout louder! Perhaps he's deep in thought?" So the prophets shouted louder and louder and slashed themselves with their swords and spears until they bled, as was their custom. By evening they were exhausted, and there was still no response. The altar to Baal remained unlit.

Then Elijah called everyone over to his altar, but it was in ruins so he repaired it. He took twelve stones, one for each of the tribes of Israel, and rebuilt the altar. He arranged his wood and cut his calf into pieces and laid them in position. When this was done he asked for several large jars of water to be poured over the altar until it was soaking wet.

Jezebel at the window
This carving is thought to depict Queen Jezebel staring out from her palace window. King Ahab had the palace built for her at Jezreel. The fact that the prophets of Baal ate with the queen shows that Baal-worship had become the kingdom's religion.

Mount Carmel
The Carmel is a mountain range that stretches from the Jezreel Valley to the Mediterranean Sea. Mount Carmel rises to 470 ft (143 m), overlooking the sea near modern Haifa. In ancient times, it was lush and green, with oak trees, olive groves, and vineyards.

"The Rival Sacrifices of Elijah and the Priests of Baal" (1545) by Lucas Cranach the Younger

He stepped forward and spoke, "O Lord, God of Abraham, Isaac, and Israel, let it be known today that you are God in Israel and that I am your servant. Answer me, O Lord, so these people will know that you, O Lord, are God." Immediately, the sodden wood on his altar burst into flames, crackling around the sacrifice and leaping high in the air. Everyone gasped in amazement and fell to the ground, crying, "The Lord—He is God! The Lord—He is God!"

Elijah gave orders for the prophets to be rounded up. "Seize the prophets of Baal! Don't let them get away!" he commanded. And the four hundred and fifty prophets of Baal were taken down the mountain and slaughtered in the Kishon Valley.

Meanwhile, Elijah walked up the mountain with his servant, through the olive groves and the oak trees. When they reached the very top, the Great Sea lay like a sheet of silver at their feet. Elijah asked the young man what he could see?

"I can't see anything," replied the servant. "Only a clear sky and a calm sea."

"Look again," said the prophet. But again the servant could see nothing.

Elijah asked him the same question seven times, and it was only then that the servant replied, "A cloud as small as a man's hand is rising from the sea." And immediately, Elijah told him to go to Ahab to say that the rains were coming. As he spoke, the sky grew black and the wind roared wildly, bringing the rain with it. Ahab rode off as fast as he could to his home in Jezreel, but Elijah, filled with the power of the Lord, ran ahead of Ahab.

Understanding the story

The local pagan god was called Baal, meaning "master" or "possessor." God was unhappy that the Israelites were worshipping Baal, so the drought continued. The prophet Elijah challenges the prophets of Baal to a contest. He gives his opponents every advantage, so when they are defeated, the Israelites are witness to God's power and superiority.

"O Lord, answer me, so these people will know that you, O Lord, are God."

Palace relic
A number of relics were discovered in the remains of King Ahab's palace. According to the Bible, the palace was adorned with ivory. Finds include ornate ivory plaques and sculptures. This piece from the palace, of a human-faced Sphinx possibly used as a decoration for furniture, dates between the 8th and 9th centuries BCE.

Vineyard
This Assyrian carving depicts a king and queen enjoying the fruits of their vineyard. Supports lift and guide the vines up off the ground. There were many vineyards at that time. The first Biblical mention of wine came in the story of Noah, who planted vines after he left the Ark.

Naboth's Vineyard

There was a vineyard next to King Ahab's residence in Jezreel, which belonged to a man named Naboth. Ahab had eyed it enviously for some time.

"Let me have your vineyard to use for a vegetable garden since it is so close to my palace," he said to Naboth. "In exchange, I will give you a better vineyard, or, if you prefer, I will pay you whatever it is worth."

But Naboth refused point-blank. "The Lord forbids that I should give you the inheritance of my fathers," he replied politely. He could not even think about it as, according to the Law of Moses, Israelites were not allowed to sell any of the ancestral lands that had been allotted to them after the conquest of Canaan.

Ahab was furious and headed back to his palace in a rage. He lay on his bed with his face to the wall and would not talk to anyone, sulking like a little boy. His wife, Jezebel, came in and could not understand why her husband was lying there on his bed in the middle of the day. "What's wrong with you?" she asked. "Why won't you eat anything?"

To begin with, he did not respond, but finally he turned over and told her about the vineyard. Jezebel looked at him in disbelief. "And you call yourself king of Israel! I ask you!" she sneered. "I'll get that vineyard for you!" Ahab turned back to face the wall.

Jezebel knew exactly what to do. Without delay, she sat down and wrote dozens of letters, forging Ahab's signature and stamping them with his own royal seal. She sent them to all the elders and nobles who lived in the city. In them, she said that there would be a day of fasting, which showed that someone had committed a serious crime. Naboth was to be seated in a prominent position among the people, and she told the elders to make sure that two good-for-nothings, who could be bribed

to do anything, were seated opposite Naboth. They would set him up, testifying that he had spoken against God. This was a crime that carried the death sentence.

The elders and the nobles did as they were told, thinking that they were carrying out King Ahab's orders. And the two villains, happy to earn their money, sat opposite Naboth and brought the charges against him. "That man sitting there has cursed both God and the king!" And Naboth was taken outside the city and stoned to death.

When Jezebel heard that her plan had worked and that Naboth had been killed, she rushed to Ahab to tell him the good news. "Get up! The vineyard that you wanted so much is yours. Naboth is dead!"

Ahab was delighted and went straight to the vineyard to inspect his prized possession. But the Lord had already spoken to the prophet Elijah, and he was there waiting for Ahab.

"You have murdered a man and stolen his property! And the Lord says that, just as the dogs licked up Naboth's blood from the roadside, so they will lick up yours! You have sold your soul and have done evil in the eyes of the Lord, and so disaster will fall on you and your descendants. And dogs will devour Jezebel by the walls of Jezreel!"

When Ahab heard these words, he was appalled and deeply ashamed. He tore his clothes, put on sackcloth, and fasted. God saw that he was truly remorseful and He spoke to Elijah again. "Because Ahab has humbled himself and is truly sorry I will not punish him, but I will bring disaster on his descendants."

Understanding the story

Naboth's relatives were given the land of the vineyard after the conquest of Canaan. Moses's Law stated that the Israelites must not sell any ancestral land. By conspiring to have Naboth accused of blasphemy, his death is a certainty. Jezebel and King Ahab are both to blame for Naboth's murder. Ahab shows remorse, but God's punishment is passed down to Ahab's son, Ahaziah, who dies childless, so ending Ahab's dynasty.

The bountiful land of the Jezreel Valley was the setting for Ahab's palace and Naboth's vineyard.

"The Lord says that, just as the dogs licked up Naboth's blood from the roadside, so they will lick up yours!"

Chariot of gold
Elijah is taken to heaven in a fiery chariot (seen in this panel above from the altar made by Nicholas of Verdun at Klosterneuburg Priory, Austria). Chariots were usually used for either ceremonies or battles. In war, two men took their positions in the chariot. The driver held the reins to control the horses, while the soldier took aim with a spear or bow and arrow. In the story, the chariot is made of fire as it has been sent by God.

Elijah's Final Journey

The prophet Elijah was walking with his disciple Elisha. He knew that his life was drawing to a close and that the Lord would soon take him up to heaven.

"I have to go to Bethel now, but you stay here," he said to Elisha.

But Elisha protested, "As surely as the Lord lives and as long as you live, I will not leave you." So they went on together and arrived in Bethel. The company of prophets who lived there came out to meet them. They greeted them both and said to Elisha, "Do you know that the Lord is going to take your master from you today?"

Golden chariot
This golden chariot was made in the Persian Empire about 500 BCE. It was part of a treasure hoard found in what is now Tajikistan.

"Yes, I know," replied Elisha, "but do not speak of it." Then Elijah told him to stay in Bethel while he went on to Jericho.

Again, Elisha protested, "As surely as the Lord lives and as long as you live, I will not leave you." So they left Bethel together and went to Jericho.

When they arrived in Jericho, the prophets who lived there met them and said to Elisha, "Do you know that the Lord is going to take your master from you today?"

"Yes, I know," replied Elisha, "but I would rather not speak of it." Then Elijah told him to stay in Jericho while he went on to the Jordan River.

Again, Elisha protested, "As surely as the Lord lives and as long as you live, I will not leave you." So they left Jericho together and traveled to the Jordan. When they got there, fifty prophets stood at a respectful distance, watching them.

They stopped by the edge of the river. Elijah took off his cloak and rolled it up. Then he bent down and struck the surface of the water with it. Immediately, the river divided and a path of dry ground stretched in front of them. Elijah and Elisha walked across together until they reached the other side. Then Elijah said to Elisha, "What can I do for you before I am taken from you?"

"What I would like, more than anything in the world, is to follow in your footsteps and be your spiritual heir," Elisha replied.

Elijah listened and was silent for a few moments. Then he said, "You have asked a difficult thing. Yet, if you see me with your own eyes as I am taken from you, you will get what you have asked for. Otherwise, not."

At that moment a chariot of fire appeared between them, pulled by blazing horses. It separated them and Elijah went up to heaven in a whirlwind. Elisha watched him disappear. And that was the last he saw of Elijah.

Elisha wept and tore his clothes in grief. He picked up Elijah's cloak, which had fallen to the ground, and held it closely to him. Then, he went back to the banks of the river and rolled the cloak up tightly, just as the great prophet had done not long before. He struck the water with it and, once again, the river divided and a path of dry ground stretched in front of him. He walked back to the other side. And the company of prophets who were watching said, "The spirit of Elijah is resting in Elisha!" They went to meet him, bowing low on the ground.

Jordan River
When prophet Elijah parts the waters of the Jordan River, it is reminiscent of other Biblical stories in which waters behave miraculously to allow a safe crossing. The Jordan River stops flowing when the priests carry the Ark of the Covenant to Jericho, while the Red Sea divides to allow the Israelites to leave Egypt.

"Do you know that the Lord is going to take your master from you today?"

Understanding the story

Elijah's time on Earth is over, and disciple Elisha (meaning "God is salvation") will be his successor. Elisha is to be Elijah's spiritual heir and literally takes up Elijah's mantle when he picks up the cloak left by Elijah. Elisha will continue Elijah's ministry. The whirlwind that carries Elijah up to heaven is another demonstration of God's colossal strength and power.

Elisha and the Woman of Shunem

Elisha often visited Shunem in the beautiful Valley of Jezreel. Whenever he was there, he was invited to dinner by a rich woman and her elderly husband.

Shunem
The town of Shunem lay 3 miles (5 km) north of the town of Jezreel, in the rich and fertile Jezreel Valley. Shunem was situated along a busy road. Elisha was a regular visitor to the town. Shunem was also the base camp for the Philistines before they waged war on Mount Gilboa.

Girded loins
When Gehazi placed his robe between his legs and under his belt, he is decribed as "girding his loins." Manual workers, like this man in Bangladesh, still do this in order to give them more freedom of movement.

The woman knew that Elisha was a prophet and a holy man of God. "Let's make a little room on the roof for him," she said to her husband. "We can put a bed and a table in it—and a chair and a lamp. We will make it comfortable for him and he can stay there when he wants to. It will be a home from home."

Elisha accepted their hospitality gratefully. One evening, as he was resting on his bed, he thought how lucky he was. He called his servant Gehazi and said, "How can I repay their kindness?"

"The woman has no son—no children at all," replied Gehazi. "And her husband is an old man—too old to father a child. She would like a son more than anything else in the world." Elisha asked him to fetch the woman immediately, and she came and stood in the doorway.

"About this time next year," Elisha told her, "you will hold your very own son in your arms!" The woman could not believe her ears. But, sure enough, about one year later she gave birth to a baby boy, just as Elisha had predicted. The woman still could not believe it and every day she gave thanks to the Lord for blessing her with a son.

The child grew, healthy and strong, and life was good for the family. But, one day, the boy went to find his father who was supervising the harvest in the fields. The boy clutched his hands to his head, howling in pain. "My head! My head! It hurts so much! I can't bear it!" His father ordered one of the servants to carry his son back home as quickly as possible.

By the time they got back to the house, the boy was almost unconscious, and the servant gave him straight to his mother. She tried to revive him, but he lay there as white as a sheet. His breathing became shallower and shallower and finally stopped altogether. His mother sat weeping. Then, slowly, she took him upstairs and laid him gently on the bed in Elisha's room.

Forcing back the tears, she went to her husband and said, "Quick! I need a donkey and one of the servants! I am going to fetch Elisha!" Moments later, she set off for Mount Carmel, where she knew she would find the prophet. When she reached Elisha, she bowed down before him and clutched at his feet, crying. His servant, Gehazi, came over to push her away, but Elsiha rebuked him. The woman told him what had happened and that her son was dead. Elisha listened and said to Gehazi,

English painter Frederic Leighton's "Elisha Raising the Son of the Shunamite" (1881)

"Tuck your cloak into your belt, take my staff, and run back to Shunem as fast as you can. If you meet anyone, don't stop, whatever you do! When you get there, lay my staff on the boy's face."

Gehazi did exactly as his master had told him, while Elisha followed with the distraught woman. But when he laid the staff on the boy's face, nothing happened. So Gehazi rushed back to tell his master.

When Elisha reached the house, he climbed the stairs and went into his room. The boy lay on the bed. The prophet shut the door and prayed to the Lord. Then he got on the bed and lay on top of the boy. As he stretched himself out, the boy's body gradually started to get warm. Elisha got up and paced to and fro across the room. Then he went back and stretched himself on top of the boy again. At once, the boy sneezed loudly seven times and opened his eyes.

Elisha summoned Gehazi and told him to fetch the boy's mother. She peeped fearfully around the door and Elisha smiled and said, "Take your son. He is alive!" She gasped and rushed in, thanking Elisha from the bottom of her heart. Then she went to her son and put her arms around him.

"At once, the boy sneezed loudly seven times and opened his eyes."

Understanding the story

Now Elisha has the spiritual powers of Elijah, he must put them to good use. Elisha performs twice as many miracles as his master did, and many of them benefit ordinary people. This reflects God's concern for all. The boy sneezes seven times as he is brought back to life, and this number represents perfection and completeness.

Syrian king
Syrian craftsmen used tusks to make ivory carvings. This Syrian king is believed to be Hazael. During Hazael's reign of 37 years, he waged war with the Israelites.

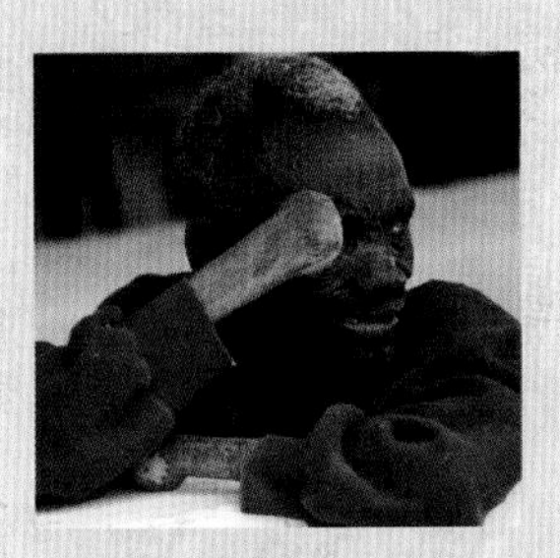

Leprosy
Namaan's skin condition may have been leprosy. This bacterial infection causes damage to nerves in the face and limbs, sometimes resulting in the loss of parts of the body. At the time, leprosy described many types of skin complaint as people could not differentiate between them.

Elisha and Naaman

Naaman was a commander in the Syrian army. He was a brave soldier and was highly regarded by his troops.

But Naaman suffered from an affliction, which made every inch of his skin white and scaly. It itched and stung, tormenting him from morning till night, and he knew that people avoided him when they could.

Recently, a young girl from Israel had been taken captive by the Syrians and she became the maidservant to Naaman's wife. The girl was horrified when she first saw Naaman and said to her mistress, "If only your husband could see the prophet Elisha in Samaria, he would cure him." That evening, Naaman's wife encouraged her husband to go to Israel. He agreed and went to the Syrian king and asked him if he might be relieved of his duties for a while. "By all means, go!" said the king. "I will send a letter to the King of Israel, asking him to cure you."

The next day, Naaman left for Israel, taking with him ten talents of silver, six thousand shekels of gold, and ten sets of the finest clothing. He was not sure how much it would cost to cure him, but he was willing to pay anything. When he finally arrived, Naaman gave his letter to the King of Israel. But, as soon as the king had read it, he erupted in fury. "Why does the King of Syria send someone to me to be cured?" he stormed. "He's just trying to pick a quarrel!" Naaman wished he had never come.

But when Elisha heard about this, he sent a message to the king. "Tell the man to come to me and he will know that there is a prophet in Israel."

Naaman went straight to Elisha's house, but Elisha did not come out to greet him. Instead, he sent a messenger to tell Naaman to wash himself seven times in the Jordan River and he would be cured. But Naaman was not happy. "I thought that he would come and wave his hands over me and call on the name of the Lord, and that I would be cured," he said. "The rivers in Damascus are just as good as the Jordan. I shall go straight home and wash myself in the waters there!"

But his servant stopped him. "Master, if the prophet had told you to do something important and difficult, you would have risen to the occasion, wouldn't you? All he wants you to do is to bathe in the waters of the Jordan and be cleansed!"

Naaman listened and reluctantly agreed. He went down to a deserted part of the river and waded into the water. He submerged himself completely, seven times, and then came out. As he stepped onto the bank, he looked down in amazement. His skin disease had completely disappeared.

Naaman went back to Elisha and said to him, "Now I know that there is no God in all the world except in Israel. Please accept a gift of thanks." But Elisha declined. "In that case, would you give me as much earth as my two mules can carry so that I can take it back with me and worship the God of Israel on Israelite soil?" asked Naaman. And Elisha agreed gladly.

But Gehazi, Elisha's servant, thought that his master should have accepted a gift from Naaman. So, filled with greed, he went back to Naaman and pretended that he came with a message from Elisha. "My master has had a change of heart!" he lied. "He wants me to tell you that there are two young prophets who have just arrived from Ephraim and they would be grateful for anything you could give them. Maybe a talent of silver and a set of clothing each?"

"By all means," said Naaman. He tied up the two talents of silver in two bags and sorted out two fine sets of clothing. And he insisted that his servants carry them back for Gehazi. But, as soon as Naaman was out of sight, Gehazi grabbed the silver and the clothes and sent the servants on their way. He went back to his own room and hid his ill-gotten gains under the bed. Then he went back to Elisha.

But Elisha looked him straight in the eye and said, "Is this the time to take money or accept clothes—or anything else for that matter? The skin disease that used to torment Naaman will now be yours. It will cling to you and your descendants forever!"

Gehazi watched in horror as his hands and arms and toes turned scaly and white. He felt a terrible itch creep up his legs and spread across his back. Naaman's affliction was now his.

Understanding the story

The miraculous healing of the Syrian soldier is an example of God's love and care extending to other nationalities. Again, the number seven features, and is symbolic in its meaning of perfection and completeness. Naaman bathes his sore skin seven times in the Jordan River and is cured. Though a foreigner in Israel, he rejects his local gods in order to worship the Lord.

After submerging himself seven times in the river, Naaman's skin is totally cleansed

The Prophet Isaiah

One day, the prophet Isaiah had a vision in the Temple in Jerusalem. He saw the Lord seated high on His throne, the train of His robe filling the whole of the Temple.

Two beautiful angels, each with six feathery wings, looked down on Isaiah from above. "Holy, holy, holy is the Lord Almighty! The whole earth is full of His glory!" they sang, as the Temple shook and filled with smoke.

Isaiah was overwhelmed by the power and majesty of the Lord, and by His holiness. He fell to his knees and cried, "I am unworthy and I am unclean! My eyes have actually seen the Lord God Almighty himself!"

Immediately, one of the angels flew down to the altar and picked up a burning coal with a pair of tongs. He placed it on Isaiah's lips, then swiftly took it away again saying, "This coal that touched your lips has taken away your guilt and made amends for your sin."

Then Isaiah heard the Lord's voice saying, "Spread the word of God. Tell the people that the Lord is coming and that they must prepare the way for Him. At first, they will not listen. There will be destruction and devastation and the land will be laid waste. But eventually, the Glory of God will be revealed. The wilderness will blossom and water will gush forth in the desert. The weak will become strong, the blind will see, and those who follow the Lord will be given strength. The Lord Himself will come down to earth and look after His flock, protecting them from evil."

Prophet Isaiah
Prophets often predicted dire consequences when the people disobeyed God. This carving depicts Isaiah (meaning "God saves"). Many of his prophecies from the 8th century BCE came true, such as the Assyrian destruction of Israel.

"Tell the people that the Lord is coming and that they must prepare the way for Him."

Understanding the story

God has a message that Isaiah must give to His people. He tells Isaiah that He will come to Earth to bring salvation, but that Isaiah will not be believed at first and will face opposition, like prophets before him. Isaiah is one of several Old Testament prophets who foretell the coming of a Messiah, and a new covenant between God and His people.

Hezekiah's Gold

The kings of Israel had grown greedy and corrupt. They and their people had turned away from the Lord, worshipping false gods and idols again.

The Lord was not pleased. He warned them through His prophets, "Turn from your evil ways. Observe my commands and decrees, in accordance with the entire law that I commanded your fathers to obey and that I delivered to you through my servants, the prophets." But no one would listen.

The neighboring Assyrians, who had a powerful army, were a threat to Israel and Judah. Now they invaded Israel, pillaging and plundering. They laid siege to the capital, Samaria, and after three years it fell to the enemy.

While Israel was occupied by the Assyrians, a king named Hezekiah came to the throne in Judah, to the south. He obeyed the Lord in everything he did. There had never been a king like him in Judah, and there never was again. He had also led his men to victory over the Philistines many times. But, when the Assyrians raced south and attacked the cities of Judah, Hezekiah had met his match. He sent a message to King Sennacherib of Assyria, saying, "Withdraw from Judah and I will pay whatever you ask."

Sennacherib demanded three hundred talents of silver and thirty talents of gold. It was a huge amount. The only way that Hezekiah could pay was by stripping the gold from the doors of the Temple in Jerusalem. But Sennacherib did not keep his word. He took the treasure and ordered his troops to besiege Jerusalem. They stopped just outside Jerusalem, calling for the king. But Hezekiah sent his officials instead. At this, the commander of the Assyrian army addressed the people of Jerusalem. "Do not let Hezekiah deceive you. Do not believe that the Lord will protect you. Has the god of any nation ever delivered his land from the hand of the king of Assyria?"

The officials went back and told Hezekiah that the Lord's name had been taken in vain. Hezekiah put on sackcloth to show his humility. Before praying, he told his officials to ask the prophet Isaiah for help.

When the officials found Isaiah, he told them, "God will defend you and save your city."

That night, the angel of the Lord flew over the Assyrian camp. When King Sennacherib got up, thousands of his soldiers were dead. He looked in horror at the sea of bodies that surrounded him, and he fled, as fast as he could, away from Jerusalem. He did not stop until he got back to his home in Nineveh.

"God will defend you and save your city."

Hezekiah's tunnel
During his reign, King Hezekiah gave orders for a tunnel to be dug underneath Jerusalem to stop the Assyrian invaders cutting off the city's water supply. Hezekiah's Tunnel still flows with water today.

Understanding the story

God punishes the Israelites' sins of greed and idol worship by unleashing the Assyrian army on the nation. In the carnage and devastation that follows, God acknowledges Hezekiah's faith, prayer, and humility. He assures the king, through Isaiah, that He will save Jerusalem and His people. King Sennacherib believes that Assyria is more powerful than God. But God proves him wrong by destroying the Assyrian army.

Josiah
Josiah's father, Amon, was assassinated by his servants. Josiah reigned 31 years from 640 BCE. He loved God from childhood and ordered many religious reforms. This is why he restored the Temple in Jerusalem. Josiah decided to renew the covenant with God after reading the lost Book of the Covenant.

Kidron Valley
Ben Hinnom was a place where children were sacrificed to the Ammonite god of fire. The location is thought to be in the Kidron Valley. The monastery of Mar Saba (above) stands on the top of the valley today. It was founded in 483 CE and is still in use today.

Josiah and the Scroll of the Law

Josiah was only eight years old when he became the new ruler of Judah, after the assassination of his father, Amon. Unlike his father and his grandfather, King Manasseh, Josiah was obedient to the Lord.

During the previous decades, the splendid Temple that Solomon had built in Jerusalem had been neglected and had fallen into disrepair. In the eighteenth year of his reign, King Josiah decided that it was time for the Temple to be restored to its former glory. He asked the high priest, Hilkiah, to gather together the money that had been collected in the Temple over the years. It would be used to finance the repairs.

While Hilkiah was finding the money and having a good look around to see what needed doing, he came across an old scroll hidden in a neglected corner of the Temple. It was festooned with cobwebs but, fortunately, the mice had not got their teeth into it. He dusted it off and saw, with amazement, that the yellowing parchment contained the Book of the Covenant. Hilkiah knew that there was only one copy in the whole of Judah and Israel, and it had been missing for many, many years. This must be it. Gingerly, he picked it up and took it to his friend, Shaphan, who was the royal scribe. Shaphan's eyes opened wide when he saw the yellowing parchment scroll and, taking Hilkiah with him, he went straight to the palace with it. He bowed low before King Josiah and then unrolled the scroll very carefully. His voice trembled as he began to read the first few lines aloud.

King Josiah reads the Book of the Covenant from the Temple

Josiah listened intently and, as he heard the beautiful words bearing testimony to the Lord, he was filled with the deepest sorrow. He sprang up from his throne and began to tear at his clothes. "My people have forgotten God's Law!" he wept. "They are selfish and corrupt and God must be so angry with them! What will happen to them?" And he begged Shaphan and Hilkiah to find out what lay in store for the people of Judah.

"Great is the Lord's anger that burns against us because our fathers have not

"My people have forgotten God's Law!"

obeyed the words of this book," Josiah said. "They have not acted in accordance with all that is written there concerning us."

Shaphan and Hilkiah went to consult a prophetess named Huldah. She was married to the wardrobe keeper in the Temple and lived in a new part of Jerusalem. She told them that the Lord was going to bring disaster on the people of Judah because they had worshipped so many different gods. But King Josiah would be spared because he was a good man and had humbled himself in front of the Lord.

When King Josiah heard this, he called everyone together in the Temple—the elders and the priests, the prophets, and all the people of Jerusalem. He stood by the great pillar, solemnly unrolled the parchment scroll of the law, and read it to them, every word. And then, in the presence of the Lord, he renewed the covenant that had been made long ago by the people of Israel to follow the Lord and to keep His commands and decrees. The people listened in silence and gave their pledge.

After this, Josiah ordered a purge of the pagan gods and the priests who bowed down before them. All the trappings of worship were to go. The statues and altars were to be removed from the Temple and then destroyed and burnt. Sacred stones and shrines to the false gods were to be smashed, ground up into fine powder, and scattered over the land. And the altar in the Valley of Ben Hinnom, where so many sons and daughters had been sacrificed in the flames by their parents, was to be reduced to dust. Then, when the whole of the country had been cleansed, Josiah commanded his people to celebrate the festival of Passover, which commemorated the Israelites' escape from Egypt.

Pagan icons
The reigns of Josiah's father and grandfather had led to the worship of pagan gods such as Ashtoreth (also known as "Astarte"). Ashtoreth was the Canaanite goddess of love and fertility, and her partner was the weather god Baal. Josiah felt so angry at the worship of pagan gods like these that he tore apart an altar dedicated to Ashtoreth.

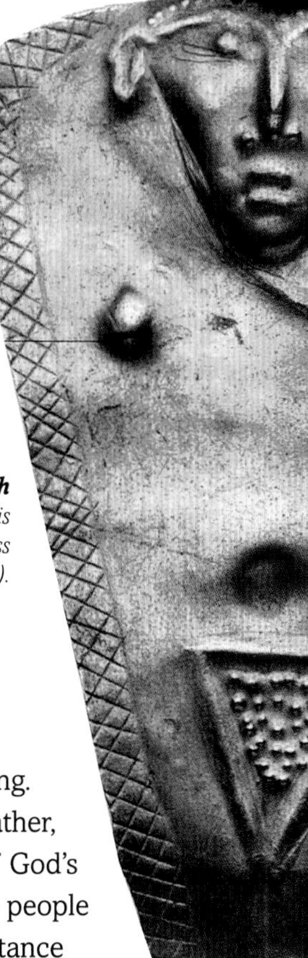

Ashtoreth
Dating back to about 1500 BCE, this gold pendant depicts the goddess Ashtoreth (meaning "womb").

Understanding the story

Josiah is mentioned in the Book of Kings as being Judah's best king. He wants to make up for the past mistakes of his father and grandfather, and save Judah from a terrible fate. The discovery of the lost book of God's Law becomes the focus of Josiah's religious reformation. He urges the people to destroy their false idols and return to God. But the people's repentance has come too late. The prophetess predicts disaster will befall Judah, though Josiah will be spared.

Jeremiah and the Potter's Wheel

The Lord told Jeremiah that He had chosen him to be a prophet. Jeremiah was astonished.

"Do not be afraid," answered the Lord. "I am with you." And He reached out His hand and touched Jeremiah gently on the lips with His fingers. "Now I have put words into your mouth," He said. "What do you see?"

"I see the branch of an almond tree in bloom," Jeremiah replied.

"That is right," said the Lord. "I am watching to see if my word is fulfilled. What else do you see?"

"I see a boiling pot, tilting away from the north," Jeremiah answered.

"It is from the north that I will bring disaster," said the Lord. "I am about to summon people to overrun Judah and punish the people for their wickedness in forsaking me and worshipping false gods. You must warn them. They will turn on you, but do not be frightened. I am with you."

The Lord sent Jeremiah to the house of a potter, who was busy in his workshop. The potter threw some clay on his wheel and shaped it with his hands. The lump of clay started to transform into a pot, but then it wobbled and collapsed in a heap. The potter scooped up the clay and started to make another pot. This time it was perfect.

The Lord spoke to Jeremiah and said, "Like the clay in the hand of the potter, so is the House of Israel in my hands! If the people repent of their evil ways, I will make them good and strong. But, if they persist in worshipping false gods, they will be destroyed. Go and tell them this."

Some time later, Jeremiah bought a clay jar from the potter. Then he went to the Valley of Ben Hinnom and summoned everybody. He told them what the Lord had said. And, to illustrate his point, Jeremiah picked up the jar and threw it on the ground, destroying it. "This is what the Lord will do to you if you do not change your ways!" he warned.

As usual, no one listened, but soon enough, Jeremiah's prophecy came true. Under Nebuchadnezzar, the Babylonian army attacked Jerusalem. After months of suffering the city was captured. King Jehoiachin and the people were exiled to Babylon. Nebuchadnezzar chose a new king, Zedekiah, to be king of Judah.

"Like the clay in the hand of the potter, so is the House of Israel in my hands."

Almond tree
The almond is symbolic because it was the first tree to flower in the spring. The Hebrew for "almond tree" is similar to "watching." The story says that God is watching to see if His word is kept by everyone.

Figs
This soft, pear-shaped fruit is mentioned many times in the Bible. Here, the figs are a metaphor for good and bad. The ripe figs are compared to repentant people whom God will forgive. The rotten figs are bad people who will be punished.

One day, the Lord showed Jeremiah two baskets of figs. One of them was full of perfect fruit. The other basket had only rotten figs. "What do you see, Jeremiah?"

"I see figs," he replied. "The good ones are very good, but the bad ones are rotten."

"Yes," said the Lord. "The people who have left Judah and gone to Babylon are like the ripe figs. They will repent and I will bring them out of captivity to be my people. But King Zedekiah and the people who remain in Jerusalem will not repent. They are rotten and I will destroy them!"

Jeremiah breaks the jar to show the people that God will destroy them if they don't change

Understanding the story

The clay jar is used as a metaphor for what will happen to the people of Judah if they do not stop worshipping false gods. A priest and a prophet, Jeremiah conveys this message from the Lord by smashing the jar on the ground. Though the people ignore him, Jeremiah is proven right. The enemy attacks and those who remain in the city will suffer God's punishment.

Nebuchadnezzar
While Jeremiah was a kind prophet, Nebuchadnezzar was a cruel king. Jeremiah viewed Nebuchadnezzar as a representation of God's anger, so he told the people to submit to his rule or face disaster. Jeremiah correctly predicts the fall of Jerusalem and the Israelites' deportation to Babylon as a result of not heeding his warning.

Cistern
Built in about 2500 BCE in a desert region of southern Israel, this deep well leads down to a cistern similar to the one where Jeremiah was trapped. Jeremiah only survives this terrible punishment because there was no water inside. Water was usually hoisted up in a bucket attached to a rope in the underground tank.

The Israelites in Captivity

For years, the prophet Jeremiah had tried to warn the people that Jerusalem was in terrible danger. He knew that they could save themselves.

"The Lord has told me that, if you leave the city and go to Babylon, you will survive," he said to them. "But if you stay here in Jerusalem, you will be killed—either by the sword or by famine or plague. It is your choice!"

The people were infuriated by his constant warnings of doom and gloom and did not believe a word of them. Some army officers decided to take action. They went to King Zedekiah in the palace. "This man Jeremiah, who calls himself a prophet, has gone too far! He should be put to death!" they said. "He is demoralizing the troops—and everybody else who is left in Jerusalem. He pretends to be concerned with our well-being but, in fact, he is doing much more harm than good!"

"Do what you want with him," muttered the king. His thoughts were far away on more important business—he was plotting how to get his own back on the Babylonians, who made his life a misery.

So the officers seized Jeremiah and tied him up. They took him to their barracks where there was a courtyard with a large, empty water cistern. They lowered him over the side. Although there was no water, there was mud at the bottom, and Jeremiah sank into it up to his waist. He was left there, helpless, with no escape.

But when a palace official named Ebed-Melech heard what they had done to Jeremiah, he went to the king and protested. "My Lord," he said. "Those men are out of order! They have done a terrible thing to the prophet Jeremiah and thrown him into a huge cistern. He can't get out and he will surely starve to death!" The king agreed that Jeremiah must be rescued.

Ebed-Melech took some old rope and a bundle of old rags. Then, with thirty men, he went to the cistern. Ebed-Melech leant over the side and peered down into the darkness. He could just see Jeremiah huddled at the bottom. "Put these rags under your arms to pad the ropes," he shouted, letting down the ropes and the rags. Jeremiah made a makeshift harness for himself and Ebed-Melech and his men slowly hauled him up to the surface.

After his lucky escape, Jeremiah renewed his efforts to warn the people of their fate, but still they would not listen. And soon, King Nebuchadnezzar of Babylon attacked the city again and laid siege to it. The people were starved into submission. After two long years,

they finally opened the gates and let the invaders in.

When the Babylonian army entered the city, King Zedekiah fled as fast as he could. The Babylonians pursued him and caught up with him on the plains of Jericho. Zedekiah's two sons were put to death in front of his very eyes. Then they put out Zedekiah's eyes with burning stakes, and they took him to Babylon, blind and bound with shackles. All the most important people were deported from Jerusalem and sent into exile in Babylon. Only the very poor stayed in Judah, working in the vineyards and the fields.

The invaders swarmed into the holy Temple in the middle of the city, looting whatever they could get their hands on. They stole the precious gold treasures that had been there since the time of King Solomon. Then they set fire to the entire building, together with the royal palace and most of the houses. The whole city went up in flames, like a tinderbox, and was burned to the ground.

"All the most important people were deported from Jerusalem and sent into exile in Babylon."

Understanding the story

Judah was a vassal of Babylon and Nebuchadnezzar had put Zedekiah on the throne. When Zedekiah plots against the Babylonians, Nebuchadnezzar attacks Jerusalem. The destruction of Jerusalem and the exile of the people are God's punishment for their disobedience. Jeremiah had repeatedly warned them of this, but their refusal to listen brings devastating consequences.

Ishtar Gate
Babylon became the capital of Nebuchadnezzar's kingdom. He had the great Ishtar Gate built in about 575 BCE as the gateway to enter the city. The gate was dedicated to the Babylonian goddess Ishtar. This reconstruction of the gate in Berlin, Germany, was made with decorative glazed bricks uncovered at the site.

Babylonian priest
This Babylonian seal depicts a bare-headed priest praying to divine symbols of two Babylonian gods. The crescent moon represents the moon god Sin and the star represents Ishtar, the goddess of love and war. Here they are each positioned on an altar.

The Golden Statue

Nebuchadnezzar had been king of Babylon for two years. He had conquered Jerusalem and brought back many of the people as slaves to his city.

One night, Nebuchadnezzar had a dream that disturbed him deeply. He summoned the wise men and asked for their help. "I have had a strange dream. I can't stop thinking about it," he told them. "Tell me what it means!"

"O King! Please live forever!" they flattered him. "Tell us your dream and we will interpret it for you."

"This is the deal," said the king. "If you cannot tell me my dream and what it means, I will have you cut into pieces and your houses reduced to piles of rubble. But, if you can interpret my dream, I will give you huge rewards and honors!"

There was a terrible silence. Not one of them had any idea what the dream was or what it meant. "O King! What you ask is impossible!" they cried. Nebuchadnezzar was furious and he immediately ordered the execution of every single wise man in Babylon.

One of them was a young man named Daniel who had been captured in Jerusalem. He had been singled out, together with a few other captives from Judah, to be taught the language and history of Babylon. They were then taken into the king's service. Daniel soon became good friends with three of the other young men. They had been given new Babylonian names—Shadrach, Meshach, and Abednego. Daniel himself was now known as Belteshazzar. All four of them were clever, but Daniel had a special gift. He could interpret dreams.

So, when he heard about Nebuchadnezzar's terrible decree, Daniel went to the king and asked if he might be allowed to try to interpret the dream. The king agreed, but first Daniel went back to his house, where he and his three friends prayed for help from God. During that night, the mystery was revealed to him and, when he woke up in the morning, he knew what the dream meant. He gave thanks to the Lord. "Praise be to the name of God forever and ever. Wisdom and power are His."

He went to Nebuchadnezzar and said, "No wise man, enchanter, magician, or diviner can explain your dream, but God in heaven can reveal the mystery. He has shown me the meaning of your dream." Nebuchadnezzar told him to go on.

"You saw a gigantic statue in your dream. The head was made of pure gold, the chest and arms of silver, the belly and thighs of bronze. The legs were made of iron while the feet and toes were half iron and half baked clay." Nebuchadnezzar listened, open-mouthed, while Daniel continued.

"As you gazed at the statue, a rock suddenly came through the air from

Daniel meets Nebuchadnezzar in this oil-on-canvas painting by Italian artist Mattia Preti (1613–1699)

nowhere and hit the statue's feet, breaking them into tiny pieces. At once, all the other parts of the statue—the gold, silver, bronze, iron, and clay—were smashed to pieces, like chaff on the threshing-floor in summer. The wind swept them away without a trace. But the rock became a huge mountain and filled the whole earth." Daniel paused for breath while Nebuchadnezzar sat, transfixed, on his throne.

"Now I will tell you what it means," Daniel went on. "You, O King, are the king of kings. The God of heaven has given you dominion and power over your people, the beasts of the field, and the birds of the air. The statue's head of gold represents you. The silver represents another kingdom that will rise after you, but it will be inferior to yours. Next, there will be a third kingdom, one of bronze, which will rule over the whole earth. Finally, there will be a fourth kingdom, strong as iron. And, just as iron can break things, so this kingdom will crush and break all others. But, as you saw, the feet and toes of the statue were made of iron and baked clay, so this will be a divided kingdom.

"The rock that destroyed these kingdoms is the Kingdom of God. It is greater than any kingdom on earth and will never be destroyed."

King Nebuchadnezzar fell at Daniel's feet crying, "Surely your God is the God of gods and the Lord of kings. He is the revealer of mysteries!" The king heaped lavish gifts on Daniel and made him governor of Babylon. He also put him in charge of the wise men. And, at Daniel's request, he gave Shadrach, Meshach, and Abednego important positions, too.

Then, he ordered a statue to be made. It was gigantic and the whole thing was

Dream interpretation
In King Nebuchadnezzar's dream, there are four kingdoms represented by the great statue. These have traditionally been identified as Babylon (gold)—the city ruins are shown above, Persia (silver), Greece (bronze), and Rome (iron). As the strength of the metals increases, so too does the endurance of each empire. The rock that turns into a mountain symbolizes the Kingdom of God—the kingdom that will last forever.

"Surely your God is the God of gods and the Lord of kings. He is the revealer of mysteries!"

"They were willing to give up their lives rather than worship any god except their own."

made of solid gold. Nebuchadnezzar summoned all the officials and told them to worship the statue. If they did not, they would be thrown into a blazing furnace.

But Shadrach, Meshach, and Abednego refused. "If we are thrown into the blazing furnace our God will save us. But even if He did not, we would never worship your golden statue," they said. Upon hearing this, the king told his men to stoke the furnace and make it seven times hotter than usual. Then he ordered his soldiers to take the three men, tie them up, and throw them into the flames. But as they did so, the flames licked out of the furnace and devoured the soldiers themselves.

The king looked into the fire. "Look!" he shouted. "I can see four men wandering around in there. They aren't tied up and they seem completely unharmed. The fourth one looks like a son of the gods!" Cautiously, he crept nearer. "Shadrach, Meshach, and Abednego," he shouted. "Come out at once!"

They obeyed and walked calmly out of the furnace, not a hair singed. Everyone crowded around them in amazement. Then Nebuchadnezzar proclaimed, "Praise be to the God of Shadrach, Meshach, and Abednego, who has sent His angel and rescued His servants! They trusted in Him and defied my command. They were willing to give up their lives rather than worship any god except their own. I decree that my people shall worship their God alone!"

Furnace
Babylonian builders fired bricks or smelted metals in huge furnaces, like this 14th-century-BCE copper-smelting furnace in Israel. Lined with bricks or stones, furnaces were usually bottle- or dome-shaped. Bellows were used to increase the temperature to 1652–1832°F (900–1100°C). Fire and furnaces are linked to God's judgement and salvation in the Bible.

A 15th-century-CE German painting, "Shadrach, Meshach, and Abednego," oil on panel.

Understanding the story

Just like Joseph in Egypt, Daniel interprets a king's dream in a foreign land. The Lord works through both Joseph and Daniel, and, though neither man seeks it, both are rewarded with high positions under the king. Once again, God shows that He has not forgotten His people in exile, protecting and guiding those who keep faith in Him.

Belshazzar's Feast

King Belshazzar gave a great banquet for a thousand of his nobles.

He ordered his servants to bring in the gold and silver cups that Nebuchadnezzar, his father, had plundered from the Lord's Temple in Jerusalem. The precious cups were filled to the brim. Belshazzar and his guests raised them high in the air. And then they drank from them, toasting their gods. But, suddenly, the king turned pale. He stared at the wall opposite him. A ghostly hand had appeared from nowhere and was floating there, all on its own. Slowly its finger wrote some words on the wall. It looked like a secret code: MENE, MENE, TEKEL, PARSIN. Then the hand melted away, leaving its message behind. Belshazzar asked his wise men what the words meant, but they were baffled.

The queen, however, knew what to do. "There is a man in your kingdom named Daniel—or Belteshazzar to his Babylonian friends. He will tell you what the writing means." Daniel was found and brought to the palace. Belshazzar showed him the writing and said, "If you can tell me what it means, you will be clothed in purple with a gold chain around your neck, and you will be made the third highest ruler in the kingdom."

"You may keep your gifts and rewards," replied Daniel. "But I will read the writing and tell you what it means." And he examined the wall carefully. Then he said, "God sent the hand you saw that wrote on the wall. MENE, MENE, TEKEL, PARSIN means three things. First, God has numbered the days of your reign. Secondly, you have been weighed on the scales and been found wanting. And thirdly, your kingdom will be divided and given to the Medes and the Persians." Belshazzar listened in horror to Daniel's words.

That very night, the Persian army launched a surprise attack on Babylon under King Darius the Mede. And, just as the cryptic words predicted, the city fell and was taken by the Medes and the Persians, and Belshazzar was killed.

Understanding the story

King Belshazzar and his guests toast their gods from the sacred cups plundered from the Temple, invoking punishment from God. Daniel's interpretation is again proven correct, as Belshazzar dies and the city is divided between the Medes and Persians that same night. Babylon's might is nothing in comparison to that of God.

"Belshazzar's Feast" (c. 1635), oil on canvas, by Dutch artist Rembrandt van Rijn

Daniel and the Lions

Lion of Babylon
Representing royalty, power, and strength, the lion was adopted as a symbol of Babylon. This reconstruction of the gateway to Babylon features a lion motif. Lion hunting was a favorite sport of Babylonian kings. Lions were also kept in captivity and bred.

After Babylon was conquered it became one of the great Persian Empire's royal cities. King Darius made Daniel one of his chief administrators and planned to put him in charge of the entire kingdom.

"May your God, whom you serve so well, rescue you,' Darius said, sadly, as Daniel was thrown inside and left to his fate."

This made the other officials at court very jealous. They tried to undermine Daniel and put him down whenever they could, but there was simply no way of getting at him. "We will never be able to pin anything on him," they said. "The only way is to make him disobey his God." And together they hatched a plan.

They went to Darius and said, "O King Darius! Live forever! We ask you to issue a decree that, for the next thirty days, the worship of any god, other than you, the King, is forbidden. Anyone caught worshipping another god will be thrown into the lions' den. Please make sure that it is written down so it cannot be changed." Darius agreed and called for the royal scribe.

Daniel heard about the decree, but went on praying to the Lord three times a day, as usual, at home in his room upstairs. The big windows opened toward Jerusalem and everyone could see him clearly, kneeling down to worship his God. His enemies gathered in the street below and watched him.

Then they went straight to the palace to denounce him. "Daniel pays no attention to you, O King. Or to the decree you put in writing," they told him gleefully. "He still prays to his God three times a day."

Darius was distressed when he heard this. Daniel was one of his most trusted men. He spent the rest of the day trying to think how

he could save him. But the conspirators were not going to give up. "Remember, O King, that, according to the law of the Medes and the Persians, no decree that the king issues can be changed."

With a heavy heart, Darius gave the order to arrest Daniel, who was seized as he kneeled at his window to pray. He was taken to the lions' den, and the king accompanied him. As they approached the enclosure they could hear blood-curdling roars from inside. "May your God, whom you serve so well, rescue you," Darius said, sadly, as Daniel was thrown inside and left to his fate.

A huge stone was rolled across the mouth of the den. Darius sealed it with his signet ring. He returned to the palace, but he could not sleep.

At dawn, he hurried to the lions' den, dreading what he would find. All was quiet. He called out, his voice trembling with fear. To his amazement, he heard Daniel saying, "O King! Live forever! My God sent His angel and He shut the mouths of the lions. They have not hurt me because I am innocent in His sight. Nor have I ever done wrong to you, O King."

Darius was overjoyed and ordered Daniel's release. The stone was duly rolled away and he walked out calmly, without even the tiniest scratch. Behind him, the lions opened their great jaws and yawned, watching him go. Darius ordered his men to arrest the conspirators. They were thrown into the lions' den, and this time, it was a very different story. Before their bodies reached the ground, the lions pounced, tearing them limb from limb. The lions devoured their flesh and lay there happily, gnawing on the bones.

Understanding the story

Though Daniel is now a powerful figure in the Persian Empire, he never loses his faith or integrity. He chooses to ignore the decree that forbids the worship of anyone but the king, and continues to pray to God. Even when he is thrown into the lions' den, Daniel is fearless because he knows he has the Lord on his side to protect him. It is a different story for the officials who tricked the king—the lions devour them without hesitation.

Drinking vessel
King Xerxes loved extravagant festivities that displayed his power and wealth to the people. Lavish furnishings and ornately decorated items of gold symbolized his success. This impressive 5th-century-BCE gold drinking vessel comes from the same period. It has been handcrafted with a repeated lotus and bud pattern around the drinking rim. The winged lion represents great strength and power.

Esther Becomes Queen

King Xerxes ruled over all the different provinces of the Persian Empire, from India to the Nile.

In the third year of his reign, he gave a lavish banquet for his nobles and military leaders at his palace in Susa. It lasted a week and was a glittering occasion. On the seventh day, when King Xerxes was in particularly high spirits, he sent for Queen Vashti. She had been entertaining her women friends in another part of the royal palace. And now, Xerxes wanted to show off his beautiful wife. But the queen refused to come.

King Xerxes exploded with fury. He had been snubbed in front of all the important dignitaries. Immediately, he called for his wise men. "According to the law, what must be done to Queen Vashti?" he asked them, still seething with rage. "She has not obeyed my command!" They told him to find a new wife who was more suitable.

Xerxes followed their advice, and emissaries were sent far and wide to find a new queen. Hundreds of suitable candidates were brought back—all beautiful and young. They were looked after well and were taught how to make themselves look even more beautiful. But it was a whole year before King Xerxes was allowed to see them and choose his queen.

One of the girls was named Hadassah—or Esther. She had been brought up by her cousin, Mordecai, after her parents died. Mordecai was a Jew who belonged to the tribe of Benjamin and he had been captured in Jerusalem by King Nebuchadnezzar. When she joined the other girls at the royal palace, Esther was warned by Mordecai not to tell anyone about her family background. He thought that Xerxes would not look kindly on a Jewish girl.

At last, after a year of preening and polishing, the girls were presented to the king. They shone like jewels as they appeared before him. It was an impossible choice. But when Xerxes saw Esther, he fell helplessly in love. He beckoned her to him immediately and sent the other girls back to their quarters. He made Esther his wife soon after, and gave a great banquet, proclaiming a special holiday.

One day, during the course of his duties at court, Mordecai overheard two of the officers, on guard at the gate, discussing a plan to assassinate Xerxes. He went straight to his cousin, Esther, and told her about the plot. She immediately informed Xerxes, and the two conspirators were arrested. King Xerxes's life had been saved. The chief scribe carefully noted this down, along with the rest of the day's events, in the Book of Chronicles.

But Mordecai was not happy when Xerxes appointed Haman, who was an Amalekite, as chief minister. The Israelites and the Amalekites had been fierce enemies since the time when the Israelites left Egypt. All the royal officials were commanded to bow down before Haman and honor him, but Mordecai refused point-blank. Haman was infuriated by Mordecai's lack of respect. When he discovered that Mordecai was a Jew, he decided that he would have him killed. And not only Mordecai—all his people, too.

Haman and his men cast the little stones known as the pur—or the lot—to choose a time for the massacre of the Jews. The lot fell on the thirteenth day of the twelfth month. Haman went straight to Xerxes. "There is a certain people whose customs are different from those of other people in your kingdom," he said. "They do not obey your laws. If it pleases the King, let a decree be issued to destroy them."

The king agreed and gave him his signet ring. "Do as you please with these people," he said. So the royal scribes were summoned and they wrote out the decrees in all the many different languages of the empire, telling the governors to kill all the Jews on the thirteenth day of the twelfth month.

When Mordecai heard the terrible news, he told Esther of Haman's plans to get rid of the Jewish people. She replied, "Go, gather together all the Jews who are in Susa and fast for me. Do not eat or drink for three days, night or day. I and my maids will fast as you do. When this is done, I will go to the king, even though it is against the law. And if I perish, I perish."

Cosmetics
It is likely that the women presented to the king would have styled their hair and worn cosmetics and perfume in their efforts to impress him and catch his eye. Mulberries (top) were crushed into juice, which was use to stain cheeks red. Kohl was used to outline and emphasize the eyes. Henna (below the mulberries) covered the palms of the hands in decorative patterns.

"There is a certain people whose customs are different from those of other people in your kingdom."

Understanding the story

On the advice of her cousin Mordecai, Esther doesn't tell King Xerxes about her Jewish family background. The king is dazzled by Esther's beauty and they wed. When Haman asks for a decree to destroy all the Jews, Xerxes grants it. Unaware that his wife is Jewish, the king does not realize the consequences of his action. Esther is prepared to risk her life in order to save the Jewish people.

"I and my people are about to be put to death like animals."

Esther Saves Her People

After Esther had fasted for three days, she put on her ceremonial robes and went to the inner court of the palace, in front of the King's great hall.

Xerxes was sitting on his magnificent throne opposite the door, deep in thought. When he saw her, his face lit up and he held out the golden scepter in his hand toward her. This was the sign that she was allowed to approach him. She smiled and went straight to him, touching the tip of the scepter.

"What is it, my dearest?" he asked fondly. "What is your request? You know I would give you half my kingdom!"

"If it pleases, my Lord, I would like to prepare a banquet for you tomorrow evening. Please come—and bring the chief minister, Haman, with you. Then I will answer your question." Xerxes agreed, gladly, knowing that his wife would make sure that he was offered all his favorite dishes.

Haman was delighted when he got the invitation and boasted about it to his wife and friends. "I am the only person that Queen Esther has invited to accompany the King to her banquet!" he gloated, pink with pleasure. Then his face darkened. "But all this gives me no satisfaction as long as I see that Jew Mordecai sitting at the King's gate!"

His wife, Zeresh, and his friends said, "Have a gallows built and tomorrow morning ask the King to have Mordecai hanged on it. Then go to the banquet and

Scroll of Esther
The story of Esther saving the Jews from death is remembered at the festival of Purim. This is a joyful celebration in which a scroll containing the book of Esther is read aloud in the synagogue. The scroll is often ornate and decorative, like this silver example. The reading receives a noisy response. At the mention of the villainous Haman's name, people boo and stamp their feet.

be happy!" The suggestion delighted Haman and he immediately ordered the huge gallows to be built outside his house.

That night, Xerxes could not sleep, so he asked for the Book of Chronicles to be brought to him. He opened the book and started to skim through it. When he came to the bit that described how Mordecai had saved his life by uncovering a plot against him, he sat bolt upright. "What honor and recognition did this man, Mordecai, receive?" he asked his attendant in the bedchamber.

"Nothing, my Lord," the attendant replied.

Early the next morning, when Haman requested an audience with the King to discuss hanging Mordecai, Xerxes asked him, "There is someone I want to honor for a great service that they did for me. How can I reward him?"

Haman's gallows

Naturally, Haman thought that the King was talking about him, and that he was about to be heaped with yet more favors. "He should be proclaimed a hero! He should be dressed in a magnificent royal robe and put on the King's horse," he replied. "Then he should be led through the streets of the city in triumph!"

"Excellent!" said Xerxes. "What a good idea! Go and get my finest robe for my servant Mordecai, put him on my very best horse, and parade him through the streets! You can walk by his side!" Haman went very pale!

That evening, Xerxes and Haman went together to Esther's banquet. The three of them sat down to eat and Xerxes repeated his question. "What is it, Queen Esther? What is your request? You know I will give you half my kingdom!"

"If I have found favor with you, O King, and if it pleases your majesty, grant me my life—that is my request," she replied. "For I and my people are about to be put to death like animals. We are going to be exterminated."

The King leaped up from the table. "What? Who is he? Where is the man who would dare do such a thing?" he thundered.

Esther stared at Haman. "That is your man. He is sitting there right in front of you! It is the unspeakable Haman," she said.

Xerxes gasped in disbelief. Then he turned and left the room, without saying anything. He paced up and down in the palace garden as the full horror sank in. While he was gone, Haman threw himself on Esther, begging for his life. He was hysterical and, just as the King returned, he was clutching at the Queen like a madman. Xerxes thought he was harming her, so he gave the order for Haman to be taken away immediately.

"There is a huge gallows just by his house," said one of the attendants, helpfully. "He had it made for Mordecai, the loyal servant who saved your life!" So they hanged Haman on the gallows he had prepared for Mordecai.

Prisoners' fate
The Bible states that Haman died on the gallows. However, hanging was rare in Persia at that time. Prisoners set to be executed were more likely to be impaled on a stake. Judean prisoners are impaled on stakes in this carving dating from c. 700 BCE.

Understanding the story

The only book of the Bible that does not include God by name is the Book of Esther. Despite this, the Lord's influence is clear as the wicked are punished and the faithful are saved. Greedy Haman's plan to destroy the Jews comes undone at the hands of two of the people he seeks to kill when Esther and Mordecai expose his plot. Esther is the king's wife and Mordecai saved the king's life, so Xerxes has the treacherous Haman hanged.

When Mordecai left the king's presence, he was wearing royal garments of blue and white, a large crown of gold, and a purple robe of fine linen. And the city of Susa held a joyous celebration. For the Jews it was a time of happiness and joy, gladness and honor.

Esther 8:15–16

Susa

Susa was the capital of the state of Elam, and later became the winter capital of the Persian kings. Today, it is the Iranian town of Shush, with a population of 65,000 people.

Stonemasonry
Rebuilding Jerusalem was a huge task, so skilled stonemasons would have carried out the work. Firstly, wooden pegs were banged into holes in the rock before water was poured over them. As the wood swelled up, the rock split. A pick was then used to saw and trim the rock into slabs. Stonemasons in the Middle East still work in this way today.

The Rebuilding of Jerusalem

Over the years, some of the people who had been exiled from Judah and taken to Babylon were given their freedom by King Artaxerxes and allowed to return home.

A few came back to court again with sad tales of the city of Jerusalem. Nehemiah, who was the cupbearer to King Artaxerxes, heard the stories and was deeply affected. He mourned and he fasted and prayed to God, asking for mercy. "I confess the sins we Israelites have committed against you. We have not obeyed the commands, decrees, and laws you gave your servant Moses. You said that if we were unfaithful we would be scattered among the nations. But if we came back to you and obeyed your commands, we would be together again and returned to your dwelling place."

That day, when he took a goblet of wine to Artaxerxes, the king looked at him and asked, "Why do you look so sad? What grieves you so deep in your heart?"

"May the King live forever!" said Nehemiah. "But why should I not look sad when the city where my fathers are buried lies in ruins and has been destroyed by fire?" And he asked the king if he could go to Jerusalem to help rebuild it. Artaxerxes agreed and helped him on his way with letters of safe passage and an armed escort. It was a journey of four months from the royal palace in Susa to Judah.

As Nehemiah reached Jerusalem, he saw that the city was in ruins. The walls were rubble, and the holy Temple and royal palace were charred. One night, he set out to inspect the city on his donkey, then summoned the people. "Let us rebuild the walls of Jerusalem!" he said. "Our great city lies in ruins. It is a disgrace. Let us pray to the Lord our God to help us!"

Some people mocked him. "You haven't a chance," they jeered.

"The God of heaven will give us success," said Nehemiah quietly. "We will start rebuilding the city."

Sanballat, the governor of Samaria to the north, was incensed when he heard that Nehemiah was organizing the rebuilding work. "What are those feeble Jews doing?" he asked. "Do they think that they can build those great walls again? Can they bring back to life the stones that have been reduced to piles of rubble?"

But, despite the resentment and threats from the neighboring countries, Nehemiah and his people started rebuilding the great wall of Jerusalem. Nehemiah put some men in front of the weakest places, armed with swords, spears, and bows, to prevent attack. "Do not be afraid," he said to them. "Remember the Lord, and fight for your brothers, your sons, your daughters, your wives, and your homes."

From then on, half of the workforce got on with building while the other half stood guard. After only fifty-two days, the walls were finished and Jerusalem stood, safe and secure, once more. The neighboring nations could not believe their eyes and they were filled with fear. They realized that the work had been done with the help of God. And the people of Judah flooded back from exile to the land of their fathers. There were more than forty-two thousand of them.

The people assembled in the square in front of the Water Gate, and Ezra brought out the Book of the Law of Moses and read it aloud. He praised the Lord and the people cried "Amen! Amen!" Together, they bowed down and worshipped God. And the Levites came to dedicate the great new walls to the Lord, and to celebrate with songs of thanksgiving and with the music of cymbals, harps, and lyres.

"Our great city lies in ruins. It is a disgrace. Let us pray to the Lord our God to help us!"

Understanding the story

The return of the exiled Jews to the Promised Land echoes the Exodus. Just like Moses before him, Nehemiah leads the Israelites to a new beginning, and a chance at a closer relationship with God. The rebuilding of Jerusalem's walls is completed quickly, to the fear of the neighboring countries, who realize that God must be helping to resurrect the holy city.

Jonah and the Big Fish

And God told His prophet Jonah that he must go to Nineveh, the capital of Assyria, to warn the people that their great walled city would be destroyed if they did not give up their wicked ways.

Sperm whale
Though the Bible describes a large fish, it was more likely to be a sperm whale. These were known to visit parts of the Mediterranean Sea, and their throats were big enough to swallow a person whole. There are personal testimonies of people who managed to survive being swallowed by whales. This is because whales must surface regularly for air, allowing the person to escape.

But Jonah did not like the people of Nineveh and did not want to see them saved, so he disobeyed the Lord. He fled to Joppa, a harbor in Israel, and boarded a ship to Tarshish, on the eastern shores of the Mediterranean.

The sea was calm and the skies were clear but, as soon as the ship set sail, dark clouds gathered and a violent storm howled across the water, whipping it into towering waves that crashed wildly onto the little ship. Terrified, the sailors prayed to their different gods and threw the cargo overboard to lighten the ship's heavy load.

Jonah, meanwhile, had fallen fast asleep below deck and was dead to the world. The captain raced down and shook him furiously. "Wake up! How can you sleep at a time like this? Pray to your God that we are saved." Up on deck the rest of the crew were busy drawing lots to find out who was responsible for their terrible predicament. It was Jonah.

The crew challenged Jonah and he admitted that the storm was his fault because he had disobeyed his God. "Pick me up and throw me into the sea, and it will become calm," he said. The sailors were doubtful about this and tried to row for shore, but the waves became wilder. Reluctantly, they threw Jonah over the side and into the sea. As if by magic, the raging waters grew calm and they were saved. The sailors, amazed and a little afraid at the

"But Jonah was angry with God for sparing Nineveh."

power of Jonah's God, offered up prayers and gave thanks.

Jonah sank to the bottom of the sea, long streamers of seaweed trailing behind him. Suddenly, a huge fish appeared out of the gloom, opened its jaws, and swallowed Jonah whole. He slid headfirst into the creature's great empty belly and stayed there, praying to God, for three days and nights in the dark.

Finally, he proclaimed, "Salvation belongs to the Lord!" The fish opened its mouth and dropped Jonah onto dry land, safe and sound.

Again, the Lord told Jonah to go to Nineveh. This time he obeyed and set off on the long journey. The king welcomed him and heeded his warning. He promised that his people would turn to God. They started to fast and wear clothes of sackcloth to show how sorry they were for their bad behavior. Even the king took off his royal robes and covered himself with sackcloth. The city was saved.

But Jonah was angry with God for sparing Nineveh. He built a shelter outside the city walls and waited there, hoping that the city would fall after all. God watched over him and planted a tall shrub to shade him from the sun. Jonah was thankful for the cool leaves. But the next day, God sent a worm that ate the roots of the plant and killed it. Despite the hot sun and strong wind, Jonah kept watch, weak and angry that the plant had died. "It would be better for me to die," he moaned.

"Jonah, why are you so angry about a plant that you did not grow or tend?" God asked. "Yet you resent my concern for the great city of Nineveh and the thousands of people who live there?"

Understanding the story

This story is about the consequences of not obeying God's orders. Jonah does not accept that God should extend His mercy to the Ninevites—who are enemies of the Israelites and are gentiles (non-Jews). The storm and the big fish are Jonah's punishment, but when he realizes the error of his ways, he is spared. When Jonah remains angry that God has spared the repentant Ninevites, God kills his plant. God is showing Jonah his error in being concerned for a plant instead of the lives of thousands of people.

The Book of Psalms

David the Psalmist
King David was a talented musician. He is said to have started the custom of composing songs for worship, and is believed to be the author behind a lot of Book of Psalms. He is seen here kneeling outside Jerusalem in a 15th-century depiction.

The Book of Psalms is also known as the Psalter. In Hebrew, it is called the Book of Praises.

It contains one hundred and fifty different prayers addressed to God, including laments, praises, and thanksgivings. Many of them are thought to have been written by King David, who was a poet as well as a singer and musician.

The very first psalm, whose author is not known, introduces the themes that recur throughout the whole book—devotion, thanksgiving, and unwavering faith in God.

It says that only those who follow the path of righteousness will ultimately be blessed by God.

"Blessed is the man who does not walk in the counsel of the wicked or stand in the way of sinners or sit in the seat of mockers. But his delight is in the law of the Lord, and on His law he meditates day and night."

In ancient Israel, the law was studied every day. A deep knowledge of the law was a way of getting closer to God.

Psalm 8, attributed to King David, celebrates man's dominion over the earth. It is a reflection of God's greatness and recognizes man's insignificance in comparison to the glory of God's creation.

"O Lord, our Lord, how majestic is your name in all the earth! You have set your glory above the heavens. From the lips of children and infants you have ordained praise. Because of your enemies, to silence the foe and the avenger. When I consider your heavens, the work of your fingers, the moon and the stars, which you have set in place, what is man that you are mindful of him, the son of man that you care for him? You made him a little lower than the heavenly beings and crowned him with glory and honor. You made him ruler over the works of your hands; you put everything under his feet: all flocks and herds, and the beasts of the field, the birds of the air, and the fish of the sea, all that swim the paths of the seas."

Psalm 23, one of the most famous psalms, is also attributed to David. It describes God as a good shepherd, looking after His sheep. Man can live free from fear because He is always there to protect and guide His flock.

"The Lord is my shepherd, I shall not be in want. He makes me lie down in green pastures, He leads me beside quiet waters, He restores my soul. He guides me in the paths of righteousness for His name's sake. Even though I walk through the valley of the shadow of death, I will fear no evil, for you are with me; your rod and your staff, they comfort me. You prepare a table before me in the presence of my enemies. You anoint my head with oil; my cup overflows. Surely goodness and love will follow me all the days of my life, and I will dwell in the house of the Lord for ever."

Psalm 121 is the second in a collection of fifteen psalms called "Songs of Ascents." These psalms were sung during the annual religious pilgrimages to Jerusalem.

"I will lift up my eyes to the hills—where does my help come from? My help comes from the Lord, the Maker of heaven and earth. He will not let your foot slip—He who watches over you will not slumber; indeed, He who watches over Israel will neither slumber nor sleep. The Lord watches over you—the Lord is your shade at your right hand; the sun will not harm you by day, nor the moon by night. The Lord will keep you from all harm—He will watch over your life; the Lord will watch over your coming and going both now and for evermore.

Psalter

Illustrated books containing the text of the Psalms together with accompanying music are called Psalters. This comes from the Greek meaning "songs accompanied by the harp." These decorative books feature illuminated initials and ornate lettering interspersed with musical notation. Shown here, the Mainz Psalter (c. 1457) was one of the first books printed in Europe. Today, Psalters are used in worship—either sung by choirs or accompanied by music.

Understanding the story

In this collection of joyful prayers to God, the message is that those who keep on the path of righteousness will receive the Lord's blessing and enter the Kingdom of Heaven. Love, devotion, and faith are themes repeated throughout. God is depicted as a good shepherd, caring and tending for His flock. He will provide all the protection and shelter His people need.

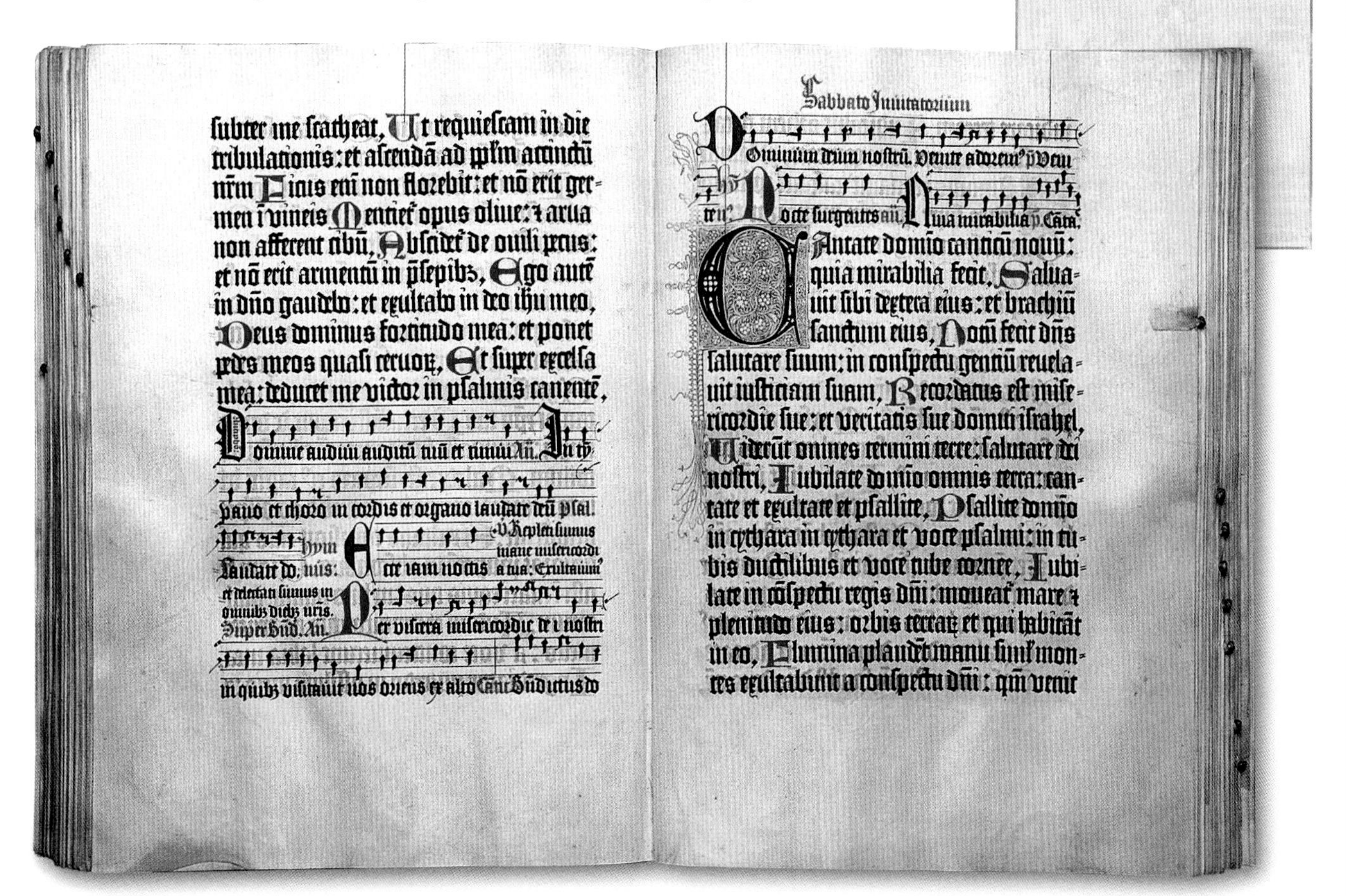

The New Testament

"I am the good shepherd. The good shepherd lays down his life for the sheep... I am the good shepherd; I know my sheep and my sheep know me."

John 10:11, 14

New Testament

The New Testament is the second part of the Christian Bible. It was written nearly 2,000 years ago, and, across 27 books, it tells the story of Jesus's life and teaching and the early Christian Church, and ends with a vision of the world's end.

Parables
Jesus often taught by using parables—short stories that appear to be about everyday life, but which have a deeper moral to learn from. In the parable of the lost sheep, a shepherd finds one of his flock that was lost. In the same way, God is overjoyed when even one sinner returns to Him.

Paul's letters
The New Testament ends with the apostle Paul's (above) letters sent to the churches he established. There are 22 letters in the New Testament, and Paul is believed to have written at least 13 of them. His writings offer guidance on the core teachings of Jesus Christ and encouragement and support for the new Church leaders.

Miracles
The New Testament is full of examples of Jesus doing extraordinary things. These miracles often fulfill prophecies from the Old Testament. They include walking on water, calming storms, reviving the dead, and healing the blind, as shown in this 15th-century-CE relief.

Gospel authors

The four Gospels ("good news") proclaim Jesus Christ as the Messiah—the savior of mankind. They cover the life of Jesus Christ, and are attributed to four authors: Matthew, Mark, Luke, and John. Each of them gave a different perspective on the birth Jesus, his life, and his impact on the world.

Mark

The earliest and shortest of all the Gospels came from Mark. His main concern was conveying Jesus's message that the Kingdom of God was coming, and there was little time left to repent. Mark tells of an emotional and temperamental Jesus, who is misunderstood by his own disciples. The work was probably intended for non-Jewish readers, and explains many Jewish traditions and words.

Matthew

This narrative was meant to prove that Jesus was the Messiah. Formerly a tax collector from Capernaum, Matthew views Jesus's miracles as evidence that he is the fulfillment of the Old Testament prophecies. His Gospel includes an angry attack on the Jewish leaders, especially the Pharisees.

Luke

A doctor by profession, Luke was the only non-Jew known to write a book in the Bible. His Gospel is a biographical account of Jesus's relationships with everyday people. He uses examples to show that Jesus helped those in need and gave salvation to all nations. His gospel is the longest of the four apostle accounts.

John

This is the last Gospel and it reads very differently from the other three. Jesus is presented as a divine being visiting earth from heaven, who explains "I have come down from heaven not to do my will but to do the will of Him who sent me" (John 6:38). John uses symbolic ideas, such as light and dark, instead of including parables and miracles.

Revelation

The last book of the New Testament was called the Book of Revelation. Written by an exiled Jewish-Christian visionary named John, it was written to help strengthen the early Christian community in the face of persecution and suffering. In Revelation, Jesus returns in glory to save the righteous from the end of the world.

Augustus Caesar
At the time of King Herod, Israel belonged to Rome. Augustus Caesar (above) ruled from 31 BCE until 14 CE. When he took power, Rome changed from a republic to an empire.

Altar of incense
Priests often burned incense on a four-horned altar similar to this one. It was the only time Zechariah could enter the Temple sanctuary—the most holy of places in Israel.

A Son for Zechariah

In the time of King Herod of Judea, there was a priest named Zechariah who served in the splendid Temple at Jerusalem. He was a descendant of Aaron, the brother of Moses, and so was his wife Elizabeth.

They were good people who lived righteous lives and obeyed all the Lord's commandments. But they were both growing old and, to their great sadness, they had no children. This was considered something of a disgrace, and their neighbors pitied them.

One day, when he was on duty, Zechariah was chosen by the casting of lots—as was the custom—to go into the inner sanctuary of the Temple to burn the incense before the morning sacrifice. It was a huge honor and privilege. He walked through the doors adorned with embroidered curtains, which hid the inner and most sacred part of the Temple. Only the priest on duty was allowed to go there. Outside, in the main part of the building, the people had gathered to pray. Zechariah approached the magnificent golden altar in front of the Holy of Holies, where the Ark of the Covenant had once stood.

Slowly, he lit the incense and little clouds of smoke danced through the air, filling the sanctuary with a sweet and heady scent. And, when Zechariah looked up, he saw an angel standing there just to the right of the altar. He nearly jumped out of his skin.

But the angel held out his hands and said to him, kindly, "Do not be afraid, Zechariah. Your prayer has been heard. Your wife, Elizabeth, will bear you a son and you are to give him the name John. He will be a joy and delight to you, and many will rejoice because of his birth, for he will be great in the sight of the Lord. He is never to take wine or other fermented drink, and he will be filled with the Holy Spirit even from birth. Many are the people of Israel that he will bring back to the Lord their God."

Zechariah listened in amazement to the angel's words. "How can this be possible?" he asked. "I am an old man already—and my wife, Elizabeth, is well advanced in years, too."

"I am Gabriel," the angel replied. "God has sent me to tell you the good news. But, because you did not believe me, you have been struck dumb. You will not be able to speak a single word until what I have just told you comes true."

Meanwhile, the worshippers, waiting outside the sanctuary, were beginning to wonder why Zechariah was taking so long. He should have come out by now.

Finally, he appeared from behind the

"God has sent me to tell you the good news. But, because you did not believe me, you have been struck dumb."

doors and stood before them, unable to say a word. He made signs with his hands, pointing to the sanctuary and to his eyes and to the air, and they realized that he had seen a vision.

When Zechariah had finished his duties in the Temple, going silently about his business, he went home to his wife, Elizabeth. He was, of course, not able to tell her what he had seen and what he had been told. But, before very long, she discovered, to her great delight, that she was pregnant. She was overjoyed. For the next few months, she stayed at home, counting her blessings. "The Lord has done this for me," she said, gratefully. "He has shown me great mercy and taken away my disgrace."

Understanding the story

Society frowned on childless women at this time, considering their situation to be a punishment from God. However, boys with a special purpose in life were often born to older, childless women, and this is the case with Elizabeth. Apart from Jesus, her son John is the only one in the New Testament to be filled with the Holy Spirit from birth. Zechariah is struck dumb because he doubts the words of God's messenger Gabriel.

Nazareth
Gabriel appeared to Mary in the quiet town of Nazareth, but today it is a bustling city. The Church of the Annunciation is in the center of the picture. It was built to commemorate Gabriel's message for Mary.

"You will be with child and give birth to a son, and you are to give him the name Jesus."

An Angel Appears to Mary

God sent His messenger, the archangel Gabriel, to find a young woman named Mary, who lived in the small town of Nazareth in southern Galilee.

Mary, like her cousin Elizabeth, was descended from Aaron, the first high priest of Israel. She was betrothed to Joseph, a carpenter who lived and worked in Nazareth, and they would be married soon. Joseph's family tree went back through the generations to David, the first king of Israel.

The angel Gabriel appeared as Mary was sitting alone in her small garden. There was no-one else around. She looked at him, astonished, as he stood there in front of her. "Greetings, you are highly favored," he said. "The Lord is with you!"

Mary was deeply troubled by the apparition, which had arrived so suddenly, from nowhere. She did not understand why he had come to find her or what he was talking about. Then, as if he could read her mind, the angel went on, "Do not be afraid, Mary, you have found favor with God. You will be with child and give birth to a son, and you are to give him the name Jesus. He will be great and will be called the Son of the Most High. The Lord God will give him the throne of his father David, and he will reign over the house of Jacob forever. His kingdom will never end."

"How can this be?" asked Mary. "I am not married."

"The Holy Spirit will come upon you and the power of the Most High will overshadow you," the angel replied. "So the holy one to be born will be called the Son of God."

Mary said to the angel, "I'm ready for whatever God wants from me! If that's His will, then let it be."

And the angel went on to tell Mary that her elderly cousin Elizabeth, who was thought to be barren, was now in her sixth month of pregnancy. "For nothing is impossible with God," he said. Then he left her standing in the garden, her thoughts full of excitement and trust.

Understanding the story

The angel Gabriel's message, known as the Annunciation ("the announcing"), predicts that Mary will be the mother of God's son. Her conception of the baby Jesus is a miracle. Though he will be human, he will also be divine.

Italian Renaissance painter Fra Angelico (c. 1395–1455) shows the angel Gabriel appearing to Mary in "The Annunciation."

The Birth of John

Mary went to the town in the hills near Jerusalem, where her cousin Elizabeth lived with her husband Zechariah.

Church of John the Baptist
Nestled in the Judean hills lies the town of En Kerem (meaning "vineyard spring"). As well as being the home town of Zechariah and Elizabeth, it is also believed to be the birthplace of John the Baptist. The remains of the church named after him are still there today.

Writing tools
As Zechariah was mute, he requested a writing tablet. In Zechariah's time, this was a wooden board covered in wax. A pointed instrument was used to scratch into the wax on the tablet. This example (right) comes from 11th-century-CE Russia, and has the Psalms of David written on it. An alternative to a wooden board was writing paper crafted from dried papyrus stems. A reed pen dipped in black ink was used to write on the papyrus paper.

Mary went into the little house and greeted her cousin warmly. When Elizabeth heard her voice, she could feel the baby in her womb leap for joy and she was filled with the Holy Spirit. "Blessed are you among women and blessed is the child you will bear!" Elizabeth cried. "But why am I so favored that the mother of my Lord should come to me? Blessed is she who has believed that what the Lord has said to her will be accomplished!"

Mary replied with a beautiful song of praise. Her sweet voice filled the air: "My soul glorifies the Lord and my spirit rejoices in God my Savior, for He has been mindful of the humble state of His servant.

From now on all generations will call me blessed, for the Mighty One has done great things for me—holy is His name.

His mercy extends to those who fear Him, from generation to generation."

Mary stayed for about three months and then went home to Nazareth. Soon after, Elizabeth gave birth to her son, and her relatives and friends and neighbors rejoiced. He was a precious gift to his parents, late in life. Eight days after he was born he was circumcised, as was the custom, and was about to be named Zechariah, after his father. But Elizabeth protested. "No! He is to be named John!" she insisted, much to everyone's surprise.

"But no one in your family has ever been named John," they replied, mystified by her sudden outburst. They turned to Zechariah and asked his opinion, using sign language because he had been struck deaf and dumb after he doubted the angel's message in the Temple. He pointed for his wooden writing tablet. Then, in big, clear letters he wrote "His name is John." There was nothing more to be said. And, immediately, his tongue woke up from its long sleep. He started to speak and was filled with the Holy Spirit, prophesying and proclaiming God's word:

"Praise be to the Lord, the God of Israel, because He has come and has redeemed His people.

He has raised up a horn of salvation for us in the house of His servant David (as He said through His holy prophets of long ago),

salvation from our enemies and from the hand of all who hate us—to show mercy to our fathers and to remember His holy covenant, the oath He swore to our father Abraham. And you, my child, will be called a prophet of the Most High; for you will go on before the Lord to prepare the way for Him, to give His people the knowledge of salvation through the forgiveness of their sins, because of the tender mercy of our God, by which the rising sun will come to us from heaven to shine on those living in darkness and in the shadow of death, to guide our feet into the path of peace." Everyone looked at each other, wide-eyed. And word soon spread that the Lord was with the baby who had been born to Elizabeth and named that day.

Benedictines
The prophecy of Zechariah has become known as the "Benedictus," after the first word in Latin, which means "blessed." The name has been adopted by many religious figures, including many popes. St. Benedict set up the first monastery in 529 CE in Italy. Today's Benedictine monks come from this religious order.

Understanding the story

Traditionally, a firstborn boy belonged to God. It was usual for Jews to name their eldest son after his father, but the angel's message sees Zechariah's son named John (Hebrew for "the Lord is gracious"). It is John who will prepare the way for the coming Messiah. When Zechariah's voice is restored, he prophesies his son's mission and proclaims that God's mercy will bring salvation to His people.

Mary and Joseph give thanks for the baby Jesus in "Nativity" by Italian painter Girolamo del Pacchia (1477–1533).

Jesus is Born

Joseph was an honorable man. He was pledged to Mary in marriage and, when he learned that she was expecting a child that was not his, he wanted to protect her from disgrace.

But, while he was considering what to do, an angel appeared to him in a dream. "Joseph, son of David, do not be afraid to take Mary home as your wife, because what is conceived in her is from the Holy Spirit. She will give birth to a son, and you are to give him the name Jesus, because he will save his people from their sins."

The Lord's words, which had been spoken by the great prophet Isaiah many years before, would now come true. And, as promised, the baby would be the son of David because Joseph, who would become his father, was a descendant of King David. And so, Joseph and Mary kept their pledge and soon they were married.

Meanwhile, the Emperor, Caesar Augustus, ordered that a census should be taken of all the people in the Roman Empire. This happened every fourteen years. It meant that everybody had to go back to their home town to register and to be counted. So Joseph and Mary set off from Nazareth in Galilee and made the long journey south to Bethlehem in Judea, where Joseph was born. They were cold and tired by the time they eventually arrived in Bethlehem, the City of David.

Bethlehem was bursting at the seams—the streets crowded, and every inn full. Mary knew that soon it would be time to give birth to her baby and she must find somewhere safe and warm. Eventually, they found some shelter. There was straw on the ground, and it was dry and protected from the cold.

That night, Mary gave birth to her firstborn. It was a boy, perfect and new. Tenderly, she nursed him and wrapped him in strips of linen, as was the custom. She laid him in the stone manger, where the animals fed. It was lined with straw and would make a comfortable little bed for her newborn son. There was nowhere else for him to sleep.

Son of Israel
God's plan stated a ruler of ancient descent would arise in Bethlehem, the town where David (above) was born. The lineage starts with Abraham, father of Israel, and continues through David to Jesus—the true son of Israel.

Town of Bethlehem
Bethlehem was crowded due to the Roman census (a survey conducted for military and tax purposes), so Joseph and Mary could not find accommodation. Today, a modern city has built up around its historic center.

Understanding the story

The angel reassures Joseph that the baby Mary is carrying is the son of God. When Joseph marries Mary, the prophecy comes true—the Messiah will be the "Son of David" because his adoptive father Joseph is a direct descendant of King David. The exact location of Jesus's birth is unknown, but Bethlehem was full, so it was probably a stable, a cave, or a poor family's home.

The Shepherds' Visit

Some humble shepherds were looking after their flocks in the fields near Bethlehem that night. It was dark and clear, with a thousand stars shining.

Shepherd's tools
These were the standard tools for a shepherd in ancient times. The hook on the end of the crook was used to grab hold of any sheep wandering astray. If a sheep fell ill or got injured, a wooden bowl could be filled with water and given to the animal to prevent dehydration.

Choir boys
Many Christian hymns began as poems and were later set to music. Hymns were traditionally sung in unison (plainsong) by a small choir of male voices. The choir of angels singing "Glory to God in the highest" is reflected in the hymn, *Gloria in Excelsis Deo.*

The men tucked their thick, fleecy cloaks around their legs to keep out the biting cold. Eagle-eyed, they watched their sheep, on the lookout for any hint of danger from thieves or wild animals.

Suddenly, the peace was shattered and an angel appeared in the sky, surrounded by a brilliant white light. The stars disappeared, outdazzled. It was the Glory of God shining in the darkness. The shepherds dropped their crooks, shielding their eyes from the blinding light.

"Do not be afraid!" the angel said, looking down at them. "I bring you good news of great joy for everyone. Today, in the town of David, a Savior has been born to you. He is Christ the Lord. This will be a sign to you. You will find a baby wrapped in cloths and lying in a manger." And then, he was joined by a whole army of angels and archangels, stretching across the sky. Their voices rang out, a heavenly choir, praising the Lord: "Glory to God in the highest and on earth, peace to men on whom His favor rests!"

As the last note lingered and died away, the angels vanished into thin air and the shepherds looked at each other in wonder. "Let's go to Bethlehem and see this thing that has happened, which the Lord has told us about," they said. They hurried off, leaving their flocks behind.

When they got to Bethlehem, they found their way to the stable where Joseph and Mary had taken shelter. They crept in quietly, past the ox, the donkey, and the sheep asleep on the ground. Through the gloom, they could just make out the figure of a tiny baby lying fast asleep in the manger, with Mary and Joseph by his side. They went over and knelt down before him. They gazed at him in awe, the angel's words ringing in their ears. Then they told Joseph and Mary about the heavenly visitation earlier that night, and the astonishing things they had been told.

After a while, they left the little family in the stable. They could not believe that they had been the first to see the newborn Savior. Dawn was just breaking and they went straight into town. Full of joy, they told everyone the amazing news that Christ the Lord had been born that very night in Bethlehem. Word traveled fast and soon the whole town knew. In the stable, Mary sat quietly, holding her baby in her arms, thinking on what the shepherds had told her. She turned their words over in her

"The Annunciation to the Shepherds" by Dutch painter Adam Colonia (1634–1685)

mind and treasured them.

The shepherds themselves returned to their flocks in the fields and found them safe and sound. They rejoiced and praised God for all the wonderful things they had heard and seen that night.

"Glory to God in the highest and on earth, peace to men on whom his favor rests!"

Understanding the story

Shepherds had a bad reputation for stealing and being unreliable, so much so that they were never allowed to give evidence in courts of law. Though society held them in low esteem, God chooses the shepherds to be the first to hear the news of Jesus's birth. This is a great honor and they go to worship the baby. Jesus is descended from David, who was also a shepherd before becoming king.

Dove of peace
When Mary offers two doves, it is a reflection of her poor economic background. However, in the Bible doves are symbolic of goodness. Today, the dove remains an emblem of the Holy Spirit, and a recognized sign of peace and love.

Old age
The only people to recognize Jesus as the Messiah are the elderly Simeon and Anna. Old age was seen as a sign of wisdom and goodness, and also as a special blessing from God, as the life expectancy at the time was low.

The Presentation in the Temple

When Mary's baby was eight days old, he was circumcised, as was the custom. And he was named Jesus, just as the angel had said.

Under the Law of Moses, every firstborn son had to be consecrated to the Lord, but Mary had to wait forty days—the time of purification—before she was allowed to enter the Temple in Jerusalem. So, it was more than a month before Mary and Joseph set off from Bethlehem with the baby Jesus, to present him to the Lord in the Temple and to dedicate him to God's service. They would make an offering of two turtle doves, as they did not have enough money to buy a lamb.

When they arrived in Jerusalem, Mary and Joseph joined the stream of pilgrims flooding into the Temple. They walked up the great steps into the outer courtyard where the money changers were doing a roaring trade. No one took any notice of the young couple with the baby, as they wove their way through the crowds. Mary and Joseph paid their tax, as everyone had to before they went into worship, sliding their money into the narrow mouth of one of the treasure chests.

An old man named Simeon had come to the Temple that day, filled with the Holy Spirit. He was a good man, virtuous and devout, and he had been told by God that he would not die before he had seen the Messiah. He went straight up to Mary and Joseph, and he knew, at once, that the baby he was looking at was the Savior he had been waiting for. Gently, he took Jesus in his arms and praised God, saying, "Sovereign Lord, as you have promised, I may now die in peace. With my own eyes I have seen the son you have sent to bring salvation to all people—a light for revelation to the gentiles and for glory to your people Israel."

Mary listened, marveling at his words. Simeon blessed them and said, "This child will be a turning point in the life of Israel and will cause the falling and rising of many. But he will make powerful enemies who will do their utmost to cause his downfall." As he passed Jesus carefully back to Mary, he added, "And a sword will pierce your own soul, too."

Then an old woman shuffled up to them out of the gloom. She was a prophetess called Anna, who belonged to the tribe of Asher. She was eighty-four years old and had been a widow for many years. The Temple was her home now and she worshipped day and night, fasting and praying. She gazed at the baby in Mary's arms, but did not touch him.

Jesus is presented at the Temple in this detail of Italian painter Giotto di Bondone's fresco cycle "Life of the Virgin" (c. 1305).

Then she gave thanks to the Lord that she had been allowed to see him and shuffled off again. She told everyone that the baby she had just seen would be the Savior of Jerusalem.

When they had finished at the Temple, Mary and Joseph left Jerusalem and went home with Jesus. He grew healthy and strong, and was filled with wisdom and the grace of God.

"With my own eyes I have seen the son you have sent to bring salvation to all people."

Understanding the story

At the Temple, Mary offers two turtle doves to show her gratitude to God and her desire to be forgiven for past sins. The Temple is packed with people, but only Simeon and Anna realize that baby Jesus is the Messiah. God chooses these two humble people because they are truly devout. Simeon recognizes that God has sent His son into the world to bring salvation to all, not just the Jews.

The Wise Men

After Jesus had been presented in the Temple, the news of his birth spread far and wide. A group of highly respected wise men traveled from the east to Jerusalem.

Astrology
Some believe the wise men came from India, Persia, and Arabia. They were most likely respected astrologers, who believed that the stars were used by God as symbols to humankind. They made use of star catalogs in their predictions.

The gifts
Offering gifts as a sign of respect and obedience was a common practice in the ancient Middle East. The expensive gifts of gold (left), myrrh (right), and frankincense (bottom), reflect the high esteem in which they held Jesus, the infant king.

Although they were not Jewish themselves they had heard about the new infant king and they wanted to pay their respects. "Where is the one who has been born king of the Jews?" they asked. "We saw his star in the east and have come to worship him."

When King Herod heard about the newborn child who was to lead the Jews, he was deeply disturbed. He thought a new king was a terrible threat to his power. He called together all his chief priests and teachers of the law and asked them where the child might have been born. "In Bethlehem in Judea," they replied. His worst fears were confirmed. Bethlehem was not very far from Jerusalem.

Secretly, King Herod summoned the wise men to the palace. First, he found out the exact time the star had appeared in the sky and then he asked them if they would go to Bethlehem on his behalf. "As soon as you find him, report to me so that I may go and worship him." He had no intention of doing this, of course, and was hatching a very different plan.

The wise men agreed and left for Bethlehem on their camels. The star still guided them on their way, shining brightly ahead in the night sky. It stopped over a little stone stable on the outskirts of town and they knew that this must be the place that they had traveled so far to find. They saw the child with his mother Mary, and they bowed down and worshipped him.

Then they opened the heavy caskets that they had brought with them from the east and laid their magnificent gifts before him. There was gold to pay tribute to him as a king, frankincense to honor him as God, and myrrh as a sign that he, too, would die. Later, when it was time to go, the wise men got back on their camels and set off on the journey home. This time they took a different route, avoiding Jerusalem completely. They had been warned in a dream that they must not go back to see Herod again, whatever happened.

Understanding the story

At this point in history, the birth of a baby was not considered a significant event. The wise men make their journey because they believe the star signifies the birth of a king, and the gifts they bring are valuable both literally and symbolically. Their worship of baby Jesus, even though they are not Jewish, shows he is a savior for all people.

Herodium
Herod reigned over Judea from 37–4 BCE. He is said to be buried at Herodium, the summer palace he had built and named after himself. Situated 7 miles (12 km) south of Jerusalem, Herodium nestled in a hollowed-out hill, protected by steep sides. The palace's four circular towers offered stunning views of Judea.

Herod's coin
King Herod never forgot his Jewish roots. He was raised in Idumea, south of Israel, where the people had converted to the Jewish faith. Instead of issuing coins bearing his image, Herod chose coins with a military helmet and star. This showed respect for Jewish law.

The Flight into Egypt

After the wise men had left Bethlehem, an angel of the Lord appeared to Joseph in a dream.

"Take the child and his mother and escape to Egypt. Stay there until I tell you, for Herod is going to search for the child to kill him."

Joseph woke immediately and jumped up. He stood there for a moment as the full meaning of the angel's words sank in. He looked down in wonder at the baby Jesus, sleeping so quietly in the little manger. Then, he went over to Mary and shook her gently. He told her about his dream and what they must do. She rubbed her eyes sleepily and listened. She gathered her things together and tenderly picked up the sleeping Jesus, as Joseph prepared the donkeys for the long journey ahead.

They left as soon as they could, creeping quietly out of the little stable into the night. Like shadows they flitted past the darkened houses, through the empty streets, and out of the peaceful, sleeping town. By the time dawn broke, they had left Bethlehem far behind and were heading into the wilderness, far from human habitation.

Meanwhile, Herod had waited and waited for the wise men to return to the royal palace in Jerusalem with news of the baby Jesus. He paced impatiently up and down his throne room. When he finally realized that he had been outwitted by the wise men from the east and that they were not coming back, he was furious. How would he find the newborn king that was such a threat to his throne now? How would he get rid of him? Mad with rage, he issued a decree that all boys under the age of two in the Bethlehem area should be killed immediately.

Herod's most trusted soldiers were dispatched at dawn to carry out his terrible order. And that very day, as Mary and Joseph hurried on their way with the infant king, every little boy in Bethlehem was butchered. Their mothers pleaded and wept for their children's lives as the soldiers obeyed the King's command. It was the massacre of the innocents that the prophet Jeremiah had predicted many years before: "A voice is heard in Ramah, weeping and great mourning, Rachel weeping for her children and refusing to be comforted, because they are no more."

Unaware of the slaughter in Bethlehem, Mary and Joseph traveled south, looking out for any sign of Herod's men. They avoided the main routes as much as they could, keeping to the ancient animal tracks that wound through the landscape. Mary held her baby tightly to her, hidden safely under her thick cloak. On and on they went, through the wild countryside, stopping only to rest at night. It was a long and difficult journey. When they reached the bleak and rocky desert, the sun beat down relentlessly on the little family.

Eventually, they arrived in Egypt—a strange and exotic land from which their ancestors had escaped so long ago. They found sanctuary there, as the angel had told Joseph, far from King Herod and his henchmen in Jerusalem.

Some time later, an angel appeared to Joseph again in a dream. "Get up," he said. "Take the child and his mother and go back to Israel, for those who were trying to take the child's life are dead." And so, the Lord's words spoken through the prophet Hosea were fulfilled: "Out of Egypt, I called my son."

On hearing this message, Joseph and Mary set off with Jesus to make the long journey home. But, when they arrived in Israel, they discovered that Herod's kingdom had been divided into three parts following his death. His cruel son, Archelaus, was now reigning over Judea. Fearful at the news, they decided to travel further north and to settle in Nazareth in Galilee, where they had lived before.

The Holy Family travel into Egypt in this detail from a panel painted by Fra Angelico (Guido di Pietro).

"Take the child and his mother and go back to Israel, for those who were trying to take the child's life are dead."

Understanding the story

The angel warns Joseph to leave Egypt before the Massacre of the Innocents. This terrible act was typical of King Herod, who killed many people—including his wife and three of his sons—in pursuit of power. Egypt was traditionally a place of refuge for the Jews in times of trouble. Their later journey out of Egypt recalls the Exodus of Moses and the Israelites to Israel.

Spiritual learning
By Jesus's time, children learned Jewish Law in special schools set up next to synagogues. The Mishnah, a written record of traditions, was part of their studies. It stated that a five-year-old is ready for the Scripture, a 13-year-old ready to fulfill the commandments, and a 20-year-old ready to pursue a religious calling. This German Mishnah is from the 13th century CE.

Bar Mitzvah
At the age of 13, a Jewish boy celebrates his Bar Mitzvah, after which time he is considered an adult. The ceremony involves reading from the Torah, (being carried here by this boy at the Western Wall of the Temple of Jerusalem). The equivalent celebration for Jewish girls is called a Bat Mitzvah.

Jesus is Found in the Temple

Mary and Joseph set off with their friends and relatives during Nisan, the first month of the year, to go to Jerusalem for the Feast of Passover.

It was held in the evening of the fourteenth day of the month, and it was important to arrive in good time. Passover celebrated the deliverance of the Israelites from Egypt and was one of the greatest feast days of the year. The roads were always crowded with pilgrims coming from all over the country. Jesus was twelve years old now, and he was allowed to go with Mary and Joseph for the first time. He was excited at the thought of going into the Temple with them and taking part in the celebrations. It would be an important moment in his life, preparing him for the next year, when, at the age of thirteen, he would be considered a man.

After the Feast, Mary and Joseph left Jerusalem and started the journey back to their home in Nazareth with everyone else. Tired after the festivities, they traveled slowly along the road toward Galilee. It was not until the evening, when they stopped for the night, that Mary and Joseph noticed that Jesus was not with them. They looked at each other, puzzled. Then they looked around, but there was no sign of him. They were both filled with a terrible, sinking feeling. Desperately, they asked people if they had seen him, but no one could help. Jesus seemed to have vanished into thin air. As night fell, Mary and Joseph turned around and headed back to Jerusalem, scouring the road as they went.

For three days they searched the city high and low, consumed with fear and hoping against hope that they would find him safe and sound. Finally, in desperation, they went back to the Temple and walked up the great steps.

Suddenly, in the inner courtyard, they saw Jesus. He was sitting on the ground, deep in conversation with some of the religious teachers. Wise beyond his years, he was asking them question after question and listening intently to their answers. The teachers were clearly amazed by his intelligence and understanding. They talked to him as if he were an adult and chose their words carefully. Mary and Joseph stood and watched, fascinated by the scene. Then they rushed forward and threw their arms around Jesus. "My son, why did you do this to us?" asked Mary, holding back the tears. "Your father and I have been so worried. We have been looking everywhere for you."

Jesus looked at them, wide-eyed.

"The Boy Jesus in Temple" by Dutch painter Adriane van der Werff (1659–1722)

"Why were you searching for me?" he asked innocently. "Didn't you know that I had to be in my Father's house?" But neither Mary nor Joseph understood what he meant. He got up and said goodbye to the teachers, then left the Temple with his parents.

Together, they set off from Jerusalem and started their journey home to Nazareth. But Mary could not stop thinking about her son, sitting there in the Temple and talking so seriously with the teachers. She turned the image over in her mind and smiled to herself.

"Didn't you know that I had to be in my Father's house?"

Understanding the story

Jesus was not born with complete knowledge of God, and this story shows the beginning of his spiritual growth. He displays his spiritual maturity in his first visit to the Temple, developing his knowledge of God through discussions with the Temple teachers. When Jesus says "my Father's house," he is showing awareness of his unique relationship with God the Father.

John Baptizes Jesus

It was the fifteenth year of Tiberius Caesar's reign as Roman Emperor. Judea, in the south, was ruled by his governor, Pontius Pilate. Galilee, in the north, was governed by Herod Antipas, son of Herod the Great.

Nearly four centuries had passed since the last of the prophets had spoken to the Jewish people. They remembered the promise that a new Messiah was coming—and a new prophet who would prepare the way for him. But they had waited a long time.

John, the son who had been miraculously born to Elizabeth and Zechariah late in life, lived a solitary life in the desert far from the Roman garrisons and Herod's splendid Temple in Jerusalem. He wandered alone through the remote countryside, preaching and baptizing the people. He had a special gift for speaking, and the words from his tongue were eloquent and pure. His clothes were made of the roughest camels' hair, held in place by a leather belt around his waist, and he lived on wild food, like locusts and honey from the desert bees. When he stopped to preach, he urged the people to turn away from evil. He told them to return to God because Judgement Day was near. And then, when they had repented of their sins, he baptized them in the cool waters of the Jordan River.

Word spread, and soon people from all over Galilee and beyond were talking about the prophet in the wilderness who could wash away their sins. They called him John the Baptist. People wanted to see for themselves and soon they started to flock to the desert to find him.

When he saw the wealthy and powerful Sadducees and the Pharisees who had come all the way from the Temple in Jerusalem, John berated them. "You brood of vipers! Repent your sins!" he said. "Do not think that you are safe just because you are the children of Abraham. Trees that produce rotten fruit will be cut down and thrown on the fire."

"What should we do?" the people asked.

"The man with two tunics should share with him who has none. And the man who has food should do the same," John replied.

"And what about us?" asked the tax collectors. "What should we do?"

"Do not collect any more than you are required to," John told them.

Then some soldiers stepped forward. "What should we do, Teacher?"

"Do not extort money and do not accuse people falsely. Be content with your pay."

The people listened and wondered whether John the Baptist might be the Messiah himself. As if he could read their minds, John said, "I baptize you with water. But one more powerful than I will come; the thongs of his sandals I am not worthy

After King Herod

When King Herod the Great died, his kingdom was shared between his three sons—Antipas, Archelaus, and Philip. From 4 BCE until 39 CE, Herod Antipas ruled Galilee (where Jesus was raised) and Perea. Archelaus controlled Judea and Samaria, while Philip ruled Iturea in the northeast of Palestine.

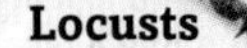

Locusts

John the Baptist had limited options for food in the desert. He resorted to honey made by wild bees. Holes inside Palestine's rocks and trees were home to thousands of these bees. Locusts were also eaten by John. They are a rich source of fat and protein, and can also be eaten raw.

The Jordan River was the last part of the Israelites' journey to freedom during the Exodus, and also the start of Jesus's ministry.

to untie. He will baptize you with the Holy Spirit and with fire. His winnowing fork is in his hand to clear his threshing-floor and to gather the wheat into his barn, but he will burn up the chaff with unquenchable fire."

Jesus came from Galilee to be baptized by John in the river. John bowed down. He knew that Jesus had never sinned and had nothing to repent. "I am the one who should be baptized by you," he said.

"No, you must baptize me," answered Jesus. "It is God's will. We must obey Him." Jesus did not want to separate himself from the sins of his people, and his baptism would be an example to his followers.

Together, they waded into the river as the crowd watched. John cradled Jesus in his arms and lowered him into the water, submerging him for a few moments. As he lifted him back out of the water, the clouds parted and a white dove flew down from heaven, bathed in light. It was the Spirit of God and it hovered over Jesus. At the same time, a voice from above said, "This is my Son, whom I love; with him I am well pleased."

Understanding the story

John the Baptist fulfills a prophecy from the Old Testament's Book of Isaiah that a voice from the wilderness will proclaim the return of the Lord. Although he has never sinned, Jesus's baptism shows that he identifies with ordinary people. Baptism represents the cleansing of sins and a fresh start. It is a promise to lead a righteous life in future.

Desert creatures
Very few creatures can survive in the barren wilderness of the desert. Eagles, scavenger vultures, and snakes, such as this desert black cobra—one of the world's most venomous snakes—are always a threat.

Satan
Depicted in this 15th-century picture, Satan (meaning "adversary") is believed to be an evil angel, opposed to God. Although it is unknown how Satan appeared to Jesus, his temptations were real and challenging.

The Temptations in the Wilderness

After Jesus was baptized he came back from the Jordan and went into the wilderness to be alone—away from the distractions of daily life.

It was a bleak and barren landscape, unbearably hot by day and bone-numbingly cold at night. His only companions were the great eagles and vultures that flew high above and the desert snakes that slithered into the shade under the hot rocks.

For forty long days and nights, Jesus fasted and prayed in complete solitude. At the end of this time, he was exhausted and weak with hunger, and the Devil came to tempt him and test his faith. "If you really are the Son of God, as you say, prove it. Turn these burning desert stones into bread."

Jesus, obedient to the will of God, refused to break his fast. He replied, "It is written that man cannot live by bread alone, but must find strength in God's words."

But the Devil refused to give up. He took Jesus to the very top of Herod's magnificent marble Temple in the heart of Jerusalem.

The Devil turned to Jesus and said, "You say you are the Son of God. Jump off the Temple! The angels will catch you."

Jesus, steadfast in his obedience to God, replied calmly, "It is written that God must never be put to the test."

The Devil remained undeterred. He took Jesus to the highest mountain peak and showed him all the kingdoms of the world spread out like a patchwork quilt beneath them. "I will make you lord and ruler of all these lands if you will just kneel down and worship me."

And, once again, unwavering in his devotion to God, Jesus replied, "Get behind me, Satan. It is written that God alone is Lord of all, and it is God alone whom you should worship."

With that, the Devil vanished and a host of angels appeared from nowhere and flew down to strengthen Jesus after his struggle.

Understanding the story

Jesus's 40 days in the desert echo the 40 years the Israelites spent there before reaching the Promised Land. Jesus is aware that he can perform miracles, yet he refuses to demonstrate these powers to the Devil. In the face of various temptations, Jesus remains resistant because he is wholly committed to God.

Russian painter Ivan Kramskoi's "Christ in the Wilderness" (1872), oil on canvas

Fishing industry
In Jesus's time, the fishing industry around the Sea of Galilee was thriving. At least four of Jesus's 12 disciples were fishermen. It was a challenging vocation, as fishermen often had to work all night cleaning their catches, drying nets, and preparing the fish for market.

Jesus Calls his Disciples

Jesus returned to Galilee and went to live in Capernaum, a little town on the shore of the big freshwater lake known as the Sea of Galilee.

One morning, Jesus was preaching at the edge of the water and, as usual, a crowd had gathered to listen. As he spoke, he noticed two little fishing boats moored nearby. Peter and his brother, Andrew, were scrubbing their nets in the water. Jesus stepped onto the boat belonging to Peter, and asked him to cast off from the shore. The little vessel plowed slowly out to sea, while Jesus sat down and carried on preaching from it. When he had finished, he said to Peter, "Put out into deep water and let down the nets for a catch."

The fisherman looked at him doubtfully. "Master," he replied. "We worked hard all night and haven't caught anything. But,

"The Miraculous Draught of Fishes" (1515–1516) by Italian painter Raphael (1483–1520)

because you say so, I will let down the net."

They headed toward the middle of the sea, and Peter threw the big cast net over the side. Suddenly, there was a great surge and the net ballooned with fish. Peter watched in amazement. He had never before seen such a catch. He signaled to his brother Andrew, far away on the shore, to join them with the other boat. Together, the brothers heaved in the haul of fresh fish. And then the two little boats turned, both piled high and perilously low in the water. They just made it back to dry land before they sank.

Two other fishermen, James and John, the sons of Zebedee, came over, astonished at the miraculous catch and, along with Peter and Andrew, they fell down to the ground, consumed with fear. "Do not be afraid," said Jesus. "Follow me and I will make you fishers of men."

So the four men left their boats and said goodbye to their families. They set off with Jesus and went with him all over Galilee as he taught in synagogues and preached by the wayside, spreading the word of God. He spoke with such authority that people were amazed and flocked to hear him. And he healed the sick and the diseased. News spread far and wide, and soon people came not only from Galilee but from Jerusalem, Judea, and far beyond the Jordan River.

One day, Jesus saw a tax collector named Matthew, counting out the money he had taken that day. He was disliked by the Jewish people because he worked for the Romans. Jesus went up to him, saying, "Follow me!" Matthew got up immediately and went with him. That evening, Jesus and his followers went to Matthew's house and sat down to eat with him. A few other tax collectors and some undesirable people joined them.

When the Pharisees saw this they were shocked. "Why does your teacher break bread with such unsavory characters?" they asked.

Jesus heard their pious words and replied, "It is not the healthy who need a doctor, but the sick. I am not looking for the righteous. I have come to find sinners. It is they who need me."

Later, Jesus went to the top of a high mountain to be on his own. He stayed there all night, deep in prayer. The next day, he came down and called all of his followers together and chose twelve disciples to his side. They were Peter and his brother Andrew, James and his brother John, Philip, Bartholomew, Matthew, Thomas, James son of Alphaeus, Simon the Zealot, Thaddeus, and Judas Iscariot.

The number 12
There are many references to the number 12 throughout the Bible. In Scripture, the number is linked to "fullness." Jacob had 12 sons, who went on to become the fathers of the 12 tribes of Israel. Jesus chooses 12 men to be his apostles. In the Book of Revelation, the depiction of a perfect Jerusalem is a city with 12 gates and 12 foundations. This 6th-century-CE mosaic shows the 12 disciples surrounding Jesus.

"Follow me and I will make you fishers of men."

Understanding the story

Jesus begins his ministry on the shores of the Sea of Galilee. His first act is to recruit his disciples, also known as "apostles," which means "messengers," because they will be tasked with telling people about the word of God. The twelve are ordinary men, but Jesus will use their human failings to establish God's Kingdom on Earth.

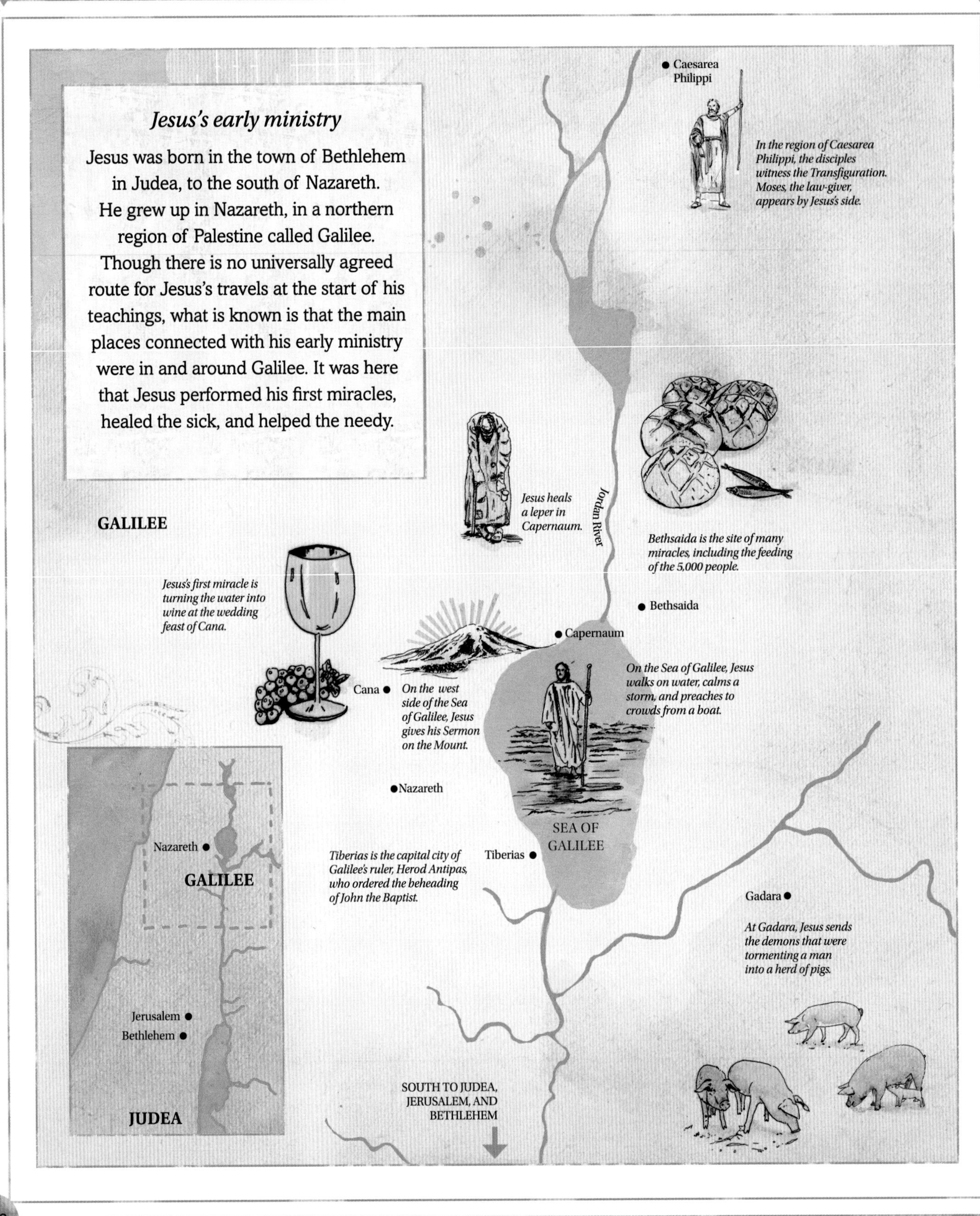
Jesus's early ministry
Jesus was born in the town of Bethlehem in Judea, to the south of Nazareth. He grew up in Nazareth, in a northern region of Palestine called Galilee. Though there is no universally agreed route for Jesus's travels at the start of his teachings, what is known is that the main places connected with his early ministry were in and around Galilee. It was here that Jesus performed his first miracles, healed the sick, and helped the needy.
Caesarea Philippi
In the region of Caesarea Philippi, the disciples witness the Transfiguration. Moses, the law-giver, appears by Jesus's side.
GALILEE
Jesus heals a leper in Capernaum.
Jordan River
Bethsaida is the site of many miracles, including the feeding of the 5,000 people.
Jesus's first miracle is turning the water into wine at the wedding feast of Cana.
Bethsaida
Capernaum
Cana
On the west side of the Sea of Galilee, Jesus gives his Sermon on the Mount.
On the Sea of Galilee, Jesus walks on water, calms a storm, and preaches to crowds from a boat.
Nazareth
SEA OF GALILEE
Tiberias
Tiberias is the capital city of Galilee's ruler, Herod Antipas, who ordered the beheading of John the Baptist.
Gadara
At Gadara, Jesus sends the demons that were tormenting a man into a herd of pigs.
Nazareth
GALILEE
Jerusalem
Bethlehem
JUDEA
SOUTH TO JUDEA, JERUSALEM, AND BETHLEHEM

The Marriage Feast of Cana

Jesus, his mother Mary, and the twelve disciples were all invited to a wedding feast at Cana, just north of Nazareth in Galilee.

Everybody was sitting in the sun as the musicians played on their harps and pipes and tambourines. The women were dancing and singing to the music. The celebrations had been going on for some days now, as was the custom, and everybody was enjoying the fine food at the banquet.

Mary, who was sitting next to Jesus, suddenly noticed that the wine had run out. There was not a single drop left although the banquet was in full swing. She turned to Jesus and told him, whispering quietly so that no one else would hear. He turned to her and said, "Dear mother, why do you involve me? My time has not yet come."

Then Mary called one of the servants over and said, "Do whatever he tells you." There were six huge stone water jars standing nearby, the kind that were used to store the water for washing before a meal or for a religious ceremony.

Jesus pointed to the jars and said to the servants, "Fill them with water, please!" The servants did as he said, slowly filling the great jars with their water carriers. It took some time. Then Jesus said to one of them, "Now pour some out and take it to the guest of honor who is sitting over there."

The servant looked at him, surprised, as this water would never normally be used for drinking. But he went to fetch a clean goblet and filled it carefully from the jar. He took it to the guest of honor who thanked him and raised it to his lips. The guest of honor had no idea that it had just been poured from the water jar. The servant watched curiously as he tasted the first few drops, and then drained the goblet.

The guest of honor called the bridegroom over and said, "Delicious! Thank you so much! Most people give their guests the finest wine first and then bring out the cheaper wine later, when the guests have had too much to drink. But you have saved the best till now!" The bridegroom glowed with pleasure. The servant was still standing there. He opened his mouth in amazement, but said nothing.

And so, Jesus turned the water into wine at the wedding feast in Cana. It was the first miracle that he performed.

Wine jar
In ancient times, water was usually stored in stone jars to be used for ceremonial washing. However, wine was kept in more decorative ceramic jars, called amphoras. This terra-cotta amphora, crafted in Lebanon during the 4th century, is a typical example. Shaped like a vase, it has two large handles for carrying the wine.

Understanding the story

Wedding celebrations usually lasted seven days. It was social humiliation for the bridegroom if the wine ran out. But Jesus's first miracle is much more than sparing embarrassment. Jesus is showing a new path to righteousness. The wine represents Jesus's blood, which will spill in order to unite the people with God.

Mount of Beatitudes

Mount of Beatitudes
The sacred spot where Jesus gave his sermon is thought to be the Mount of Beatitudes—a low hill near Capernaum with views over the Sea of Galilee. This church stands atop the mount today.

The Sermon on the Mount

So many people had come to listen to Jesus that he went up the mountain to speak to the crowd from there. The words he spoke are known as the Beatitudes, from the Latin for "blessed."

"Blessed are the poor in spirit, for theirs is the kingdom of heaven.

Blessed are those who mourn, for they will be comforted.

Blessed are the meek, for they will inherit the earth.

Blessed are those who hunger and thirst for righteousness, for they will be filled.

Blessed are the merciful, for they will be shown mercy.

Blessed are the pure in heart, for they will see God.

Blessed are the peacemakers, for they will be called sons of God.

Blessed are those who are persecuted because of righteousness, for theirs is the kingdom of heaven."

The great crowd listened from a distance, drinking in his words. Jesus continued, "Do not think that I have come to destroy the law or the words of the prophets. I have come to uphold them. The law must be obeyed. You are the light of the world, do not hide it. Let your light shine brightly before men so that they may see your good deeds and praise your Father in heaven.

"You have heard it said that you must not kill. But do not be angry with your brother, either. If you have quarreled with him, be reconciled. Forgive anyone who has made you angry. You have heard it said, 'An eye for an eye, a tooth for a tooth.' But I tell you, do not resist an evil person. If someone strikes you on the right cheek, turn the other cheek to him, also. Some people say that you must love your neighbor and hate your enemy. But I tell you to love your enemies and pray

for those who persecute you.

"Do not boast about your good deeds. When you give to the needy, do not announce it with trumpets as the hypocrites do in the synagogues and on the streets. When you pray to the Lord, do it quietly, without being seen. Go into your room, close the door, and pray to your Father, who is unseen. You do not need to babble like the pagans, who think the more words they use the more they will be heard.

"Pray simply to God, using words like these: Our Father, who is in heaven, hallowed be your name. Your kingdom come, your will be done on earth as it is in heaven. Give us this day our daily bread and forgive us our sins, as we forgive those who sin against us. Do not lead us into temptation, but deliver us from evil.

"I tell you not to worry about what you will eat or wear. Life is more than food and the body is more than clothes. Consider the ravens. They do not sow or reap, they have no storeroom or barn. Yet God feeds them. The lilies of the field do not labor or spin, but God clothes them in splendor.

"Do not store up treasures for yourself on earth, where moth and rust destroy. Store up treasures in heaven, where thieves do not break in and steal. No one can serve two masters. You cannot serve both God and money.

"Do not judge, or you, too, will be judged. Why do you criticize the speck of sawdust in your brother's eye when you have a plank in your own eye? First, take this out, then you will see clearly to remove the speck from your brother's eye.

"Ask and it will be given to you, seek and you will find. Watch out for false prophets because they come to you in sheep's clothing, but inwardly they are ferocious wolves.

"You have heard my words. If you put them into practice, your house will be safe. The rain will come and the wind will blow and the floodwaters will rise, but it will not fall down because the foundations are built on rock."

Understanding the story

In his sermon, Jesus is teaching God's will on Earth. Jesus attempts to clarify the true meaning of God's Law. He guides the people, explaining that those who lead a spiritual life without revenge in their hearts will be the triumphant ones. God is the ultimate judge, who will reward the righteous in heaven and punish unrepentant sinners.

"*Blessed are the meek, for they will inherit the earth...*
Blessed are the pure in heart, for they will see God.
Blessed are the peacemakers, for they
will be called children of God."

Matthew 5:5, 8–9

Goat herder
This boy is looking after goats in Israel's Negev Desert, a sight that would have changed very little since Jesus's time. Jesus taught that people needed to have the same openness, humility, and lack of pretention as children to be able to enter the Kingdom of Heaven.

Healing the Sick

People came from all over Galilee to hear Jesus teach and huge crowds followed him wherever he went.

Reed-roofed houses
In Jesus's time, most homes were small dwellings, built from mud bricks or uneven stones. Many of them had just one large room. The roofs were flat for a variety of reasons. It was easier to dry fruit, grain, and clothes on flat roofs, and in very hot weather, people could even sleep on them. Outside, a flight of steps led up to the roof. In Galilee, the flat roofs were crafted from layers of reeds and mud laid on top of supporting wooden beams.

One day, in Capernaum, a leper approached Jesus, ringing a little bell and shouting, "Unclean!," "Unclean!" People fled from him. The poor man's skin was white and scaly and his clothes were tattered and torn. He went up to Jesus and knelt down on the ground before him. "Lord, if you are willing, please cure me!" he begged. Jesus looked at him and, filled with compassion, he reached out and touched him on the hand. "Of course I am willing," he said. "Be clean!"

Immediately, the leprosy vanished and the man's skin became soft and smooth. He was completely cured, and he bowed down low on the ground in thanks. Jesus said to him, "See that you don't tell anyone. Just go and show yourself to the priest who will confirm that you are healed. And make sacrifices, as Moses commanded." But the man was so overwhelmed by the miracle that he rushed around telling everybody. And, as a result, even more people came to Jesus to be healed. He was mobbed wherever he went.

A few days later, Jesus was preaching in a house, full of people. Some people could not even get into the little house but stood outside, trying to hear a word or two. As the day wore on, more and more people arrived, including a man who was completely paralyzed. He was carried by his friends, but their hearts sank when they saw the huge crowd of people. They had come from far away and they were determined to get to Jesus. Carefully, they carried their friend up the outside steps and onto the little flat roof. Then they cut a big hole in the roof, and gently lowered him down into the house on his mat. He landed just in front of Jesus.

Jesus saw the faith they had and he said to the paralyzed man, "My son, your sins are forgiven." The Pharisees and the teachers of the law, who had been there since crack of dawn, looked shocked and raised their eyebrows. "Who is this fellow who speaks such blasphemy?" they said to each other. "Who can forgive sins but God alone?"

Jesus, who could read their minds, said, "Why are you thinking these things in your hearts? Tell me, which is easier? To say 'Your sins are forgiven' or to say 'Get up and walk?' " And he turned to the paralyzed man and said, "Get up, take your mat, and go home."

Immediately, the man sprang to his feet in front of everyone, praising God. He bent down and picked up the mat he had been lying on and went home. Everybody watched him in amazement and gave thanks to God. "We have seen remarkable things today!" they said to each other.

"We have seen remarkable things today!"

Jesus heals the leper in this 12th-century-CE mosaic from the cathedral of Monreale, Sicily, Italy.

Understanding the story

Touching a leper is regarded as dirty, yet Jesus ignores this and reaches out to him. By miraculously healing the sick, Jesus demonstrates his close relationship with God. The growing crowds are amazed at the healings they are witnessing, but what really matters is that God has given Jesus the authority to forgive their sins.

The Centurion's Servant

Jesus preached all over the country, drawing bigger and bigger crowds. But he always went back to Capernaum on the northern shore of the Sea of Galilee.

Capernaum was a busy fishing town and Jesus used it as his base during his ministry. He performed many miracles there. Like so many others, a Roman centurion had heard the stories about a teacher named Jesus, who preached the word of the Lord and had astonishing powers. The centurion had a much-loved and most loyal servant, who had been with him for many years. The servant had fallen dangerously ill and was now on the brink of death.

The centurion did not know what to do. He wondered whether he might ask for Jesus's help. He thought about it for some time and, finally, enlisted the help of some elders from the synagogue in Capernaum. He asked them if they would go to Jesus on his behalf. They agreed, gladly, as they liked the Roman centurion and were fond of his old servant.

The elders approached Jesus and begged him to come to the centurion's house to save the life of the servant. "Our friend, the Roman centurion, is well-deserving of this," they said to Jesus. "He loves our nation and has built a synagogue." Jesus listened with interest and agreed to go with them.

Roman army
Roman soldiers wore protective armor, weaponry, and hobnail sandals. A soldier wore the same as his officer, except the centurion's armor was decorative. Only centurions wore metal leg protectors, known as greaves (above).

Capernaum
The thriving fishing town of Capernaum was where Jesus was based during his ministry in Galilee. It was also home to Peter and other disciples who were fishermen. This synagogue was built in the 4th century CE on the site of the former synagogue where Jesus often taught.

He was not far from the house, where the servant lay so dangerously ill, when the centurion himself came out to meet Jesus. He was a fine figure of a man, resplendent in his shining chain mail, but he greeted Jesus respectfully. "Lord, do not trouble yourself for I do not deserve to have you come under my roof," he said, bowing low. "That is why I did not even consider myself worthy to come to you. But I know that, if you just say the word, my servant will be healed. For I myself am a man well acquainted with authority. I am used to giving orders to soldiers and having them obeyed."

When Jesus heard this he was astonished and said to his followers, "I tell you the truth, I have not found anyone in the whole of Israel with such great faith." And, without further ado, the centurion turned around and went home to find that his servant, who had been at death's door, was completely recovered.

Centurion's helmet
Roman military soldiers wore the galea (a special metal helmet) to protect their heads in battle. A protective visor extended to cover the forehead. Metal cheek plates came down low to guard more of the face, while metal flairs protected the neck area. The ears and eyes were left uncovered so that soldiers could hear and see clearly on the battlefield. The precise design of these helmets depended on a soldier's ranking and his army. Higher-ranked officers wore more prestigious helmets, with crests of feathers or horse's hairs adorning the tops.

"I have not found anyone in the whole of Israel with such great faith."

Understanding the story

Faith can not only change situations, but save lives. The centurion is a Roman military officer responsible for about 80 soldiers, but it is his deep religious belief that impresses Jesus. This unfaltering faith results in the servant's full recovery from the brink of death, proving that there is salvation for those who truly believe.

Jesus Calms the Storm

One evening, Jesus and his disciples were walking by the Sea of Galilee. It had been a beautiful day and the orange ball of the sun was sinking low in the sky.

The waters were calm and tranquil, and the fishermen were preparing for the night ahead. "Come, let us go to the other side," said Jesus. They climbed into their little fishing boat, the disciples took the oars, and they sailed out to sea.

A gentle breeze tickled the water and soon Jesus had fallen asleep, lulled by the rocking motion of the boat. The disciples looked at him and smiled at each other. On and on they rowed and they were far out at sea when, without warning, the sky darkened. A sudden violent wind appeared from nowhere, whipping the waters into gigantic waves. Water crashed down onto the little boat, threatening to swamp it. Jesus was still fast asleep in the stern of the boat.

"Master! Master! Wake up! Save us! We are going to drown!" the disciples shouted, shaking him. Jesus opened his eyes and got to his feet, holding the side of the boat. He lifted his arm above the sea, which raged below, and said to the waves, "Quiet! Be still!"

Immediately, the waters calmed and the wind dropped. The Sea of Galilee lay flat once more. The disciples looked at each other, pale with fear and amazement. "How great is he? Even the winds and the water obey him!"

"Christ Stilling the Tempest" by Danish painter Anker Lund (1840–1922).

Understanding the story

Located in a basin bordered by mountains, the Sea of Galilee is known for its sudden storms. Jesus orders the wind and waves to return to calm, and they obey him. The disciples see for themselves that he is able to control even the powerful forces of nature. They are in awe of his abilities and their faith grows stronger.

Assyrian demon
In the Bible, evil spirits called demons are shown as being in league with Satan against God. At the time of Jesus, it was believed that demons could possess people, causing disease and mental illness. This statue depicts an Assyrian demon.

Monastery
At the spot where Jesus released the demons from the disturbed man are the ruins of a Byzantine monastery. The site in Kursi was discovered in 1967 during excavations for a new road.

The Possessed Man

Jesus and the disciples crossed the sea and landed in the country of the Gadarenes. As they stepped out of the boat, a man rushed up to Jesus, screaming and gibbering.

The man was bleeding, with cuts on his arms and legs. His wrists and ankles were bound in chains and his torn clothes were filthy. He was possessed with demons and had lived among the tombs of the dead for years, terrifying anyone who came near.

He fell at Jesus's feet, clutching at his robes with blackened hands. "What do you want with me, Jesus, Son of the Most High God? I beg you, do not torture me!"

"What is your name?" asked Jesus politely.

"My name is Legion," he replied. "Because I have so many demons inside me."

Jesus listened and looked at the huge herd of pigs, rooting around on the hillside that led down to the sea. "Be off!" he said to the demons possessing the wild man. "Go and find a new home. Go to the pigs. There are plenty of them, at least two thousand. Leave this man in peace."

Obediently, the evil spirits swarmed out of the man toward the herd. They possessed the pigs like a terrible virus. The creatures squealed and shivered. Then, they charged down the hill. They ran to the edge of the cliff and straight over it and into the sea below. They plunged under the water and drowned.

The astonished herdsmen who had been looking after the pigs rushed off to tell everyone. Naturally, people came to have a look. But when they arrived, all they saw was a normal man, sitting at Jesus's feet, talking quietly. And not a pig in sight.

People were confused by what they saw. They asked Jesus and his disciples to leave. As they left, the man who had been cleansed of his demons, begged to go with them. But Jesus turned to him and said, "Go home and tell everyone what God has done for you."

Understanding the story

The demons inside the possessed man recognized Jesus's power and did as he asked of them. Jews believed that pigs were the dirtiest of animals, so when the pigs drown, it is symbolic of the removal of the man's uncleanliness. Those who benefit from Jesus's miracles want to stay with him, but Jesus asks the man to spread the news of God's mercy.

Place of worship
Dating from the 3rd century CE, this synagogue in Baram, Galilee, is much more elaborate than the simple synagogue run by Jairus. As head of the synagogue, Jairus would have maintained the building and organized religious services.

Mourning music
Public displays of grief were the usual response when someone died. It was customary for musicians to play haunting and sorrowful pieces during the week-long period of mourning. The reed pipe was one of the instruments played at this time because of its high-pitched, wailing sound.

Jairus's Daughter

Jesus got back to the other side of the Sea of Galilee and a crowd was waiting for him on the shore.

One of the leaders of the synagogue, a very important man named Jairus, came up to him in a terrible state. He fell at Jesus's feet, pleading with him to come to his house. His only daughter, a little girl of twelve years old, lay there dying.

As Jesus went with Jairus through the crowd, he was jostled and squashed by people trying to get near him. Among them was a woman who had been ill for many years, suffering from bleeding. She had tried everything, but nothing stemmed the flow. "If only I can touch his cloak, I will be healed," she said to herself. She inched herself toward him, weaving her way through the crowd and finally got near enough to touch the edge of his cloak with her fingers. At once, her bleeding stopped and she was released from her suffering.

Jesus stopped in his tracks and turned around. "Who touched me?" he asked.

People shook their heads, denying it was them, and the disciples said, "Master, there are so many people crowding around you! How can you ask who touched you?" But Jesus kept turning his head and looking around to see who it was. Eventually, the woman bowed down before him, trembling with fear, and told him the truth.

"Daughter," said Jesus, "your faith has healed you. Go in peace and be freed from your suffering."

While he was speaking to the woman, some men came to Jairus with bad news. "Your daughter is dead," they said. "Why bother the teacher any more? There is no point in him coming with you now."

But Jesus ignored them. "Don't be afraid," he told Jairus. "Just believe and she will be healed." And he continued on his way to the house, taking only three of his disciples with him—Peter, James, and John. As they approached, they could see the flautists playing music for the dead, and the people outside, weeping and sobbing. "Why all this commotion and wailing?" Jesus asked. "The child is not dead but asleep!" But the mourners did not believe him.

He and the disciples went into the house with Jairus and his wife. Their daughter was lying on her bed, cold and still. Jesus bent over her and took her small hand in his. "Little girl," he said softly. "I say to you, get up!" Her eyelashes fluttered and opened and she smiled. Then she stretched and yawned and jumped off the bed and ran to her parents. Astonished, they clutched her tightly to them and looked at Jesus in amazement. He gave them strict instructions not to tell anyone what had happened. And he told them to give her something to eat.

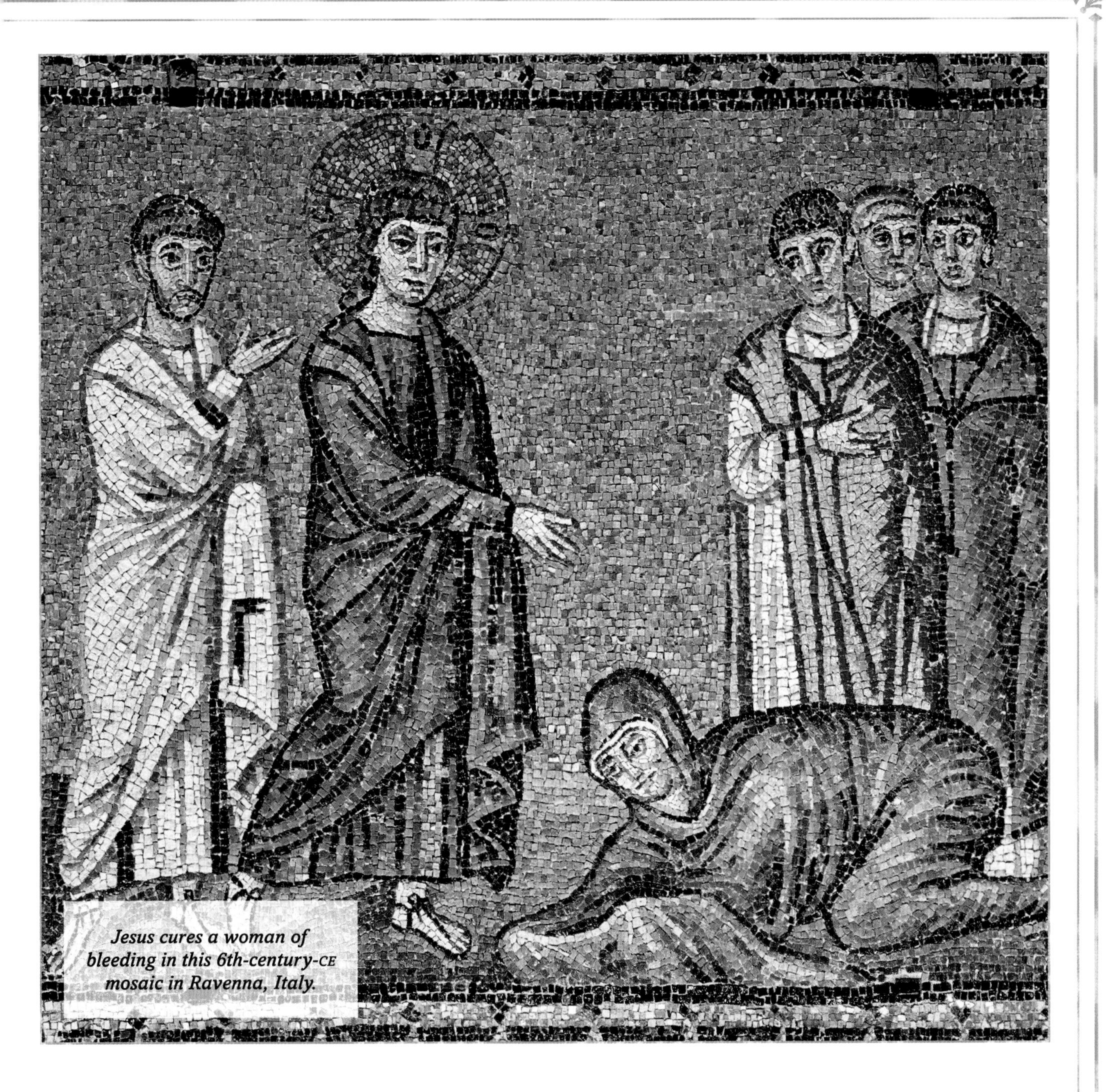

Jesus cures a woman of bleeding in this 6th-century-CE mosaic in Ravenna, Italy.

Understanding the story

Jesus heals both the suffering woman and the sick girl in response to their faith. Though the woman's illness has condemned her to a life of loneliness, the belief that contact with Jesus will cure her is rewarded. While Jairus knows his daughter has passed away, Jesus reminds him to have faith, and she returns to life. Faith is stronger than death.

The Sower

Jesus went to the lake to preach and a large crowd gathered to hear him. There were so many people that he got into a little fishing boat and spoke to them from that.

Sower's bag
In ancient times, farmers sowed seeds by hand from bags like this one. The method was called broadcasting—walking up and down the fields, scattering seeds over the soil. Farmers prayed for their seed to yield a bountiful harvest.

They listened from the shoreline, where the wading birds wandered to and fro, and from the bulrushes, where the waterfowl watched from their nests. Other people perched on the rocks or sat quietly on the soft green grass. Jesus's voice rang out across the water, clear as a bell, telling them a parable.

"A farmer went out to sow his seed. As he scattered it, some fell along the path and the birds came and ate it up. Some fell on rocky places where there was not much soil. It sprang up quickly, but when the sun shone the plants were scorched and they withered because they had no roots. Other seed fell among thorns, which grew up and choked the plants. And the remaining seed fell on good soil where it produced a fine crop and multiplied greatly—by thirty, sixty, or even one hundred times." Jesus paused briefly and then added, "He who has ears, let him hear."

At first, the crowd had listened quietly but, as Jesus went on, a few of them started to shuffle their feet and whisper to each other. They wondered why the preacher, who had such a growing reputation, was telling them a simple story about an ordinary farmer sowing his seeds. Others stayed silent, listening to every word that Jesus said.

Later, when everyone had gone home

and the disciples were alone with Jesus, they asked him why he spoke in parables. Jesus replied, "You are my disciples and I explain to you the secrets of the Kingdom of Heaven, but to everybody else I speak in parables."

And, because even the disciples themselves did not always understand the details of every parable, he explained the meaning of the story he had just told.

"The farmer sowing the seed is sowing the word of God. Some people are like the seed along the path; no sooner is the word sown in them than Satan comes along and takes it away. Other people, like the seed sown on rocky places, hear the word with joy. But, because they have no roots, they quickly collapse and lose their faith when there is any trouble or opposition. Still others, like the seed sown among the thorns, hear the word but are choked by the worries and desires of this life. The remaining people, like the seed sown on good soil, hear the word and accept it. The seed can only grow in those people who live their lives according to the word of God."

Jesus told them that, although parables were not always easy, people must listen to them with an open heart and a receptive mind. Only then could the truth take root. They must search hard for the hidden meaning and take the message to heart.

The farming year
In October, the fields were sown and then plowed to bury the seed. This ancient plow was used to scratch through the tough soil. Flax was harvested in the new year, wheat and barley were gathered in the spring, and fruit was ripe by late summer. Jesus's parables often made comparisons with farming.

Understanding the story

The word parable comes from the Greek word "parabole," meaning a comparison. Jesus's simple stories about everyday life carried a deeper meaning. Jesus hoped people would take the hidden message to heart. In the sower parable, Jesus is the farmer who sows words rather than seeds. He explains that his words will not grow inside everyone. Jesus reveals the hidden meaning to his disciples because he is aware that his ministry will soon pass to them.

"The farmer sowing the seed is sowing the word of God."

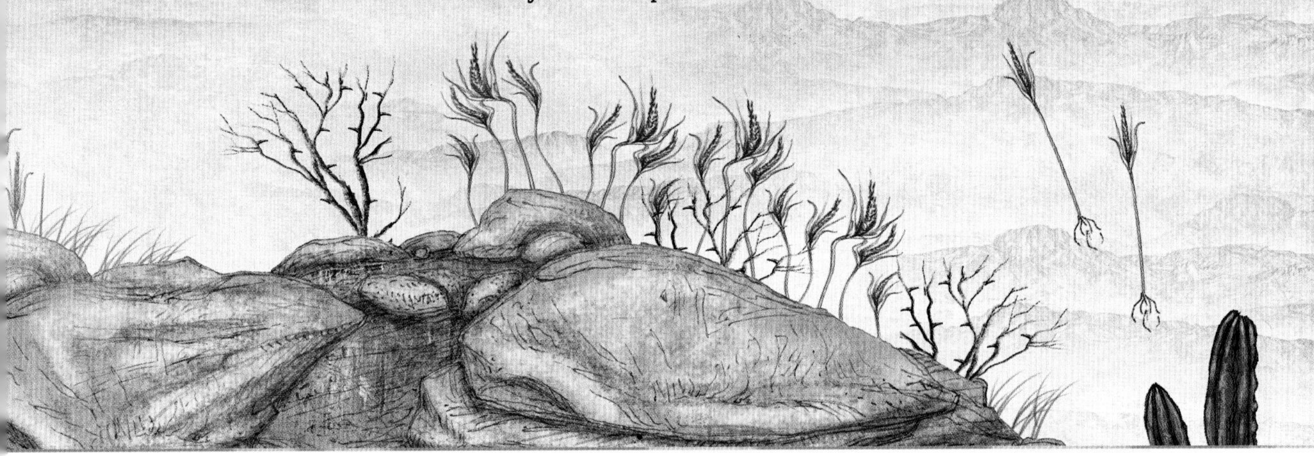

The Death of John the Baptist

Herod Antipas, the ruler of Galilee, respected and feared John the Baptist. But his wife, Herodias, hated the holy man because he had spoken out against her marriage to Herod.

Machaerus fortress
Herod Antipas's hilltop palace is shown here from an aerial perspective. It lies to the east of the Dead Sea in what is now Jordan. Although the New Testament does not say exactly where John the Baptist's imprisonment and execution took place, a Jewish historian named Josephus claimed that this was the site.

"It is not lawful for you to have your brother's wife," John had told Herod one day. Herodias wanted to have John put to death for his insolence, but Herod refused. He admired John and knew that many of his people held him in the highest esteem and thought that he was a great prophet. Herod did not want to risk an uprising. But, after much persuading, he did agree to have John arrested and put in prison.

Soon after, a huge banquet was to be held in the palace to celebrate Herod's birthday. It had taken months of planning. The guest list included all the highest officials and the most important men in the whole of Galilee. The leading lights of the Roman army would also be there, in full military dress. It would be a glittering occasion.

When the great day came, all the guests sat down to a sumptuous feast. The finest wine flowed and musicians played on their harps and lyres. Then, Herodias's young daughter, Salome, appeared in front of her stepfather and his guests, a picture of beauty and grace. She smiled sweetly to the king and started to dance for him, her dress floating around her and flowers nodding in her long, dark hair. Effortlessly, she turned this way and that, holding her tambourine high in the air. Everyone watched, entranced by her. And Herod himself was spellbound, unable to take his eyes off her. When she had finished, he beckoned her over and kissed her fondly on both cheeks. "Whatever you ask, shall be yours," he promised. "Even half my kingdom!" And he swore this on oath in front of all his guests, raising his goblet of wine.

Salome ran over to her mother, Herodias, who had been watching her daughter dance. "What shall I ask for?" whispered Salome.

"The head of John the Baptist on a plate!" said her mother.

Salome went straight back to Herod and repeated her mother's words. "I would like you to give me the head of John the Baptist on a plate," she said.

Herod looked at her in horror, but he had sworn an oath in front of all his guests and he had to keep it. So he gave orders for his executioner to go to the prison to behead John the Baptist. He waited, sick to the stomach, while Herodias gloated.

At last the doors opened, and a servant entered carrying the bleeding head of John the Baptist on a large silver platter. A trail of

"The Beheading of St John the Baptist" oil on canvas, by Niccolo de Simone.

Greek dancers
In Jesus's time, the cultural influences of both Rome and Greece were apparent. It was customary for the Greeks to hire female dancers to provide entertainment at special feasts and celebrations. This scene of young women dancing is taken from the lid of a Greek vase.

blood stained the marble floor as he walked toward Salome, who reluctantly accepted her prize. She walked across the room, blood dripping around her feet, and offered the platter to her mother. Herodias gazed at the severed head of John the Baptist, and her dark eyes gleamed with satisfaction.

As soon as John's disciples heard the news, they went to the prison and took the body of John the Baptist and laid it in a tomb. When Jesus was told, he took a boat and went away to mourn and pray for his cousin.

Understanding the story

King Herod must keep his word because he has sworn a public oath to honor whatever Salome wants. The terrible beheading of John the Baptist is devastating to his cousin Jesus. This event is a turning point in Jesus's ministry. He tells his disciples to spread the same message as John, but he also gives them the power to perform miracles.

Fish as a symbol
A recurring theme in Jesus's life and teachings is fish. Several of the disciples were fishermen, and Jesus told them they would be "fishers of men." Fish became an important symbol for early Christians, and the motif is included on some tombs. Fish are shown in this 4th-century-CE mosaic from the Church of the Multiplication in Tabgha, said to be the site of the miraculous mass feeding.

"They do not need to go away,' Jesus replied. 'You can give them something to eat here."

The Feeding of the Five Thousand

Jesus and his disciples tried to get away on their own for a little while, and they went to Bethsaida. But, as usual, the crowds followed them.

When Jesus saw the crowds, he smiled. He would never turn them away, whatever happened. They brought him their sick and he healed them.

By the time the sun was low in the sky, everybody was tired and hungry. The disciples came to Jesus and said, "It has been a long day. And we are far from anywhere. Why don't you send the crowds away to find food for themselves?"

"They do not need to go away," Jesus replied. "You can give them something to eat here." The disciples laughed and said, "How can we do that? There must be at least five thousand of them!"

Then Andrew, the brother of Peter, spoke up, "There is a boy here who has five small barley loaves and two small fish. But how far will they go among so many?"

Jesus told the disciples to divide the people into groups of fifty or a hundred and make them sit down on the grass. The people sat patiently, waiting to see what would happen.

Meanwhile, Jesus took the loaves and the fish from the boy and, looking up to heaven, he gave thanks and started to break the first loaf into pieces. He gave them to the disciples to take around. The disciples could not believe it. There was more than enough for everybody. And then Jesus did the same with the fish—turning two small sardines into many thousands. Everybody tucked in gratefully—all five thousand of them. And, even after everybody had finished, there was still enough bread and fish left over to fill twelve baskets.

Understanding the story

This miracle not only proves Jesus's power to the disciples, but also echoes the story of the feeding of the Israelites in the wilderness through Moses. Once again, God reaches out to feed His people, this time through His son Jesus. The crowds are provided with spiritual and bodily sustenance by God.

Jesus feeds the masses in this detail from a fresco by Italian Francesco Pagani (c. 1502–1548).

Later that night, the boat was in the middle of the lake, and he was alone on land. He saw the disciples straining at the oars, because the wind was against them. Shortly before dawn he went out to them, walking on the lake. He was about to pass by them, but when they saw him walking on the lake, they thought he was a ghost. They cried out, because they all saw him and were terrified.

Mark 6:47–50

The Sea of Galilee
Jesus found his first followers among the fishermen of the Sea of Galilee, a large freshwater lake. In the 1st century CE, several hundred fishing boats regularly worked the lake. It is still known for rich fishing and sudden storms.

Sea of Galilee
The Sea of Galilee is a large freshwater lake, 13 miles (21 km) long and 8 miles (13 km) wide. It experiences sudden strong winds and powerful storms because warm air above the lake mixes with cool air from the Mediterranean.

Fishing boat
This 1st-century-CE fishing boat, discovered on the northern shore of Galilee, is about 29 ft (9 m) in length. It was made of oak and cedar wood, and it is probable that its hull was once coated with tar to prevent it letting in water.

Jesus Walks on the Water

The crowds went away, talking of the miracle of the loaves and fish, and the disciples said goodbye to Jesus. They got back into their boat and started to row home.

Jesus stood on the shore, watching them go. Then he walked up the mountainside. When he got to the top, he could see the boat making its way across the calm water. He sat there, alone as night fell, praying to the Lord.

The disciples rowed on through the darkness toward the other side. They were far from the shore now and the inky water stretched around them, merging with the sky. The disciples were making good progress when, out of nowhere, the wind whistled in, whipping up the waves. The disciples gripped tight to their oars and battled on.

Then, in the distance, they saw a strange sight. It looked like a man walking over the water. The figure came nearer and nearer, gliding silently through the gloom and over the moonlit sea. The disciples rubbed their eyes and looked at each other in terror as the apparition approached. Now they could see that his sandalled feet were walking on the water as if it were solid ground.

"It's a ghost!" they cried, shivering with fear.

But then the familiar voice of Jesus said, "Do not be afraid. It is only me." The disciples stared at him in amazement.

Then Peter said, "Lord, if it is you, tell me to come to you on the water."

"Come!" said Jesus, and he held out his hand.

Peter got up and climbed over the side of the boat, not taking his eyes off Jesus. He put his feet down on the surface of the water and walked slowly toward his master.

But when Peter looked down at the water and at the waves, his courage failed him, and he began to sink. "Lord! Save me!" he cried.

Jesus reached out his hand and caught him. "You of little faith," he said. "Why did you doubt?" He took Peter back to the boat and together they climbed in. Immediately, the wind died down, the waves vanished, and the sea lay calm and tranquil.

The disciples looked at Jesus in awe and said, "Truly you are the Son of God!"

"Do not be afraid. It is only me."

"Peter Walks on Water" (1806) by German painter Philipp Otto Runge (1777–1810)

Understanding the story

The disciples' faith in Jesus grows stronger once they see him walk on water. Initially, Peter is able to walk across the water because of his faith in Jesus. It is significant that he sinks at the moment his fear takes over and he begins to doubt Jesus. The seemingly impossible can be achieved with faith.

The Good Samaritan

First aid
The Samaritan used wine and olive oil to dress the wounds of the injured Jew. Wine was applied first to act as an antiseptic before the cuts were coated in olive oil to soothe and protect. The wounds were then covered in linen bandages.

One day, a lawyer asked Jesus a difficult question, trying to trick him. "What must I do to gain eternal life?"

"You know what the law says," replied Jesus. "What does it tell you?"

The lawyer thought for a while and then answered him. "Love the Lord your God with all your heart and with all your soul and with all your strength and with all your mind. And you must love your neighbor as you love yourself," he said finally.

"Good—that is quite right," answered Jesus. "Remember these words every day of your life."

The lawyer frowned.

"But who is my neighbor?" he asked.

So Jesus told him a story. "A man was traveling along the lonely road from Jerusalem to Jericho through the desert land. Suddenly, he was ambushed and attacked by robbers. They stripped him of his clothes and everything he had, beat him savagely, and left him at the side of the road to die.

"Soon after, a priest walked along the road, through the heat and the dust. But when he saw the man lying there, covered in blood, he crossed over and hurried past on the other side of the road. Next, a Levite, who helped the priests in the Temple, appeared, but when he caught sight of his fellow Jew, bleeding and injured, he too crossed over quickly to the other side of the road and carried on his way. Then a Samaritan arrived and, when he saw the man lying there, he stopped and knelt down. And, although Jews and Samaritans were not the best of friends, he showed the poor man the utmost kindness, unlike the priest and the Levite. The Samaritan dressed his terrible wounds and bandaged them up. Then gently, he lifted the injured man onto his own donkey and took him to the nearest inn, where he looked after him.

"The next day," Jesus continued, "when the Samaritan was getting ready to go, he gave the innkeeper two silver coins and asked him to look after the injured man. As he left, the

The rocky road from Jericho to Jerusalem is 17 miles (27 km) long, and provided many hiding places for robbers.

Samaritan also asked the innkeeper to let him know next time he stayed if he owed any more money."

At the end of the story, Jesus paused and asked the lawyer, "Which of these three people do you think was a neighbor to the man who fell into the hands of the robbers?"

"The one who showed kindness," the lawyer said. "The Samaritan."

"Exactly," said Jesus. "Go and do likewise."

"And you must love your neighbor as you love yourself."

Understanding the story

Jesus is telling the lawyer that love knows no nationality, religion, or limit. People should love others without reservations, just as God loves His people. The priest and the Levite follow the letter, but not the spirit, of religious law. The Samaritan is the only one who shows the injured man true love.

The Transfiguration

When Jesus got to the region of Caesarea Philippi he asked his disciples, "Who do people say I am?"

"Some say you are John the Baptist, others say Elijah, Jeremiah, or one of the prophets," they said.

"But what about you?" Jesus asked the disciples. "Who do you say I am?"

"You are the Christ, the Son of God," Peter replied. No one else said anything.

Jesus smiled at Peter and said, "Blessed are you, Peter. God, my Father in Heaven, revealed this to you. You are my rock and on you I will build my church. I will give you the keys to the Kingdom of Heaven." But he warned the disciples not to tell anyone that he was Christ. He said that, in time, he would go to Jerusalem and suffer at the hands of the elders, the chief priests, and the teachers of the law. He told them that he would die, but would rise again after three days.

Peter protested, "This cannot happen, Lord."

Jesus turned on him and said, "Get behind me, Satan! Do not speak like that. You are only thinking of yourself and not the will of God." Jesus went on to tell his disciples that, to follow him, they must give up all their worldly riches. "For whoever wants to save his life will lose it, but whoever loses his life for me will find it. What good will it be for a man if he gains the whole world yet forfeits his soul?"

A week later, Jesus took Peter, James, and John to the top of a nearby mountain to pray. It was a long and hard climb. As soon as they got to the highest peak, Jesus was transfigured in front of their very eyes, and a dazzling light radiated from deep within him. His face was illuminated, like the brightest sun.

Just then two men appeared from nowhere and began talking to Jesus. The disciples recognized them as Moses the law-giver and Elijah the great prophet. The three disciples watched in amazement.

Then, as Jesus, Moses, and Elijah were speaking, a bright cloud came down from the sky and enveloped them. And a great voice inside the cloud said, "This is my Son, whom I love. With him I am well pleased. Listen to him."

The disciples could not believe their ears and fell to the ground, hiding their eyes. But Jesus came and touched them. "Get up," he said. "Do not be afraid." They opened their eyes and looked around. Moses and Elijah had vanished and Jesus was by himself again, standing alone.

Then the three disciples came back down the mountain with Jesus, and he said, "Until I have risen from the dead, do not tell anyone about what you saw today."

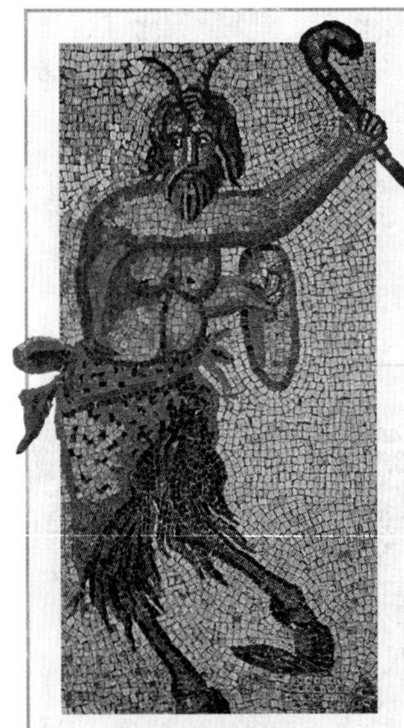

Mosaic of Pan
Caesarea Philippi was built by Philip II, the son of Herod the Great. It was originally called Paneas, after the goat-footed Greek god Pan, shown here on a Roman mosaic.

Keys to the Kingdom
The keys to God's Kingdom are a symbolic reward for Peter's good work. Jesus is asking Peter to open the door of Christian faith to the world. Peter will have a leading role in establishing the Christian Church.

Understanding the story

Jesus begins to prepare his disciples for the fulfilment of his mission with his death on the cross. Peter protests, but Jesus tellingly uses the same words he used to banish Satan in the desert. Through the amazing experience of Jesus's transfiguration, the disciples catch a glimpse of his true glory and power—greater even than that of Moses and Elijah, the greatest prophets of the Old Testament.

Jesus's final journey

The transfiguration prepares the disciples for their master's death. Jesus leaves Galilee and begins a long journey toward Jerusalem, traveling through Judea and into Perea. He shares parables with his disciples and followers and performs many miracles. In the days leading up to his crucifixion, Jesus stays close to Jerusalem.

NORTH TO GALILEE

Jesus passes through Jericho where he heals the blind man and converts Zacchaeus the tax collector.

Jericho

JUDEA

Jesus's triumphant arrival in Jerusalem on a donkey fulfils the Old Testament prophecy of the Messiah.

Jesus's donkey is taken from Bethphage.

Jesus is arrested in the Garden of Gethsemane on the Mount of Olives.

Jordan River

PEREA

Jesus spends some time in Perea (modern-day Jordan) where he blesses the children and talks to the rich young man.

Jerusalem

Mount of Olives

Bethphage

KIDRON VALLEY

Bethany

Jesus is crucified on a rocky hill at Golgotha, just outside Jerusalem.

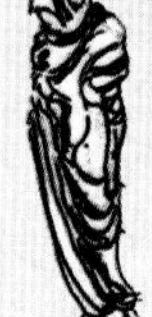

Jesus visits Martha and Mary in Bethany, and returns later to raise Lazarus from the dead.

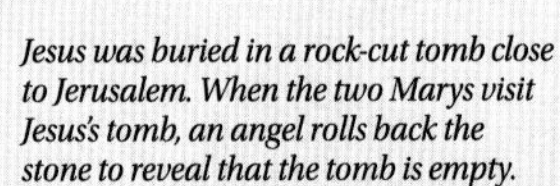

Jesus was buried in a rock-cut tomb close to Jerusalem. When the two Marys visit Jesus's tomb, an angel rolls back the stone to reveal that the tomb is empty.

DEAD SEA

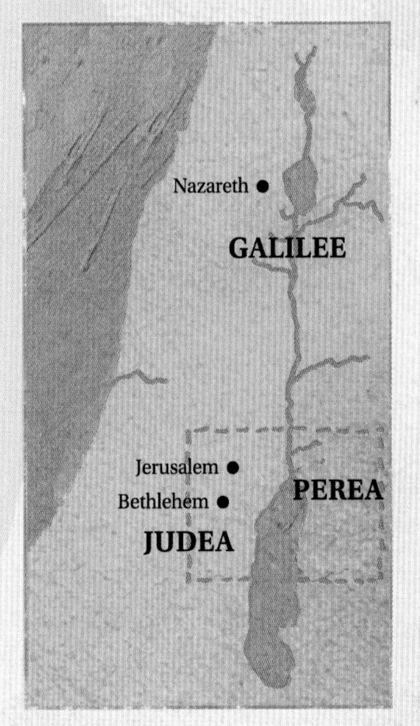

Mary, Martha, and Lazarus

There was a man named Lazarus, who lived in Bethany with his sisters, Mary and Martha. Jesus had stayed in their house one day, and Mary had spent many hours sitting at his feet, listening to him.

Mary absorbed every word Jesus said. Her sister, Martha, on the other hand, bustled about, cleaning the house and preparing the food. Eventually, she moaned to Jesus, "Lord, it is not fair that my sister has left me to do the work."

"Martha," Jesus replied gently. "Mary is quite right. It is much more important to listen to my teaching than to worry about cooking and cleaning."

Weeks later, Lazarus lay seriously ill. His sisters tried to make him better, but to no avail. They sent word to Jesus that their brother was on the brink of death.

When he got the message, Jesus said, "This sickness will not end in death. No, it is for God's Glory so that God's Son may be glorified through it." He did not rush to Bethany but stayed where he was for two more days. Then he said to his disciples, "Let us go back to Judea. Our friend Lazarus has fallen asleep. But I am going to wake him." The disciples looked at each other, puzzled, not realizing that Jesus was talking about death rather than sleep.

When they got to Bethany, they discovered that Lazarus had died four days earlier. He had been buried immediately, as was the custom, his body washed and wrapped in linen, scented with aloes and myrrh. Then it had been laid in a tomb in the hillside. As Jesus and the disciples approached, Martha ran out to meet them. Mary stayed in the house, mourning with her relatives.

"Lord," said Martha to Jesus, "If you had been here, my brother would not have died. But I know that even now God will give you anything you ask for."

"Your brother will rise again," replied Jesus. "I am the resurrection and the life. He who believes in me will never die. Do you believe this?"

"Yes, Lord," she answered. "I believe that you are the Christ, the Son of God, who has come into the world." Then she ran to the house and called Mary. "The teacher is here."

Mary went out to meet Jesus, accompanied by the other mourners. They had heard so much about the preacher who healed the sick that they wanted to see him for themselves.

Mary fell at his feet, sobbing, "Lord, if you had been here, my brother would not have died." Jesus was deeply moved

Household tasks
At the time of Jesus, women had many duties to perform each day in order to keep the household running smoothly. Women like Martha woke early in order to prepare the food, make bread, and light fires for cooking. Since the matriarch was responsible for all the domestic decisions, she was a highly respected member of the family.

"I am the resurrection and the life. He who believes in me will never die."

"Did I not tell you that if you believed you would see the Glory of God?"

"The Raising of Lazarus" (1857), oil on canvas by French painter Léon Bonnat (1833-1922)

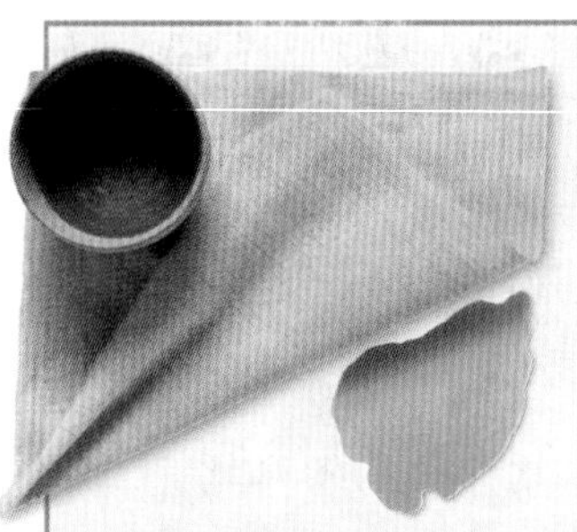

Preparing for burial
When someone died, their body was prepared for burial. This happened soon after the death in order to prevent excessive decay. The body was first washed and wrapped in a sheet or covered in bandages. Those who could afford it were wrapped in linen. Aloes (the juice of the aloe plant) and myrrh (the fragrant gum from tree bark) were often placed between the folds of the fabric.

by her sorrow and the tears of her family.

"Where have you laid him?" he asked.

"Come and see, Lord," she replied, tears running down her cheeks. Jesus wept.

One relative remarked, "See how he loved Lazarus, too."

But another replied, "If he can make a blind man see why did he not prevent Lazarus from dying?"

Together, they went to the tomb of Lazarus. It was a cave, and a huge rock had been rolled across the entrance to seal it. Jesus said, "Take away the stone."

Martha asked, "But Lord, are you sure? There will be a terrible smell."

He said, "Did I not tell you that if you believed you would see the Glory of God?"

The strongest men heaved the stone away from the entrance. Jesus looked to the heavens and said, "Father, I thank you that you have heard me. I know that you always hear me, but not everybody does."

Then, in a loud voice, Jesus shouted into the tomb, "Lazarus! Come out!" After a few moments, a shadowy figure appeared from the gloom. It was Lazarus, brought back to life from the dead. He was still wrapped in the linen strips of his shroud and a cloth was draped over his head.

Understanding the story

Death is depicted as sleep on many occasions in the Bible. Jesus is keen to teach his disciples that death is nothing to fear because the spiritual life is eternal. Martha's faith in Jesus makes her believe that he can help her brother rise from the dead. By bringing Lazarus to life, Jesus proves to all that he is the son of God.

Lost and Found

All sorts of people had gathered round Jesus to hear him speak, including some tax collectors and criminals.

The Pharisees, who thought it essential to uphold the law at all times, were not happy with this. "Look at him! He makes sinners welcome!" they said to each other, stroking their long white beards. Jesus started to speak, telling the people a parable about a shepherd and his sheep.

"There was a shepherd who had a large flock of one hundred sheep. He looked after them carefully out in the fields, watching over them day and night. But one day, he was counting his sheep and one was missing. He counted again, just to be sure. There were only ninety-nine. So, leaving the ninety-nine behind to graze on their own, the shepherd went to look for the missing sheep. He searched high and low, never giving up hope.

"Eventually, he found the sheep and, joyfully, he put it on his shoulders and carried it home. He called his neighbors and friends together and asked them to give thanks and celebrate with him because he had found his lost sheep."

And then, Jesus explained the story to them. "In the same way, there will be more rejoicing in heaven over one sinner who repents than over ninety-nine righteous people who do not need to repent." The crowd listened intently as he went on to tell another parable.

"There was a woman who had ten silver coins, but she lost one of them. She knew that it must be somewhere in the house. But she had no idea where. So she lit her lamp, took her broom, and swept the house thoroughly from top to bottom, searching for it. She looked in every corner, under each stick of furniture and rush mat and, at last, she found it hidden behind her stone water jar. She called her friends and neighbors together, asking them to rejoice with her. 'I am so happy that I have found my silver coin!' she told them."

And, when he had finished, he added, "In the same way, there is great rejoicing amongst the angels in heaven when even one sinner repents."

The Good Shepherd
Sheep are vulnerable creatures, dependent on shepherds for food, water, and protection. In the Old Testament, God's tender love and care is compared to a shepherd looking after his flock. In the New Testament, Jesus identifies with this role and calls himself the Good Shepherd. By protecting and ultimately dying to save his flock, Jesus's devotion and self-sacrifice for all of humanity is clear.

Understanding the story

The self-righteous Pharisees are unhappy that Jesus has welcomed tax collectors and criminals to listen to him speak; yet Jesus's point is that the repentance of just one sinner is cause for celebration. In the same way that the shepherd is delighted to locate one missing sheep and the woman is thrilled to find her missing coin, there is much reason to rejoice when a lost soul finds salvation with God.

The Prodigal Son

Jesus told the crowd a parable about a rich farmer who had two sons and what happened when one of his sons left home.

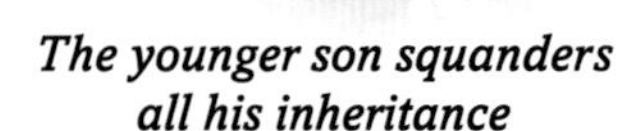

The younger son squanders all his inheritance

Inheritance
The younger son's request for his inheritance before his father had even passed away showed great disrespect. To then waste the money made the situation even worse.

"One day, the younger son came to him and said, 'Father, give me my share of your estate.' His father, who was a kind man, agreed, and divided his property equally between his two sons. Soon after, the younger son took his share of the inheritance, said goodbye to his father and brother, and left home. He went far away to a different country, settled there, and started a new life quite unlike the one he had left behind. He lived it up day and night, drinking and dancing with his wild new friends and spending his money in the most extravagant way. It did not take him long to get through the whole of his fortune and soon nothing was left. Then, to add to his woes, there was a terrible famine in his adopted country and people began to die of hunger.

"The young man was desperate and did not know what to do. Eventually, he had to swallow his pride and work as a lowly farm laborer, tending pigs out in the fields. His own stomach was so empty that he eyed the pigs' food enviously and wondered about stealing some of it. Hunger gnawed at him day and night and his thoughts turned to home. Finally, he said to himself, 'Even my father's humblest servants will have something to eat and food to spare and here am I starving to death.' He knew that he had sinned against heaven and against his father, and that he must make amends.

"He set off on the long journey, and when he got close to his home, his father saw him and his eyes filled with tears. He ran to meet his son with his arms outstretched and hugged him warmly. And the son said to him, 'Father, I have sinned against heaven and against you. I am no longer worthy to be called your son.'

"But his father would have none of it and told his servants to fetch the finest robe that could be found. He dressed his son in it, put a ring on his finger and sandals on his feet. 'Bring a fattened calf and kill it,' he ordered his servants. 'We shall have a great feast to celebrate. For this son of mine was dead and is alive now. He was lost and he is found.' The celebrations began.

"Meanwhile, the elder son had been working in the fields. When he came

"He was lost and he is found."

home at the end of the day, tired and hungry, he was amazed to hear music and dancing in the house. He asked one of the servants what was going on, who replied, 'Your brother has come home and your father has killed the fattened calf because he is back safe and sound.' The older brother could not believe it. Anger swelled within him and he could not bring himself to set foot in the house.

"His father went out to plead with him, but his son shouted at him, 'All these years that he has been gone, I have slaved away for you and never disobeyed you. And you have never given me so much as a miserable goat to say thank you. But when your precious young son comes home after squandering every last penny, you kill the fattened calf for him!'

"His father replied, 'My son, everything that I have is yours and I love you dearly. But we have to celebrate and give thanks because this brother of yours was dead and is alive again. He was lost and is found.' "

Jesus looked at the crowd and said, "Like the father in this parable, God will open His arms to all those who repent. He will rejoice when they return to Him!"

The father is overjoyed to see his younger son return home

Understanding the story

The word "prodigal" is used to describe someone who spends money wastefully. Jesus explains that God does not hold grudges for past mistakes. As long as the sinner repents, he will be forgiven and accepted. Even the return of a son who insulted and abandoned his family is celebrated after he asks for forgiveness for his errors.

Ring and sandals
The gifts the father bestows on his repentant son are symbolic of his forgiveness and acceptance. The giving of a ring grants the son authority over the servants. Only the family wore sandals in the house, so the father makes his son wear them to welcome him back.

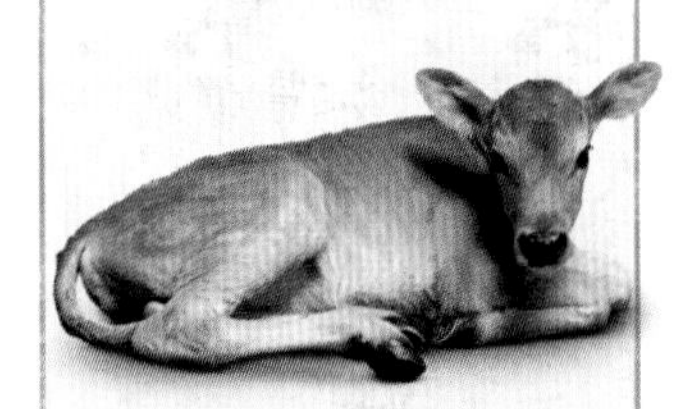

Fattened calf
It was traditional for wealthy families to honor a very special occasion by killing a calf (fattened on milk) and feasting on it. By doing this, the father makes it clear that the return of his son is cause for great celebration.

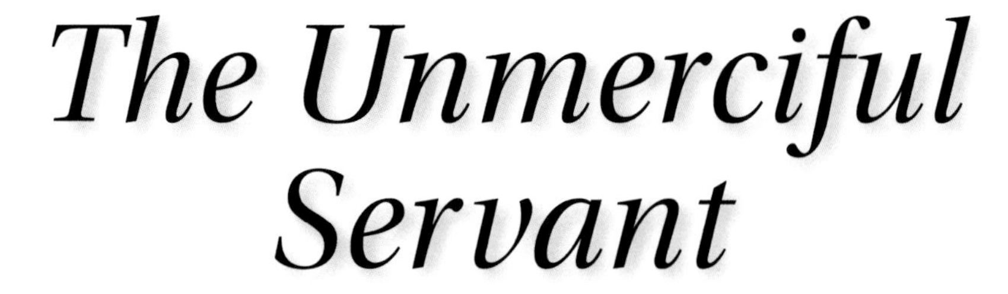

The Unmerciful Servant

Servants
There are many examples of servants in ancient times. Most servants were slaves, and their working day involved long hours and hard work. They received no wages for taking care of the house, from cleaning and running errands, to cooking, as seen in this 1st-century-CE Roman relief of a servant preparing a meal. However, the Bible's recurring message is that everyone should be a true servant of God, and Jesus is the best example of this selflessness.

Peter came to Jesus one day and said, "Lord, how many times should I forgive my brother when he sins against me? Up to seven times?"

Jesus answered, "I tell you, not seven times but seventy times seven." And he told the disciples a parable. "There was a king who was very kind and often used to lend his servants money when they were in need. The time came for the accounts to be settled, so he called everybody to him, one at at time. A servant owed him ten thousand talents, which was an extremely large sum of money. The king asked for the debt to be settled, but the servant had nothing and could not pay him back. So the king ordered that the man and his wife and all his children should be sold as slaves in order to raise the money.

"Distraught, the servant fell down on his knees before the king. 'Be patient with me, I beg you, my Lord!' he pleaded. 'I will pay back everything!' The king was a merciful man and took pity on him. He decided to cancel the debt—all ten thousand talents of it—and let the man go.

"Not long after, the servant met one of his friends who worked at the palace and owed him one hundred denarii. It was not a large amount of money. As soon as the servant saw his friend, he shouted, 'I want that money you owe me! Pay me back now!' And he grabbed his friend around the throat and started to beat him.

"Gasping for breath, the man fell to his knees and begged for mercy. 'Be patient with me, please!' he cried. 'I will pay you back!' But his tormentor refused and had

"The Unmerciful Servant", oil on canvas, attributed to Dutch painter Willem Drost (1633–1659)

Denarii
These shiny silver coins are ancient Roman currency. Called denarii, they were the coins that were most commonly used in Jesus's time. The coin was first issued in 211 BCE, and it was common for the ruler of Rome to have his profile on one side of the coin. One denarius was worth about a day's wages to a soldier. The quality of the silver changed in line with the economic climate. Eventually, denarii came to be made of copper with a silver coating, to save on cost.

the man thrown in prison until he could pay his debt.

"When the other servants in the palace heard about this they could not believe it. They were so distressed that they went straight to the king and told him. He immediately summoned the servant to whom he had showed such kindness. 'You wicked man,' he said. 'I canceled all of your debt because you begged and pleaded with me. Should you not have had mercy on your fellow servant, just as I had on you?' And then, boiling with rage, he sent the man to prison to be punished, until he could pay back all of the money he owed."

At the end of the parable, Jesus said, "This is how my heavenly Father will treat each of you, unless you truly forgive your brother from the bottom of your heart."

Understanding the story

This parable explains why people should treat each other how they would wish to be treated. God is like the king, who cancels a debt that his servant can never repay. Yet the servant has his friend imprisoned for a far smaller sum. When the servant himself is thrown in prison, Jesus is warning that God will punish those who do not show true forgiveness.

"Be patient with me, I beg you, my Lord! I will pay back everything!"

Lazarus and the Rich Man

Jesus told the disciples a story about a rich man and a beggar, and what happened to them after they died.

"There was a rich man who dressed in purple and the most expensive linen. He lived in the lap of luxury in a splendid house, surrounded by every comfort and waited on hand and foot. The food he ate was the very finest, and the wine he drank was the best. But, at his gate, there lay a poor beggar, named Lazarus. He was a pitiful sight, and his body was covered in weeping sores. He was starving and longed to eat any scraps of food that might fall from the rich man's table.

"The time came when Lazarus died and the angels carried him up to heaven. Soon after, the rich man also died and his body was buried with all due ceremony. But he was taken straight down to hell, where he suffered the most terrible torment, roasting day and night in the flames. He looked up to heaven and saw Abraham, the father of his people, with Lazarus by his side. So he called up to him, 'Father Abraham!' he cried. 'Have pity on me and send Lazarus to dip his finger in water and come and cool my tongue! I am in agony!'

"Abraham looked down at him and shook his head slowly. 'My son,' he said. 'Remember, in your life you had everything, while Lazarus had nothing. He has now earned his comfort here in heaven, while you are being punished in hell. And besides, there is a great chasm between heaven and hell and no one can bridge it.'

" 'Then I beg you,' pleaded the rich man. 'Send Lazarus to my father's house, for I have five brothers. Let him warn them what has happened to me.'

" 'They have Moses and the prophets. Let them listen to them,' said Abraham.

" 'But they won't!' the rich man protested, as the flames licked around him. 'But, if someone from the dead goes to them, they will repent.'

"Again, Abraham shook his head. 'If they do not listen to Moses and the prophets, they will not listen if someone rises from the dead.' "

"Remember, in your life you had everything, while Lazarus had nothing."

Understanding the story

Many rich people thought that their wealth was a reward for their righteousness, and so heaven was assured. However, it is Lazarus who goes to heaven after his hellish existence on Earth where the rich man ignored him. The disturbing glimpse of burning hell is Jesus's warning of what lies ahead for those who make money their life's meaning rather than God.

The Pharisee and the Tax Collector

Jesus told this parable about the dangers of being self-righteous and looking down on other people.

Prayer items
For prayer time, Jewish men wore tallit (special shawls) and kippah (skull caps) to show their respect to the Lord. People did not read prayers from books, but many worshippers carried small Torah texts in small containers on their bodies. Prayers were usually said by candelight. These days, a nine-branched candelabrum, called a menorah, is used during Hannukah, the Jewish festival of lights, and books are used for prayer.

"Two people went to the Temple to pray. One was a Pharisee and the other was a tax collector. The Pharisee stood up importantly, sure in the knowledge that he had observed all the Lord's commandments. Catching the priest's eye, he raised his head high in the air and started to pray to the Lord. 'God, I thank you that I am not like other men who commit crimes and sins, and I also thank you that I am not like that tax collector over there. I devote my life to you and am obedient in all things, fasting twice a week and giving a tenth of all I have to helping other people.'

"But the tax collector stood modestly some way away. Nobody took any notice of him. He did not think himself worthy enough even to raise his eyes toward heaven, so he bowed his head to the ground. 'God have mercy on me,' he prayed. 'I am a sinner.' "

Jesus concluded, "Now this was the man, rather than the Pharisee, who went home with God's blessing. For everyone who puffs themselves up and exalts themselves will be humbled. And those who are meek and humble will be exalted."

"God have mercy on me,' he prayed. 'I am a sinner."

Understanding the story

Jewish society looked up to the piety of the Pharisees and down on tax collectors, whom they considered dishonest. Jesus is saying that there is no place for self-importance before God. The Pharisee is boastful of his achievements, while the tax collector is humble and admits to being a sinner. His desire to repent means the tax collector is the one who will enter God's Kingdom.

Jesus and the Children

On their way back to Capernaum, the disciples had been arguing. Jesus asked them what they had been quarreling about.

They had, in fact, been arguing about which of them would be considered the most worthy in the eyes of God, but they did not want to tell him. They were ashamed of themselves and kept quiet. But Jesus knew exactly what was in their minds. Sitting down, he beckoned all twelve disciples to him. They gathered around to listen. "If anyone wants to be first," he said to them, "he must be the very last and the servant of all."

Then a group of women arrived and came up to Jesus. They asked him if he would bless the children that they had brought with them. They clustered around him expectantly, babies in their arms and little children at their feet. It was quite a crowd and the disciples started to push the mothers away, telling them to stop bothering Jesus. But Jesus, who never turned anyone away, said to the disciples, "Let the little children come to me. Do not stop them for the Kingdom of Heaven belongs to them."

He took one little boy and lifted him gently onto his lap. The child looked up at him, wide-eyed, "Whoever welcomes one of these little children in my name, welcomes me," said Jesus. "And whoever welcomes me, welcomes the one who sent me. I tell you the truth. Unless you change and become like little children, you will never enter the Kingdom of Heaven." And he stretched out his hand and blessed each baby and child in turn, as their smiling mothers watched. The disciples stood back, quietly listening.

Understanding the story

Children are just as important as adults to Jesus. He believes that all members of the community are equal. In order to enter the Kingdom of God, everyone must have complete faith in the Lord, just as a child has faith in his or her parents. Their humility and trust are a lesson to all.

"Suffer the Little Children to Come unto Me" (1854) by Mexican artist Juan Urruchi (1828–1892)

The Rich Young Man

As Jesus went on his way, a young man ran up to him and fell down on his knees before him.

"Good teacher," he asked, "what must I do to gain eternal life?"

"You know the commandments. You must follow them," Jesus answered.

"Teacher," the young man said. "I have kept all the commandments since I was a boy."

Jesus smiled at him. "Now all you have to do is to sell everything you have and give it to the poor, then come and follow me. You will have treasure in heaven." The young man was filled with sorrow when he heard this because he came from a very wealthy family. As he walked away, Jesus said to the disciples, "I promise that it is easier for a camel to go through the eye of a needle than for a rich man to enter the Kingdom of God."

Like most people, the disciples thought that wealth and prosperity were a sign of God's blessing. "Who then can be saved?" they asked.

Jesus replied, "All things are possible with God."

"Lord, we have left everything behind to follow you!" said Peter. "What will happen to us?" he asked.

"Anyone who has left their homes and their fields and their families behind to follow me will receive one hundred times as much and will recieve eternal life," Jesus answered.

"All things are possible with God."

Understanding the story

Jesus explains that living by the Ten Commandments is not enough. Though the rich man believes his prosperity is a blessing from God, Jesus dismisses material wealth. He tells him to give his money to the poor and make God his priority. Jesus is not rejecting the man, but warning him that riches can ruin a close relationship with God.

"Christ and the Rich Young Ruler" by German painter Heinrich Hofmann (1824–1911)

Zacchaeus the Tax Collector

On his way to Jerusalem, Jesus passed through the city of Jericho. People had heard so much about the teacher from Galilee that they lined the streets to watch him go by.

Among them was a man named Zacchaeus, who was an extremely wealthy tax collector. But he was a short man and was stuck at the back of the crowd, unable to see anything. He stood on tiptoes and craned his neck, but could not even catch a glimpse of Jesus. Determined not to lose his chance, he darted ahead and spotted a shady sycamore tree growing nearby. He heaved himself slowly onto the lowest branch and climbed up through the dense, green leaves to get a bird's-eye view of Jesus as he came along. The rest of the crowd watched him, surprised to see a fully grown man, and a tax collector at that, sitting in a tree.

All the while, Jesus was walking slowly along the road, talking to the people. When he got to the sycamore tree he stopped in his tracks and looked up. "Zacchaeus, come down immediately," Jesus said. "Please would you take me to your house? I would like to stay there."

The tax collector could not believe his ears and slithered down the tree, landing at Jesus's feet. He dusted himself off and, bowing low, he said that he would be honored and glad to welcome Jesus to his house. They carried on along the road as the crowd watched, surprised to see the two deep in conversation together. They did not like Zacchaeus because he worked for the Romans and they did not trust him. "Can you believe it?" they muttered to one another. "Jesus is going home with that sinner!"

But, when they got to the house, Zacchaeus said to Jesus, "Look, Lord. Here and now I promise to give half of my possessions to the poor. And, if I

Tax collectors
The Romans employed Jewish tax collectors to gather monies, believing they could bring insider knowledge of people's finances. As a result, tax collectors were disliked.

Sycamore tree
Weary travelers found shade under the sycamore-fig trees lining Israel's roadways. In the Bible, figs can represent good (ripe) and bad (rotten). Old Testament prophet Amos was a farmer of sycamore figs before God's calling.

have ever cheated anybody out of anything, I will pay back four times that amount."

Jesus smiled and said to him, "Today salvation has come to this house. This man is, indeed, a son of Abraham. What was lost has been saved."

Understanding the story

The repentant tax collector risks his dignity by climbing a tree in order to see Jesus. Most Jewish people believed tax collectors were dishonest and impure, so they react angrily when Jesus befriends one. Yet, Zacchaeus expresses remorse and vows to make amends many times over. Jesus shows forgiveness and welcomes him back into Jewish society.

The Wedding Feast

One of the leading Pharisees had invited Jesus and the disciples to eat at his house.

There were many other guests and, as they were sitting at the table, Jesus told them a parable. "The Kingdom of Heaven is like the king who prepared a magnificent wedding banquet for his son. All the guests had been invited and everything had been prepared. He sent his servants out to summon the guests, telling them that the celebrations were about to begin. But, although, they had all accepted their invitations quite some time ago, the guests began to make excuses.

" 'I have just bought a field and I have to go and inspect it now!' said one, looking the other way. 'Please send my apologies!'

" 'I have just bought five teams of oxen and I'm on my way to try them out now!' said another. 'I am so sorry!'

" 'I have just got married myself so I am afraid I can't come!' said still another. 'Please excuse me!'

"The servants went back to tell their master the bad news. Not one of the guests was coming. The king was furious. 'They did not deserve to come to the banquet anyway!' he stormed. 'Go into town and pick up anyone you can find. It doesn't matter who they are! The more the merrier! Invite them all!' The servants did as they were told and brought back dozens of people, glad to be invited so unexpectedly to the wedding feast.

"The king came in and was pleased to see all the guests. But he noticed one disrespectful man sitting at the table who was not wearing wedding clothes. Going up to him, he said, 'Friend, how did you get in here without wearing wedding clothes?' The man looked at him and said nothing.

"Immediately, the king ordered his servants to seize the man. 'Tie him up, hand and foot, and throw him out into the darkness,' he said."

And, after he had finished telling the parable, Jesus looked round the table and said, "So it is with the Kingdom of Heaven. Many are invited in, but only those with the right spirit are chosen."

Ketubah
The marriage ceremony is sealed with a contract, called the Ketubah (above), which states the groom's obligations toward the bride. This is read aloud during the service and displayed in the home after the event.

Understanding the story

Those who reject Jesus's message are turning away from God. Jesus is warning the Pharisees that their place in the Kingdom of Heaven is not assured. They were invited first, but they have refused. They are breaking their commitment to God. Only those who respond to Jesus's message will enter God's Kingdom.

The Wise and Foolish Maidens

Jesus told another parable to explain the Kingdom of Heaven. It was about ten bridesmaids at a wedding.

Oil jar
Lamps were in everyday use in ancient times, so households kept supplies of oil in large jars. This was poured into the lamps before the wicks were lit. As oil provided light for only three hours, it was important to store extra oil.

"They had helped the bride to get ready and were waiting excitedly for the groom to arrive at her house. Then they would escort the couple back to the groom's house for the wedding ceremony. When evening came, it seemed unlikely that the groom would come that day, so they settled down for the night. But five of them—the wise ones—decided that they would keep enough oil for their lamps to light the wedding procession, if the groom should arrive during the night. The other five—the foolish ones—let their lamps burn out.

"At midnight there was a shout, 'Quick, wake up, he's here!' The wise bridesmaids hurriedly lit their lamps, but the foolish ones had no oil.

" 'Lend us some,' they said, 'Please!'

"But the others replied, 'No, we can't. There may not be enough for all of us!'

"So the foolish young women hurried away to try to buy some oil, while the wise ones greeted the groom and proceeded with him and the bride to the groom's home, where the wedding ceremony started.

"Later, the five foolish bridemaids arrived and knocked at the door. But the groom refused to let them in. 'It's too late,' he said. 'You've missed your chance.' "

Jesus paused for a moment and then he said, "And so, always be prepared. You do not know the day or the hour when I will return."

Understanding the story

In this parable, the groom represents Jesus, while the bridesmaids are his followers, and the wedding ceremony is the Kingdom of Heaven. It is the bridesmaids who are prepared for the groom's arrival who accompany him to the wedding ceremony. Jesus explains that he could come at any time. Those who live by God's word will always be prepared for his arrival and will gain entry to the Kingdom of Heaven.

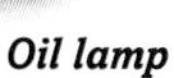

Oil lamp
Oil was poured into the hole in the middle, and a wick was fed from the smaller hole on the side into the well of oil and lit. This oil lamp dates from about 70 CE.

The Parable of the Talents

Jesus told another parable about the Kingdom of Heaven. It was about a master and his three servants.

Talents
In Palestine, at the time of Jesus, people often used weights instead of coins. With three currencies in place, the weight system was based on shekels (pictured). The heaviest weight was a talent, which equaled about 66 lb (30 kg). It represented approximately 3,000 shekels or 6,000 denarii. This was a very large sum—the equivalent of many years' wages.

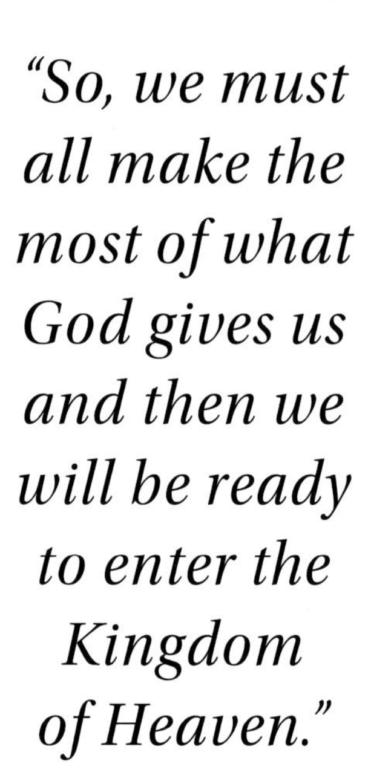

"So, we must all make the most of what God gives us and then we will be ready to enter the Kingdom of Heaven."

"The master called his three servants together and asked them to look after his money for him while he went on a journey. He gave them different amounts of money, according to their ability. To the first servant he gave five talents, to the second servant he gave two talents, and to the last servant he gave one talent.

"The first two men cleverly put the money to work for them and soon doubled the amount that they had been given. But the third man went and dug a hole in the ground and hid his money there.

"After a long time away, their master returned and wanted to know what had happened to his money. The first servant came to him and said, 'Master, you gave me five talents and I have turned them into ten.'

"The second servant said, 'I have doubled your money, as well. You gave me two talents and I have since made two more.'

"Their master was very pleased with them and said, 'Well done. You are good and faithful servants. You have both worked hard with what I gave you. I will put you in charge of all sorts of things now.'

"Then the servant who had been given one talent came and said, 'Master, I have always known that you are a hard man, harvesting where you have not sown and gathering where you have not scattered seed. So I was afraid and hid your talent in the ground. See, here is what belongs to you.' And he held out the talent.

"His master was furious and replied, 'You worthless and lazy man! Why didn't you put my money on deposit in the bank? Then, at least, when I returned I would have got the interest. Take the talent from him and give it to my servant who has ten talents.' And, with that, he gave orders for the man to be thrown out of the house."

Explaining the parable, Jesus went on, "The two servants who used their abilities to the full to benefit their master are rewarded, but the other man loses everything. So, we must all make the most of what God gives us and then we will be ready to enter the Kingdom of Heaven."

Understanding the story

This parable is not about financial failure. The word "talent" here means aptitude. As long as an individual makes the most of their abilities, they will be welcomed in the Kingdom of God. By choosing the safe option of burying the talent, the third servant has failed to recognize his full potential and is punished by losing everything.

Jesus Enters Jerusalem

It was the week before Passover, and Jesus and the disciples were on their way to Jerusalem. They came to Bethphage on the Mount of Olives and stopped for a little while.

Jesus sent two of the disciples into the village. "You will find a donkey tied up there, with her young colt. Untie them both and bring them to me. If anyone asks you what you are doing, tell them that the Lord needs them." And so the words of the prophet Zechariah would now come true. Many years before, he had said, "See, your king comes to you, gentle and riding on a donkey, on a colt, the foal of a donkey."

The disciples fetched the two animals and spread one of their cloaks over the colt. Then Jesus climbed on the colt, and they set off down the hill. The olive trees cast a dappled light, protecting them from the sun. Although the little donkey had never been ridden before, he was good-tempered, and plodded down the path, taking Jesus to Jerusalem. The disciples walked by his side.

Soon, they were joined by other pilgrims, also going to celebrate Passover. Word spread that the teacher who could heal the sick had traveled all the way from Galilee and was on his way to Jerusalem. People stared in wonder and whispered that he was the Messiah. They clustered around him and gradually the crowd swelled. Some people took off their cloaks and laid them on the ground in front of him as he passed. Others climbed up the tall trunks of the date palm trees and cut branches to scatter beneath the donkey's feet. They praised Jesus and called his name, shouting, "Hosanna to the son of David! Blessed is he who comes in the name of the Lord!"

Some of the Pharisees were shocked to hear the people calling Jesus "son of David" as this was the special name for the expected Messiah. "Teacher! Can't you control your disciples?" they said.

"I tell you," replied Jesus, "If they keep quiet, the stones will cry out." And he rode on.

At last, the procession approached the city walls. But as he drew near, Jesus wept, knowing that before long Jerusalem would be destroyed again. "The day will come when your enemies will surround you on every side," he said, as if talking to the holy city itself. "They will destroy everything because you did not recognize God's coming."

Many pilgrims had gathered in the city already. They watched in astonishment as Jesus and his followers streamed through the gate, heading toward the Temple.

"Blessed is he who comes in the name of the Lord!"

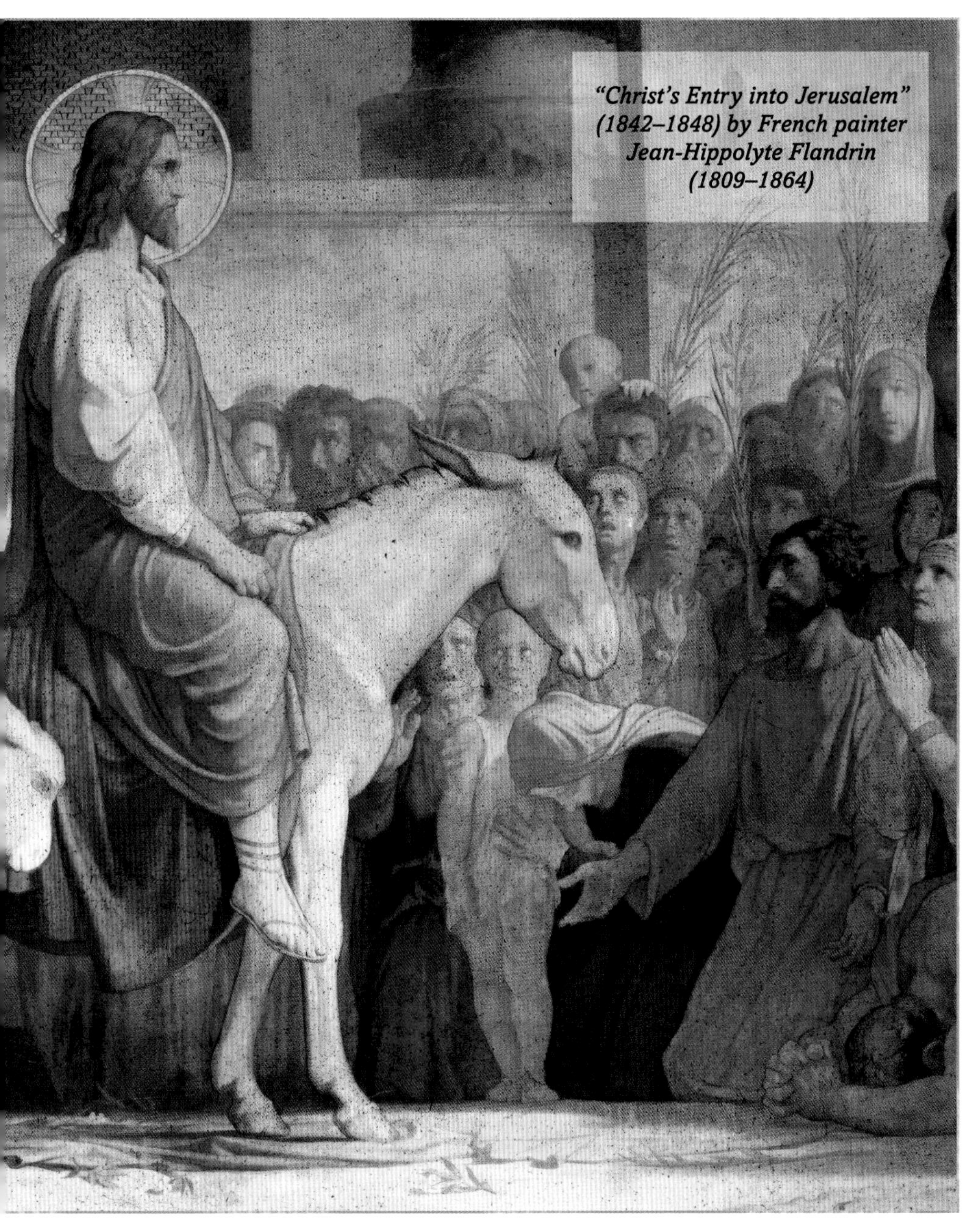

"Christ's Entry into Jerusalem" (1842–1848) by French painter Jean-Hippolyte Flandrin (1809–1864)

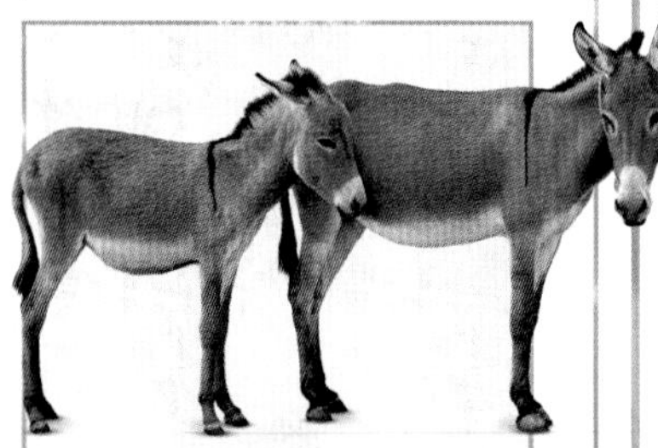

Donkeys
During times of peace, it was traditional for kings to ride on donkeys. An ancient prophecy in the Old Testament stated that a king would come in peace to Jerusalem. Jesus's arrival on a colt (a young donkey) is a symbolic act that fulfills the prophecy.

Palm leaves
In ancient times, palm leaves symbolized victory. This is why the people lay the leaves down on Jesus's path. They are sharing in his triumphant arrival. Although these leaves resemble branches, they grow from the top of the date palm's tall trunk.

Understanding the story

When Jesus rides in on a donkey, the Jewish crowds realize the significance. Jesus is the Messiah Zechariah promised them. During Jesus's time, Herod the Great and his sons had enlarged and beautified Jerusalem. Jesus is reduced to tears because he knows that the city will soon be destroyed, and he will be crucified.

Jesus and the Temple Traders

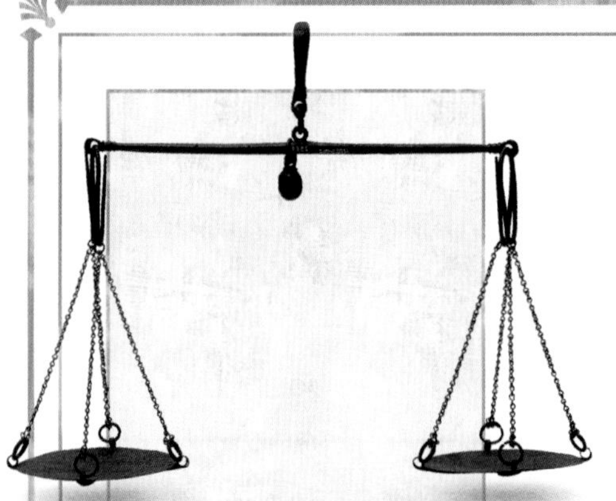

Scales
In Biblical times, traders used metal scales like these to weigh out money and products. Some people worked as money exchangers, converting foreign currency into shekels for visitors to use in the Temple and making an unfair profit. Jesus objected to them robbing those going into the Temple to worship, so he threw them out of the Temple.

Jesus walked up the great steps and into the courtyard that led into the Temple. He looked around sadly. It was like a bustling marketplace, full of people buying and selling their wares as fast as they could.

Cattle and sheep stood lined up in the sun, waiting to be sold for sacrifice, flicking their tails to keep the flies away. Doves and pigeons cooed pitifully in their baskets beside them. The traders haggled loudly, all determined to get the very best price. The money exchangers sat at their tables, competing with each other furiously. They raked in the foreign coins with greedy fingers, changing them into shekels at the worst possible rate. The pilgrims waited for their money to be handed back so that they could go into the Temple.

Overwhelmed with sorrow and filled with rage, Jesus walked straight up to the nearest money exchanger, grabbed his table, and turned it over. The man sat there, unable to believe his eyes, as his money cascaded to the ground. Jesus went to the next table and did the same. One by one, he turned over all the tables, the coins bouncing and rolling into every corner of the courtyard. Everyone watched in utter amazement.

Then, Jesus went up to the traders, who had by this time stopped their haggling and were watching open-mouthed. "It is written that my house will be a house of prayer," he thundered. "But you have turned it into a den of thieves." And he began to drive them out of the Temple. Filled with fear they ran, taking their animals with them. The money exchangers followed, hot on their heels. Before long, the courtyard had been cleared completely.

The pilgrims walked quietly into the Temple to pray, and Jesus started to heal the sick. They crowded around, waiting to be cured by him, but the chief priests and the teachers of the law watched with pursed lips. And, when they heard the children singing "Hosanna to the son of David," they marched up to Jesus. "Do you hear what these children are saying?" they demanded indignantly.

"Yes," replied Jesus. "Have you never read the psalm that says it is the lips of children that praise God most sweetly?"

As the sun set, Jesus left Jerusalem and went back to Bethany for the night. The

"It is written that my house will be a house of prayer."

next morning, he returned with the disciples to begin teaching in the Temple. The chief priests and the elders came up to him in front of everybody and asked, "Who gave you the authority to come and teach here?"

"I will ask you one question," Jesus replied. "If you answer me I will tell you by what authority I am here. Was my cousin John given the right to baptize by God or by men?"

The chief priests and elders scratched their heads and could not make up their minds. "If we say that God gave him the right, then Jesus will ask us why we did not believe John the Baptist. But if we say that men gave him the right, then the people will stone us because they believed that John was a prophet."

So, reluctantly, they turned to Jesus and said, "We don't know."

"In that case," replied Jesus, "neither will I tell you by what authority I am here."

Understanding the story

By throwing the traders out of the Temple, Jesus is showing his authority. The religious leaders challenge his authority. They are indignant that the children are calling Jesus "son of David"—the promised king who will deliver them from Roman oppression. By asking a question that the priests and elders will not answer, Jesus discredits them publicly.

Market
This busy street market echoes the bustle of biblical times. In Jesus's day, Jerusalem had a population of 60,000.

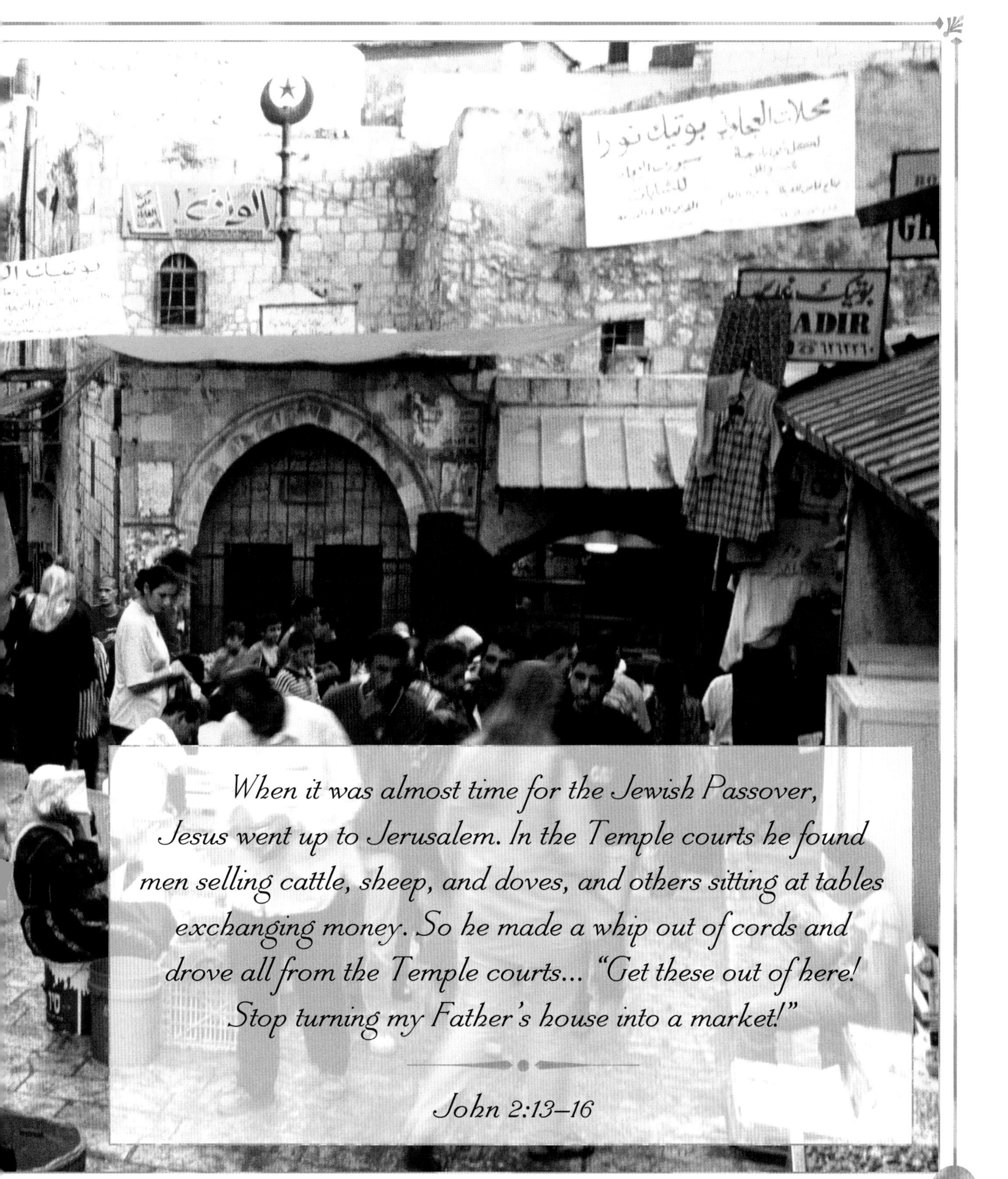

When it was almost time for the Jewish Passover, Jesus went up to Jerusalem. In the Temple courts he found men selling cattle, sheep, and doves, and others sitting at tables exchanging money. So he made a whip out of cords and drove all from the Temple courts... "Get these out of here! Stop turning my Father's house into a market!"

John 2:13–16

Perfume bottles
Aromatic oils, fragrant perfumes, and cosmetics were carried in jars and vases made of alabaster and glass. By using the expensive ointment, Mary demonstrates Jesus's important status, and that he won't be with the disciples for long.

Anointing for burial
Before a burial, a special ointment was often used to anoint the body. This was imported from India into Palestine. Mary anoints Jesus with the oil of the spikenard plant, which grows in the Himalaya Mountains.

Judas's Betrayal

The priests and the elders had seen Jesus ride into Jerusalem and they had watched him teaching the people and healing the sick.

They had also witnessed him driving the traders and the money exchangers out of the Temple. They knew that his following was growing by the day and that people were calling him the Messiah, the king that had been promised to the Jewish people for so long. The teacher from Galilee was a thorn in their flesh, challenging their authority and putting their livelihoods at risk. Something had to be done.

In the evening, they gathered secretly at the house of Caiaphas the high priest to try to find a solution. They racked their brains and talked long into the night, discussing how they could get rid of Jesus once and for all. They must find some way of arresting him that would not attract too much attention, and then find grounds to have him executed. "But let's wait till after Passover, shall we? We do not want to cause a riot." They all agreed.

Jesus and the disciples had gone to Bethany, a short distance away, and were staying in the house of Lazarus and his sisters Mary and Martha. There was to be a great feast and Martha had spent all day preparing and cooking. Jesus sat down at the table, in the place of honor, with the disciples and Lazarus around him, while Martha started to serve the food.

As she was doing this, her sister Mary went up to Jesus, carrying a beautiful alabaster jar. It was filled with nard, which was an expensive and aromatic ointment, made with the oil of the spikenard plant. Kneeling at his feet, she broke the jar open and carefully poured the nard over his feet. Then she bent down and wiped his feet clean with her hair. The exotic perfume wafted through the air, filling the house.

But one of the disciples, named Judas Iscariot, objected. "What a waste!" he said. "That nard must be worth at least a year's wages! Why did you not sell it and give the money to the poor?"

"Leave her alone," Jesus replied. "She has done a beautiful thing. The poor you will always have with you and you can help them any time you want. But you will not always have me. When Mary poured perfume on my body, she did it to prepare me for burial. What she just did will be remembered always."

Soon after, Judas left the other disciples and went to the chief priests and the elders and told them that he was willing to betray Jesus. "What are you willing to give me if I hand him over to you?" he asked.

The priests and the elders were delighted and immediately counted out thirty pieces of silver and put them into his hand. From that moment on, Judas did not leave Jesus's side, waiting for an opportunity to hand him over.

Understanding the story

Jesus's enemies are not just the Pharisees, chief priests, Romans, and Herodians, but within his own inner circle too. It is not clear why Judas decides to betray Jesus, but once he makes his decision, the priests and the elders reward him with money. Any disloyalty to Jesus goes against the word of God, but Judas's acceptance of financial rewards makes the betrayal even worse. Today, the phrase "thirty pieces of silver" is commonly used to express betrayal.

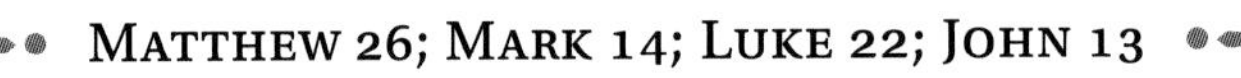

Preparing for the Passover

It was just before Passover and Jesus knew that the time had come for him to leave this earth and go to his Father in heaven.

Upper room
The Coenaculum, or "dining room" shown here, is thought to be the upper room, where the washing took place. It is now part of a Muslim mosque on Mount Zion in Jerusalem. Upstairs rooms were often used as entertaining spaces for visitors.

Jesus's disciples, wanting to make sure that everything would be ready for the Passover Feast, came to him and asked, "Where do you want us to prepare the meal?"

Jesus told two of them, Peter and John, to go into Jerusalem. "As you enter the city," he said, "you will meet a man carrying a jar of water. Follow him to a house and go in with him. Ask the owner of the house to show you the room where your teacher will celebrate Passover with his disciples. He will take you upstairs to a large room where you will find everything you need. Stay there and start to prepare the Passover meal."

Peter and John did exactly as Jesus had said, making all the preparations and laying out the food for the Feast. In the evening, Jesus and the other disciples arrived at the house, went upstairs, and sat down.

But, before they started to eat, Jesus got up from the table and knotted a towel around his waist. He fetched a basin, which he filled with clean water. He bent down and started to wash the feet of the disciple sitting next to him. Then he dried them carefully with the towel wrapped around his waist. When he had finished, he moved to the next disciple and did the same. Slowly, Jesus worked his way around the table, washing the feet of each of his disciples. Peter watched, unhappy, and when it came to his turn, he objected.

"Lord, why are you kneeling down to wash my feet?" he asked.

"You do not realize what I am doing now," said Jesus. "But later, you will understand."

"No," replied Peter. "You will never wash my feet!"

"Unless I wash your feet, you are not part of me," answered Jesus.

"Then, Lord," said Peter, "not just my feet, but my hands and my head as well."

Jesus shook his head. "A person who has had a bath needs only to wash his feet. His whole body is clean. And you are clean, though not every one of you is," he replied, looking around the table at the twelve disciples. He knew exactly who was going to betray him.

When Jesus had finished, he sat at the table. "Do you understand what I have just done?" he asked them. "Now that I, your Lord and teacher, have washed your feet, you should also wash one another's feet. I have set you an example. You are all equal. No servant is greater than his master. You should do as I have done for you."

Understanding the story

Washing feet is a symbolic Jewish ritual of cleansing. Jesus cleans all the disciples' feet, teaching them that no man is more important than another. He even washes the feet of the disciple he knows will later betray him. As well as serving God, Jesus's disciples will lovingly serve each other without complaint.

Water and washing
In ancient times, it was customary for servants to wash dust off the feet of house guests. But in the Bible, washing was not just about keeping clean. It was a process of self-purification and cleansing. In other stories, Pilate washes his hands to rid himself of guilt, John the Baptist performs baptisms in water, and Namaan bathes his sore skin.

"You are all equal. No servant is greater than his master. You should do as I have done for you."

The Last Supper

Jesus and the twelve disciples sat quietly, eating their Passover Feast together. "I have been looking forward to this last meal with you," Jesus said. "Next time, it will be in the Kingdom of Heaven."

He took a loaf of unleavened bread, blessed it, and broke off a large piece. He gave it to the disciples and said, "Take it and eat. This is my body given to you. Do this in remembrance of me." At the end of the meal, he took his cup of wine, gave thanks, and offered it to them. "Drink from it, all of you. This is my blood, the blood of the covenant, which is poured out for many for the forgiveness of sins. I tell you, I will not drink of the fruit of the vine from now on until that day when I drink it again with you in my Father's kingdom."

And then he looked at the disciples and said, "I tell you the truth, one of you is going to betray me."

The disciples shook their heads in dismay and disbelief. "Surely not me, Lord? Surely not me?" they all said.

"It is one of the twelve," replied Jesus. "One who is eating with me. The Son of Man will go just as it is written about him. But woe to the man who betrays me. It would be better for him if he had not been born."

Peter turned to the disciple who was sitting next to Jesus and whispered, "Ask him which one he means."

Leaning toward Jesus, the disciple said, "Lord, who is it?"

"I will give this bread to him," Jesus answered. He tore a piece off the loaf. The disciples watched his every move. He dipped the bread into a dish in front of him, carefully removed it, and gave it to Judas Iscariot.

"Surely, not me, Rabbi?" gasped Judas, taking the bread. The color drained from his face.

"Yes, it is you," said Jesus. "What you are going to do, do it quickly." Judas looked at him in dismay, then rushed out of the room. He fled into the night. Nobody tried to stop him.

Later, Jesus and the other disciples prayed together and then left the house to go to the Mount of Olives.

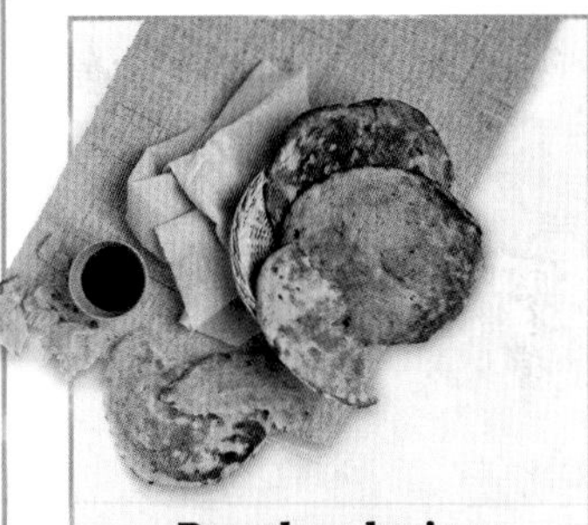

Bread and wine
Unleavened bread is eaten at passover to remember that the Israelites left Egypt so swiftly that the bread had no time to rise. The bread and wine Jesus shares with his disciples has become a reminder of his ultimate sacrifice for the world.

Judas Iscariot
One of Jesus's 12 original disciples, Judas was the only one who didn't come from Galilee. Iscariot is Hebrew for someone from Kerioth in southern Judea. He was group treasurer, in charge of all the money.

"One of you is going to betray me."

Understanding the story

The passover meal commemorates the Israelites' escape from Egypt. The Lord's last supper welcomes the new era of the Church. The bread and wine represent Jesus's body and blood. In the Christian Church, this meal is a service of remembrance called "Holy Communion."

"The Last Supper" by Italian painter Bartolome Carducci (1554–1610) shows the scene at Jesus's final meal.

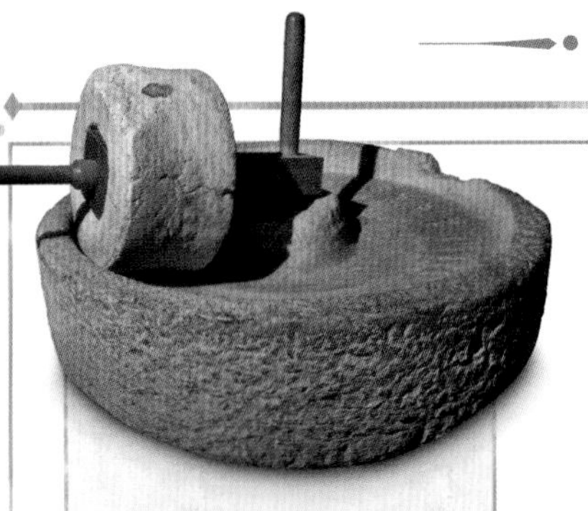

Oil press
Situated on the lower slopes of the Mount of Olives, Gethsemane (meaning "oil press") was one of Jesus's favorite places. Olives were brought here to be pressed. Ancient olive presses like this turned olives into oil. Olives were widespread in Judea, and olive oil became the region's biggest export.

The Garden of Gethsemane

Jesus and his twelve disciples crossed the valley and walked slowly up the stony path to the garden of Gethsemane.

It was a quiet and tranquil spot, just outside the city walls, where the wild flowers and figs flourished and the ancient trees shook their silver leaves in the gentle breeze. Jesus and his disciples often came here to be alone, far from the hustle and bustle of the Temple.

"Stay here while I go and pray," Jesus told his disciples. And he chose three of them to take with him—Peter, James, and John. He was deeply distressed and knew that, come what may, death was drawing near. "My soul is overwhelmed with sorrow," he told them. "Stay here and keep watch

The kiss that betrays Jesus is shown in a mosaic from a 6th-century church in Ravenna, Italy.

while I pray." He went further through the darkness before kneeling on the ground. "Father, if it is possible, please take this cup of suffering from me. But let your will, not mine, be done," he prayed.

An angel appeared silently before him, a sign from God, helping to give him strength in his anguish. He went on praying. When he had finished, he returned to the three disciples and found them asleep. He woke them up and asked, "Could you not even stay awake for one single hour? Please keep watch and pray that you will not fall into temptation. The spirit is willing but the flesh is weak." For the second time, he went away and prayed. And again, when he came back, he found them sleeping. They did not know what to say. For a third time, Jesus went and prayed and came back to find the three disciples asleep.

"Are you still sleeping?" he asked. "Enough! The hour has come. The Son of Man is betrayed into the hands of sinners. Get up. Let's go. Here comes my betrayer."

While Jesus was still speaking, Judas arrived with the elders, the chief priests, and the soldiers. Their flaming torches lit up the dark hillside. Judas had told his group, "The one I kiss is the man you are after. Arrest him." Then, Judas went straight up to Jesus and greeted him with a kiss on the cheek.

Jesus looked at him and asked him sadly, "Judas, are you betraying the Son of Man with a kiss?" Immediately, the soldiers seized Jesus and arrested him. But, before they could take him away the disciple Peter, who had a sword, drew it from his side and lunged at one of the guards, slicing off his right ear. And Jesus reproached him, "Put it away. All those who live by the sword will die by the sword." And he gently touched the guard's bleeding head and healed it, making his ear whole again.

Jesus looked at the elders and the chief priests and the soldiers and said to them, "Do you think that I am leading a rebellion? Is that why you have come out with swords and clubs to capture me? I have sat in the Temple teaching, day after day. You could have arrested me there, but you did not." Then he added, "This is all taking place so that the scripture and the writings of the prophets will be fulfilled."

And, as the soldiers bound his wrists, the disciples were overwhelmed with terror and fled into the night, deserting Jesus.

Roman sword
The High Priest and his council employed a police force to act on their behalf. These soldiers had the authority to arrest suspected wrongdoers. They carried weaponry that was easy to handle, similar to the gladius (short sword) shown here. Jesus preached against the use of violence, which is why he rebukes Peter and heals the injured guard.

Understanding the story

Gethsemane was a picturesque location favored by Jesus, yet it is here that Judas commits his act of betrayal. A kiss was a common greeting between friends or a sign of respect between teacher and disciple. Jesus tried to be both friend and teacher to Judas. Jesus's despair and anxiety reveals his humanity—he fears the physical pain to come.

The Garden of Gethsemane
Since the 4th century CE, this olive grove in east Jerusalem has been identified as the Garden of Gethsemane, where Jesus prayed on the night before his death.

They went to a place called Gethsemane,
and Jesus said to his disciples, "Sit here while I pray."
He took Peter, James, and John along with him,
and he began to be deeply distressed and troubled.
"My soul is overwhelmed with sorrow to the point of
death," he said to them. "Stay here and keep watch."

Mark 14:32–34

Peter's Denial

"This very night, before the cock crows, you will disown me three times."

On the Mount of Olives, before his arrest, Jesus had said to his disciples, "This very night, you will desert and betray me."

Peter looked at him in disbelief. "I will never leave you!" he protested.

"I tell you the truth," Jesus replied. "This very night, before the cock crows, you will disown me three times."

"Even if I have to die with you, I will never disown you!" Peter declared. The other disciples all said the same.

But now, Jesus had been arrested and taken from the Garden of Gethsemane to the house of Caiaphas the high priest to be tried by the Sanhedrin, the powerful council of elders and chief priests. The other disciples had disappeared, fleeing into the night, and it was Peter, alone, who followed Jesus. He kept a safe distance and watched as Jesus was taken inside. He went into the courtyard and sat down with the guards around the fire to warm his hands, waiting to see what would happen.

The night was dark, but the flames leapt and jumped in the air, lighting up their faces. A young servant girl came up behind Peter and peered at him. "You were with Jesus of Nazareth, weren't you?" she said.

"I don't know what you are talking about," replied Peter nervously, glancing at the guards around the fire. He got up quickly and went toward the gate of the courtyard. Another girl came up, pointing at him. "This fellow was with Jesus of Nazareth," she said to the people with her.

Again, Peter denied it. "No, I swear I do not know that man!" he cried.

After a while, another man who had been watching came up and said, "But surely, you must be one of the disciples? I can tell from your accent. You are from Galilee."

Enraged, Peter swore, for the third time, that he did not know Jesus.

Immediately, he heard an unearthly cry piercing the night air. It was a cock crowing. And, as if a dagger had been plunged deep into his heart, Peter remembered Jesus's words—"Before the cock crows, you will disown me three times." He staggered out of the courtyard into the night, far from the high priest's house, weeping silently.

Understanding the story

Many homes kept roosters, and their crowing marked the coming of day. When the cock crows for the third time, Peter remembers Jesus's words. Night has passed and with the new day dawning, the realization of Peter's denial dawns on him. He had been sure that he would never disown Jesus, yet in a moment of weakness, he fails. As Jesus had said, the spirit is willing, but the flesh is weak.

Jesus and the Sanhedrin

Jesus was brought before the Sanhedrin, the Jewish council made up of all the chief priests, elders, and teachers of the law.

The high priest, Caiaphas, presided over them all. A string of witnesses had been bribed to appear with trumped-up evidence against Jesus. One by one, they stepped forward and told their stories, and one by one they were dismissed.

Finally, two men came forward and said, "This fellow, Jesus, said that he could destroy the Temple of God and rebuild it single-handed in three days."

The high priest looked at Jesus. "Are you not going to answer? What is this testimony that these men are bringing against you?" he asked. Jesus said nothing.

"I charge you, under oath by the living God, to tell us if you are Christ, the Son of God," the high priest ordered.

"If I tell you, you will not believe me," Jesus replied.

"Are you, then, the Son of God?" asked the men who made up the Sanhedrin.

"You are right in saying I am," Jesus answered.

"What blasphemy!" said the high priest, tearing at his clothes. "Why do we need any more testimony or witnesses? We have heard it from his own lips!" And he turned to the assembled Sanhedrin. "What do you think?"

"He should be put to death!" replied the holy men. They surrounded Jesus, spitting at him and slapping him.

When Judas heard what had happened, he was overwhelmed with remorse. He went to the Temple and tried to give back the thirty silver coins that he had accepted in return for betraying Jesus. "I have sinned," he said bitterly. "I have betrayed innocent blood."

Then Judas flung the coins down on the Temple floor and went away and hanged himself. The holy men picked up the money from the floor and counted it. They decided that they would use it to buy a field that belonged to a potter, which they would use as a burial place for foreigners. It became known as the Field of Blood.

"Are you, then, the Son of God?"

Ceremonial clothes
The High Priest's lavish costume included a linen garment called an ephod, worn like a tunic. Gold and colored threads were woven together to symbolize the riches of the Lord. A jeweled breastplate to represent the 12 tribes of Israel was worn over the ephod. The high turban emphasized the High Priest's authority.

Understanding the story

The High Priest presided over the Sanhedrin (Greek for "council"), but many Jews shunned him because he was appointed by the Romans. By saying that he is the Son of God, Jesus has given the Sanhedrin cause to accuse him of blasphemy, a crime punishable by death under Jewish law.

Jesus and Pontius Pilate

Very early the next morning, the Sanhedrin had reached a unanimous verdict—Jesus should be put to death.

They bound his hands and took him to appear before Pontius Pilate, the Roman governor of Judea. The chief priests and the elders began to accuse him again, in front of Pilate. Jesus stood in front of them, saying nothing. "They are accusing you of so many terrible things. Why don't you reply?" asked Pilate from his judge's seat. But Jesus said nothing.

"Are you the king of the Jews?" he asked.

"Yes," replied Jesus. "It is as you say."

Pilate turned to the priests and elders and said, "I see no reason to charge this man." But the Sanhedrin would not give up. "He has incited people all over Judea with his teaching," they insisted. "Where will it end?" So Pilate agreed to punish Jesus and put him in prison.

Each year, at the Feast of Passover, the people were allowed to choose a prisoner who would be released from jail. Pilate went out and asked the crowd, "Which of the two do you want me to set free—Barabbas the murderer, or Jesus?"

But the chief priests and the elders had already told the crowd what to do and there was a great roar as the crowd shouted "Barabbas!"

"And what do you want me to do with Jesus?" Pilate asked.

"Crucify him!" they shouted.

Pilate called for a bowl of water and washed his hands in front of everyone. "I am innocent of this man's blood," he said. And, with that, he gave the order for Jesus to be flogged and crucified.

The soldiers took Jesus away, stripped and beat him. They put him in a robe and made a crown of thorns for his head. Then they made him hold a wooden staff and knelt down mockingly in front of him. "Hail, king of the Jews!" they jeered. When they had tired of their fun, they put his own clothes back on before taking him away to be crucified.

Understanding the story

The Sanhedrin have no authority to carry out their verdict, only the Roman governor can impose the death penalty. The Romans did not recognize blasphemy as a crime, so the Sanhedrin present Jesus as a political activist. Pontius Pilate believes Jesus is innocent, but is so keen to please the religious leaders that he agrees to have him crucified.

Ritual washing
A bowl and jug like these would be used for ritual washing. This process of purification was a symbolic way of cleansing the soul. Pilate washes his hands to show he wants no involvement in Jesus's death.

Crown of thorns
A symbol of royalty, power, and honor during Jesus's time, crowns also feature in the stories of King Solomon's Wisdom and God Chooses David. However, this crown was woven from thorny branches and was only placed on Jesus's head so the Roman soldiers could ridicule the idea of him being king.

Jesus is Crucified

The soldiers led Jesus away to be crucified outside Jerusalem. He was made to carry the wooden cross.

Jesus's followers gathered behind him. He stumbled on the stony path, and the soldiers beat him on. Then they seized a man named Simon from Cyrene and made him help Jesus carry the cross the rest of the way.

At last, they arrived at Golgotha, a rocky, skull-like hill. At nine o'clock in the morning, they crucified Jesus, nailing him to the cross and hoisting it high in the air. Above him, they put a mocking sign saying "This is Jesus, the king of the Jews." Two common criminals were crucified with him—one to the right and one to the left. And the soldiers had already begun to share out his clothes between them, casting lots to see who would get what.

Looking down from his cross, Jesus said, "Father, forgive them, for they know not what they do."

Mary Magdalene, Mary the mother of the disciple James, and Jesus's mother sat not far away. The crowds had begun to gather and started to taunt Jesus. The chief priests and the elders and the teachers of the law also

"The Crucifixion", oil on canvas by German painter Hans Muelich (1516–1573)

Via Dolorosa
The path along which Jesus is believed to have carried his cross in Jerusalem is known as the Via Dolorosa, or "way of grief," and is now a Christian pilgrimage route.

made fun of him. Even one of the criminals by his side joined in. But the other rebuked him, saying, "We are punished justly, but this man has done no wrong! Jesus, remember me when you are in heaven!"

Jesus replied, "I tell you the truth. Today you will be with me in paradise."

At noon, the sky suddenly darkened and night fell. It lasted for three long hours. Then, as the first rays of light appeared again, Jesus cried out in a loud voice, "My God, my God, why have you forsaken me?" Soon after, he took his last breath. At that exact moment, the curtain in the Temple in Jerusalem was torn in two from top to bottom. At the same time, the earth trembled and shook and rocks split in two.

The soldiers guarding Jesus looked up, terrified. "Surely, he was the Son of God!" they whispered to each other.

In the evening, a man named Joseph of Arimathea went to Pontius Pilate. He was an important member of the Jewish council, but also a follower of Jesus. He asked Pilate if he might be allowed to bury Jesus's body. Pilate agreed, and so Joseph went to Golgotha. With the help of a man named Nicodemus, Joseph took the body down from the cross. He anointed it with myrrh and aloes, as was the custom, and wrapped it in a clean linen cloth. Then Joseph and Nicodemus carried the body to a tomb that had been cut out of the rock. They rolled a big stone across the entrance to keep the body safe.

Understanding the story

Jesus has absolute faith in God and knows his death on the cross will not be in vain. His purpose on Earth was to take away the wall of sin between God and His people, and the act of self-sacrifice achieves God's will. When Jesus dies, the Temple curtain rips apart to symbolize that the path to God is open.

Cross
Jesus's suffering on the cross has become the most recognized symbol of Christianity, and can be seen at many places of worship. Crosses are often made from precious materials, such as this one, made of gold.

Burial tomb
Jesus's tomb would have looked like this example above. It was cut from rock and sealed with a great rolling stone. The body of Jesus was laid on a rocky ledge cut into one of the tomb walls. The stone was then rolled into place to protect the tomb.

Mourning
Grief was not a private emotion in ancient times. When mourning the dead, people made their feelings known with very public displays. They wailed, ripped their clothes, beat their chests, and tipped ashes over themselves to show their devastation.

The Resurrection

It was the day after the Sabbath and, just as dawn was breaking, Mary Magdalene and her friend, who was also called Mary, went to the tomb where Jesus had been buried.

It was two days since he had died. The entrance had been sealed tightly with a huge stone, and Pontius Pilate had sent two soldiers to guard it around the clock. The chief priests and the Pharisees had warned him that the disciples might try to steal the body to make it look as though Jesus had risen from the dead. Pilate wanted to avoid this at all costs. They all remembered Jesus saying that he would rise again after three days.

The two Marys were just approaching the tomb when the earth beneath them started to shake violently. At the same time, an angel of the Lord appeared, shining in glory. He went over to the tomb and slowly rolled away the great stone from the entrance. The women watched, amazed, and peered into the gloom. The tomb was empty. There was no sign of Jesus.

The angel sat on the stone, as dazzling as lightning, his clothes white as snow. The two guards shielded their eyes helplessly and shook with fear. Then they both fainted as the angel began to speak to the two women. "Do not be afraid, for I know you are looking for Jesus, who was crucified," he said. "He is not here. He has risen, just as he said. Come and see the place where he lay. Then go quickly and tell his disciples that he has risen from the dead and is going ahead of you into Galilee. There you will see him."

The two women—filled with joy, but also a little afraid—hurried away as fast as they could to find the disciples. Suddenly, Jesus himself appeared in front of them. "Greetings," he said. They both fell at his feet, worshipping him.

"Do not be afraid," Jesus reassured them. "Go and tell my brothers to go to Galilee. There they will see me."

Understanding the story

Jesus's tomb was sealed and guarded because the religious leaders feared that his followers would take Jesus's body to fake his resurrection. The empty tomb, the angel's words, and Jesus's appearance before the two Marys all confirm that a miracle has taken place. Jesus's resurrection assures his followers that victory over death, and eternal life, are possible for those who live in the way he preached.

"The Resurrection of Christ" from German artist Matthias Grünewald's Isenheim altarpiece (c. 1515)

Emmaus
All that is known of the village of Emmaus is that it was near Jerusalem. The exact location remains unclear. There is speculation as to several places being the possible site, including the town of Emmaus Nicopolis, where this 12th-century-CE church is located (above).

Journey to Emmaus
This sculpture from the Spanish monastery of Santo Domingo de Silos in Burgos shows Jesus on the road to Emmaus with his unsuspecting followers. Jesus carries a pouch and stick typical of those used by pilgrims on journeys.

The Road to Emmaus

Later that day, two of Jesus's followers were returning to a village called Emmaus, not far from Jerusalem.

They were deep in conversation as they walked along, discussing the big events of the last few days. Another man came up quietly and joined them along the way. It was Jesus, but they did not recognize him.

"What are you talking about?" he asked. "It must be important."

One of them, named Cleopas, asked in disbelief, "Are you the only person in Jerusalem who does not know what has happened? Have you not heard about Jesus of Nazareth? He was a great prophet. Our priests and rulers sentenced him to death and crucified him. We had hoped that he was the one who was going to save Israel. They crucified him two days ago. But, this morning, some of our women friends went to his tomb and it was empty. And they saw a vision—an angel appeared and told them that Jesus was still alive!"

Jesus smiled and said, "How foolish you are! Do you not understand that Christ had to suffer before he could enter His glory?" He explained everything that the prophets had foretold.

As they reached Emmaus, the companions urged Jesus to stay the night. He agreed and went into their house. They sat down to eat. Jesus took the bread, gave thanks to God, broke it, and gave it to the two men. In that second, they realized who he was—and he vanished from sight, as if he had never been there.

"Did you not feel something wonderful happening when he was explaining the scriptures to us just now?" Cleopas said to the other man. Immediately, they returned to Jerusalem to tell the disciples that they had seen Jesus.

Understanding the story

The two disciples are part of a wider group of Jesus's followers. They do not realize they are dining with Jesus until he reenacts the Last Supper meal. Jesus's words of comfort reassure the pair that his death was a necessary part of God's plan for humankind's salvation. This renews their faith, reminding them that Jesus is always there.

Doubting Thomas

Nails
These large nails resemble the ones used for Jesus's crucifixion. They were usually banged through a person's wrists and sideways through their ankles during a crucifixion. In the Bible, Jesus is described as bearing the marks of the crucifixion on the palms of his hands.

As the disciples were talking in a house, Jesus suddenly appeared among them. "Peace be with you!" he said.

They looked at him in terror and did not know where he had come from. They thought that he was a ghost. "Why are you so worried?" Jesus asked. "Look at my hands and feet. Feel them. They are mine. Touch me and see—I am flesh and blood, like you. I am no ghost."

Tentatively, they went to him, looking him up and down with fearful eyes. They touched him quickly, their hands darting out uncertainly, to see if he was real. And then they smiled with relief at each other, knowing that it was Jesus standing there with them. He asked them if they had any food and they gave him a plate of grilled fish. He ate it while they all watched.

But one of the disciples, Thomas, who was known as Didymus, had not been with them at the time. Later, when they told him that they had seen Jesus, he did not believe them. "Unless I see the wounds in his hands and in his side with my own eyes and feel them with my own fingers, I will not believe it!" Thomas said.

A week later, all the disciples had gathered together, including Thomas. The doors of the house were closed and locked so that no one could get in. But, all at once, Jesus was standing there with them. "Peace be with you!" he said. And he turned to Thomas and said, "See my hands. Feel the holes where the nails went in. Look at my side. Feel the wounds. Stop doubting, Thomas, and believe."

Cautiously, Thomas stretched out his hand and looked at Jesus's wounds. Then he drew back, ashen-faced and said, "My Lord, my God!"

Jesus replied, "Because you have seen me with your own eyes, you now believe. But blessed are those who have not seen but still believe!"

Thomas examines Jesus's wounds in "Christ and Doubting Thomas" by Italian painter Paolo Cavazzola (1486–1522)

Understanding the story

The disciple Thomas refuses to believe in Jesus's resurrection until he witnesses and touches the marks of the crucifixion himself. Jesus lets Thomas feel his wounds just as he ate the fish in front of the disciples—to prove that he really had risen from the dead. He is not a ghost. Thomas's doubts vanish, but Jesus reminds him that those who have faith without proof are truly blessed.

The Last Breakfast

"Peter, do you truly love me?"

One evening, some of the disciples were together by the Sea of Galilee when Peter decided that he wanted to go fishing. His companions said that they would like to go, too.

So they all got in the boat and set off, rowing far out to sea where the waters were usually teeming with fish. They cast their net over the side again and again, but each time they hauled it back up, it was empty. They fished all night, but caught nothing.

Early the next morning, just as dawn was breaking, they gave up and headed back to shore. As they approached, they saw a man standing there, watching them.

"Friends," he called to them, across the water. "Have you caught any fish?"

"No!" they shouted back. "Not one."

"Throw your net over the right-hand side of your boat and you will find some."

They did as he said, letting the net down from the boat into the water. Immediately, it swelled, full of fish. They tried to haul the net in, but it was so heavy that they could not lift it out of the water. The disciples were amazed.

Then John looked at the man standing on the shore again, and suddenly he recognized him. His face lit up with joy. "It is the Lord!" he said to Peter. At this, Peter jumped over the side of the boat and swam as fast he could through the water to Jesus, his robe billowing around him. The other disciples followed in the boat, towing the bulging net behind them.

When they had landed, they saw that a fire had been lit and a row of fish was grilling in the flames. Loaves of bread were laid out by the side.

"Bring some of the fish that you have caught," said Jesus. Peter dragged the huge net ashore. It was bursting with large fish—one hundred and fifty-three

altogether—but the net was not torn or broken. "Come and have breakfast," said Jesus.

All the disciples had recognized him by now. It was the third time that he had appeared to them after he had been raised from the dead. He offered them the fish and the bread, and they all tucked in.

When they had eaten their fill, Jesus said, "Peter, do you truly love me?"

"Yes, Lord," replied Peter. "You know that I love you."

"Feed my lambs," said Jesus. And he asked again, "Peter, do you truly love me?"

"Yes, Lord," answered Peter again. "You know that I love you."

"Take care of my sheep," said Jesus. "Peter, do you truly love me?"

Peter was hurt because Jesus had repeated the same question three times. "Lord, you know all things. You know that I love you," he replied.

Again, Jesus said, "Feed my sheep." Then Jesus foretold how Peter would be martyred and crucified. "I tell you the truth. When you were younger you dressed yourself and went wherever you wanted. But when you are old, you will stretch out your hands and someone will dress you and lead you where you do not want to go." Then Jesus said to Peter, "Follow me."

Understanding the story

From all the disciples at the breakfast, Jesus singles out Peter for a special conversation. At Jesus's trial, Peter had disowned him three times, which is why Jesus questions his love three times. By asking him to care for his sheep, Jesus is making Peter leader of the disciples and putting him in charge of the early Christian community.

Night fishing
When a night's fishing is fruitless, Jesus provides a huge catch. This is similar to his miracle of feeding the 5,000 people. Jesus once told his disciples they would be "fishers of men," and the fish became an early Christian symbol.

Peter's martyrdom
Jesus explains to Peter that he will be crucified and martyred (a person who dies for their faith). Christian tradition says that Peter was crucified upside down, because he told his executioners that he was not worthy to die in the same way as Jesus.

Chapel
In the 12th century, the Chapel of the Ascension was built by the Crusaders high upon the Mount of Olives. The chapel is built around the rock that marks the spot where Jesus is believed to have ascended to heaven. Today it is a pilgrimage site.

Clouds
A cloud covers Jesus on his way up to heaven. Clouds can be seen as a symbol of God's glory and eternal presence. For example, in the Old Testament, God guided Moses and the Israelites through the desert in a pillar of cloud.

Jesus is Taken up to Heaven

Jesus told the eleven disciples to go to a mountain in Galilee. He met them there and they prayed with him.

Then he told them, "With my authority in heaven and on earth, go and spread the word. Make disciples of all nations, baptizing them in the name of the Father and of the Son and of the Holy Spirit. Teach them to obey everything I have commanded you. And surely, I am with you always and forever, to the very end of time."

For the last forty days, since he had risen from the dead, Jesus had appeared to the disciples, talking about the Kingdom of God. On one occasion, when he had been eating with them, he had told them, "Do not leave Jerusalem, but wait for the gift my Father promised, which you have heard me speak about. For John baptized with water, but in a few days, you will be baptized with the Holy Spirit."

The disciples asked him, "Lord, are you then going to restore the kingdom to Israel?"

"It is not for you to know the times or the dates the Father has set. But you will receive power when the Holy Spirit comes on you. And you will be my witnesses in Jerusalem and in Judea and Samaria and to the ends of the earth."

As he finished speaking, he was taken up in the air in front of their eyes, and a cloud enveloped him, hiding him completely. The disciples were looking up into the sky when, suddenly, two men dressed in white appeared, standing beside them.

"Men of Galilee," they said. "Why do you stand there looking at the sky? This same Jesus, who has been taken from you into heaven, will come back in the same way you have just seen him disappear."

Then the disciples returned to Jerusalem. When they got there they went upstairs to the room where they were staying. They knelt down in prayer together with some women and Mary the mother of Jesus, and his brothers. And they knew that they must choose someone to replace Judas, the disciple who had betrayed Jesus. Two names were put forward—Joseph, known as Barsabbas, and Matthias.

They appealed to the Lord for help. "Lord, you know everyone's heart," they prayed. "Show us which of these two you have chosen to replace Judas." Then they cast lots and Matthias was chosen to become the twelfth disciple.

Understanding the story

The number of days Jesus spends with his disciples between resurrection and ascension is significant because 40 represents completion. His work on Earth is now done and the disciples must spread the word of God, not just across Israel, but all of the world, without Jesus's physical presence. Before he ascends to heaven, Jesus explains that he will always be there in the form of the Holy Spirit—the spirit of God on Earth.

Tongues of Fire

It was Pentecost and Jerusalem was crowded with people celebrating the Jewish harvest festival.

Wind and fire
Both the violent wind and the flames that flicker over the heads of Jesus's disciples are manifestations of the Holy Spirit. In the Bible, God's presence is often indicated by fire, such as when He speaks to Moses from inside a burning bush.

Pentecost
The Jewish harvest festival was called Pentecost. It celebrated the end of the annual grain harvest, but it also commemorated God giving the Law to Moses in the Ten Commandments. This detail from an altar depicts the gathered disciples being touched by the Holy Spirit at Pentecost.

Jesus's disciples and the wider group of Jesus's followers met quietly in Jerusalem, encouraging each other and waiting for the fulfilment of Jesus's promise about the gift of the Holy Spirit. They did not have to wait for long.

On the day of Pentecost, the disciples were sitting together when suddenly, a violent wind howled through the house, whistling around every corner and rattling every door. Then, shining tongues of fire appeared from nowhere, darting brightly through the air. They hovered for a moment before coming silently down, one little flame settling over the head of each person like a flickering crown. It was the Holy Spirit, filling them all, as Jesus had promised. When they started talking to each other, they found that they were speaking many different languages from strange and exotic countries. And they could all understand every word.

When they went out into the streets to teach, the people listened to them in astonishment. "Aren't these men from Galilee? How are they able to speak so many languages? We can all understand them, no matter where we come from—Parthia,

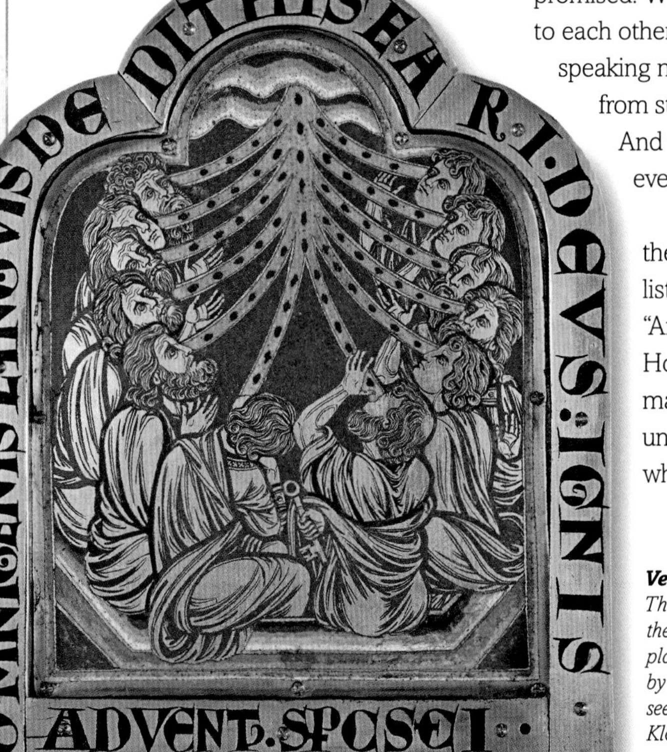

Verdun Altar
This 12th-century portrayal of the Pentecost is one of 45 copper plates that comprise an altar made by Nicholas of Verdun and can be seen in the Chapel of St. Leopold, Klosterneuburg Priory, Austria.

Egypt, Crete, Mesopotamia. It is incredible! We can all hear them spreading the word of God."

Then Peter stood up and addressed the crowd, describing the miracles that Jesus had performed in God's name. "God raised Jesus to life and we are all witnesses of the fact. Exalted to the right hand of God, he has received from the Father, the Holy Spirit, and has poured out what you see and hear. Let all Israel be assured of this: God has made this Jesus, whom you crucified, both Lord and Christ."

Their hearts touched, the people asked, "Brothers, what shall we do?"

"Repent and be baptized, every one of you, in the name of Jesus Christ, for the forgiveness of your sins," said Peter. "And you will receive the gift of the Holy Spirit. This is a promise to you and your children and to all whom our Lord God will call. Save yourselves." The crowds flocked to hear the disciples speak that day and at least three thousand people were baptized.

Language barriers
Language plays an important part in the Bible. Here, the barriers of language are removed as the Holy Spirit enters the disciples. Everyone is now sharing the same language— the word of God. This is the opposite of what took place at Babel, when God punished the people and they could no longer understand each other.

Understanding the story

From the Greek word for "50," Pentecost was held 50 days after Passover. It is called the Feast of Harvest in the Old Testament, during which Jews thanked God. People from many different countries were in Jerusalem for the feast. God removes all language barriers so everyone can understand His word. This event is seen as the founding of the Christian Church.

"It is incredible! We can all hear them spreading the word of God."

Beautiful gate
The Temple gate called Beautiful was probably made of Corinthian bronze and located on the east side. Many of the grand outer gates resembled this model reconstruction. The sick or disabled would often gather at the Temple gates to beg for alms or assistance.

Western wall
The only part of Herod's temple still standing today is the Western Wall. It is often called the Wailing Wall because Jews go there to publicly mourn the destroyed Temple. They also give thanks to God and kneel at the wall for prayers.

Peter the Healer

One day, Peter and John were going to the Temple to pray. They went through the Court of the Gentiles and approached the magnificent gate called Beautiful.

As they drew near they saw a man, who had been crippled since birth, being carried there by his friends. This was where he sat, day after day, begging for alms. As soon as he saw the disciples, he asked them for some money.

"Look us in the eye," said Peter. The beggar fixed him with a sad gaze.

"Silver or gold I do not have," Peter continued. "But what I have, I will give you. In the name of Jesus Christ, walk!" And, taking him by the right hand, he gently helped him up. The beggar got to his feet, shook his legs, wriggled his toes, and took a few cautious steps. Then he took a few more, his face lighting up with joy. Praising the Lord, he walked with Peter and John into the Temple itself to pray. People stopped to stare, hardly able to believe their eyes. When the prayers were over, Peter and John came out and made their way through the outer courtyard to Solomon's Colonnade. They started to teach, and the crowds thronged around them. The beggar who had been cured stood beside them for all to see.

"Why does this amaze you?" asked Peter. "Do not think that we made this man walk. We did nothing, but faith in the name of Jesus cured him. The God of Abraham, Isaac, and Jacob, the God of our fathers, has glorified His servant Jesus." And he went on, teaching and preaching to the people, telling them to repent their sins in the name of Jesus.

The priests, the Sadducees, and the Temple guard had all been watching and listening from the shadows. They were angry that the disciples were teaching in the Temple and proclaiming that Jesus had risen from the dead. They seized Peter and John and put them in prison for the night. But, despite this, the people who had listened to them had been convinced by their teaching and wanted to be baptized. By now, there were more than five thousand followers of Jesus.

The next morning, Peter and John were brought before the Sanhedrin—the Jewish council. The chief priests, the elders, and the teachers of the law had all assembled, with the high priest presiding. "By whose authority were you teaching in the Temple?" they demanded.

Peter, filled with the Holy Spirit, replied, "Rulers and elders of the people. If we are being called to account for an act of kindness shown to a cripple and are asked how he was cured, know this: It is by the name of Jesus Christ of Nazareth, whom you crucified but whom God raised from the dead, that the man stands before you, healed."

The council listened and were astounded

Saint Peter heals the lame man in this detail from a 16th-century-CE tapestry based on a cartoon by Italian artist Raphael.

by the courage of Peter and John. They were surprised that the disciples were ordinary, uneducated men and took note that these were the kinds of men who had been Jesus's companions. They were not sure what to do and ordered them to leave for a few moments.

"Everybody knows that they have performed a miracle and we certainly cannot deny it. But we must stop word spreading," they said to each other. They called Peter and John back in and ordered them to stop teaching in the name of Jesus.

"Judge for yourselves whether it is right in God's sight to obey you rather than God. For we cannot help speaking about what we have seen and heard," Peter replied. The Sanhedrin did not think it would be safe to punish them, seeing as so many people had seen the miracle. So they cautioned Peter and John, and let them go.

Solomon's Colonnade
Two rows of great stone columns attached to a cedar roof comprised Solomon's Colonnade. It was located on the east side of the Temple's outer court. Jesus taught here regularly, so it became a favorite spot for early Christians.

Understanding the story

Jesus had sent out his disciples in partners during their apprenticeships, and Peter and John were often together. Now they are the leading disciples, they tell the people that faith in Jesus results in miracles of healing. Many of those listening to the teachings convert to Jesus on the spot. The council is against the idea of resurrection from the dead, but Jesus's resurrection is the main message of the new Church.

Damascus
This city in the southwest of Syria was home to a large Jewish community. Saul's conversion is said to have taken place near this Roman gate in the city, and after his conversion, he was known as Paul, the Roman version of his name.

Saul's Journey to Damascus

Saul was a strict Pharisee, who observed all the Jewish laws and customs. He persecuted Jesus's disciples and their followers zealously, and was one of the great enemies of the early Church.

"This man is my chosen instrument to spread my word to the gentiles and their kings—and to the people of Israel."

One day, he went to the high priest in Jerusalem asking for letters to the synagogues in Damascus, giving him authority to arrest any Christians he found there and bring them back to Jerusalem. He set off on the long journey with his companions. As they were drawing near to Damascus, a blinding light suddenly streaked down from the heavens. Saul fell to the ground in terror, hiding his face, and he heard a loud voice, saying, "Saul, Saul, why do you persecute me?"

"Who are you, Lord?" asked Saul, fearfully.

"I am Jesus, whom you are persecuting," the voice replied. "Now get up and go into the city and you will be told what you must do." Saul's companions stood, speechless and rooted to the spot. They had heard the voice, but had not seen the light.

Slowly, Saul lifted his head and opened his eyes to look around. But he could see nothing. He was totally blind. His companions helped him up, amazed and astonished by what had happened, and together they slowly made their way along the road to Damascus. For three long days, Saul stayed in the city, blind and unable to eat or drink.

There was a man named Ananias, who lived in Damascus and was a follower of Jesus. One day, the Lord appeared to him in a vision and said, "Ananias! You must go to the house in Straight Street and ask for a man named Saul. Lay your hands on him and restore his sight."

"Lord," answered Ananias, "I have heard so much about this man and all the terrible harm he has done to your followers in Jerusalem. He has come here to Damascus with authority from the chief priests to arrest your people."

"Go!" said the Lord. "This man is my chosen instrument to spread my word to the gentiles and their kings—and to the people of Israel. I will show him how much he must suffer for my name."

Ananias did as the Lord had commanded. He found Saul and laid his hands on him and said, "Brother Saul, the Lord—Jesus who appeared to you on the road as you were coming here—has sent me so that you may see again and be filled with the Holy Spirit." Saul opened his eyes and his sight was restored. After three days, he could see properly again. He looked around, seeing the world with fresh eyes. Then, weak with hunger, he asked for some food to regain his strength.

For the next few days, Saul stayed with Jesus's followers and preached the word with them. He went into the synagogues to teach, telling the Jews that Jesus was the Son of God. Everyone was astonished. But, day after day, Saul preached the word of Jesus and more and more people came to hear him.

Some of the Jewish people thought that he was becoming a threat, however, and plotted to kill him. But Saul heard of the plan and, with the help of some of his followers, was lowered over the city walls in a basket and escaped.

At first, when he got back to Jerusalem, the disciples were afraid and could not believe the change in him. They did not trust him. But one of them, called Barnabas, explained that Saul had seen and heard the Lord on the road to Damascus. He also told them that Saul had preached fearlessly in the name of Jesus. When they heard this, the disciples welcomed Saul into their fold and told him to stay with them.

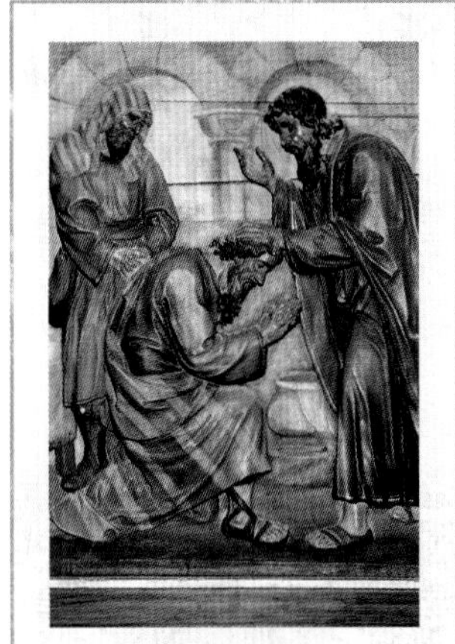

Ananias
A devout Christian who later becomes a martyr, Ananias has the trust of God. But when he is told to visit Saul, Ananias is uncertain due to Saul's reputation. God reassures him that this is missionary work, so Ananias baptizes and heals Saul.

"The Conversion of St. Paul" (1767) by French artist Nicolas-Bernard Lépicié shows God's light shining on Saul.

Understanding the story

Saul was a Pharisee and a Roman citizen. His oppression of Christians threatened to ruin the early Church, yet he literally sees the light when his sight is restored. Saul's conversion to Jesus starts the spread of Christianity right around the Mediterranean world as he fulfills his mission to preach the word of God and convert others to Christianity.

Joppa
The picturesque city of Joppa, now known as Jaffa, is one of the world's oldest seaports and features in both the Old and New Testaments. Located on a rocky ledge overlooking the Mediterranean Sea, it is said to have been founded by Japheth, a son of Noah.

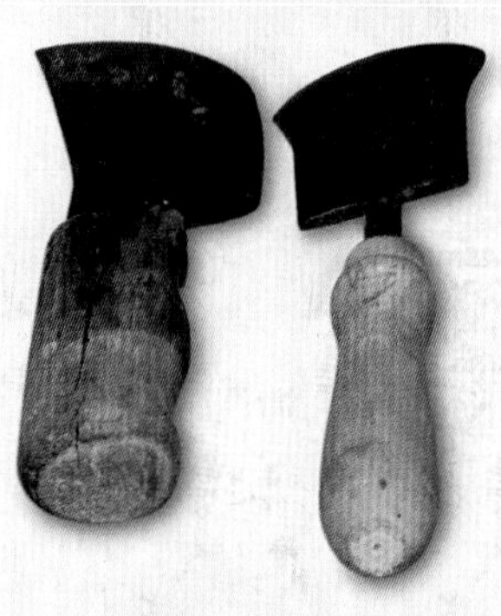

Tanner's tools
Working as a tanner was a dirty job. Making leather took time and effort. Hair and fat were first scraped off animal skins using tools like these. The tough skins were then drenched in lime and plant juices to soften them. The stench of the skins was so bad that tanners lived away from the townsfolk.

Peter and Cornelius

Cornelius lived in Caesarea. He was a centurion with the Italian regiment and, like the rest of his family, was God-fearing and devout, praying regularly and giving to the poor. He was a gentile.

One day, at about three o'clock in the afternoon, he had a vision. An angel appeared to him saying, "Cornelius!"

"What is it, Lord?" he asked fearfully.

"You must send some of your men to Joppa to get Peter. He is staying with Simon, the tanner, who has a house by the sea," replied the angel. Cornelius summoned two of his servants, as well as one of his most trusted soldiers. He told them to go to Joppa to fetch Peter immediately.

At about noon the next day, Peter went up on the roof to pray. He was hungry, and while the meal was being prepared for him, he fell into a trance. He saw heaven opening above him and something that looked like a large sheet being lowered to earth by its four corners. Inside, were all kinds of animals and reptiles and birds. Then a voice told him, "Get up, Peter! Kill and eat!"

"Surely not?" he said, knowing that Jews were forbidden from eating such creatures. "I have never eaten anything impure or unclean."

"Do not call anything impure that God has made clean," the voice answered. This happened three times and then the sheet was taken back up to heaven. Peter sat there puzzling about what it all meant. Meanwhile, the men who had been sent by Cornelius had found the house and stopped by the gate to ask for Peter. The Holy Spirit told Peter that three men were looking for him. "Get up and go downstairs. Go with them for I have sent them," it said.

So, the next day, Peter and some of his companions set off with the men to Caesarea. Cornelius was waiting for him and, as Peter came into the house, Cornelius fell at his feet. Peter looked down at him, smiling, and made him get up again. "Stand up," he said. "I am only a man myself." He went on inside the house and was surprised to find a large gathering of people there. "You know it is really against our law for a Jew to associate with gentiles," he said. "But God has shown me that I should not call any man impure or unclean. So when I was sent for, I came without any objection. May I ask why you sent for me?"

Cornelius told him about his vision a few days earlier. "So I sent for you immediately and it was good of you to come," he said politely. "Now we are all here in the presence of God to listen to everything the Lord has commanded you to tell us."

Peter began to speak. "I now know that God does not have any favorites but accepts anyone, from any nation, who fears him and does what is right." And he went on to tell them about Jesus's ministry in Galilee and Judea and the miracles that he had performed in God's name. The crowd listened, hanging on his every word. They were filled with the Holy Spirit and began to praise God, much to the amazement of Peter's companions. But Peter reproached them, saying, "Can anyone keep these people from being baptized? They have received the Holy Spirit, just as we have."

After this, Peter left to go back to Jerusalem, where the other disciples and followers of Christ criticized him for mixing with gentiles. In reply, Peter told them about his vision and described how the Holy Spirit had come down on Cornelius and his friends and family. "So, if God gave them the same gift as He gave us, who was I to think that I could oppose God?"

When they heard this, the disciples had no more objections and praised God, saying, "So then, He has even allowed the gentiles to be saved."

Understanding the story

The Jewish disciples criticize Peter for dining with gentiles, but his vision of the Holy Spirit convinces him that his actions are right. Ancient laws of Israel are overthrown as Peter takes charge of the Church and leads Jesus's followers. The message is clear—God welcomes everyone regardless of nationality.

"Peter Baptizing the Centurion Cornelius" (1709) by Italian painter Francesco Trevisani (1656–1746)

Herod Agrippa
King Herod Agrippa was ruler of Galilee, Perea, Judea, and Samaria. His grandfather, Herod the Great, tried to kill the baby Jesus, and his brother-in-law, Herod Antipas, beheaded John the Baptist and executed Jesus. This coin from about 37–44 CE bears the head of Agrippa in profile.

Stephen's death
The first Christian martyr was a preacher of the early Church named Stephen. He was stoned to death in about 34 CE by the Sanhedrin (Jewish leaders) in Jerusalem. This painting depicts him dying for his faith.

Peter in Prison

King Herod Agrippa was the grandson of Herod the Great. He had recently been made king of Judea by his friend, Emperor Claudius.

Herod persecuted the Christians relentlessly and had James, the brother of John, put to death. Then, during the Feast of Passover, Peter was arrested and thrown into prison. He was closely guarded, day and night, by four different teams of soldiers. Herod was planning to bring him out to stand trial once Passover was over. The other disciples and followers of Christ prayed constantly for Peter.

The night before he was due to stand trial, Peter was sleeping in his cell between two soldiers, his wrists bound in chains. Sentries stood guard at the door. Suddenly, an angel of the Lord appeared and a bright light filled the cell. The angel touched Peter gently on his side. Peter woke up with a start and could not believe his eyes.

"Quick! Get up!" said the angel urgently, and the chains fell off Peter's wrist. Then the angel continued, telling him what to do. "Put on your clothes and your sandals. Wrap your cloak around you and follow me."

Peter looked at him uncertainly and followed him out of the cell, as if he was in a dream. They passed one lot of guards and then another, and came to the great iron gate that led out of the prison and into the city. It opened obediently for them, swinging back on its hinges of its own accord. Silently, Peter and the angel swept through it, out into the night air. They walked together down the deserted street right to the very end, and then the angel disappeared into thin air. Peter pinched himself and realized what had happened. "Now I know, without a doubt, that the Lord sent his angel and rescued me from Herod's clutches," he said. "He also saved me from my fate at the hands of the Jewish people."

Peter went straight to the house of Mary, the mother of Mark, where people had gathered to pray. He knocked at the door and a servant girl, named Rhoda, came to answer it. But when she recognized Peter's voice, she was so overjoyed that she forgot to open the door and rushed back, crying, "Peter is at the door!"

"You are out of your mind!" they all said, knowing that Peter was in prison. But when she insisted that it was Peter at the door, they laughed at her, saying, "It must be his ghost!"

All the time, Peter kept knocking at the door and finally, when Mary and all her friends opened it, they were astonished. Peter gestured with his hand for them to be quiet and then told them exactly how the Lord had rescued him.

In the morning, when the soldiers discovered that Peter had escaped, there was pandemonium. They searched the prison from top to bottom, but there was

"St. Peter's Release from Prison" by Spanish painter Felix Castello (1602–1656) shows the angel's visit.

no sign of him. When he heard the news, Herod was furious and cross-examined all the guards. He then gave orders that they should be executed.

Catacombs
Facing persecution, early Christians were forced underground. They built burial sites, called catacombs, that were also sometimes used as places of worship. Tombs and coffins were placed in recesses within the walls of the chambers, such as in the The Via Appia Antica catacombs in Rome (above).

"Now I know, without a doubt, that the Lord sent his angel and rescued me from Herod's clutches."

Understanding the story

Herod opposes the early Church and punishes Christians for their beliefs in an attempt to gain popularity with the Jews. Those with true faith refuse to give in to Herod's constant persecution. Instead, they pray and God answers. Peter receives divine intervention in prison when an angel of the Lord helps him to escape. God sometimes assists those in need in the most miraculous of ways.

The Adventures of Paul

Saul was a Roman citizen and was now known by his Roman name, Paul. He was worshipping at the church in Antioch with Barnabas when the Holy Spirit told them that they had been chosen to spread the word of Jesus further afield.

So, sixteen years after the crucifixion, Paul set off on his first mission to convert people of all beliefs—both Jews and non-Jews—to Christianity. Over the next twenty years, he would make three long missionary journeys around the Mediterranean and Middle East and into Europe. He followed the main trade routes, going from city to city, by sea or road.

On this first journey with Barnabas, Paul traveled first to Cyprus in the Mediterranean. They landed in the capital, Salamis, and preached in the synagogue there before going all over the island, teaching and talking to the people. Then they crossed the sea to Perga in Asia Minor and traveled on inland to Antioch in Pisidia.

On the Sabbath, they were preaching in the synagogue there, and Paul was telling the Jews about Jesus's death and resurrection. He explained that the only way to God was through Christ. They were invited back to speak again the next week and a huge crowd gathered to hear them. Seeing that they were attracting such an enormous following of different people, some Jews felt jealous and threatened. They started to attack the two disciples.

"We had to speak the word of God to you first," said Paul and Barnabas. "But since you reject it and do not consider yourselves worthy of eternal life, we now turn to the gentiles." And they told them what the Lord had said: "I have made you a light for the gentiles, that you may bring salvation to the ends of the earth." And, despite the opposition, Paul and Barnabas continued to spread the word of Jesus. But their Jewish opponents were determined to get rid of them and, with backing from the most prominent people in Antioch, managed to get them expelled from the city.

The disciples carried on with their travels. They went to Lystra, a city in the remote Roman province of Galatia. One day, as Paul was preaching, he saw a crippled man in the crowd. His legs were bent helplessly beneath him and he was sitting on the ground. He was listening to every word.

Paul looked at him and could see that he had the faith to be healed. He called to him, "Stand up on your feet!" At once, the man jumped up and began to walk, a look of amazement on his face.

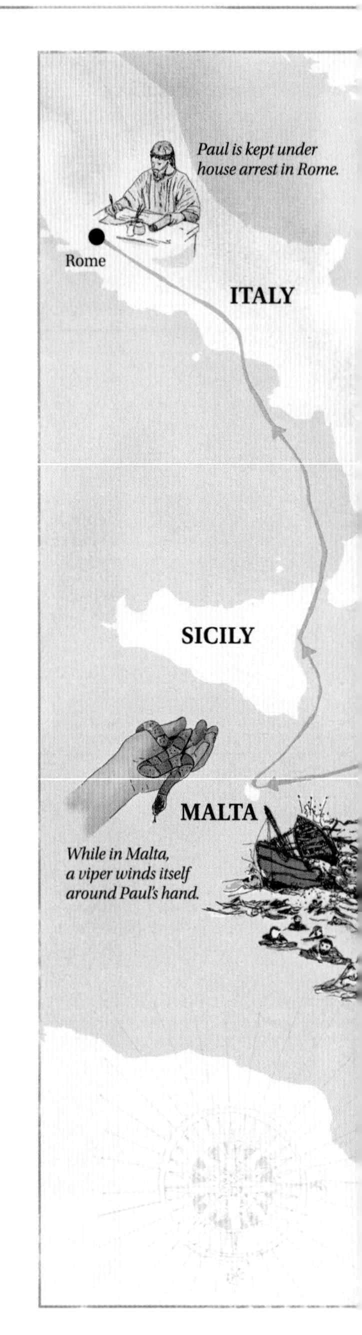

"We now turn to the gentiles."

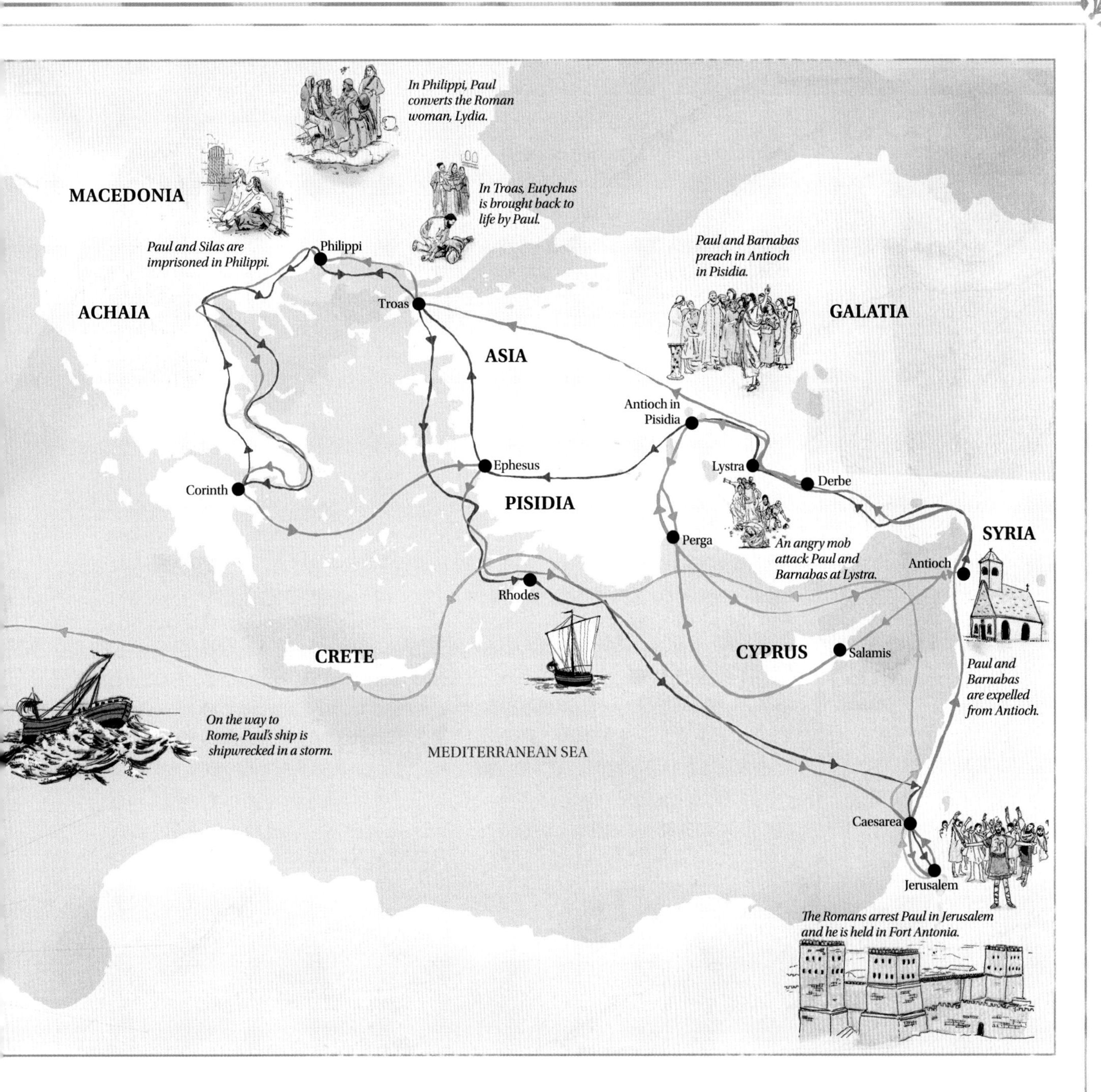

Paul's travels

Paul went on three missionary journeys to convert Jews and non-Jews to Christianity. He traveled all around the Mediterranean, Middle East, and into Europe. The first journey included Cyprus and a sea crossing to Perga in Asia Minor before traveling inland and returning home. The second trip to mainland Europe was longer, including a stay in Corinth for 18 months. The third took in a variety of cities he had previously visited, as well as two years in Ephesus before returning to Jerusalem. His final journey was to Rome, where he was due to stand trial.

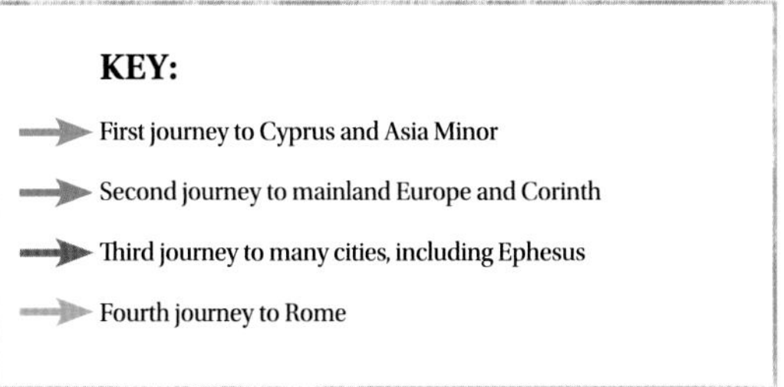

Barnabas
Paul never traveled alone. Barnabas (meaning "Son of Encouragement") was a Jew from Cyprus who converted to the new Christian religion. He accompanied Paul on his very first missionary journey and helped with his teachings in the synagogues.

Zeus
The people of Lystra gave Barnabas the name of Zeus—the Greek god of thunder and ruler of heaven. He is seen here on this silver brooch. According to legend, Zeus visited Lystra and destroyed the town when the inhabitants did not welcome him.

The crowd watched, astonished by the miracle. "The gods have come down to us in human form!" they cried joyfully—and they insisted that Barnabas was Zeus and that Paul was Hermes. The priest at Zeus's temple, just outside the city, brought a bull to be sacrificed and wreaths to honor them. Paul and Barnabas were horrified. "What are you doing?" they asked. "We are only human like you. We are bringing you good news, telling you to turn from these worthless things to the living God, who made heaven and earth and sea and everything in them."

Some Jews, who had followed them from Antioch, had joined the crowd and started to stir up trouble. In a flash, the mood changed and the mob started to hurl stones at the disciples. They drove them out of the city and left them, for dead, outside the walls. The disciples had been badly injured, but were still breathing. Their followers went to them and looked after them, taking them back into Lystra.

On Paul's next journey, a few years later, his companion was Silas. They traveled through Syria and Cilicia, and across Asia Minor to Macedonia. When they arrived in Philippi, they went down to the river to find a place to pray, and to speak to the women who were gathered there. One of them was called Lydia. She was a wealthy Roman business woman, and was a believer. She and all her household were baptized, and she invited Paul and his companions to stay with her.

One day, as they went down to the river to pray, Paul and Silas met a slave girl, who could predict the future. She made a lot of money for her owners by telling fortunes. She followed Paul wherever he went, screaming like a mad woman. At last, at the end of his tether, Paul turned around and said to the spirit who was possessing her, "In the name of Jesus Christ, I command you to come out of her!" Immediately, the spirit left and the girl stood by his side, wondering what had happened. But, when her owners discovered that their slave girl had lost her magic powers, they were furious and dragged Paul and Silas off to appear before the magistrates. Paul and Silas were thrown into prison, and, after a flogging, they were put under close guard in an inner cell.

At about midnight, Paul and Silas were praying and singing hymns to God. The other prisoners were listening to them. Suddenly, there was a violent earthquake and the foundations of the prison shook. At the same time, the doors to the cells opened and all the chains binding the prisoners fell to the floor. The jailer awoke with a start and saw, to his horror, the doors swinging to and fro. He assumed that all the prisoners had escaped and drew his sword, ready to kill himself. But he heard Paul, saying, "Don't harm

"We are bringing you good news, telling you to turn from these worthless things to the living God"

yourself! We are all here!" Calling for the lights, the jailer rushed into the cell and fell at Paul's feet, trembling. "What must I do to be saved?" he asked.

"Just believe in the Lord," answered Paul. The jailer washed the men's wounds and dressed them. He took them to his house and gave them food to eat. Then he and his family were baptized, and they were filled with joy because they had found God. The next morning, the magistrates gave the order for Paul and Silas to be released.

On his third missionary journey, Paul spent a long time in Ephesus—a wealthy seaport and trading center in the Roman province of Asia. A craftsman named Demetrius worked there, producing silver shrines to the goddess Artemis. He had always done very well for himself, but now, when he saw how many people were being converted by Paul, he was worried. He called all his fellow craftsmen together to discuss the problem. Soon an angry mob had gathered and they seized two of Paul's companions. Paul, himself, wanted to talk to the crowd, but his disciples stopped him, worried for his safety. Eventually, the city clerk arrived and managed to quieten things down. Soon afterward, Paul left Ephesus and set off for Macedonia.

In the city of Troas, Paul and his followers gathered in a room on the third floor of a house. Paul talked to them long into the night. One young man named Eutychus was sitting on a window sill, listening. His eyes began to grow heavy and he fell fast asleep. His body leaned toward the open window. Finally, he fell through it. His friends rushed down and picked up his lifeless body. Paul joined them and put his arms around Eutychus. "Don't be alarmed," he said. "He is alive!" Immediately, Eutychus started breathing again. His friends looked at each other in astonishment and then took him home.

Understanding the story

Paul is one of the first missionaries appointed by the Church to spread the word of God. Formerly Saul (his Hebrew name), Paul (his Roman name) changes his name to show his standing as preacher to the gentiles (non-Jews). He dedicates himself to this task in the face of great hardship. Though people react to Paul and his companions with hostility, they are committed to bringing the Gospel to all.

Sacrifice
Jews regarded animal sacrifice as an essential way to honor the Lord. The tradition is depicted on this Greek bowl from the 5th century BCE. However, the early Church called a halt to the ritual. Paul pointed out that Jesus's death was the last sacrifice, and no other lives needed to be lost.

Artemis
The Greek goddess of fertility, hunting, and the moon was Artemis. This statue of her is on display in Ephesus, Turkey. Ephesus was the site of a great temple to Artemis, where thousands of visitors came to worship.

Paul is Arrested

Together with his companions, Paul arrived in Caesarea and stayed with a disciple named Philip. Days later, a prophet named Agabus arrived from Judea.

Under arrest
Paul is arrested by the Roman soldiers in this detail from the crypt of St Victor Basilica in Marseilles, France. The Romans saved Paul from certain death, but his arrest put him at the mercy of the legal system that had crucified Jesus.

Agabus took Paul's belt from him and tied his own hands and feet with it, saying, "The Holy Spirit says that this is the way you will be treated by the Jews in Jerusalem. They will hand you over to the Romans."

When they heard this, Paul's followers begged him not to go back to Jerusalem. But he said, "Why are you weeping? I am ready not only to be bound, but also to die in Jerusalem for the name of the Lord Jesus."

When Paul got to Jerusalem he went to the Temple, where a group of Jews accosted him, shouting, "This is the man who teaches people to turn against us and our Temple! He has even brought Greeks into the Temple, where foreigners should never go! He has defiled this holy place!"

More people came running to join them, from all parts of the city, and soon there was an angry mob, baying for Paul's blood. They seized him and dragged him out of the Temple. When news of the disturbance reached Claudius Lysias, the commander of the Roman troops in Jerusalem, he rushed down with his soldiers. As they approached, the rioters stopped beating Paul and a hush descended on the crowd.

Claudius Lysias arrested Paul. Then he tried to find out what he had done, but the crowd started shouting. The commander could not make sense of it at all. He ordered that Paul should be taken and imprisoned in Fort Antonia, where the Roman troops were garrisoned. As the soldiers led him away, the crowd followed, chanting, "Away with him!" Paul had to be carried by the soldiers for his own safety.

Before he went into the fort, Paul asked to address the people. The commander agreed, so Paul stood on the steps, protected

Agabus predicts St. Paul's suffering in this oil and pastel on paper by French artist Louis Chéron (1660–1725).

by the guards, and spoke in Aramaic. "I am a Jew, born in Tarsus in Cilicia, but brought up here in Jerusalem. I was trained in the law of our fathers and was just as zealous as any of you. I persecuted many Christians here in Jerusalem and was about to do the same in Damascus. But on the way there, I saw a brilliant light and I heard the voice of Jesus, and then I was baptized. From that moment on, I have spread the word to Jews and gentiles alike."

The angry crowd listened, then started shouting, "Rid the earth of him! He's not fit to live!" The commander told the soldiers to take Paul to prison to be flogged. As they prepared him, Paul said to the soldiers, "Are you sure that it is legal for you to flog a Roman citizen who hasn't even been found guilty?" Claudius Lysias was filled with alarm because he knew that he had no right to treat a Roman citizen like this. He agreed to release him, but insisted that Paul was brought before the Sanhedrin.

Paul stood before the council of elders, priests, and teachers of the law, and said, "My brothers, I have fulfilled my duty to God in all good conscience this day." The high priest's face darkened with fury. He ordered his men to hit Paul in the mouth.

"God will strike you!" said Paul, still reeling from the blow. "You sit there to judge me according to the law, yet you yourself violate the law by commanding that I be struck." At this, there was uproar in the Sanhedrin as the Pharisees and the Sadducees started quarreling among themselves. It became so violent that Claudius Lysias ordered his men to take Paul back to the fortress.

There, the Lord appeared to Paul and said, "Take courage! As you have testified about me in Jerusalem, so you must also testify in Rome."

Meanwhile, more than forty Jews had gathered together to hatch a plot to kill Paul. They swore an oath not to eat or drink anything until he was dead. They asked the chief priests and the elders to persuade the commander to bring Paul out again to appear before the council. They would be waiting to ambush him and take him away to be killed. But Paul's nephew heard about the conspiracy and went to the prison to warn him. Paul asked him to tell the commander, which the young man duly did. Claudius Lysias listened, and then made arrangements for Paul to be taken to Caesarea so that the Roman governor there could hear his case. That very night, Paul was escorted out of Jerusalem, flanked by an armed guard of two hundred soldiers, seventy horsemen, and two hundred spearmen.

Caesarea
The capital and main seaport of Roman Judea, this stunning marble city was named after Roman emperor Augustus Caesar. The coming and going of boats in the great walled harbor helped to spread the Christian message across the Mediterranean.

"Take courage! As you have testified about me in Jerusalem, so you must also testify in Rome."

Understanding the story

In Jerusalem, Jews object to Paul's preaching and he is imprisoned. Paul remains unaffected, keeping his faith in God while turning the tables on his accusers and questioning them. As a Roman citizen, he uses his right to be tried before the Roman governor in Caesarea. As he sets off from Jerusalem under armed guard, Paul prepares for another missionary journey in the name of the Lord.

Soon the whole city was in an uproar.
The people seized Gaius and Aristarchus, Paul's traveling companions from Macedonia, and all of them rushed into the theater together. Paul wanted to appear before the crowd, but the disciples would not let him. Even some of the officials of the province, friends of Paul, sent him a message begging him not to venture into the theater.

Acts 19:29–31

The Theater of Ephesus
Around 57 CE, Paul's preaching led to a riot in the theater of Ephesus, in what is now Turkey. Seeing Christianity as a threat to Artemis, their mother goddess, the people shouted, "Great is Artemis of the Ephesians!"

Paul's Journey to Rome

St. Paul's Bay
The location of Paul's shipwreck is said to be St. Paul's Bay in Malta. The Bible mentions the ship hitting a sand bank, which accurately describes the sandy ridge out to sea at St. Paul's Bay. The ill-fated journey occurred in winter, when unpredictable weather in the Mediterranean made sailing problematic.

"You should have taken my advice. But keep up your courage because not one of you will be lost."

At last, after so many accusations had been made against him, Paul set off to stand trial before Caesar in Rome.

He was handed over to a centurion named Julius, and together they boarded a ship for Italy. They sailed along the island of Crete, making slow progress. Conditions grew worse, and the waves grew bigger and bigger. Paul warned the sailors, "Men, I can see that our voyage is going to be disastrous and will bring great loss to ship and cargo." But no one would listen and they sailed on.

The winds grew stronger and the waves towered above them, threatening to smash the ship to pieces. Even the sailors were terrified now and began to throw the cargo overboard. The storm raged on for days, the sun and the stars disappeared, and everyone gave up hope.

Paul stood up, as the waves crashed over the deck, and said to them all, "You should have taken my advice. But keep up your courage because not one of you will be lost. Only the ship will be destroyed. Last night an angel of the Lord stood beside me and told me that I would stand trial before Caesar and that God will protect us."

For two long weeks, the ship was driven across the Adriatic Sea from Crete. At last, to their great joy, the sailors saw a bay with a sandy beach and headed for it as fast as they could. But, as they approached, the ship ran aground and began to break up, pounded by the waves. The centurion ordered everybody to jump overboard and to swim for shore or to float in on planks of wood. Against the odds, they all reached land safely.

They discovered that they had arrived on the island of Malta, where the people gave them a warm welcome. They lit a big fire and Paul helped them gather brushwood. But, as he put it on the flames, a viper slithered out and wound itself tightly around his fingers. When the islanders saw the poisonous snake hanging from his hand, they looked at each other and said, "This man must be a villain. He has escaped from the sea, but justice has caught up with him now." But Paul just shook the snake from his hand and into the fire, where it sizzled and shrank to nothing. Paul was completely unharmed. The people watched in amazement and changed their opinion about him. Now they thought that he must be a god. Publius, the chief official of Malta, welcomed Paul and his companions to his house and for three days, he entertained them. Paul found out that Publius's father lay dangerously ill in bed and so he went to see him. Paul prayed and laid his hands on him and healed him. When word of the miracle got around the island, people flocked to Paul to be cured.

After three months in Malta, it was time to set off on the last leg of the journey to Rome. Once they had arrived there, Paul was allowed to live in a house on his own, with a soldier to guard him. He called together all the leaders of the Jews and talked to them about his arrest and why he had come to Rome to appear before Caesar. He stayed in the house, under guard, for two years and welcomed all those who came to see him, preaching the Kingdom of God and teaching about the Lord Jesus Christ.

Understanding the story

The storm at sea is terrifying, but Paul maintains his belief that God will ensure he reaches Rome. The ship breaks up at Malta, or "Melita" as the Romans call it, which means "refuge"—so-called because the natural harbors were a safe dock for ships. During the three months in Malta, Paul preaches the word of God to the community and heals the sick locals. As a result, the Christian message continues to spread.

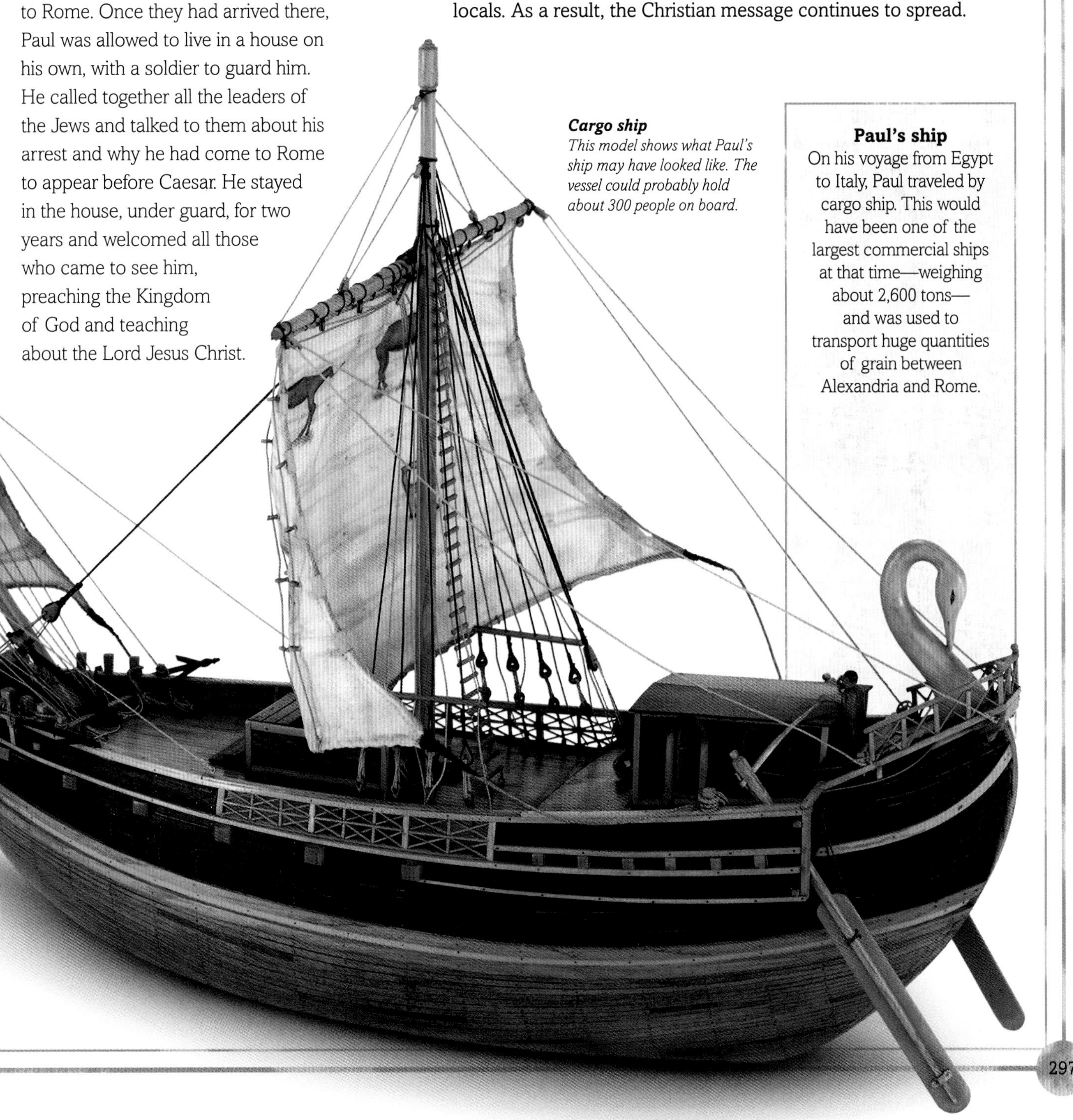

Cargo ship
This model shows what Paul's ship may have looked like. The vessel could probably hold about 300 people on board.

Paul's ship
On his voyage from Egypt to Italy, Paul traveled by cargo ship. This would have been one of the largest commercial ships at that time—weighing about 2,600 tons—and was used to transport huge quantities of grain between Alexandria and Rome.

Paul's Letters

During his missionary journeys, teaching the word of Jesus, Paul helped to establish churches around the Mediterranean countries. He kept in touch by writing letters.

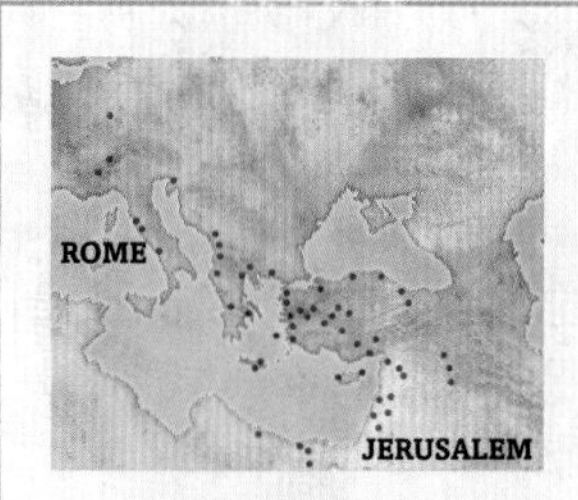

New churches
The teachings of Paul and missionaries like him resulted in the spread of Christianity at a rapid rate. This can be seen on this map, which highlights the locations of new churches across the eastern Mediterranean.

Paul's letters
Paul wanted to spread the word of God, and his writings ensured that Christianity still gained followers despite his absence. His letters have been reproduced ever since, such as in this medieval manuscript.

The letters were taken, over land and sea, by envoys to be read at church. Even his opponents admitted that the letters were "weighty and strong." Thirteen letters in the Bible bear Paul's name. Most were for Christian communities.

The earliest letter was probably to the Galatians and was written in about 49 CE, after his first missionary journey. The letters to the Thessalonians were written from Corinth on his second journey. Two letters to the Corinthians and one to the Romans followed on his last missionary journey. In 61 CE, he was in prison for two years. During this time he wrote to the Colossians, Philemon, the Ephesians, and the Philippians. His final letter, the second one he wrote to Timothy, was probably written in Rome when he was imprisoned again and was awaiting execution.

Some letters dealt with problems, such as in 1 Corinthians, when Paul warns members of the newly established Church about the dangers of division. He compared the Church to a human body. "The body is a unit, though it has many parts. So it is with Christ. We are all baptized by one Spirit into one body and we were all given the one Spirit to drink. Now, the body is not made up of one part, but of many. If the ear should say, 'Because I am not an eye, I do not belong to the body,' it would not, for that reason, cease to be part of the body. If the whole body were an eye, where would the sense of hearing be? If the whole body were an ear, where would the sense of smell be? In fact, God has arranged the parts in the body just as He wanted them to be."

Paul also wrote to the Corinthians about Love. "If I speak in the tongues of men and of angels but have not love, I am only a resounding gong or a clanging cymbal. If I have the gift of prophecy and can fathom all mysteries and all knowledge, and if I have a faith that can move mountains but have not love, I am nothing."

Then he described love in words, "Love is patient, love is kind. It does not envy, it does not boast, it is not proud. It is not rude, it is not self-seeking, it is not easily angered, it keeps no record of wrongs. Love does not delight in evil but rejoices in truth. It always protects, always trusts, always hopes, always perseveres. When I was a child, I talked like a child, I thought like a child, I reasoned like a child. When I became a man, I put childish things behind me. Now these three remain: faith, hope, and love. But the greatest of these is love."

Paul wanted to establish relations with the Church in Rome, and use it to spread the word of Jesus. In a letter to the Romans, he writes this important passage:

While under arrest, Paul dictates his letters

"For I am convinced that neither death nor life, neither angels nor demons, neither the present nor the future, nor any powers, neither height nor depth, nor anything in all creation, will be able to separate us from the love of God that is in Jesus Christ our Lord."

Understanding the story

For 20 years, Paul traveled around Europe and the Middle East, determined to convert people to Christianity. He and his companions often faced persecution from those who viewed the Gospel as a threat to their traditional ways. During these journeys, Paul wrote engaging letters in vernacular Greek (koine) on papyrus paper, including advice and encouragement for his newly established Christian communities.

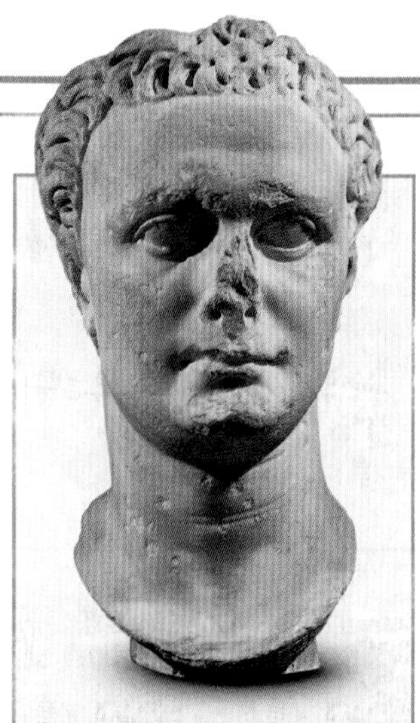

Emperor Domitian
It is likely that Domitian (81–96 CE) was the Roman emperor at the time of John's vision. He was seen as a cruel and unstable emperor. John wrote Revelation to give strength to repressed Christians and remind them that God would overthrow evil. The Roman Empire is depicted in the book as a blaspheming beast.

Alpha and Omega
The Greek alphabet consists of 24 letters, with Alpha the first letter and Omega the last. When Jesus says he is the first and the last, these are God's words. The Lord was there at the beginning of all things and will be there at the end. Everything is God's creation and His presence is eternal.

The Book of Revelation

About thirty years after Paul's last journey, the Christians were still suffering terrible persecution at the hands of the Romans.

They had been tortured and burned and crucified for their faith. Others, such as the disciple John, had been exiled. One Sunday morning, on the island of Patmos, John had an extraordinary vision of Judgement Day, with God triumphing gloriously over evil. From out of nowhere, he heard a voice, loud and clear, like a trumpet, saying, "I am Alpha and Omega, the first and the last. Write down what you see." And the voice told him to send what he wrote to seven churches in the province of Asia, as a message of hope and encouragement to his fellow Christians.

Immediately, John turned around to see who had spoken to him. He saw seven golden candlesticks and, standing among them, someone who looked like Jesus. When John saw him, he fell flat at his feet, but Jesus said, "Do not be afraid! I am the first and the last. I am the living one. I was dead, and behold I am alive forever and ever! And I hold the keys of death and Hades."

John looked up and saw a door opening to heaven above him. God was sitting on a magnificent throne, which flashed with lightning and rumbled with thunder. A beautiful rainbow arched above it. Twenty-four elders sat in a circle on their thrones. Seven torches blazed by God's throne, and a sea of glass stretched away into the distance. And John could see four astonishing creatures that looked like a lion, an ox, a man, and an eagle. But they each had six wings and their bodies were covered with dozens and dozens of eyes staring in different directions. In unison, the four of them chanted, "Holy, holy, holy is the Lord God Almighty who was, and is, and is to come."

In His right hand, God held a large scroll, and all seven of its seals were intact. John wept bitterly because he knew that there was no one worthy enough to break the seals. But then he saw what looked like a lamb, except that it had seven horns and seven eyes. It went up to God and took the scroll from Him. Immediately, the elders fell off their thrones and threw themselves down in front of the lamb. They knew it was the Son of God. After a moment, the many-eyed creatures joined them, bowing low on the ground and folding their wings neatly behind their backs to worship.

Hearing a choir of heavenly voices, John looked up and saw a host of angels. "Worthy is the lamb, who was slain, to receive power and wealth and wisdom and strength and honor and glory and praise!" they chorused.

The lamb started to break open the seals. His seven eyes stood out on stalks as the scroll slowly unrolled to reveal the suffering that was in store. Disaster upon disaster was shown being unleashed on the world and on mankind—war, earthquake, famine, pestilence, plague. And afterward, came Judgement Day, with God sitting on His throne, as it thundered and flashed beneath Him. The great Book of Life lay open on His lap, while everybody, great and small, lined up before Him to be judged.

But, at the very end of his vision, John saw a new heaven on earth. It was the Holy City, the new Jerusalem. The walls were made of solid jasper and the gates were carved out of pearl. The foundations were encrusted with precious jewels on every side. Water from the river of life flowed down the middle of the great street. On each side of it stood the tree of life, rustling with healing leaves and heavy with fruit. John heard a loud voice coming from the throne above, saying, "Now the dwelling of God is with men, and He will live with them. They will be His people, and God Himself will be with them and be their God. He will wipe away every tear from their eyes. There will be no more death or mourning or crying or pain, for the old order of things has passed away!"

John records his vision at Patmos in this detail from an oil-on-panel triptych from 1479 by German artist Hans Memling.

Understanding the story

This is the last book of the New Testament, detailing a vision of Judgement Day (the John in this story is not the original disciple). Though some of its contents are shocking, its purpose was to make the Christian faith stronger at a time when the Roman authorities were quashing the religion. The number seven features strongly in the Book of Revelation because, in Hebrew tradition, this symbolizes perfection.

People of the Old Testament

AARON
The first High Priest of Israel and older brother of Moses. Together with Moses, he tried to persuade Pharaoh to free the Israelites.

ABEDNEGO
Babylonian name given to one of Daniel's three Judean friends, who were thrown into the furnace by King Nebuchadnezzar.

ABEL
Adam and Eve's second son, who was a shepherd. He was murdered by his jealous brother, Cain.

ABIGAIL
King David's beautiful wife, who had first been married to the wealthy Nabal.

ABRAHAM
Chosen by God to be the forefather of the Israelite nation. Abraham was married to Sarah, but through her maidservant Hagar, he had a son named Ishmael. Sarah later bore him a second son, Isaac, whose grandsons were the ancestors of the twelve tribes of Israel.

ABSALOM
King David's son, who rebelled against his father in an attempt to seize the throne. He was killed by David's army chief, Joab.

ADAM
The first man created by God and husband of Eve. In Hebrew, Adam means "man" and also humankind.

Balaam

AHAB
A king of Israel who lived in the time of Elijah. Ahab was married to Jezebel, a Phoenician princess, and allowed her to promote the worship of Baal, a pagan god.

AMNON
King David's first son, who loved his half-sister Tamar. He was killed by his half-brother Absalom.

ARTAXERXES
King Artaxerxes of Persia allowed his cupbearer Nehemiah to go back to Jerusalem and help in the rebuilding of the city.

ASHER
Jacob's eighth son, the second of two boys born to him by Zilpah, who was his wife Leah's maid. Asher was the founder of one of the twelve tribes of Israel, which settled in northwest Canaan.

BALAAM
A soothsayer from Mesopotamia, Balaam was summoned by Balak to curse the Israelites. Instead, having seen the angel of the Lord, he blessed them.

BALAK
King of Moab at the time when Israel entered Canaan. He had asked Balaam to curse the Israelites.

BATHSHEBA
First married to the soldier Uriah the Hittite, she later became the wife of King David, who had plotted the murder of Uriah so that he could marry her. She was the mother of Solomon.

BELSHAZZAR
A Babylonian ruler who had asked Daniel to help interpret the mysterious writing on the wall.

BENJAMIN
Jacob's twelfth and youngest son, and his wife Rachel's second and last child. He was the only full brother of Joseph and founder of the smallest but very important tribe of Israel.

Delilah betrays Samson

BILHAH
A maidservant to Jacob's wife, Rachel. She gave birth to two of Jacob's sons—Dan and Napthali.

BOAZ
A Bethlehem farmer, who married Ruth. He was the great-grandfather of King David.

CAIN
First son of Adam and Eve, who killed his younger brother, Abel. Cain was a farmer.

CALEB
One of twelve spies sent ahead by Moses to check out Canaan, the Promised Land.

CYRUS
Founder of the Persian Empire. Under his rule (c 559–530 BCE), the Israelites were allowed to return to Judah from Babylon.

DAN
Jacob's fifth son and founder of one of the tribes of Israel. His mother was Bilhah, the maidservant of Jacob's favorite wife Rachel.

DANIEL
An Israelite who was exiled to Babylon. Daniel had a gift for interpreting dreams. He was also thrown into the lions' den by King Darius, but miraculously survived.

DARIUS
In the Book of Daniel, Darius the Mede is described as ruler of Babylon after its conquest in 539 BCE by the Persians. He threw Daniel into the lions' den.

DAVID
The Bethlehem shepherd boy who became the greatest king of Israel. He is also attributed with being the author of many psalms.

DELILAH
The beautiful Philistine woman who betrayed Samson to the Philistines—she tricked him into revealing the secret of his strength, which was his hair.

DINAH
The daughter of Jacob and his first wife Leah.

EBED-MELECH
A palace official who rescued the prophet Jeremiah from the pit.

ELI
The High Priest who looked after Samuel when he was a boy and trained him. Eli's own two sons were wicked, and were eventually killed in battle. Samuel took over from Eli as the next High Priest.

ELIJAH
One of the greatest prophets of Israel. He confronted Ahab when Ahab tried to encourage his people to worship the pagan god Baal. According to the Bible, he was taken up to heaven in a whirlwind.

Daniel

ELIMELECH
Husband of Naomi. He was from Bethlehem, but died in Moab.

ELISHA
Disciple and successor to the prophet Elijah. He was an important prophet in Israel during the 9th century BCE.

ELKANAH
The husband of Hannah and father of Samuel.

ESAU
Son of Isaac and Rebekah and twin brother of Jacob. He gave his birthright to Jacob for a bowl of stew. He was then tricked out of his father's blessing by Rebekah and Jacob.

ESTHER
Jewish wife of the Persian King Xerxes. She prevented the massacre of the Jewish people.

EVE
In Genesis, Eve was the first woman created by God. She was deceived by a serpent in the garden of Eden. She ate from the forbidden tree, and persuaded Adam (her husband) to eat the fruit. God banished them from Eden because they had disobeyed Him.

GAD
Jacob's seventh son and the founder of one of the tribes of Israel. His mother was Zilpah, who was the maidservant of Jacob's wife Leah.

David slays Goliath

GIDEON
A judge (an Israelite tribal leader) during the 12th century BCE, who defeated the Midianites and Amalekites.

GOLIATH
At the time of King David, Goliath was the leading warrior of the Philistine army. He challenged the Israelites to fight with him. David took up the challenge and killed him with a single stone.

HAGAR
The maidservant of Sarah, who was married to Abraham. She was the mother of Abraham's son Ishmael.

HAM
One of Noah's three sons.

HAMAN
An Amalekite who was made chief minister by the Persian King Xerxes. He plotted to massacre the Jews. Haman was sentenced to death when his plans were discovered.

HANNAH
The wife of Elkanah and mother of the prophet Samuel. She was blessed by the High Priest Eli as she prayed for a child. Her prayers were answered, and she bore a son named Samuel.

HEZEKIAH
A wise king of Judah, who obeyed God's laws.

ISAAC
The son of Abraham and his wife Sarah, who was born to them late in life. He was the father of Jacob and Esau, and the grandfather of the founders of the twelve tribes of Israel.

ISAIAH
An important 8th-century-BCE prophet, who warned the people of Israel what would happen if they did not obey God's commandments.

ISHMAEL
Abraham's son and half-brother of Isaac. His mother was Hagar, the maidservant of Abraham's wife, Sarah.

ISRAEL
The name God gave to Jacob, meaning "He strives with God." He was the grandson of Abraham and the son of Isaac.

ISSACHAR
Jacob's ninth son, who founded one of the tribes of Israel. His mother was Jacob's wife Leah and he was her fifth son.

JACOB
Son of Isaac and Rebekah, Jacob became known as Israel. He cheated his twin brother, Esau, out of his inheritance. He had twelve sons who became the founders of the tribes of Israel.

JAPHETH
One of Noah's three sons.

JEREMIAH
A prophet who warned the people of Judah that they would be destroyed if they did not listen to God's word.

JESSE
A farmer in Bethlehem. Jesse had eight sons. The youngest, David, was chosen by God to be the second king of Israel, after Saul.

JETHRO
A priest in the land of Midian and the father-in-law of Moses.

JEZEBEL
A Phoenician princess and King Ahab's scheming wife.

JOAB
The commander of King David's army.

JONAH
A prophet who tried to escape God's calling to save the city of Nineveh. He was swallowed by a big fish, but survived.

Jonah

JONATHAN
The eldest son of King Saul and a close friend of David.

JOSEPH
Jacob's eleventh son—but the first with his favorite wife, Rachel. Joseph founded one of the tribes of Israel but, as a boy, was sold into slavery in Egypt. He later rose to a position of great power and was the savior of his own people.

JOSHUA
Successor of Moses. Joshua led the people of Israel across the Jordan River into Canaan.

JOSIAH
Became king of Judah when he was only eight years old. He repaired the Temple in Jerusalem.

JUDAH
Jacob's fourth son, who founded one of the twelve tribes of Israel. His mother was Jacob's first wife, Leah.

LABAN
The brother of Rebekah, uncle of Jacob, and father of Leah and Rachel.

LEAH
Daughter of Laban, sister of Rachel, and first wife of Jacob. Mother of Reuben, Simeon, Levi, Judah, Issachar, Zebulon—and one daughter, Dinah.

LEVI
The third son of Jacob and Leah and founder of the Levite tribe of Israel, which was set aside for the service of God.

Moses

LOT
Abraham's nephew who lived in Sodom. His wife was turned into a pillar of salt as she fled from Sodom and Gomorrah.

MESHACH
One of Daniel's three Judean friends, who were thrown into the furnace by King Nebuchadnezzar.

MICHAL
Saul's daughter who became David's first wife.

MIRIAM
The sister of Moses and Aaron. Miriam danced and sang with the Israelite women after they had crossed the Red Sea.

MORDECAI
The cousin of Esther and her foster father. Mordecai saved King Xerxes's life.

MOSES
A Levite by birth, but brought up at Pharaoh's court. He led the Israelites out of slavery and received the Law from God on Mount Sinai.

NAAMAN
The commander of the Syrian army whose skin disease was healed by Elisha.

NABAL
A wealthy but mean Calebite, married to Abigail—who later became the wife of David.

NABOTH
A vineyard owner in Samaria whose death was engineered by King Ahab's wife, Jezebel.

NAOMI
A widow who was the mother-in-law of Ruth.

NAPHTALI
Jacob's sixth son. He founded one of the tribes of Israel. His mother was Bilhah, the maidservant of Jacob's wife, Rachel.

NATHAN
A prophet who rebuked King David for committing adultery with Bathsheba and arranging the death of her husband, Uriah.

NEBUCHADNEZZAR
The king of Babylon who captured Jerusalem and took the people of Jerusalem into exile.

NEHEMIAH
A cupbearer to King Artaxerxes. He was allowed to go back to Jerusalem and help in the rebuilding of the city.

NOAH
Built an ark as instructed by God so that he and his family, together with the animals he took, would survive the flood. Noah was the father of Shem, Ham, and Japheth.

ORPAH
The daughter-in-law of Naomi and sister of Ruth.

POTIPHAR
Pharaoh's captain of the guard, who bought the young Joseph as a slave in Egypt.

RACHEL
Jacob's favorite wife and the mother of Joseph and Benjamin.

RAHAB
The woman who hid two Israelite spies in her house in Jericho and helped them to escape.

REBEKAH
The wife of Isaac and the mother of Jacob and Esau.

REHOBOAM
Inherited the throne of Israel from his father, Solomon, but the nation divided under his rule.

REUBEN
Eldest son of Jacob and his wife, Leah, and ancestral head of one of the tribes of Israel.

RUTH
The Moabite daughter-in-law of Naomi. She married a farmer named Boaz.

SAMSON
He possessed super-human strength because of his long hair. A sworn enemy of the Philistines, Samson was betrayed by Delilah.

SAMUEL
Son of Elkanah and Hannah. He was the prophet who anointed Saul and David as kings of Israel.

SARAH
Abraham's wife and the mother of Isaac.

SAUL
A Benjamite, Saul was chosen by God to be the first king of Israel. He was the father of Jonathan.

SENNACHERIB
The ruler of Assyria whose army besieged Jerusalem in the reign of King Hezekiah.

SHADRACH
One of Daniel's three Judean friends.

SHEBA
The queen who visited King Solomon to see for herself if he was as wise as everybody said.

SHEM
Eldest of Noah's three sons.

Saul attacks David

SIMEON
Jacob's second son with his wife Leah. He was the founder of one of the twelve tribes of Israel.

SOLOMON
Son of David and Bathsheba. He was the third king of Israel. Solomon built the Temple in Jerusalem and was renowned for his wisdom.

Samson

URIAH
Married to Bathsheba, Uriah was a loyal soldier. He was sent to his death by King David.

VASHTI
Xerxes's first wife, who refused to obey her husband and was thus banished.

XERXES
The Persian ruler who divorced his wife Vashti to marry Esther.

ZEBULON
Jacob's tenth son, who founded one of the twelve tribes of Israel. His mother was Leah, Jacob's first wife.

ZEDEKIAH
The puppet king chosen by Nebuchadnezzar to rule Judah after Jerusalem had been conquered by the Babylonians.

People of the New Testament

AGABUS
A prophet who predicted that Paul would be imprisoned.

ANANIAS
A follower of Jesus, who restored Saul's sight after he had been left blinded on the road to Damascus.

ANDREW
A fisherman from Galilee and one of Jesus's twelve disciples. He was the brother of Peter.

ANNA
A prophetess who recognized the baby Jesus as the Messiah when he was presented in the Temple.

AUGUSTUS
First emperor of Rome (c. 31–14 CE). Born Octavius, but took the name Augustus, which means "lofty." Jesus was born during his reign.

BARABBAS
The criminal who was chosen by the crowd to be set free instead of Jesus.

Jesus

BARNABAS
Paul's companion on his first missionary journey.

BARTHOLOMEW
One of Jesus's twelve disciples who was, reputedly, flayed alive, and the patron saint of tanners.

CAIAPHAS
The high priest at the Temple in Jerusalem when Jesus was arrested and crucified.

CLEOPAS
One of two men who met Jesus on the road to Emmaus after Jesus had risen from the dead.

CORNELIUS
A Roman centurion in Caesarea. Together with his family, he was converted to Christianity by Peter.

DEMETRIUS
A silversmith in Ephesus. Demetrius made shrines to the goddess Artemis. When Paul's teaching threatened his livelihood, he started a riot against Paul.

ELIZABETH
The cousin of Jesus's mother Mary, and mother of John the Baptist. She was married to Zechariah, and had been childless for many years. According to the Gospel of Luke, an angel told Elizabeth she would have a son.

EUTYCHUS
The young man who fell out of the window while Paul was preaching. According to Acts 20, Eutychus was brought back to life by Paul.

GABRIEL
Name of an angel, or heavenly messenger, who appears four times in the Bible.

HEROD AGRIPPA
Grandson of Herod the Great. As king of Judah (c. 37–44 CE), he persecuted the Christians to gain favor with the influential Jews.

HEROD ANTIPAS
Herod the Great's son, who ordered the beheading of John the Baptist at the request of his niece, Salome. Antipas was tetrarch (ruler) of Galilee and Perea (4 BCE–39 CE).

HEROD THE GREAT
King of Judea (c. 37–4 BCE) at the time of Christ's birth, and responsible for rebuilding the Temple.

HERODIAS
Herod Antipas's wife and granddaughter of Herod the Great. She told her daughter, Salome, to ask for John the Baptist's head because he proclaimed her marriage to Herod as being immoral.

JAIRUS
The head of the synagogue whose daughter was healed by Jesus.

JAMES
Son of Zebedee, brother of John, and one of the twelve disciples.

JAMES
Son of Alphaeus, James was one of the twelve disciples.

JESUS
Thought by Christians to be the Son of God and the Messiah. He was born in Bethlehem to Mary and Joseph.

JOHN
Son of Zebedee, brother of James, and one of the twelve disciples. John was very close to Jesus and is thought to be the author of the fourth Gospel. He was present at the transfiguration and in the garden of Gethsemane.

JOHN THE BAPTIST
Son of Elizabeth and Zechariah and cousin of Jesus. John was a Jewish holy man and prophet, who called on people to repent, and offered to baptize them.

JOSEPH
A carpenter who lived in Nazareth. He was married to Mary, the mother of Jesus. Joseph was descended from the house of David.

JOSEPH
Also known as Barsabbas, he was one of the two men whose names were put forward to replace the disciple Judas, who had betrayed Jesus.

JOSEPH OF ARIMATHEA
A wealthy follower of Jesus and member of the Sanhedrin. He took Jesus's body down from the cross and buried it in a tomb.

JUDAS ISCARIOT
Son of Simon Iscariot and one of the twelve disciples. Judas betrayed Jesus for thirty pieces of silver. He later killed himself.

JULIUS
A Roman centurion who escorted Paul to Rome.

LAZARUS
The brother of Martha and Mary, who lived in Bethany. According to John's Gospel, Jesus raised him from the dead.

LUKE
A physician and thought to be the author of Acts and the Gospel of Luke. He accompanied Paul on his missionary journeys.

LYDIA
A rich business woman who lived in Philippi. She was baptized by Paul, and became his first European convert.

Judas

MARK
Accompanied Paul and Barnabas on their first missionary journey, and is thought to be the author of the Gospel of Mark.

MARTHA
The elder sister of Lazarus and Mary, and friend of Jesus. Martha lived in Bethany.

MARY
Married to the carpenter Joseph, Mary was the mother of Jesus.

MARY
The sister of Martha and Lazarus, who lived in Bethany. She was a very close friend of Jesus and anointed his feet with perfume before his death.

MARY
The mother of the disciple James. Together with Jesus's mother Mary and Mary Magdalene, she was present at Jesus's crucifixion.

MARY MAGDALENE
A follower of Jesus. Mary Magdalene was present when Jesus was crucified, and was the first witness of his resurrection. In the Bible, Jesus appeared to her first and told her of his coming ascension into heaven.

MATTHEW
Also known as Levi, Matthew was a tax collector from Capernaum. He was one of the twelve disciples, and is also thought to be the author of the first Gospel.

MATTHIAS
The man who was chosen to replace Judas Iscariot as one of the twelve disciples.

Paul

NICODEMUS
Together with Joseph of Arimathea, Nicodemus helped to take Christ's body down from the cross and prepare it for burial.

PAUL
Born a Pharisee in Tarsus, Paul was at first a persecutor of the Christians. But he was converted after he saw a vision of Jesus, changing his Hebrew name of Saul to Paul. He spread the word on his missionary journeys and helped to build up the early Church.

PETER
A fisherman and brother of Andrew, Peter was one of the twelve disciples. During the trial of Jesus, he denied knowing him three times. He was the first disciple chosen by Jesus Christ. His original name was Simon, but Jesus renamed him Cephas, meaning "rock" in Aramaic. He is better known by the Greek version of his name, Peter, which also means rock.

PHILIP
One of the twelve disciples. He came from the town of Bethsaida.

PONTIUS PILATE
The Roman governor—or procurator—of Judea from c. 26–36 CE. Pilate condemned Jesus to death although he knew Jesus was innocent.

PUBLIUS
The governor of Malta when Paul and his companions were shipwrecked. Paul helped to heal Publius's father.

RHODA
The servant girl who answered the door to Peter after he had escaped from prison.

SALOME
The daughter of Herodias, who danced for her stepfather, Herod Antipas. As a reward for pleasing him, she asked for the head of John the Baptist on a plate.

Salome

Angel Gabriel appears to Zechariah

SAUL (see Paul)
Hebrew name for Paul.

SILAS
Paul's companion on some of his missionary journeys.

SIMON
One of the twelve disciples, sometimes known as Simon the Zealot.

SIMON
A tanner from Joppa. Peter was staying at Simon's house when he had a vision.

SIMON OF CYRENE
The man from Cyrene who helped Jesus to carry the cross.

STEPHEN
The first Christian martyr, who was stoned to death by some Jews.

ZACCHAEUS
A wealthy tax collector who climbs a tree to be able to see Jesus, and later repents his sins.

ZECHARIAH
Married to Elizabeth, who was the cousin of Jesus's mother, Mary. Zechariah was the father of John the Baptist. According to Luke's Gospel, he doubted the angel's prophecy that he would have a son. As a result of his disbelief, he was struck dumb.

Zacchaeus climbs a tree to see Jesus

Index

A

B

C

D

E

L

M

N

O

S

T

U

V

W

X

Y

Z

Acknowledgements

Dorling Kindersley would like to thank Smiljka Surla and Katie Knutton for additional design; Carron Brown for the index; Hazel Beynon for proofreading; Rebecca Warren for Americanization; Matilda Gollon, Ashwin Khurana, and Jenny Sich for additonal editing; and Sophia Abadzis and Bryce Patterson for editorial assistance.

The publisher would like to thank the following for their kind permission to reproduce their photographs:

(Key: a–above; b–below/bottom; c–center; l–left; r–right; t–top)

8 akg-images: MPortfolio / Electa (bl). **Corbis:** Dr. Trever John C. Ph.D. (tl). **Getty Images:** DeAgostini (br). **9 Corbis:** Alinari Archives (tr). **Dorling Kindersley:** Ellen Howdon / Courtesy of Glasgow Museum / Glasgow City Council (Museums) (cl); Dominic Winter (br); Laurence Pordes / Courtesy of the British Library / By permission of The British Library (bl). **10 The Bridgeman Art Library:** Bibliotheque Nationale, Paris, France (tl); De Agostini Picture Library / M. Carrieri (bl); The Stapleton Collection / Private Collection (bc). **11 akg-images:** (bc). **Corbis:** Richard T. Nowitz (tc). **SuperStock:** Bridgeman Art Library, London (cr). **14-15 The Bridgeman Art Library:** Basilica di San Marco, Venice, Italy / Giraudon (c). **16 Alamy Images:** ASP Religion (bl). **Corbis:** Richard T. Nowitz (tl). **16-17 SuperStock:** Bridgeman Art Library, London / Victoria & Albert Museum, London. **17 The Bridgeman Art Library:** Musee des Beaux-Arts, Caen, France / GIraudon (c). **Corbis:** Peter Langer / Design Pics (br). **20 Corbis:** Michael Interisano / Design Pics (clb). **21 Alamy Images:** Peter Barritt (c). **23 Dorling Kindersley:** Peter Hayman / British Museum / The Trustees of the British Museum (crb/adze, crb/drill, crb/chisel). **24 Corbis:** Bruno Morandi (tl). **26 Corbis:** Nik Wheeler (clb). **27 Corbis:** The Gallery Collection (tc). **28 Corbis:** Ed Kashi (tl). **29 Getty Images:** A. De Gregorio / De Agostini Picture Library (t). **30 Alamy Images:** Christine Osborne Pictures (clb). **33 Corbis:** Inge Yspeert (crb). **34 Corbis:** Roger Tidman (clb). Getty Images: David Silverman / Getty Images News (tl). **36 Alamy Images:** Jon Arnold Images Ltd (tl); Zev Radovan / www.BibleLandPictures.com (clb). **37 Corbis:** Ted Spiegel (clb). **SuperStock:** DeAgostini (c). **38 Corbis:** Frans Lemmens (clb). **Getty Images:** Rizwan Tabassum / AFP (tl). **40 Dorling Kindersley:** Powell-Cotton Museum, Kent (tl). **42 Corbis:** Dean Conger (clb). **SuperStock:** Robert Harding Picture Library Ltd (tl). **43 The Bridgeman Art Library:** Galleria Sabauda, Turin, Italy (c). **45 The Bridgeman Art Library:** Louvre, Paris, France / Giraudon (bc). **46 Corbis:** Yannick Tylle (tl). **49 Alamy Images:** Rosemary Behan (cr). **Getty Images:** Time & Life Pictures (tr). **50 Alamy Images:** Gianni Dagli Orti / The Art Archive (tl). **52 The Trustees of the British Museum:** © The British Museum (clb). **Corbis:** Alfredo Dagli Orti / The Art Archive (tl). **54 Corbis:** Robert Harding World Imagery (cr). **55 Alamy Images:** Ivan Vdovin (crb). **Corbis:** Sandro Vannini (tr). **56-57 Corbis:** Stefano Amantini (c). **58 Werner Forman Archive:** Egyptian Museum, Berlin (tl). **59 Alamy Images:** Gianni Dagli Orti / The Art Archive (tr). **60 The Bridgeman Art Library:** Giraudon (cl). **Getty Images:** De Agostini (tr). **62 Alamy Images:** Zoo Imaging Photography (tl). **Corbis:** The Gallery Collection (bl). **66 Alamy Images:** Gianni Dagli Orti / The Art Archive (tl); fotofacade.com (cl). **67 Alamy Images:** Ancient Art & Architecture Collection Ltd (tr). **70 Corbis:** Christie's Images (bc); Richard T. Nowitz (clb). **72 Alamy Images:** Nathan Benn (clb). **Dorling Kindersley:** Peter Anderson / Bolton Metro Museum (tl). **73 The Bridgeman Art Library:** Harris Museum and Art Gallery, Preston, Lancashire, UK (tc). **78 Alamy Images:** Gianni Dagli Orti / The Art Archive (clb). **Dorling Kindersley:** Rough Guides (tl). **79 Corbis:** Richard T. Nowitz (cr). **80 akg-images:** Bible Land Pictures (bl). **Corbis:** Sandro Vannini (tl). **81 Alamy Images:** Zev Radovan / www.BibleLandPictures.com (crb). **Corbis:** Sandro Vannini (tr). **82 Getty Images:** Bronze Age / The Bridgeman Art Library (tl). **83 Getty Images:** Science & Society Picture Library (crb). **86-87 Alamy Images:** Dennis Cox. **88 Corbis:** Hans Georg Roth (clb). **90 Alamy Images:** Zev Radovan / www.BibleLandPictures.com (tl). **91 SuperStock:** Universal Images Group (tc). **92 Corbis:** Gianni Dagli Orti (bl). **93 Alamy Images:** Ilan Amihai / PhotoStock-Israel (crb); Collection Dagli Orti / The Art Archive (tr). **94 Alamy Images:** Zev Radovan / www.BibleLandPictures.com (cl). **97 Corbis:** JosÈ F. Poblete (cr). **100 Corbis:** Atlantide Phototravel (tl). **101 The Bridgeman Art Library:** Musee des Beaux-Arts, Caen, France / Peter Willi (cl). **102 Alamy Images:** Hanan Isachar (tl); Zev Radovan / www.BibleLandPictures.com (cb). **104 akg-images:** Erich Lessing (cl). **105 akg-images:** Bible Land Pictures (br). **106 Alamy Images:** Zev Radovan / www.BibleLandPictures.com (tl). **Corbis:** Hans Klaus Techt / APA (clb). **109 Alamy Images:** Hanan Isachar (tr). **Corbis:** Hanan Isachar (crb). **111 The Bridgeman Art Library:** Dura-Europos Synagogue, National Museum of Damascus, Syria / Photo © Zev Radovan (c). **112 Corbis:** Richard T. Nowitz (tl). **116 Corbis:** William James Warren (tl). **117 Corbis:** Steve Kaufman (tr). **118 Alamy Images:** Vignon, Claude / The Art Gallery Collection (tl); Shay Levy / PhotoStock-Israel (clb). **119 Corbis:** Francis G. Mayer (tc). **120 Alamy Images:** Itsik Marom / Israel images (cl). **Getty Images:** Werner Forman / Universal Images Group (tl). **121 The Bridgeman Art Library:** Musee National de la Renaissance, Ecouen, France / Peter Willi (bc). **122-123 Corbis:** Annie Griffiths Belt (c). **124 Alamy Images:** Zev Radovan / www.BibleLandPictures.com (tl). **125 Corbis:** Gianni Dagli Orti (tr). **127 Corbis:** Wolfgang Kaehler (tr). **Dorling Kindersley:** Judith Miller / Wallis and Wallis (cr). **128 Getty Images:** Getty Images News (bc). **130 Corbis:** Gianni Dagli Orti (tl). **Getty Images:** Alinari Archives (clb). **131 Dorling Kindersley:** Karl Shone / David Donkin (t). **132 Alamy Images:** WILDLIFE GmbH (bl). **133 The Bridgeman Art Library:** Noortman Master Paintings, Amsterdam / Private Collection (cl). **Corbis:** Herve Collart / Sygma (cr). **134-135 Corbis:** Frank Lukasseck (c). **137 Alamy Images:** islandspics (crb). **138 Alamy Images:** Duby Tal / Albatross (cl). **Corbis:** Gianni Dagli Orti (tl). **139 The Bridgeman Art Library:** Gemaeldegalerie Alte Meister, Dresden, Germany / © Staatliche Kunstsammlungen Dresden (tc). **140 akg-images:** Bible Land Pictures (tl). **Getty Images:** G. Nimatallah / De Agostini (clb). **140-141 akg-images:** Israelimages (bc). **142 akg-images:** Erich Lessing (b). **Corbis:** Alfredo Dagli Orti / The Art Archive (tl). **143 Corbis:** Hanan Isachar (tr). **144 Alamy Images:** www.BibleLandPictures.com (tl). **Corbis:** David Bathgate (clb). **145 The Bridgeman Art Library:** Private Collection (tc). **146 Alamy Images:** Phoenician / The Art Gallery Collection (tl). **Corbis:** Tim Graham (clb). **148 Corbis:** Christophe Boisvieux (tr). **149 Dorling Kindersley:** Rough Guides (tr). **150 Art History Images:** Holly Hayes (tl). **Corbis:** Richard T. Nowitz (clb). **151 Dorling Kindersley:** Alan Hills and Barbara Winter / The Trustees of the British Museum (br). **152 Corbis:** Richard T. Nowitz (tl). **154 Alamy Images:** www.BibleLandPictures.com (clb). **Getty Images:** A. Dagli Orti / De Agostini (tl). **156 Corbis:** Nik Wheeler (tl). **Werner Forman Archive:** British Museum, London (cl). **157 Alamy Images:** Images&Stories (tr). **The Bridgeman Art Library:** Bonhams, London, UK / Private Collection (tl). **158 The Bridgeman Art Library:** Ancient Art and Architecture Collection Ltd. (clb); The Barnes Foundation, Merion, Pennsylvania, USA (cb). **159 Corbis:** Michele Falzone / JAI (tr); (br). **160 Corbis:** Jon Arnold / JAI (tl). **162 Corbis:** Gianni Dagli Orti (bl). **163 Dreamstime.com:** Steve Lovegrove (tr). **164 Alamy Images:** Zev Radovan / www.BibleLandPictures.com (b). **165 Alamy Images:** Zev Radovan / www.BibleLandPictures.com (tr). **166-167 The Bridgeman Art Library:** (c). **168 Corbis:** Wolfgang Kaehler (tl). **170 Corbis:** Denis Scott (cl). **172 akg-images:** Joseph Martin / Russian National Library (l). **173 The Bridgeman Art Library:** The Royal Collection © 2011 Her Majesty Queen Elizabeth II (b). **174-175 Alamy Images:** Ivan Vdovin (c). **176 The Bridgeman Art Library:** Sherborne, Dorset, UK / Photo © Neil Holmes (cr). **Dorling Kindersley:** Jamie Marshall (cl). **177 Alamy Images:** The Art Archive (cl, tc). **Corbis:** Historical Picture Archive (c). **Getty Images:** De Agostini (crb). **SuperStock:** DeAgostini (tr). **178 Alamy Images:** Zev Radovan / www.BibleLandPictures.com (clb). **Corbis:** Bettmann (tl). **180 Alamy Images:** National Geographic Image Collection (tl). **181 Corbis:** Alfredo Dagli Orti (c). **182 Alamy Images:** Duby Tal / Albatross (tl). **Corbis:** Anatoly Maltsev / epa (bc). **183 Corbis:** Arte & Immagini srl (tr). **184 The Bridgeman Art Library:** Agnew's, London, UK / Private Collection (c). **185 Dreamstime.com:** Farek (tr). **186 Corbis:** Del Castillo / epa (clb). **Dreamstime.com:** Vitaly Korovin (cla). **187 The Bridgeman Art Library:** Maidstone Museum and Art Gallery, Kent, UK (tc). **188 Dreamstime.com:** Jackq (tl); Zurijeta (clb). **190 Corbis:** Stapleton Collection (tl). **192 Alamy Images:** Hanan Isachar (tl). **Corbis:** Nir Alon / Demotix (clb). **193 The Bridgeman Art Library:** Museo di San Marco dell'Angelico, Florence, Italy (bl). **194 The Bridgeman Art Library:** Library of the Hungarian Academy of Sciences, Budapest (tl). **Corbis:** Nathan Benn / Ottochrome (clb). **195 Getty Images:** Superstock (tc). **197 Alamy Images:** MARKA (cl). **198 The Bridgeman Art Library:** Giraudon (clb). **SuperStock:** Minden Pictures (tl). **199 Corbis:** (c). **200 Corbis:** (bc); Shai Ginott (tl). **201 The Bridgeman Art Library:** Baptistry of Ariani, Ravenna, Italy (tr). **203 Getty Images:** De Agostini (tr). **206-207 Corbis:** Yonathan Weitznam / Reuters (c). **208 Corbis:** David Sutherland (tl). **209 Getty Images:** The Bridgeman Art Library (tc). **210 Dorling Kindersley:** Tina Chambers and James Stevenson / University Museum of Newcastle (tl). **Dreamstime.com:** Noam Armonn (clb). **212 SuperStock:** (br). **213 Corbis:** Hanan Isachar / JAI (cl). **Getty Images:** A. Dagli Orti / De Agostini Picture Library (tl). **214 Corbis:** Hanan Isachar / Godong (tl). **Dorling Kindersley:** Tim Ridley / Church's Ministry among the Jews (cl). **215 The Bridgeman Art Library:** Sant'Apollinare Nuovo, Ravenna, Italy / Giraudon (tc). **216 Dreamstime.com:** Han Van Vonno (tl). **218 Corbis:** Richard T. Nowitz (tl). **219 The Bridgeman Art Library:** Agostini Picture Library / A. Dagli Orti (tl). **Getty Images:** G. Dagli Orti / De Agostini (tr). **221 Corbis:** Elio Ciol (c). **222-223 Getty Images:** John Arnold (c). **224 Alamy Images:** Hanan Isachar (clb). **Corbis:** Hanan Isachar (tl). **225 Corbis:** The Gallery Collection (tc). **226 Dreamstime.com:** Cristi180884 (tl). **227 Alamy Images:** BibleLandPictures.com (tc). **228 Alamy Images:** Sonia Halliday Photographs (tl). **Corbis:** Philippe Lissac / Godong (clb). **231 Corbis:** Mamoun Wazwaz / Xinhua Press (tr). **232 SuperStock:** Art Archive, The (tr). **233 Alamy Images:** Zev Radovan / www.BibleLandPictures.com (tr). **234 Getty Images:** Insy Shah (clb). **235 Dorling Kindersley:** Ermine Street Guard (tr). **236 Alamy Images:** Gianni Dagli Orti / The Art Archive (bl). **237 Alamy Images:** Zev Radovan / www.BibleLandPictures.com (crb). **The Bridgeman Art Library:** Wallace Collection, London, UK (tl). **238 iStockphoto.com:** Selahattin Bayram (bc). **240 The Art Archive:** Queretaro Museum Mexico / Gianni Dagli Ort (br). **242 Dreamstime.com:** Marilyn Barbone (cl). **Getty Images:** G. Dagli Orti / De Agostini Picture Library (tl). **245 Alamy Images:** Zev Radovan / www.BibleLandPictures.com (cr). **Corbis:** Kenneth Garrett / National Geographic Society (tr). **246 Alamy Images:** Zev Radovan / www.BibleLandPictures.com (cl). **249 akg-images:** Erich Lessing (cl). **Getty Images:** Travel Ink / Gallo Images (tr). **252-253 Corbis:** Atlantide Phototravel (c). **254 Alamy Images:** Zev Radovan / www.BibleLandPictures.com (tl). **Dorling Kindersley:** Judith Miller / Helios Gallery (clb). **256 Alamy Images:** Israel images (cl). **257 Getty Images:** T.J. Kirkpatrick / Getty Images News (tr). **258 Alamy Images:** Collection Dagli Orti / The Art Archive (cl). **259 The Bridgeman Art Library:** Prado, Madrid, Spain (c). **260 Alamy Images:** The Art Gallery Collection (bc). **Corbis:** Richard T. Nowitz (tl). **261 Dorling Kindersley:** Ermine Street Guard (cr). **262-263 Rex Features:** Francis Dean (c). **266 Corbis:** Bojan Brecelj (tr). **267 Fotolia:** gavran333 (cla). **Getty Images:** A. De Gregorio / De Agostini (tl). **268 The Art Archive:** Academia BB AA S Fernando Madrid / Gianni Dagli Orti (br). **269 Corbis:** Hans Hildenbrand / National Geographic Society (tr). **270 Dreamstime.com:** Compuinfoto (tl). **271 SuperStock:** Fine Art Images (c). **272 Corbis:** Alfredo Dagli Orti / The Art Archive (cl); Hanan Isachar (tl). **273 The Bridgeman Art Library:** Agostini Picture Library / A. Dagli Orti (bc). **275 Alamy Images:** Colin Underhill (crb). **Getty Images:** Chris Caldicott / Axiom Photographic Agency (tr). **278 akg-images:** Erich Lessing (bc). **Dorling Kindersley:** Emma Firth (tl). **279 Corbis:** Francis G. Mayer (tr). **280 The Bridgeman Art Library:** Holyland Tourism 1992, Ltd (tl). **281 Alamy Images:** Forray Didier / Sagaphoto.com (tr). **Getty Images:** DeAgostini / A. De Gregorio (tl). **282 SuperStock:** imagebroker.net (tl). **283 The Bridgeman Art Library:** John Mitchell Fine Paintings / Private Collection (bl). **Getty Images:** C. Sappa / De Agostini (tr). **284 Dreamstime.com:** Ermess (cl). **285 The Bridgeman Art Library:** Photo Christie's Images / Private Collection (cr). **286 Alamy Images:** Zev Radovan / www.BibleLandPictures.com (tl). **Corbis:** Francis G. Mayer (clb). **287 The Bridgeman Art Library:** Caylus Anticuario, Madrid, Spain (tl). **Dorling Kindersley:** James McConnachie / Rough Guides (tr). **290 Alamy Images:** Helene Rogers / ArkReligion.com / Art Directors & TRIP. **Corbis:** Hoberman Collection (bc). **291 Getty Images:** G. Dagli Orti / De Agostini (tr). **292 akg-images:** Erich Lessing (tl). **The Bridgeman Art Library:** Musee des Beaux-Arts, Caen, France / Giraudon (bl). **293 Corbis:** Hanan Isachar / JAI (tr). **294-295 Corbis:** Michele Falzone (c). **296 Getty Images:** De Agostini (tl). **297 Dorling Kindersley:** National Maritime Museum, London (b). **298 akg-images:** (clb). **300 Dorling Kindersley:** Alamy (clb). **Getty Images:** A. Dagli Orti / De Agostini Picture Library (tl). **301 SuperStock:** Bridgeman Art Library, London (tr)

Jacket images: *Front:* Mary Singleton / Mary's Folk Art; *Back:* Dorling Kindersley: Julian De Narvaez fcla, fcra, fcl, fclb; *Spine:* Mary Singleton / Mary's Folk Art: tc

All other images © Dorling Kindersley
For further information see: **www.dkimages.com**